EACH ONE A HERO

EACH ONE
A HERO

Kisho Kurokawa

The Philosophy of
Symbiosis

KODANSHA INTERNATIONAL
Tokyo • New York • London

Note: Following customary practice, Japanese names for historical figures (predating 1868) are given in the traditional Japanese manner (that is, surname preceding given name), whereas names after that date are reversed, with given name first.

Translated from the original Japanese edition of *Shin Kyosei no Shiso*, Tokuma Shoten, 1996, by Jeffrey Hunter and Centre Franco-japonais d'Echanges Techniques et Economiques. Edited by David B. Stewart.

This book was published with the cooperation of the Executive Committee of the Kisho Kurokawa Retrospective Exhibition.

Distributed in the United States by Kodansha America, Inc., 114 Fifth Avenue, New York N.Y. 10011, and in the United Kingdom and continental Europe by Kodansha Europe Ltd., 95 Aldwych, London WC2B 4JF. Published by Kodansha International Ltd., 17-14 Otowa 1-chome, Bunkyo-ku, Tokyo 112, and Kodansha America, Inc.

CONTENTS

C H A P T E R   3

SYMBIOSIS IN THE ECONOMY

C H A P T E R   4

TRANSCENDING MODERNISM

C H A P T E R   5

THE PHILOSOPHY OF CONSCIOUSNESS-ONLY AND SYMBIOSIS

CHAPTER 10

MAN AND NATURE

CHAPTER 18

CHALLENGE OF ASIA, CHALLENGE OF ECO-MEDIA CITY

EPILOGUE

LIBERATION FROM CRAVING AND IGNORANCE

INTRODUCTION

Toward a Deeper Understanding of Symbiosis

In 1991, I revised the original 1987 edition of *The Philosophy of Symbiosis*. In that year, Academy Editions of London issued a large-format, illustrated English edition of this book, as well as a separate paperback text without illustrations (1994). By that time, *symbiosis* had become a key issue. In the beginning, I had combined the Buddhist idea of coexistence (or, more properly, co-living) with the more strictly biological notion of symbiosis; now, however, the term enjoys a certain vogue and no longer needs presentation as a novel concept. My book has become increasingly popular overseas as well as in Japan, probably as a result of the many lectures I have given all over the world on the philosophy of symbiosis.

The English text of *The Philosophy of Symbiosis* is available on my Internet home page, and every day up to two thousand readers access this site. Many overseas users have reacted with surprise to *The Philosophy of Symbiosis*, exclaiming that this concept has opened their eyes or even radically changed their view of life. Others, however, have voiced the opinion that the philosophy of symbiosis—being based on Buddhist precepts—may not be relevant to cultures and ways of life founded on other religions. Moreover, some have protested that my interpretation of symbiotism, or symbiosis, differs too greatly from the original biological meanings of these terms.

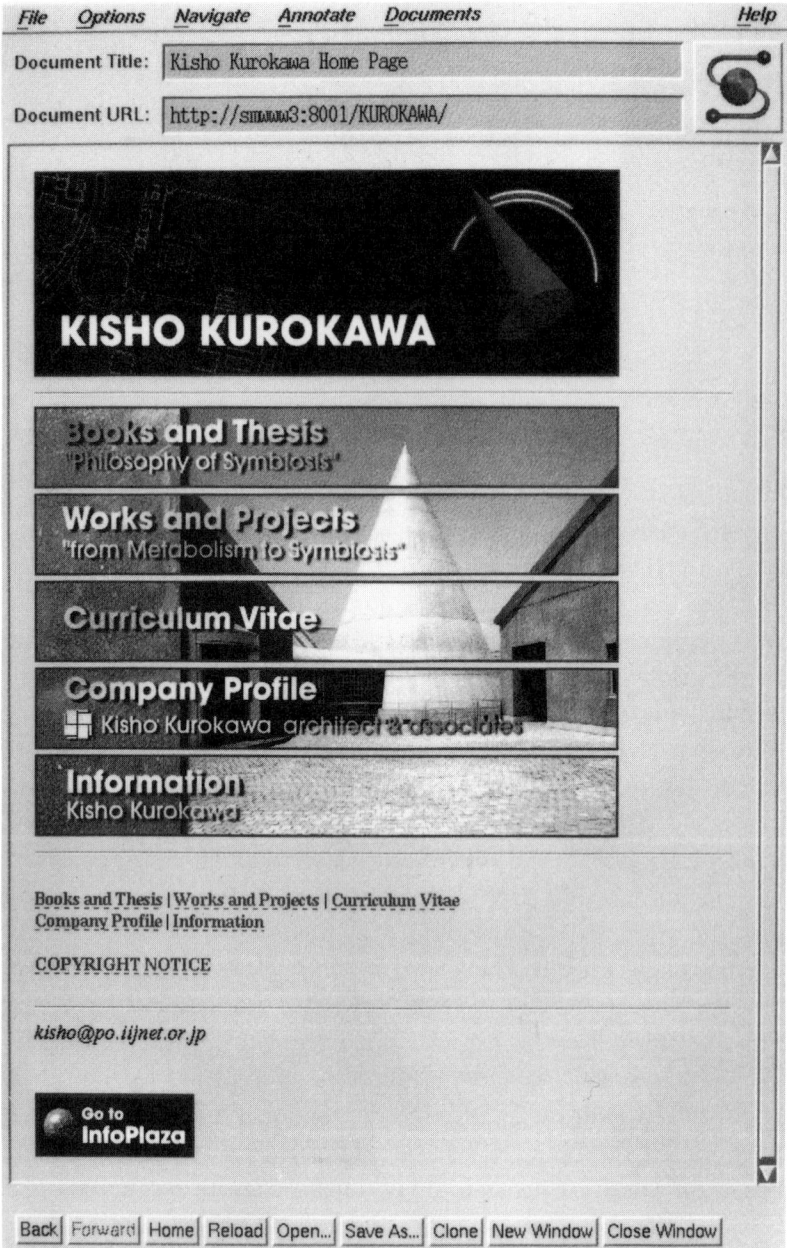

The author's home page (http://www.kisho.co.jp).

I have advocated the philosophy of symbiosis for nearly four decades now. I believe that it must become the dominant philosophy of the twenty-first century, encompassing all fields of endeavor. I first began developing the concept when, as a middle-school student, I was exposed to the *Tomoiki Bukkyo* doctrines of Co-living Buddhism advocated by Benkyo Shiio. Since I have often expressed my view that Co-living Buddhism has its roots in the Consciousness-Only philosophy of fourth-century India, some have mistaken the philosophy of symbiosis for a mere extension of Buddhist thought.

Although the philosophy of symbiosis does indeed include Buddhist thinking, I consider it a *new* philosophy that has expanded to embrace a global field. Moreover, it clearly differs from symbiotism, or symbiosis, in their biological senses. Without doubt, the philosophy of symbiosis is deeply linked to traditional Japanese cultural aesthetics and beliefs; however, it certainly does *not* stress Japanese cultural uniqueness.

My philosophy of symbiosis also echoes much of the thought and philosophy of Western culture since Greek and Roman times, including the atomic theories of Democritus and Cretius and the view of nature propounded by Leibniz. Still, Western society, supported by a rationalistic dualism, took its modern form chiefly from the late nineteenth to the early twentieth centuries. An analogous process occurred in Japan. Japan's modernization, beginning with the Meiji Restoration of 1868, followed the pattern set by the West. During that modernization, Japan's culture, as based on a philosophy of symbiosis, was disparaged as being vague, ambiguous, and outmoded.

Thus, for some time, I have considered the Edo period as the precursor of my philosophy of symbiosis—before the beginning of the rapid modernization and Westernization of the Meiji age.

In this significant regard, the new philosophy of symbiosis is intended to revitalize Japan's traditional culture, whose decline began with the Meiji period. At the same time, I think of it as a philosophy capable of overcoming the present impasse in Western thinking, whether European or American.

Readers may be surprised that this book deals with a range of subject matter that extends far beyond my own fields of specialization, which comprise architecture, city planning, land-development planning, and what in Japan is called social engineering. Today, however, if one hopes to arrive at plausible solutions for the twenty-first century, one must adopt a long-term, comprehensive, and integrated point of view.

Definition of Symbiosis and Its Origins

We are clearly entering an era in which knowledge and understanding are undergoing a paradigm shift[1]—the beginning of a major groundswell, of significant and wide-ranging changes in overall structure affecting all fields and areas worldwide. In such times, the only way to deduce the future is to search out overall changes in an integrated manner, transcending the vertical division of labor and specialization that emerged during the process of modernization. No amount of specialized understanding or knowledge in any individual field is of particular use in this endeavor. One must adroitly peruse all fields of endeavor, both vertically and horizontally, to discern the subtle signs of future orientation.

The philosophy of symbiosis not only bridges the fields of art, culture, politics, economics, science, and technology. It also takes into account the symbiosis apparent in many dimensions: including symbiosis between human beings and nature, art and science, reason and sensibility, tradition and advanced technology, local and global features, past and future, one generation and another, cities and villages, oceans and forests, abstraction and symbolism, part and the whole, body and spirit, conservatism and revolution, and development and preservation. This has led to a call that the definition and conceptual boundaries of symbiosis should be clarified.

Since this concept and the philosophy flowing from it are, relatively speaking, still in their formative stages, I feel that it is still too early to present a dictionary definition. However, the following differences may be noted between symbiosis and the related concepts of harmony, coexistence, or compromise:

• Although symbiosis encompasses opposition and contradiction, it refers to new, creative relationships born from competition and tension.

- Symbiosis refers to a positive relationship in which the participants necessarily attempt to understand each other, despite mutual opposition.
- Symbiosis refers to relationships that spark a level of creativity impossible for either party to achieve alone.
- Symbiosis refers to relationships in which the participants try to broaden their shared ground, all in respecting the individuality of the other and the "sacred zones" that each considers inviolable, such as religion and cultural traditions.
- Symbiosis is positioning one's own existence within the larger biological scheme of giving-and-receiving.

By way of contrast, let us now define the concepts of *coexistence*, *harmony*, and *compromise*.

Coexistence describes relationships—such as that which existed between the United States and the former Soviet Union—where hostile participants, each of whom may wish to exterminate the other, nonetheless avoid destruction and continue to coexist.

Harmony describes relationships in which there are no basic points of contention, and where any differences that do exist are coordinated in a balanced manner.

Compromise refers to a relationship such as a moratorium, in which shared ground is achieved passively and without any particular intention to build a creative new relationship between parties whose interests are in opposition.

By contrast, when two parties have a symbiotic relationship, the establishment of this relationship often includes a moratorium period or a spatial buffer zone where the parties actively maintain their relationship through opposition, competition, and struggle. As we shall see, the moratorium and buffer zone play important roles in the formation and development of my philosophy of symbiosis as a theory of intermediary space.

In the revised edition of *The Philosophy of Symbiosis*, the notions of intermediary space and sacred zones were supplemented, and a new chapter, "Toward the Evocation of Meaning," added. In the present comprehensive edition, the overall chapter structure has been reorganized, existing chapters revised, and the following new chapters added: "Toward an Age of Symbiosis," "From the Machine Age to an Age of Life," "Symbiosis in the Economy," "Intermediary Spaces," "Abstraction Rendered Symbolic," and "Symbiosis in Asia," as well as a new introduction.

It is my hope that *Each One a Hero: The New Philosophy of Symbiosis* will reach a larger audience and foster further acceptance of this philosophy in the century to come.

Cooperation *and* Competition

Not only in the East, but across the world, a great conceptual revolution is taking place—but so quietly that it has gone largely undetected. This is not the birth of a new ideology, like capitalism or communism; nor is it the advent of a new philosophy to replace that of Kant or Descartes. Yet the new currents of thought that are arising around the world will have a greater effect on us than any ideology or systematic philosophy, for they are unarguably changing our way of life and our ideas of what it is to be human. This great, invisible change I identify as the philosophy of symbiosis.

Although I began to study the philosophy of symbiosis nearly forty years ago, its real origins go back to 1923, the year Benkyo Shiio, the eighty-second leader of modern Buddhism (Zojoji, Daihonzan, and Jodoshu) initiated a new movement called *Tomoiki Bukkyo Kai*, or the Co-living Buddhist Association. As Professor Shiio also served as president of the Pure Land Sect's Tokai Gakuen, where I attended middle school, I had the good fortune to hear his lectures in person. I remember once asking him this question: "Buddhism teaches that the Buddha resides in all people, animals, and plants, and that it is wrong to kill any living thing. But even a vegetarian diet requires that vegetables be consumed. Isn't that a contradiction?"

I remember Professor Shiio's reply for its clarity and directness: "It is acceptable to take the necessary minimum. When people die, their bodies become ashes that enrich the soil and allow plants to live. Those plants then allow animals to live. As this cycle continues, one both supports life and receives support for one's own life, and a reciprocal life-giving relationship is established."

Even earlier than this, at the end of World War II, when I was an elementary school pupil, American culture suddenly entered Japan, even though the United States and England had only recently been denounced as savage. My childish heart was enchanted with America's materialistic culture, but at the back of my mind I wanted to resist any materialistic way of thinking. I believe that many of my generation felt the same way.

I began to feel a strong desire to rediscover Japanese traditions. I entered Kyoto University, which offered the kind of environment I had been seeking. From that time on, I continued to seek out consciously things Oriental and Japanese, rather than things typical of the West.

Thus, I discovered Co-living Buddhism through Professor Shiio as a middle-school student, and by the early 1960s, following my university career, it had become a part of my consciousness. In reaction to the machine-age principles of modernism, I participated in the Metabolism movement, believing that cities and buildings should be considered according to the life-principle of metabolic systems, or as a function of biology. In preparing to launch this movement, I read *Toyojin no Shii Hoho* (Oriental Thinking, 1948–49; most recently: *Selected Works of Hajime Nakamura*, Vols. 1-4, Shunju Sha) by Hajime Nakamura, then professor of Indian philosophy at Tokyo University. This book examines the manner in which Buddhism was translated and modified to suit divers national traditions as it spread from India to Tibet, Thailand, China, the Korean peninsula, and Japan. By tracing the propagation and changes of Buddhist thinking in Asia, one could grasp the astonishing diversity of the vast region known simply as "Asia." For me, this was an eye-opening discovery.

I thus turned my interest to India, believing that the roots of Co-living Buddhism might be found there. After reading books on the life of the Buddha and a variety of other subjects, I became aware of Consciousness-Only thinking, and surmised that this must be the origin of Co-living Buddhism. So, as a sophomore at university, I began a rather serious study of Consciousness-Only philosophy. Not many materials on the subject had been translated into Japanese at that time, so I read translations in classical Chinese. However, I found this difficult, so I attempted to learn Sanskrit in the belief that studying the original texts would prove more rewarding. I became increasingly convinced that beyond Buddhism, symbiosis would become the center of the philosophy that might sustain me as a person. In the course of the nearly forty years since, I have followed an individual approach in developing my own philosophy of symbiosis.

The Philosophy of Symbiosis Predicts Paradigm Shift

I used the word "symbiosis" in place of Professor Shiio's concept of "co-living" because in Japanese the former has the same pronunciation as the biological concept of symbiotism—another of my interests. I also wanted to found my own philosophy applying Buddhism to a broader range of fields. In 1979, when the Japan Inter-Design Forum was established, I wrote *Kyosei no Jidai* (The Age of Symbiosis). Thereafter, in 1980, I served as the first chairman of the Yokohama Inter-Design Conference and selected "Toward the Age of Symbiosis" as the theme of its international meeting, to which I invited Paolo Soleri,[2] Andrzej Wajda,[3] Françoise Choay, Renzo Piano,[4] and others. There, I predicted that symbiosis would become a major concept.

I then proceeded to give lectures in Japan on the philosophy of symbiosis with increasing frequency. Oddly, although my book had not yet been published abroad at that time, many politicians and students in the countries I visited told me they were indeed aware of my philosophy of symbiosis. Apparently, photocopies of my lectures were being circulated, albeit without permission.

Before the fall of the U.S.S.R., the Soviet Architects' Union asked me to lecture. I made the following statement: "Many minorities exist within the Soviet Union. I believe that an age of symbiosis will eventually arise, and when that happens, minorities that have been enclosed within the framework of federalism will want to return to ways of life based on their own traditional cultures. They will begin to speak their own distinctive languages again and will become more independent. When such a time comes, the federation of the Soviet

Union will become much looser than at present, and a time of restructuring toward a richer nation will begin."

This was not intended as an incitement to political acts; I was simply stating what I believed must one day come to pass. However, the system at the time being what it was, my words may have been considered subversive. Perhaps for that reason, certain students who had attended the lecture without permission secretly recorded it in English and transcribed it into Russian.

I must have given some thirty lectures on the philosophy of symbiosis in Czechoslovakia, Bulgaria, Hungary, Romania, the former Yugoslavia, and other Eastern European nations. My intentions were merely to discuss the philosophy of symbiosis and to forecast the coming era, but the Eastern Europeans seemed anxious to interpret my words as prophecy. Each of my lectures in Moscow and Eastern Europe—intended for young students—was, in fact, attended by crowds exceeding one thousand people, who surrounded me and made it difficult to move.

Opposing Whilst Cooperating

Criticism of Japan—"Japan bashing"—has been popular recently. American congressmen or other officials smashing a Toyota product with sledgehammers is perhaps the quintessential image of this trend. But a similar impulse can be easily observed in Japan itself, where, as the proverb states, "The nail that sticks out is hammered down." Japanese society has inherited a long tradition of human relations cast in a feudal mode, which dictates that those with special talents, those with unique personalities, or those who achieve sudden success be attacked and ostracized by their peers. In an isolationist or protectionist era, when it is sufficient to guard the status quo and shun all external influences, individuality and achievement are despised as destabilizing factors, and they are feared for the deleterious effects they may have on the established order. The fact that most Americans engaged in Japan bashing are protectionists further testifies to the truth of this claim.

The elimination of the spirit of protectionism, both in trade and in the form of group loyalties that exclude all outsiders, is a universal struggle and a universal goal. But to pursue that goal also means that we are plunging into an age of confrontation: between beneficence and danger, between personalities, and between cultures. It will no longer do simply to hammer down the nail that sticks out. We can no longer solve anything by attacking unique or extraordinary individuals. We are living at the start of an age of symbiosis, in which we will recognize each other's differing personalities and cultures while competing, and in which we shall cooperate while yet opposing and criticizing each other.

Will the traditional Japanese reverence for harmony, the emotional and spiritual commitment to consensus, function effectively in this age of symbiosis? If we define harmony and consensus as undercutting all individuality and exceptional ability, as forcing all to bend to the will of the group, then that tradition will find itself at sea in the age of symbiosis. Nor is there much hope for a harmony served by cowering before the strong, and so failing to put forth one's own position forcefully.

When positions, or standards, of cultural value are in disagreement, it is *not* necessary for one side to defeat the other and force its values on its opponent. The two parties can instead search for common ground, even while remaining in opposition. The success of this approach depends upon whether one has the desire to understand one's opponent. The intermediate space and sacred zones I shall discuss further on are thus necessary conditions for the establishment of symbiosis.

In the international arena the age when strong countries made all the rules, when they forced their ideologies on all other nations, is coming to an end. Nation and city will gradually achieve an equal status, and cities will grow increasingly autonomous, engaging in their own foreign relations, trade, and cultural exchange. Minority peoples will also become equal in status to nations and larger federations—such as the EU or NAFTA—and parallel to these they, too, will engage in foreign relations, trade, and cultural exchange.

This is the tide of the age of symbiosis.

My symbiosis, which includes opposition and competition, can frequently be observed in nature. This is a major reason that I chose the term "symbiosis" rather than coexistence, harmony, or peace.

The Death of God and the Icon

Hitherto, society taught that all humankind is equal before God. For those with faith, God was absolute and instructed humanity in its proper course. Even after the masses ceased to believe in such a God, mass society created substitutes: heroes and "superstars."

There comes a time when each of us notices that his or her life has not proceeded exactly as we might have wished. To compensate for this disappointment, we may transfer unrealized dreams to a hero or an idol of some sort. This ideal image, or icon, becomes our goal. Society comprised this God, this ideal or icon, on the one hand and, on the other, the great body of humankind—Heidegger's *das Mann*. But suddenly in the present age, God, as well as the ideal and the icon, are dead. We have lost even our heroes and our superstars. Though stars may still be born, they soon fall to earth and are consumed in the blink of an eye.

Meanwhile, for most of the nations of the world, Western society and Western culture have continued as both ideal and goal. As a result, developing countries have made every effort to approach, however gradually, the ideal that the West represents. Progress has been identified with mere Westernization.

Societies that cherish this ideal refuse utterly to recognize the value or meaning of other cultures. For them, modernization is Westernization. It is a universal conquest by a single culture.

Japan, in particular, from the time of the Meiji Restoration in 1868, consciously chose this path. With progress as its rallying cry, our nation spared no pains in its grinding efforts to modernize. Years ago, Tokyo, and especially the Ginza district, was regarded as a major symbol of this trend. Enraptured by the icon of the Ginza, towns across the archipelago dubbed their main shopping streets as the local Ginza, and little Ginzas sprouted all over Japan, like bamboo shoots after rain.

And so, was it that Japan set out in pursuit of Western society and, eventually, surpassed it? This would be a ridiculous point to argue—for there can be no question of a society either overtaking, or not, another society of a completely different nature. Nor can we speak of superiority or inferiority among cultures. Each culture treads a different path; it is not as if we were all on one large athletic field, competing against each other.

Recently we Japanese often hear the claim that we have overtaken the West and no longer have any goal to aim for. This is a misunderstanding. True, the aim of society up to now, with its faith in the icon of progress, has crumbled. Without an ideal, the concept of progress becomes meaningless; but now that superstars are fading, it has become possible for each of us to play the role of hero.

A Mirror Society

Film stars of the old days, whose names were synonyms for the ideals of male and female beauty, have passed from the scene; today's stars achieve only a more ordinary human scale. When we view everyday entertainers on our living-room television screens, we succeed in conceiving of ourselves as stars too. This is the beginning of a mirror society in which we define ourselves through the activity of observing others, where *others* are a mirror in which we see ourselves. Since we no longer find peace of mind in God, we are forced to find it in looking about us. The present is an age when we are all absorbed with those around us.

Modern society offers great opportunities for each to emphasize his or her own individuality and fabricate a unique identity. We have taken the first step into an age of differentiation, which values signs and symbols; the possibility that myriad unique individuals may flourish in symbiosis, that we may see the birth of a symbiotic society respecting very different cultural spheres, lies just over the horizon.

I have purposely said "possibility" because the road will not be an easy one. A mirror society easily fragments into a conformist, absolutist society. This danger is particularly strong in Japan, where the strictures of the feudal village—which for centuries rejected nonconformists and those of exceptional talent—remain alive in people's minds. A mirror society is in danger of turning conformist to forestall ostracization.

When, for example, a corporation succeeds in a certain venture, the rest follow in a thundering herd. Many Japanese businessmen, on the pretext of socializing, go out drinking night after night with their workmates and colleagues to communicate the message: "I am just like you. We're the same sort. No need to worry that I have any special talent, any real individuality." They are preserving the village truce. And, by the same token, they are jealous and spiteful of anyone who does show special talent, anyone who *succeeds*.

The danger of a regressive mirror society spans the worlds of the university, business, government, and the arts. Those who dare to violate the strictures of conformity are denounced and the value of their achievements is challenged. This is a long-accepted practice in Japan.

To repeat, the age of heroes and superstars is finished. But recognizing and evaluating the individual worth of others is a fundamentally different activity from the process of making heroes. From the fair and proper evaluation of diverse cultures—different talents and different personalities—is born a newly discriminating spirit, and the foundations are prepared for a society of symbiosis.

The End of Universality

In the age of symbiosis the ideals of universality and equality, which before passed unchallenged, will cease to apply. Until now, the most widely acknowledged form of universality has been technology. It was believed that technology, which brought wealth and happiness to the masses, would unify and homogenize the entire world, regardless of differences in development or culture among nations. Cars, nuclear power plants, and the glass-and-steel of modern architecture were supposed to engender happiness in the deserts of the Middle East, the tropical cities of Southeast Asia, and the loess plains of China, and make people the same.

We no longer believe this to be true: technology will *not* take root when it is cut off from culture and tradition. The transfer of technology requires sophistication: adaptation to region, unique situations, and local custom. When the technology of one culture is introduced into another with a different lifestyle, it is impossible to ensure success. For instance, even if, in the future, atomic fusion is perfected and becomes economically viable, is it necessarily a good idea for such plants to spread across the globe as the universal means of energy? Probably not. If the per capita income of the Chinese reaches the level of Japan, will it be a good idea for China to become a mass automobile society? Probably not. Each cultural sphere will devise unique technologies to create a distinctive lifestyle.

In the twenty-first century fusion, fission, water-generated electrical plants, and new energy such as bio-mass will exist in symbiosis. This will not be because some regions are too poor to introduce nuclear fusion generators, but because different societies must opt for different technologies.

A Mix-and-Match Age: Jekyll and Hyde

In contrast to the first half of the twentieth century, during which the concept of progress influenced improvements in the quality of materials and general standard of living, in the future, *creativity* will be the concept that expresses the richness of our divers standards of living. We shall no longer have a unified goal toward which we progress; instead, people will make the discovery of fluid, mix-and-match goals their aim. As long as Paris fashion reigned as the model of style, other designers were required merely to imitate. But in an age of mix-and-match, fashions from different periods, genders, and functions are recombined and juxtaposed. Unlike epochs of hierarchy, when conventions of time, place, and occasion prevail, in the mix-and-match age we can find delight in reading the sensibility that has dictated multiple choices in each new combination.

Ours will be a heterogeneous age where people can pursue different activities at the same time. It will be a time of a broad and flexible "Jekyll and Hyde" sensibility that can freely juxtapose sacred and profane, a Paris model with farmer's overalls; a creativity that can, through subtle recombination, bring us novelty. We shall, in other words, see an age in which a richly creative, or, so to say, schizophrenic, personality rules supreme. Sincerity and insincerity will live side by side, the distinction between work and play will fade, formal and casual will lose their meaning in fashion as in lifestyle.

How enjoyable it may be to live in this new age of symbiosis remains to be seen. The world will be a more difficult place, though it will be "hard" in a way different from the present interpretation of that word. The age of the individual, of pluralism and diversification, in which each person will express his or her individuality and be responsible for making individual choices, will bring the joy of discovering what is different and unique. Each of us will need to make continual efforts to acquire the skills allowing us that pleasure. Unless we cultivate our sensibilities, it will be difficult either to make new discoveries or to be creative. Compared to a bygone age of conformism when we could be lazy, we shall have no choice but to take the first steps along a difficult path leading to a richly creative life.

1

TOWARD AN AGE OF SYMBIOSIS

Post-Industrial Paradigm Shift: Symbiosis between Production and Information

I call the founding order of the twenty-first century an order of symbiosis, or an age of symbiosis.

The world is changing continually. It can happen that small changes—not very noticeable in themselves—accumulate so that, after some time, one realizes a major change has resulted. Other times, what seems at first to be a major, revolutionary change disappears or comes to affect only one specific field. However, the changes that now face humanity are the result of major transitions in economics, science and technology, art and culture, politics, thought, philosophy, society, and lifestyle. They amount to a major structural change or paradigm shift. Such global-scale paradigm shifts, affecting all fields, do not occur more than once in several hundred years.

These major changes are still underway. Of course, it is only a prediction that they will ultimately lead to a new order, an age of symbiosis. However, the signs pointing to the age of a new order of symbiosis can be observed and even verified in many areas.

First, we already have the shift from an industrial society to an information-oriented, or post-industrial, society. An industrial society mass produces uniform products, shapes the average human being—Heidegger's *das Mann*—and finally molds a homogeneous society. In contrast, the hallmarks of an information-oriented society are information-added value, individuality and creativity of the individual, and strong regional cultural identities. Already, more than 70 percent of Japan's GDP is from nonmanufacturing sectors. Moreover, the information-added value of design has become vital to competition in the remaining industrial and manufacturing sectors.

A society which stresses individuality and creativity will naturally become a diverse society, moving away from an age dominated by large organizations, large businesses, and macro-engineering. The present age is one in which smaller, venture-type enterprises can boldly challenge large businesses. Its weapons are managerial individuality, special ability and know-how, and individual creativity. Of course, this will also be an age of competition—through individuality and creativity—one in which diverse values exist in symbiosis. In such an age, each person needs to become conscious of his individuality and hone his creativity in order to succeed. In this sense, ours will be the beginning of a more demanding age than that of industrialized society.

As the nations of the world, both large and small, begin to awaken to their native cultures, this will produce an age of oppositions and friction among cultures, including religions. But meanwhile, the world is becoming borderless through the development of transportation and communications. It has become nearly impossible for any society to remain closed, not just economically, but also in the areas of science, technology, art, and culture. It is essential that our world aim for symbiosis among differing cultures through dialogue and good will, in spite of opposition and competition.

Linear to Nonlinear: Symbiosis between Developed and Developing Countries

Secondly, there is a change from Walt Rostow's formula of linear development through economic stages toward a nonlinear economic development. In 1960 the American economist Rostow was acclaimed for his theory of economic stages, according to which developing countries pass through a "takeoff" stage leading to a stage of maturity, and then to a stage of highly developed consumer culture. Western Europe, as well as the U.S. and Japan, have passed through each of these stages to become, first, industrialized, and then, mass-consumption societies. These three regions have now already become information oriented.

However, information orientation is also affecting newer nations and the so-called NIES (newly industrializing economies),[1] regardless of each country's "stage of development." With just a parabolic antenna, anyone may receive satellite broadcasts and other communications. In the blink of an eye, the Internet is linking the world's computers and building personalized global communications without distinction between "advanced" and "developing" countries. Everyday, more than 2,000 persons access my own home page, from all kinds of societies. They can peruse my work, read my books, respond to a questionnaire, and then participate in discussions.

This means that the order of information-oriented society is no longer pyramidal or tree-shaped. Instead, we are approaching a new age of economic symbiosis, in which countries at all stages of economic development can play a part in the world economy, making full use of their own available resources, industrial structures, climates, natural features, and cultures. The recent rapid progress of the NIES and other developing nations of Asia would, of course, have been impossible without intensive economic support and investment from advanced nations. Still, it is indisputable that Rostow's stage theory of economic development has lost much of its attractiveness.

As I shall explain, I am currently involved in planning Malaysia's new international hub airport, with its five runways, and Eco-Media City (a city of symbiosis), which utilizes an information infrastructure. The new airport uses the latest high technology and is one of the world's largest passenger and freight facilities, twice the size of the New Kansai Airport. Eco-Media City is expected to become the world's first experimental city combining ecotechnology with multimedia potential.

In physical terms, container freight shipping is also growing rapidly in the Asian region. Singapore presently handles the largest volume of container freight, followed by Pusan, Kaohsiung, and

Hong Kong. However, as active strategies for constructing information infrastructures are pursued in Asian countries, especially Singapore, there is a possibility that these may surpass the level of Europe's information infrastructure within ten years. In addition, economic spheres that span national borders are multiplying within Asia, including the Baht Economic Bloc,[2] the Northern Triangle, and the Golden Triangle of Southern Asia. Transportation and information are propelling the industrialized-era hierarchy of advanced, NIES, and developing nations into a new age, and forming a new distribution of industrial functions and economic and informational networking. Here, neither American supremacy nor Japanese economic leadership can continue to dominate the picture simply on account of titular membership in the G7[3] league of advanced nations, or because of America's military and nuclear strength. Asia's new configuration in the age of symbiosis is already evident.

Power to Authority: Symbiosis between Economy and Culture
    Thirdly, we are witnessing a shift from an age of power to one of authority. The end of the Cold War has not only led to a reduction of the U.S. and Russian military establishments, but also accelerated defense cutbacks in the nations formerly under the nuclear umbrellas of the two superpowers. As the international outcry against France's nuclear testing program proves, there is an unstoppable tide toward military cutback and disarmament.
    In the past, powerful countries have used military and economic strength to maintain world order. Science and technology have underlain this military and economic might. However, the time has come to end a world order maintained by might alone. A new era is beginning in which the authority of culture and traditions can no longer be ignored in foreign relations or economic activities.
    In the near future, only those leaders who explain and justify their actions to the people and show an understanding of art and culture, will receive the world's respect. They will be expected to discuss their dreams for the future and propose realistic strategies for achieving those dreams.
    China's military strength and population of more than one bil-

lion are not the only reasons China cannot be ignored as a major nation. With a history of several thousand years, China possesses a great culture and tradition, and this alone would lend authority. Moreover, the world at large perceives authority in the bold attitude of leaders who evince a definite awareness of China's own millennial cultural traditions. Malaysia's Prime Minister Mahathir and Deputy Prime Minister and Minister of Finance Anwar are two further outstanding Asian leaders, whom I shall discuss further, and at length, later on.

An Age of Life Principle: Symbiosis between Reason and Sensibilities

Fourthly, one may note a shift from the age of Mediterranean civilization toward an age of Pacific and, in particular, Asian civilization. In fact, this change parallels the shift away from an age of mechanical principles in the twentieth century toward an age of life principle. Details will be left for a later chapter. Here, I shall just touch on the most important points.

The twentieth century has been an age of macro-technologies and their visible applications, including steam engines, electricity, nuclear power, aircraft, and automobiles. In contrast, the technologies of the coming twenty-first century will be invisible or difficult for the eye to perceive, such as biotechnology, computer-based communication, soft technology, micro-machines, and ecotechnology.

It has already become difficult to achieve efficient organization and verification through mere analysis, assembly of parts, and a pursuit of mechanical principles. That is, the logic of reason and science alone no longer suffice. This implies that the age of modernist, rationalist dualism—with its historical development centered around the Mediterranean basin—has met an obstacle. For instance, both ecotechnology and biotechnology take life and nature itself as their resources and cannot be developed through scientific analytical methods alone. The nations of Asia enjoy an extremely favorable setting, as illustrated by the tropical forests and climatic conditions of Malaysia, which boasts abundant nature with an overwhelming number of living species. In addition, the people of Asia have maintained symbiotic lifestyles as dependent upon sensibility as upon reason.

Multimedia technology has also shifted rapidly from written documents and charts to such areas as three-dimensional simulation using imaging and animation. The creativity and rich sensibilities of designers and artists are much in demand in the creation of software as well as for its effective use. This is just one reason for predicting the dawn of an "age of Asia."

Age of the Matrix

Fifthly, a transition has begun from a linear order of radial structures with a single center, or treelike structures with a trunk, or axis, giving rise to branches; instead, we now have a preponderance of holonic, network, or matrix structures which are noncentric and directionally diverse, and whose parts may even be autonomous.

This has been termed a shift from radial to belt-shaped structures. A change toward this new type of order is expected, particularly in land-use and urban planning, as well as in all aspects of social systems. It can be interpreted as a symbiosis of parts with the whole.

A Symbiosis of Diversity: Non-Bourbakian Models, Complexity, and Immunity Network

Sixthly, there is a movement in divers academic fields from Bourbakian toward non-Bourbakian models.

The term "Bourbaki" originated in the pseudonym of a group of French scholars preoccupied with the rigor of a certain prototype of logical formation. Since the goal of this group was to pursue consistency and wholeness, the term came to connote modern science and philosophy as a whole from Euclid to Darwin.[4]

I will discuss non-Bourbakian models in another chapter. These include Koestler's Holon, Riemann's geometry, Prigogine's dissipative structures, Haken's synergetics, Mandelbrot's fractal geometry, Edgard Morin's theory of "noise," the theory of chaos, Margulis's continuous symbiosis theory, Scott Russell's *soliton*, David Bohm's implicated order, F. David Peat's synchronicity, and the biologist

Rupert Sheldrake's theory of morphogenesis. The systems thus modeled are sometimes said to belong to the "complex sciences."

Professor Ken-ichi Nishiyama of Saitama University refers to the age of these complex sciences as the age of an "immunity network." Non-Bourbakian systems are nonlinear, that is not connected sequentially. They emphasize flexible, horizontal styles of relationship and take chance and improvization into consideration. They tend to stress the potential of "chaotic" situations and aim for a symbiosis of diversity.

To state the case succinctly, over the past ten years the leading edge in all areas of scholarship has turned toward symbiosis. Nishiyama provides the notable interpretation that information transmitted via the neural system, which could be termed Bourbakian, is "smooth," while the immune system is informed by "sticky" data. This system thus undertakes crisis management using the mutual relationships maintained by diverse immune cells as information sites. They are like an informal community whose elements may at first appear disparate, but are protected from crises through constant vigilance that sharpens sensitivity to contingencies; the invading foreign body (or "noise") is, therefore, dealt with by means of a sort of improvization.

Homo Movens: Borderless Society

Seventh, there is today a shift from the agricultural, or fixed and disparate, societal grouping toward a nomadic, or mobile, society. In the 1970s, I published the book "*Homo Movens*" (admittedly a neologism) in which I predicted the birth of a mobile, borderless society. And in the 1980s, I wrote a sequel, *The Era of the Nomad*. This predicted that the lifestyle of people in the twenty-first century would be of a new type. I also hypothesized that cities of the information age would play the same role as oases in nomadic cultures.

Unlike the adventurous exchanges of the age of maritime discovery or the sites of near-global exchange in the Silk Road era, the age of *Homo Movens* in which we are now living is an age of transport at astounding speeds. Nor is this mobility experienced as something adventurous, but rather as the everyday life of ordinary people. In the twenty-first century, HST (hypersonic transport) will link New York and Tokyo in four hours, while Maglev trains travel between Tokyo and Osaka in 60 minutes at the speed of some 550 kilometers per hour.

The world will be interlinked by the global information infrastructure (GII) with capacities as high as gigabits per second. Furthermore, an information infrastructure using satellite broadcasting and communications, as well as high-capacity digital radio, will provide a network over the entire globe. With just a portable information terminal, people will be able to travel worldwide while exchanging not only text and images, but also three-dimensional simulation data. The essential feature of this age of electronic communications will be that people can send and receive information in real time without distinction between advanced and developing nations, while interactive information exchange will be commonplace. It is no longer necessary to rely only on so-called mass media, which transmit information one-way outbound from the "center."

In settled agricultural societies, experienced elders were relied on, with collective decision-making the most effective method of crisis management. Peace was ensured as long as people obeyed commands from above and eschewed selfish behavior.

In relationships such as families, communities, cities, and nations—as well as blocs of neighboring regions and blocs of neighboring countries—the scope of human behavior has gradually expanded during the process of transition from agricultural to industrialized society. There has been a shift from Gemeinschaft to Gesellschaft[5]—in other words, from a community-based society to a society of relationships based on company affiliation. In "*Homo Movens*," I used the term "time communities" to describe relations of solidarity among those living in different locations but connected in various ways at certain moments in time—such as people attending the same school, working in the same company, or belonging to the same club, or those who are drinking buddies or belong to a single church or sect.

Business is also approaching an age of borderless multinational corporations, both large and small, of global industries, and of international network enterprises. Thus Japan's Sumitomo Corporation has recently decided to move its operations headquarters for electrical appliances and computer-related products from Japan to Singapore. Virtually all Japanese makers of electrical appliances, audiovisual equipment, and personal computer-related items now have parts depots and assembly plants in Southeast Asia, from where they export to Europe and America. Likewise, there is no real need even to maintain a head office in Japan. All business organizations, including banks, securities firms, transport companies, general contractors, and universities, are at present moving toward internationalization and global networking. It goes without saying that the same holds for tourism.

New Nomadism: A New Lifestyle in the Era of Symbiosis

I call this new world of movement and communication characterized by *Homo Movens*, "the Era of the New Nomad." Nomadic peoples live by traveling, with their livestock, in groups ranging from several hundred to several thousand people. For such groups, oases function as valuable places to obtain information, recruit personnel, and exchange goods in markets. When they encounter other tribes in the desert in the course of their migrations, they need to be able to judge quickly while still far away—at least 1000 meters away, even at night—whether those tribes are friend or foe. If they are not vigilant, twenty or thirty heads will roll in an instant when the two groups pass. They also need the ability to determine, from the scent and moisture content of wind, the direction where there is grass, rain, or an oasis. Their capacity for accurate nighttime navigation is due to sensibility toward nature and training to observe the night sky.

Men and women, adults and children, all have particular roles in a nomadic group, which sometimes moves at great speed. Each individual actively fulfills his or her responsibilities. Since environmental shifts and encounters with enemies often occur suddenly, there is little time to contest the judgments of elders or parents. Nomadic groups need to achieve instantaneous teamwork—improvizational, intuitive, and interactive—without holding lengthy discussions. Not only the life of the individual, but also the fate of the group depends on constantly maintaining a state of symbiosis of reason with sensibility.

In this dimension, the human order and lifestyles of the twenty-first century may resemble those of nomadic peoples more than agricultural societies. It will be a new nomadic age—a non-Bourbakian social order.

Ecotechnology: Symbiosis among Agriculture, Industry, and Information Technology

Eighth, the order of the twenty-first century will present an age of symbiosis among primary, secondary, and tertiary industry. It was formerly surmised that in its move toward an information-oriented society, the world would progress from the stage of primary activities or industries (agriculture, fishery, forestry, and animal husbandry) to that of secondary ones (manufacturing, which itself would progress from heavy to light, then from mass consumables to the precision activities of computer-making, electronics, and robotics) and, finally, reach the stage of tertiary industry (service and information). However, this now seems an outdated theory.

In the twenty-first century, agriculture will evolve as a major growth area. At present, mankind needs roughly 100 million tons of cereals, 100 million tons of feed grains, and 100 million tons of marine edibles. As the standard of living gradually rises in developing counties, instead of direct cereal consumption, such as rice or wheat for bread, people will shift to a meat-eating lifestyle, feeding grain to cattle, pigs, chicken, and sheep. This will lead to a rapid increase in consumption. China, which in the past had been a food-exporting nation, has already become a net importer for this reason, as is the former Soviet Union. At present, the U.S. is the only net food-exporting nation. Prices soar worldwide whenever grain production falls due to adverse weather in the U.S.

The standard of living in developing countries is expected to rise rapidly in future, especially throughout Asia. It is estimated that by the year 2020, Indonesia and other countries may have economies larger than Germany's. An increasing escalation in food demand, particularly for cereals and grains, is also predicted as a result of population growth in China and other Asian nations.

For reasons such as these, the twenty-first century will be an age of major growth in agriculture and also one of expanded demand for fishery and forestry products. In the new, or revived, primary industries of agriculture, fishery, and other ecotechnologies that will adapt to this vast market, higher quality and major productivity gains will be made possible by symbiotic strategies such as those inherent to biotechnology and genetic engineering. Investors from advanced nations will be greatly attracted to Asian nations which have an abundant nature, fertile soil, and favorable climate year round, particularly those of Southeast Asia.

In addition to the direct linkage of agriculture with biotechnology, we are approaching an age of symbiosis between primary and secondary industry, in such forms as agricultural product processing and hydroponics, not to mention the symbiosis among primary, secondary, and tertiary industries with multimedia; for example, a distribution and sales system that benefits from the Internet.

There will be increasing demand for a life of symbiosis with nature. However, in addition to the recreation styles of the past, in which people headed for the ocean or the mountains to enjoy nature after finishing work, a new age will begin of symbiosis of cities with forests and nature, in which, for example, nature is incorporated in cities themselves by the creation of artificial forests. Thus, in addition to forestry, with its timber production for construction needs and raw materials for pulp, there will be a growing demand for living, rooted trees, especially deciduous ones, for use in urban landscaping of streets and parks. It will be necessary to cultivate such seedlings on a vast scale.

As I shall later relate, 50 percent (some 50 million tons) of the world's annual fish catch of 100 million tons is taken from just 0.1 percent of the entire ocean area. In such locations, nutrition from deciduous forests flows down rivers into oceans and phytoplankton is produced. Therefore, in order to redevelop inshore fishery, it is essential to stress joint strategies between forestry and fishery, and the symbiosis of forests and the ocean.

Finally, in order both to preserve the diversity of species and to develop improved varieties, more attention must be paid to techniques of genetic preservation and improvement. Centers for preservation and registration of the world's species should be established in Asia, especially in countries, such as Malaysia, which have outstanding natural conditions and climate.

Security in an Age of Symbiosis

Ninth is the question of what kinds of security systems will be needed in the world of the twenty-first century. I will not go into detail here since I discuss this elsewhere in the book, but the world's former system of security based on military power, especially the nuclear umbrella of late unhappy memory, is no longer sufficiently effective.

Just as a police force is needed to maintain order in civilian society, the U.S. plays a necessary role as a policing nation, and is one pillar supporting the world's security. This is expected to remain the case in the twenty-first century. However, the age has come to an end in which the U.S. and the Soviet Union, with their opposing ideologies of socialism and democracy, attempted to ensure the protection of countries in their own spheres of influence under a canopy of military and nuclear power.

An age of symbiosis is beginning among differing cultures, including small countries which formerly were relatively unknown. In this age, any country may well aim to become independent, taking pride in its cultural identity and/or religion, regardless of the size of the country and whether or not it is rich. In such an age, a guarantee of security backed up only by American military power will be insufficient. At the same time, both Japan and Germany are conscious of a past history which makes it difficult to exercise leadership based on economic potential. Moreover, a dispersion of economic power is occurring, especially in Asia. By about 2020, neither Japan, the U.S., nor Germany will retain superpower status.

In such an age of symbiosis among differing cultures, it is necessary to construct a security framework combining military, economic (including food), cultural (including religion), and environmental security. Humanity no longer faces death from military crises alone.

New crises are divers and will invariably include disruptions in economic and financial systems, environmental balance, food supply, and religious and cultural life. Because of the need for multilateral security, I advocate that economic aid be determined from a global viewpoint, like the Japanese contribution of one trillion yen during the Gulf War, as well as flexible combinations of aid to advanced countries and to less developed ones. Hence, my strong support for Premier Mahathir of Malaysia's EAEC[6] proposal. That is, while APEC offers the guarantee of security in the Pacific region by the U.S. military superpower, regional alliances such as NAFTA,[7] and EAEC in Southeast Asia, address the need for more divers types of "security," including concerns regarding economy, culture, and the environment. As I shall have cause to repeat, APEC and EAEC definitely do not conflict with one another.

Japan, in particular, requires this kind of new thinking which takes the twenty-first century into consideration. Instead of working to become a leader in Asia, Japan should place its support behind symbiosis in Asia, and should itself become a participating practitioner of the philosophy of symbiosis.

Life as an Information Site

A final—tenth, and inclusive—change is the shift from the age of mechanical principles to an age of life principles. A new definition of life might be "an information site that continually evokes meaning while perpetuating dynamic relationships."

The very life principle itself can be characterized as a dynamic "order" with continuous recycling and metabolism, sometimes under-, going transformations or metamorphoses, and existing in symbiosis with differing demands. As early as 1958, I objected to the CIAM[8] movement and its principles of modern architecture based on mechanical analogy, and I predicted that the twenty-first century would be an age of life principles. That was thirty-nine years ago, and my prediction seems ever closer to becoming reality.

The new founding order based on life principles means not only the end of bilateral ideological opposition—between socialism, on the one hand, and capitalism, freedom, and democracy, on the other—but also the end of an age in which power and supremacy could be achieved on the basis of territorial, military, and techno-economic development and expansion. A nation can no longer become a world leader simply because it has an extensive land area, possesses military power and nuclear weapons, or has massive economic strength.

Instead, information, traditions and culture, economic and technical prowess, and an unpolluted natural environment are all essential conditions for becoming a world leader. Since even developing countries can be rich in these, the small countries of the world and Asian countries, in particular, will suddenly come to play an important role. Though military and economic strength foster power, it is traditions and culture that produce authority. Dualist opposition between economically advanced and developing nations will no longer apply. The old system of security based only on military or nuclear might will also cease to function.

The former Soviet Union, an empire of suppressed minorities, could not avoid crumbling. Belgium long ago separated into Flemish- and Walloon-, or French-speaking regions, forming a federation. In contrast to the Soviet Union, China's unique modernization process is taking a path at odds to dualistic opposition of the recent past, introducing the principles of a market economy while maintaining a nominally socialist system. This can be seen as a large-scale experiment in the principles of symbiosis. China is likely to become a world leader if it gradually expands the principles of symbiosis while avoiding sudden political changes and proceeds to form a loose and equitable federation among its more than fifty minority nationalities.

Taking the place of superpowers and federations, the role of regional blocs will increase. In addition to the field of economics, factors of cultural, religious, and linguistic affinity among neighboring countries will be emphasized in the formation of regional units, such as the EU, NAFTA, and EAEC. Our age of diversity is, in fact, a reason for countries to seek out closer relationships. This kind of bloc formation differs from the protectionist, closed blocs of former ages. Instead, we shall see loose, flexible relationships among highly independent countries. An age of dynamic rapport is beginning in which nations will maintain free, open-minded relations with other nations of the world even while belonging to a bloc.

Friendly relationships among countries and solidarity within blocs is not necessarily limited to military security and trading activities. A mutual respect gained through cultural exchange will come to exert the same force as that of military and economic strength.

I have here stated my predictions for the founding philosophy of the twenty-first century, symbiosis, from a variety of aspects. I believe I have made it clear how, from every angle, these predictions converge in a single doctrine. The philosophy of symbiosis thus lays a foundation of universal scope and intent for the twenty-first century that is now virtually upon us.

2

FROM THE MACHINE AGE TO AN AGE OF LIFE

Twentieth Century: Age of the Machine Principle

Industrial society inspired the ideal of modern architecture. The steam engine, train, automobile, and airplane freed humanity from labor and permitted us to journey into a realm of the unknown. The Model T Ford made the possession of an automobile, until then the privilege of the rich, available to the masses. Le Corbusier[1] declared the home a "machine for living," Sergei Eisenstein[2] called cinema a machine, and the Italian Futurist Marinetti[3] also spoke of a poem as a machine. Le Corbusier was fond of placing the latest-model automobile in front of his completed works, and the Futurist city of Antonio Sant'Elia was an expression of mechanical dynamism. Not only for artists and architects but for the general public as well, the machine was a longed-for savior that would blaze a trail for humanity's future.

The age of the machine valued models, norms, and ideals. The success of the Model T offers abundant proof of this. The masses were satisfied, and as the machine seemed to promise the rosiest of futures, no one thought to doubt. In this manner, the middle class shaped itself into the ideal market for the machines it mass-produced. As a natural result, architects saw their clientele gradually change from royalty and the extremely wealthy to a growing middle class.

The International Style architecture that became the prototype of

Henry Ford's Model T: the first completely mass-produced vehicle.

modern building was thus an expression of the models and norms of the age of the machine. This International Style was brought into being by the capitalists who manufactured such products and the middle class that used them. Nor should we forget that the models, norms, and ideals of the age of the machine were championed by the spirit of universality fundamental to European civilization; from the age of Greece and Rome similar precepts have characterized Western thought. To take an important example, the "Catholic" of the Roman Catholic Church means, in fact, "universal."

Westernization—Index of Progress

The age of the machine was an age of the European spirit, an age of universality. We can say, then, that the twentieth century has been characterized by Eurocentrism and Logocentrism (this latter concept posits one ultimate truth for the world, attainable via human intelligence). Such an attitude results in a society valuing science and technology over art, religion, and culture, domains in which feeling and sensitivity play a major role.

The great reform movement that swept Japan from the last years of the Edo period (1603–1867) through the Meiji period (1868–1912) as we modernized and internationalized, was modeled on the letter and spirit of Western civilization. It had no other goal than to measure progress by degree of Europeanization. Thus, Japanese architects of the time debated ardently about which mode of Western building to adopt. Such well-known Western-style works of the period as survive today—Tokyo Station, the Bank of Japan, the old Supreme Court, and the Yokohama Specie Bank—were all products of this policy. Western food and Western clothing enjoyed a vogue. Modernization was pursued in every field by adopting Western models in education, the economy, government, and the legal system.

This worship of the West, and the inferiority complex that is the other side of the same coin, persisted in large measure in postwar Japan. For architects, such as Togo Murano,[4] Seiichi Shirai,[5] Kunio Maekawa,[6] and Kenzo Tange,[7] Western architecture was an absolute, almost sacred ideal. Whenever Murano received a new commission, he always began work by traveling to Europe and sketching details of well-known monuments. This tendency continues today with the likes of Arata Isozaki[8] and certain younger architects, who, by some strange and inexplicable twist of fate, prize Western architecture over their own tradition.

The idea of "architecture for architecture's sake" that we hear from Hans Hollein[9] and Arata Isozaki has much in common with the old Logocentrism. The architecture with a capital "A" that Isozaki advocates—architecture as form—and Noam Chomsky's[10] deep linguistic structure and universal grammar are all examples of the Logocentrism and universality that characterized the age of the machine.

Humanism played an important role in the late medieval period by liberating humankind from the age of God. But in the machine age, the human race has allowed itself to succumb to the delusion that, with machines in its employ, it has attained the role of God and can now rule both the world and the universe. Today, humanism has become synonymous with anthropocentrism and Logocentrism. This emphasis on human superiority in the machine age is counterproductive in the present age of life, with its emphasis on the restoration of the environment and ecological thinking.

Aesthetically speaking, the ideals of the age of the machine were economy, simplicity, precision, purity, and maximization of function, as well as abstraction and clarity. The architecture of the machine as envisioned by Le Corbusier shared the purity that we can see in his early paintings. It had to exemplify a norm, just as the Parthenon was seen to do. Finally, it had to possess the clarity and force of the Mediterranean sun, which resolves all into light and shadow. The Parthenon, viewed in such context, is the definitive and eternal monument to the European spirit.

When Bruno Taut and Walter Gropius visited Japan and praised the Ise shrine and Katsura Detached Palace as embodying the norms of modern architecture, they were praising simplicity, abstraction, and freedom from ornament. To be sure, they focused only on those aspects that reflected their own modernist convictions.

Some argue that the formal aspect of today's architecture should be high-tech—meaning, basically, quotations from machine technology. In borrowing the forms of Russian Constructivism, the Pompidou Center by Richard Rogers and Renzo Piano, and Norman Foster's Hong Kong and Shanghai Bank headquarters both seem at first glance representative machine-age works, but in fact they are quite recent. While architecture of the earlier twentieth century was often simple and efficient, expressing the Logocentrism of the European spirit, the works just mentioned are neither particularly rational nor efficient. In them, the image of the machine exists as surface; it is autonomous, and constitutes a decor—an experiment in transition from the age of the machine to an uncertain future.

I have said that abstraction was one of the characteristics of the machine-age aesthetic. Indeed, abstraction was common to all the arts of the modern period: architecture, painting, sculpture, and literature, as well as philosophy.

When Le Corbusier discussed Purism in art, he wrote that the world was composed of such abstract forms as cones, cylinders, and cubes. The simplicity favored by modern architecture was a device for achieving this abstraction. The simplification of process that yielded increased production and the simple clarity aimed for in

Norman Foster's Hong Kong and Shanghai Bank, now Hongkong Bank.

modern architecture were regarded as triumphs of reason over the plurality and variety of real life. Modern architecture sought to banish historical expression, decoration, and *topos*.

Yet geometrical form is not the exclusive possession of modern architecture. In ancient cultures, geometrical forms—the pyramids of Egypt, the circle and square referred to in the Chinese *Huai-nan-zi*,[11] the keyhole-shaped tumuli of China and Japan, and the conical Tower of Babel—were thought of as mystical shapes expressing the ultimate being of the universe. The Revolutionary-period French architect Claude-Nicolas Ledoux frequently employed geometrical forms in his works. Yet the circles and spheres he used were more expressions of symbolism and mysticism than of "pure" abstraction—an idea to which I shall return.

Persistence of the European Spirit?

I have said that the age of the machine was an age of the European spirit, and I would now like to expand on this. Edmund Husserl, in his *Crisis of European Sciences and Transcendental Phenomenology* (1936), defines the twentieth century as the age of objective rationality. The fundamental tendency of the natural sciences, geometry, physics, and psychology in the age of modern rationality has been to objectivize—reflecting the conviction that a single truth underlies all reality. These sciences seek, through analysis, to reduce reality to measurability, thereby creating a norm based on a unified world view. This is remarkably similar to the process through which a machine may be reduced to its parts or by which standardized products are distributed universally throughout the world.

This vision of the world—an objective rationality and modern rationalism—was progressively elaborated by Euclid, Galileo, Newton, Lavoisier, and Darwin. Fundamental to the rational sciences is the formally axiomatic Bourbakian compilation of mathematical principles of 1939 onward, with its rejection of visual apparatus in favor of the possibilities of logical analysis. Such objective rationalism represents the absolute, orthodox current of European thought—the current of thought in which through the ages we may situate Plato, Aristotle, Descartes, Hegel, Chomsky, and Habermas. The universalism of the Catholic Church, which is the backbone of European religion, operates in a similar fashion. At the start is a single ideal existence: God. The dualism that lies at the base of this stream of thought is the same mechanical principle that makes all reduction and analysis possible. The world is perceived as sets of opposites: part and whole, flesh and spirit, science and art, good and evil, life and death, humanity and nature, and, finally, intellect and feeling. The notion of majority rule, the basic tenet of democracy, is also a dualistic choice between "yes" and "no." The most advanced manifestation of dualism is the computer. The principle by which thought can be simulated through the repeated choice between 1 and 0 at superhuman speeds must surely be the apogee of such a philosophy. In this dualistic world ambiguous, vague, and multivalent zones are rejected. Contradictory elements, the symbiosis of opposing existences, and mixed states are all treated as chaotic or irrational.

The architecture and arts of the age of the machine have employed analysis, structure, and organization to achieve a universal synthesis. This closely resembles the process of creating a machine, in which parts are assembled in such a way as to be able eventually to perform a certain function. Ambiguity, the intervention of foreign elements, accident, and multivalent elements are excluded. Instructions must not be literary or poetic, they must be firmly prescriptive. Indeed, a linear circuitry is the norm.

Thus, schools must be school-like, hospitals like hospitals, offices like offices, and homes like homes. But is there really any objective standard for a school, defining what it is like? In fact, differences among hospitals—hospitals for the aged, psychiatric hospitals, emergency facilities, examination and diagnostic facilities— can be more marked than the difference between a hospital and a school. In the real world, there is no abstract "humanity" with a capital "H"; humanity includes men, women, adults, children, Mr. A and Ms. B.

The twentieth century is wrestling with these contradictions as it nears its end. The fact that the end of the age of the machine is approaching concurrently with the end of Eurocentrism, Logocentrism, and industrial society itself, has aroused unrest throughout the world. Will the curtain on the twenty-first century be raised by revolutions in all of these realms? Will the new age begin with the rejection of the machine and the age of the European spirit? I think not. The new century will carry with it the burden of the previous 150 years—which will exist in symbiosis with a new philosophy, a new technology.

Architecture of the Age of Life Principle

In contradistinction to the bygone machine age, I call the twenty-first century an age of life. As I said earlier, my work over the past four decades has consistently raised a challenge to the machine and heralded the architecture of life. I co-founded the Metabolism movement in 1959 and consciously selected its terms and key concepts from the vocabulary of life-principles. Machines do not grow, change, or metabolize of their own accord. By contrast, "Metabolism" was the natural choice for a keyword to announce the beginning of the age of life principle.

The astonishing *plurality* of life stands in sharp contrast to machine-age concepts such as homogeneity and universality. As a result of the combination of individual cells and the genetic information transmitted by the spiral configurations of DNA, each individual life is unique. For some time we have been reexamining Darwin's theory of evolution. We must challenge his claim that the human species stands at the peak of its evolutionary climb; that notions of economic prosperity and technological culture peculiar to ourselves should serve as selection criteria for all living beings.

Labels like "undeveloped," "developing," and "developed" nations represent a notion of progress similar to Darwin's. The economic and technological advances of an age when universality prevailed are now topics of intense reflection and revision. In the new age it is the

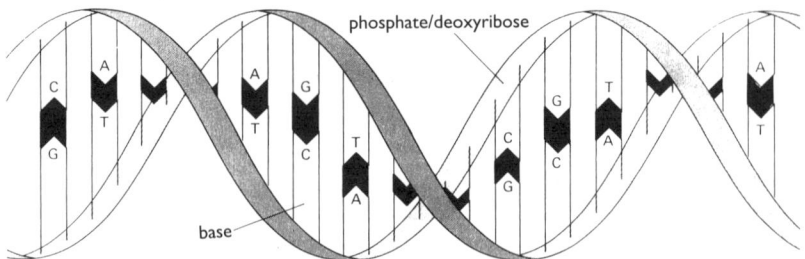

Helical structure of DNA (*Molecular Biology of the Cell*, Garland Publishing, 1983).

very plurality of life that has value. Our renewed interest in the environment and the increasing importance given to ecology aim at preserving this diversity.

A new overture to diversity is evident in the economic and technological sectors of society. We must insist on a symbiosis of heterogeneous cultures as the goal of our economies and technologies. We must move from a concept of economic assistance and technology transfer toward an agenda of perpetual transformation—discovering ways for existing advanced and traditional technologies to exist in symbiosis. Henceforward, technology will have to be adapted in ways appropriate to each region.

For example, in India, even today, dried cow dung supplies most of the energy for cooking fires. The Indians regard cows as sacred beasts, and the use of cow dung for fuel is an inseparable part of Indian culture and life. As Indian energy policy, would it not be best to combine the use of atomic energy, hydroelectric power, and cow dung in the most workable combination? This type of accommodation of technology—so that old and new exist in symbiosis—is what we may expect in the age of life.

By analogy, the intercultural architecture that I have advocated for some time is a hybrid approach, in which elements of different cultures exist in symbiosis—an architecture attuned to the environment through the symbiosis of tradition and advanced technology. Differences are precisely the proof that we are living beings; and it is these differences that create meaning.

Function vs. Heredity and Meaning

In Japan, nonmanufacturing industries already account for more than seventy percent of the GNP. Such nonmanufacturing industries as banking, broadcasting, publishing, computer software research, education, graphic and product design, and the service and distribution sectors do not produce goods per se; instead, they produce added value.

Information society and the information industries are based on the production of distinctions and of meaning. People buy clothes based on the added value of their design. As Jean Baudrillard has reminded us, a fair percentage of all pianos manufactured are never played; they stand in the living room, keyboards untouched. Such pianos are not purchased for their function as musical instruments but as symbols communicating that the purchaser enjoys music, or has the wealth to buy such an instrument. In industrial society, this phenomenon is regarded negatively. But, in information society, these untouched pianos possess a meaning of their own.

Postmodern architecture has, in its way, grasped this transition from industrial to information society. This is a notion now regarded with interest even in the fields of physics, science, mathematics, and philosophy. It is unfortunate for architecture that the postmodern has been defined in an extremely narrow fashion, as a particular style. Yet the failure of postmodern architecture in this narrow sense demonstrates the hopelessness of any attempt to return to the modern architecture of the machine age.

Just as the plurality of life is ensured by heredity, architecture acquires its plurality through the inheritance of tradition. This occurs at many levels and there is no single method. The Japanese style of architecture called *sukiya* employs a strategy by which historical forms are adhered to, while new techniques and materials are introduced to produce gradual change. The *sukiya* architecture of Sen no Rikyu, Furuta Oribe, Kobori Enshu (see chapter 7) and, in more recent times, Isoya Yoshida[12] and Togo Murano, are all examples of this. My own *sukiya* architecture, which I call *hanasuki*, is another example of this symbiosis of past and present. In Europe, Palladio's architecture affords an example from the sixteenth century of inherited tradition.

A second method of conserving tradition is to *fragment* historical forms and place elements freely throughout a new work of architecture, the method of "recombining." Following this strategy, the original meaning that such historical forms once held is subverted, and in their recombination the pieces acquire a fresh multivalent significance.

Yet another approach to reexpressing the architectural past is to highlight the ideas, aesthetics, and lifestyles that underlie historical symbols and forms. Tangible symbols and forms are manipulated intellectually, thus creating a sophisticated mode characterized by abstraction, irony, wit, twists, gaps, and metaphor. Deciphering such elements in contemporary buildings requires a broad knowledge of tradition and a sharp sense of humor. Clearly, one's approach to historical tradition will depend upon the context in which a work is to be set.

What Robert Venturi,[13] the father of eclectic postmodernism, Michael Graves,[14] and Arata Isozaki have in common is not only that they all lean too far in the direction of the historical, but that their works are an extension of Eurocentrism. Nor should we ignore that each of these three architects is subtly influenced by a feeling of inferiority toward Europe common to both Japan and the United States.

Symbiosis and "New Tech"

In decided contrast to this, symbiosis is made possible by a reverence for the sacred zone between different cultures, opposing factors, and diverse elements—not to mention extremes of dualistic opposition. The sacred zone of another's individuality, or a region's cultural tradition, is an unknown territory deserving of respect. If, however, our sacred zones are too all-encompassing, effort must be made to achieve extended dialogue and exchange. Insistence that all aspects of a particular people's lives constitute an inviolable sacred zone, such as an exclusive nationalism or closed regionalism, is not conducive to symbiosis.

A second condition necessary to the achievement of symbiosis is the presence of intermediary space. Intermediary space is important because it encourages opponents to abide by common rules, to reach a common understanding. I refer to this as "tentative understanding." Intermediary space does not exist as a tangible commodity; it is itself tentative and dynamic. The presence of intermediary space makes possible a vibrant symbiosis that incorporates opposition.

Always, as the mutual penetration and mutual understanding of two opposing elements proceeds, the boundaries of intermediary space are in flux. The possibility of such an intermediary space reveals the life-principle, in all its ambivalence and multivalence.

Tolerance, a lack of clear-cut boundaries, and the interpenetration of interior and exterior are particular features of Japanese art, culture, and architecture. The many essays I have written over three decades on various aspects of Japanese culture—such as *ma* (interval in time or space); *engawa* (veranda); the concept of *senu hima*, the moment of silence between thought and act as described by Zeami in his treatises on the Noh drama; "street space"; Rikyu grey; permeability as transparency; lattices; and *hanasuki*—all have been attempts to pursue this idea of an intermediary space. The thread of Buddhist thought that runs through all Japanese culture is itself a philosophy of symbiosis, with the result that, for me, there is a strong natural connection between architecture of the age of life and Japanese culture. And, of course, this is distinguishable in my work.

Intermediary space can occasionally engender metamorphosis. Metamorphosis is one of the special features of the life process: a larva is transformed into a butterfly, an egg into a bird or a fish. No life-principle is more sudden or extreme. Architecturally speaking, such elements as gates, atriums, and all manner of large-scale or otherwise unusual spaces move people because we perceive some sort of leap into the extraordinary—a sudden drama that cannot be explained by mere function. Such intermediary spaces as streets, plazas, parks, waterfronts, bits of townscape, city walls, city gates, rivers, landmark towers—as well as urban infrastructures, such as freeways—play a role as stimuli enriching the existence of individual buildings.

I think it may now be clear why, in the thirty-eight years since I began my architectural career in 1959, I have chosen metabolism, metamorphosis, and symbiosis as key terms and concepts to express the principle of life.

Philosophies supporting the establishment of an architecture of the age of life can indeed be found in the history of Western thought, but in the face of an overpowering tradition of dualism and objective rationalism they are a small minority. Unlike Plato and Aristotle, who represent the mainstream of ancient Greek thought, Democritus and the pre-Socratics expounded a theory of naturalism based on atoms. Leibniz, Spinoza, and Wittgenstein regarded nature as within us and possessing a formative power. Heidegger advocated a "culture of hearing" as opposed to the mainstream Western "culture of sight." Merleau-Ponty rejected Descartes's mind-body dualism. Lévi-Strauss exposed the relativity of all cultural values with his theory of structuralism. Deleuze and Guattari proposed the rhizome as a model for a new order of multiplicity and variety. More recently, Baudrillard spoke of an "autonomy of the façade" and the death of the economy. Derrida advocated the deconstruction of Eurocentrism and Logocentrism. Julia Kristeva imagined a plural "I," which she called a polylogue. The mathematician David Boehm discovered "implicated order," which in terms of a nonlinear analysis explains phenomena of the natural world previously thought to be random. Mandelbrot conceived of a fractal geometry. Arthur Koestler postulated the Holon, a symbiosis of part and whole. There were Prigogine's dissipative Structure and Haken's synergetics, which speak for themselves, and Adorno's nonidentity, which rejects the whole. Foucault urged the deconstruction of modern rationality and flight from the center. Umberto Eco contributed his exciting novels *The Name of the Rose* and *Foucault's Pendulum*. Post-Webern serial music composers such as Stockhausen and Boulez, the latter only recently dead, made their mark as well. While the philosophy and science of the machine age were epitomized in the axioms of the Bourbakian model of mathematical logic, the new philosophy, science, literature, and music of the age of life will all be "problematic"—linked to that philosophy of symbiosis I have advocated for the past nearly four decades.

Not only science and philosophy, but technology as well, are facing a major transformation as the age of life dawns. While technology of the machine age—corresponding to the age of modern architecture—was visible, embodied by the steam engine and the automobile, the main players in the technology of the age of life will be communications, biotechnology, genetic engineering, and other "invisible" sciences. As opposed to the "high-tech" architecture of the age of the machine—created as a metaphor for the machine—the "new-tech" architecture of the age of life will be faced with the extremely difficult problem of expressing these invisible technologies. So-called autonomy of the façade will allow for the birth of a new symbolic architecture. Expressions of technology will proceed on a parallel course within an "autonomy of the façade" in the age of life, while the spirit of invisible technologies will be abstractly or symbolically expressed.

My own architecture pursues a revisionist thesis rooted in this age of life principle, based on three key concepts: metabolism, metamorphosis, and symbiosis.

3

SYMBIOSIS IN THE ECONOMY

ASPEN/1979

It was toward the end of 1978 that I received a telephone call from my friend Lou Dorfsman, a graphic designer and then vice-president of CBS. "Would you agree to be chairman of the 1979 Aspen International Design Conference?" he asked. Aspen, Colorado, was originally a silver-mining town, and after the mines were closed, it was redeveloped as a resort. Three famous events are held each year in Aspen: the Aspen Music Festival, the Seminar of the Aspen Research Institute, and the Aspen International Design Conference. The latter is not only a meeting of architects and designers; philosophers, business people, government officials, and politicians also participate. It is held yearly in summer.

During the next six months I devised a private plan to turn several aspects of Japanese culture, usually identified as unique, into the principal themes of discussion. Among these were some that are well understood by Americans. On the other hand, certain features of life in Japan that Americans tend to equate with their own culture are, in fact, quite different. My intention was to clarify these.

After discussing my ideas with Dorfsman, I decided to make the theme of the conference "Japan and the Japanese"—in search of a path of symbiosis for the U.S. and Japan. Symbiosis among different cultures was a theme that I had promoted since the 1960s.

Aspen International Design Conference (1979).

The themes I selected for symposia were diverse: "Rice," "Decision by Consensus," "Isolationism," "The Hedge," "The Veranda," and "The Bullet Train." (I decided to express these topics in Japanese, hence, "*Kome*," "*Ringi*," "*Sakoku*," and so forth.) These themes were keywords not only for understanding something important about Japan, but also, I believed, for discovering a way to achieve symbiosis between America and Japan.

In the symposium on "Rice," for example, we reached the conclusion that California rice was just as delicious as Japan's *koshihikari*, but then went on to discuss the fact that in California rice included none of the cultural elements that are part of rice production in Japan: folk crafts, folk songs, festivals, saké-making, and farming life. My conviction that, for Japan, rice is a "sacred cow," that rice *is* culture, and my opposition to the complete liberalization of rice imports from the United States has continued from the 1979 Aspen conference to the present day.

In the discussion on "Decision by Consensus," we tried to evaluate the traditional Japanese decision-making method of working from the bottom of the organization up, in a democratic, consensus-style fashion—as opposed to the top-down decision-making style of the American corporate world. The discussants concluded that even such an apparently different method might well be adopted in the United States.

In the discussion on "Isolationism," an interesting idea was proposed. Instead of regarding Japan during the Tokugawa, or Edo period (1603–1867), as completely isolated from the rest of the world, perhaps it was possible to note a dynamic semi-isolationism, under the shield of which the country took in actively only what it wanted, rejecting the rest.

In the sessions on "Hedges" and "Verandas," Japanese traditions relating to the symbiosis of human beings and nature, as well as of architecture and nature, were dealt with.

Sakyo Komatsu,[1] writer; Heisuke Hironaka,[2] mathematician; Issey Miyake,[3] fashion designer; Tohru Haga,[4] professor of Tokyo University; Nagisa Oshima,[5] film director; Masuo Ikeda,[6] artist; Toshi Ichiyanagi,[7] composer; Tadanori Yokoo,[8] graphic designer; and Yotaro Kobayashi,[9] CEO of Fuji Xerox—all came from Japan to the Aspen conference, which was very productive.

Both Japanese and English were official conference languages, so at first there was resistance to and criticism of my decision to express the symposia themes in Japanese only. This was the first time that a conference had ever been held in the United States in which Japanese was heard with such regularity and frequency. At the end, I was moved when an American government official walked up to me, shook my hand, and remarked, "This conference demonstrated for the first time that English, too, is no more than a regional language. I feel as if my eyes were fully opened for the first time. Thank you." Another participant declared, "I feel as if I understand at last the way in which Japanese tradition and contemporary Japanese life are linked. I am convinced that Japan and the United States can live in symbiosis."

YOKOHAMA/1980

At its closing, the 1979 Aspen International Design Conference left an enormous impact on the more than two thousand American professionals and students who attended, as well as on the Japanese panelists. What we all learned from the conference was that it was possible to erect a common ground on which different cultures could meet, as long as differences were openly acknowledged. After returning to Japan, many of the Japanese panelists sought to continue to discuss further the topics raised at the Aspen Conference, and the Japanese Inter-Design Forum was founded with this aim. The idea was to choose a different location outside Tokyo each year as a site.

The first conference was held the following year, in Yokohama, and I took on the joint role of organizer and chairman. The main theme was "Toward the Age of Symbiosis." From outside Japan, we invited the French critic and urban-planning scholar with whom I had been discussing the idea of symbiosis since the 1960s, Françoise Choay; the Polish film director Andrzej Wajda; the architect Paolo Soleri, who was building an eco-city in the Arizona desert; Renzo Piano, the co-architect of the Georges Pompidou Center; and the legendary desert poet Alias Adonis.[10] Japanese participants included those who had been present at the Aspen conference, plus philosopher Takeshi Umehara,[11] critic Daizo Kusayanagi,[12] art critic Shuji Takashina,[13] art critic Ichiro Hariu,[14] critic Shichihei Yamamoto,[15] Noh actor Hideo Kanze,[16] writer Taichi Sakaiya,[17] writer Hisashi Inoue,[18] composer Yasushi Akutagawa,[19] film director Masahiro Shinoda,[20] writer Yuusuke Fukada,[21] architect Tadao Ando,[22] and others.

I still marvel today at how many significant issues were raised in discussion at the various symposia on the symbiosis of nature and humankind, and the symbiosis of different cultures.

Nature and Imposition

Paolo Soleri, originator and architect of the experimental city called Arcosanti in the Arizona desert, put forth the idea that the symbiosis of humankind and nature was one in which human beings continuously create new things and, in doing so, perpetuate change on an unfeeling, insentient nature. To live in symbiosis with nature required a policy of total transformation.

In contrast to this viewpoint, Shichihei Yamamoto declared that Paolo Soleri's "symbiosis" was merely of a Western type, creating an ambiance in which no Japanese could live. According to Yamamoto, the Japanese observe and merge with nature, and whatever did not accomplish that was "unnatural." Symbiosis in this Japanese interpretation, then, was an imminent harmony. That differences in cultures that were so largely reflected in the discussion of symbiosis offered a hint for carrying such discussion to a still deeper level.

Another stimulating issue was raised by the Arabian poet Alias Adonis, also a logician and interested in the semantic theories of Structuralism. He addressed the trend then apparent throughout the Third World for Western culture to impose upon and to trivialize local culture; at the same time traditional cultures repelled any creative reform offered by contemporary culture, and political regimes exploited the customs and traditions of the masses to preserve their own hold on power. Symbiosis, he insisted, would be impossible as long as traditional cultures did not liberate themselves from both Western culture and the stagnating force of their own traditions.

The issue of potential obstructions to the arrival of an age of symbiosis as raised by Yamamoto and Adonis, percolated in my mind, until finally I organized my thoughts on the subject in my 1987 book, *The Philosophy of Symbiosis*.

Roots of the Philosophy of Symbiosis

It may be of interest for me to explain at somewhat greater length how it is I came to champion the philosophy of symbiosis.

When I was at middle school, the principal was Dr. Benkyo Shiio, a professor of Buddhist philosophy and author of many works, including *Kyosei Hokku Shu* (Verses on Co-Living), *Kyosei Bukkyo* (A Buddhism of Co-Living), and *Kyosei Kyohon* (Manual of Co-Living), but at that time I had not yet read any of his books. However, the lectures that Professor Shiio gave on Buddhism remain firmly fixed in my mind. "Human beings," he declared, "cannot live without eating meat and vegetables. They cannot survive without inorganic minerals. Not only that, but we are alive because all sorts of bacterial life forms live in our digestive organs. Human beings are kept alive by other life forms and by nature itself. And when people die, they become ashes and return to the earth, where they in turn are eaten by plants, animals, and other forms of life." This relation of giving life and being given life is the relation of "co-living" (*tomoiki*). While symbiosis is the most basic teaching of Buddhism, Professor Shiio's message is, evidently, none other than the message of environmentalism and ecology so important today.

The Consciousness-Only philosophy of India has also served as a guiding theme for my personal life. For example, my home on the eleventh floor of an apartment building in the Akasaka district in Tokyo contains a garden and replica of the teahouse by Enshu Kobori that was part of his Fushimi residence at Kyoto. I have christened this tea room "Hut of Consciousness-Only." And my name as a practitioner of the art of tea is Yuishikian Kuchu, or "Suspended in Emptiness of the Consciousness-Only Retreat." I was given this name by the tea master Michio Kondo, in reference to my tea room suspended in space, on the eleventh floor.

I have no intention of discussing the philosophy of Consciousness-Only in detail here, but a basic concept of the philosophy is the *alaya*, or unconditioned stream of consciousness. The *alaya* consciousness does not distinguish pairs of opposites, such as good and evil, body and spirit, human beings and nature. Instead, it posits an intermediary zone in which such pairs exist together in symbiosis.

Here, these opposing, contradictory elements exist together in a state of undifferentiation, as at all boundaries and peripheries. Because it is undifferentiated, *alaya* produces dense and deeply significant shades of meaning.

Since Western culture is founded in a dualist opposition, it rejects undifferentiated and ambiguous elements as irrational, incomprehensible, and unscientific. However, economic achievement, science, and technology have played an enormous role in the modernization of the West. Nothing scientific could have been attained without the dogma of modern rationalism—with its oppositions and dualist outlook.

But today the world has embarked on a critical period of transition to a new age, and it is not in the least surprising to find rationalism being questioned, while intermediary zones, previously rejected by the West, are being reevaluated in economics, science, and technology.

It need not be emphasized that the philosophy of Consciousness-Only, as part of the fabric of Mahayana Buddhism, has broadly influenced Japanese culture and the Japanese people. If I may give one further example, let us look at the traditional Japanese aesthetic—that of symbiosis.

I personally gave the name *hanasuki* to an aesthetic that seeks to create rich significance by allowing or causing different elements to exist in symbiosis.

In his *Kadensho*, the Noh actor and playwright Zeami wrote, "When playing a night scene, bring daylight to it, and when playing an old man, bring a youthful feeling to it; when you play a demon, do it with gentleness." Zeami called this process of bringing diverse or opposing elements together to create a deeply expressive richness, *hana*.

It is often thought that the Japanese are vague, specifically that Japanese politicians are so vague that no one can ever know what on earth they are saying. The aesthetic of symbiosis that I call *hanasuki* is not this kind of vagueness, which can't be pinned down one way or another. It is an ambiguity produced purposely and creatively, ambiguity as a new essence altogether. This Buddhist concept of symbiosis and the symbiotic aesthetic of traditional Japanese culture cannot, as Shichihei Yamamoto suggested at Aspen, be applied in contemporary international society as it is at present.

However, Japan—which has become an international economic power—is now expected to play a major role in the construction of a new world order, whether or not its people wish to. Monetary contributions are important, of course, but I believe it is even more essential for our country to participate directly in the creation of a new order of culture. I should like to see us, therefore, recast the philosophy of symbiosis we find in Japanese Buddhism and traditional aesthetics in a way that is useful to ourselves and our contemporaries.

Transition

The Soviet Union has collapsed, the Cold War is over, America is searching for a new role, and various national groups are declaring their independence—what kind of new structure are these developments leading to?

In 1960, the largest-ever international design conference was held in Japan. As a young architect, I helped with the preparations, and—with several other architects and critics—founded the Metabolism movement. We were concerned with how we might face the relentless domination of Western culture; my conclusion was a declaration of "the age of life."

Once it had been accepted that Western culture was the most advanced culture, all "minor" cultures were inherently unmodern, and every step they took toward Western culture was regarded as progress. The question of whether traditional culture had to be abandoned for the sake of economic progress was, so to speak, on the lips of all developing and Third World nations.

Japan had rejected Westernization, cutting itself off during the Edo period. Subsequently, the great transformation of Japan wrought by the determined efforts of the Meiji government resulted in Japan categorizing all traditional culture as unmodern and becoming an outstanding pupil in the school of Westernization, until it had achieved such astonishing economic results that it seemed to outstrip its teachers.

But the position that Japan finds itself in today is clearly a dangerous one, on the very edge of a precipice. Its teacher, the Western world, is engaged in serious self-criticism, and is beginning to identify new goals. This will leave Japan an honors student without a school, and the fact of the matter is that Japan does not know how to respond.

Diversity in an Age of Life

The reason Western culture stood at the undisputed peak of modern civilization was that all aspects of philosophy and practice were orchestrated like a grand symphony, moving forward in a unified direction. The rationalism and dualism that dominated philosophical thought from Aristotle to Descartes, Darwin's "survival of the fittest" theory of evolution, the belief in the universalism of the Catholic Church, the doctrine of scientific proof, the Bauhaus[23] school of art that celebrated the glories of industrialization, the poets and artists who sang paeans to the age of the machine, capitalism with its praise of competition, the industrial products mass-produced in factories and sent to the far corners of the world—all of these were interrelated in a grand, easily grasped social program. This spirit is embodied in the law of survival of the fittest, based on free competition; in the rule of domination of the weak by the strong; and in modern scientific technology and economic law, which reject all ambiguity and difference in favor of speed, efficiency, and standardization.

The spirit of the age of life, on the contrary, is symbiosis—an ever-changing dynamic balance, unforeseen mutations, metabolism, cycles of growth, the preservation of unique individuality through genetic codes—and multiplicity. These are the horizons of the spirit of the age of life.

The signing of the Biodiversity Treaty at the 1992 Environmental Summit in Brazil announced the beginning of the age of life. However, if you subscribe to Darwin's evolutionary doctrine of "survival of the fittest," the extinction of species is a natural phenomenon we can and should do nothing about. Why, then, are we now trying to protect species on the edge of extinction? We should see in this the

Environmental Summit in Brazil and signing of treaty on biodiversity (1992).

birth of a new value system for the age of life, which regards the survival of a wider variety of life forms as a richer kind of existence. The new age will treasure the distinct cultures of minority peoples and aim for the symbiosis of distinct cultures.

In the field of biology, various arguments are calling for the abandonment of Darwin's theory of evolution. *Newsweek*, some years ago already, introduced biologist Lynn Margulis's theory of symbiosis, which is gradually coalescing with the most widely held opinions in the field and contributing to the demise of Darwin's theory. The "Sharing Theory" of the late Dr. Kinji Imanishi has also attracted attention as a revision of Darwinian evolutionism. Within species, Dr. Imanishi noted a tendency to create a boundary and then to live in symbiosis, sharing the essentials of life.

Added Value and Leisure

In the economic sphere, the relations between medium- and small-sized companies and giant enterprises will also change, as will the relations between the multinationals and their regional partners. Up to now, the larger the company, the more centralized and efficient management system it was able to create, and capital investment on a large scale contributed to the manufacture of high-quality, low-cost products in large quantities. Medium and small-scale companies were "developing companies" that would someday become giant enterprises or would ally themselves to large enterprises as subcontractors. As we can see from the example of the automobile industry, subcontractors were in the end completely absorbed by the centralized management systems of the larger enterprises. By contrast, in the new age, medium and small-scale companies will exist in symbiosis with giant enterprises, just as local enterprises will with the multinationals.

In an information society, the desire for added value and variety, even in manufactured goods, will force the system toward diversification. Soon, even manufacturing plants will be very different from the kind of factory immortalized in Chaplin's *Modern Times* (1936). Today, when nonmanufacturing industries account for seventy percent of Japan's GNP, large scale no longer necessarily possesses any merit for the production of added value. It may well be that the crisis which some years ago confronted IBM, a firm that hitherto had pursued growth without looking back, is related to this major change in the economy of our times.

Leisure is also an issue. I was once asked by a French government official why it was that Japanese businessmen and civil servants seemed unable to discuss culture. He had clearly identified this as a weakness. In the West, people work to obtain the means to enjoy their lives, for the emotion and joy they receive from cultural experiences, not merely for the sake of work itself. In contrast, most Japanese politicians and business people appear to believe that personal enjoyment and cultural activities exist only as a byproduct of commerce; that once you have attained a certain degree of freedom from economic need, you can enjoy "hobbies." For the Japanese, then, art and culture—far from being national goals—are mere diversions. When economic development becomes the unique goal of a society, the country becomes a machine directed toward expansion. In fact, something that simply grows larger and larger without any higher purpose or goal is a monster.

Debate on Symbiosis in the Business World

For the business world that motivates industrial society, to entertain the concept of symbiosis represents a dramatic conversion the likes of which Japan has not seen since the heady days of the Meiji Restoration. But what is most conspicuously lacking in this discussion among business leaders is the concept of a goal appropriate to the symbiotic society of the age of life—which must replace the industrial society of the machine age.

In the debate on symbiosis, two essays have attracted my attention. One is by Yotaro Kobayashi, CEO of Fuji Xerox; it appeared in the *Sankei Shinbun* under the title, "A Philosophy of Symbiosis for Japan." The other is by Akio Morita of Sony and was serialized in *Bungei Shunju* under the title, "Japanese-style Business in Crisis."

Kobayashi cites three issues with regard to symbiosis. The first is defining the actual conditions that must exist in order to say that industry and consumers coexist in symbiosis, or that Toyota and Fiat, or Japan and France, do the same. The second is that:

> While Japan may talk about symbiosis, it is naive to suppose that Japan's competitors will simply repay Japan's symbiosis in kind. We must take care not to lapse into a one-sided Japan-style symbiosis, and it is important for Japan to realize that at times a certain stubbornness will be required.

The third point he raises is that "Symbiosis is not a goal in itself, but a modus vivendi and necessary condition that a person, an industry, or a nation must attain to be and act as it truly wishes to." On the other hand, Kobayashi does imply that since the Japanese ideal is to become a nation with a high standard of living—or so-called "standard of living giant," *seikatsu taikoku*, a neologistic spin-off from the term "economic giant"—the philosophy of symbiosis is the necessary means to achieve that goal.

If symbiosis is simply a method for achieving a goal (or ideal), there is really no need to employ the term. "Adjustment," "compromise," "mutual understanding," or "cooperation" would serve as well and be easier to grasp. If we regard symbiosis as no more than a means, then, as Tsuneo Iida has said:

> The cartel is the easiest method for getting along with one's competitors. If you recast the notion of symbiosis in economic terms, you have a cartel. When Keidanren starts talking about symbiosis, it must be because they wish to shift their method of coming to terms with environmental issues, regional problems, and foreign industry.

Thus, in an interview in *Nihon Keizai Shinbun*, J. Dowling of the Japan-U.S. Economic Council expressed doubts about symbiosis, remarking that it might even be in violation of the U.S. anti-monopoly and anti-trust laws. Apparently, the objections raised to symbiosis in business and industrial circles arise from a deeply rooted methodology opposed to the very idea at the heart of symbiosis. Dowling later read my *Philosophy of Symbiosis* in English and wrote me a skeptical letter about it, from which I quote:

> Reading your *Philosophy of Symbiosis*, I learned of the intellectually challenging and stimulating concept of symbiosis as a new world order. But the problem is that symbiosis as discussed in Japanese industry is very close to government-managed trade and market sharing. I am concerned that it is unlikely to encourage innovation, and that it could well obstruct the growth that competition ought to bring in its wake.

By contrast with this, Akio Morita's main argument is that Japanese industrial products, which are of high quality and sell in great numbers, are produced under a different set of circumstances than prevail in non-Japanese industries. All the same, perhaps, Japanese industry should also try to approach the conditions that prevail in Western industry, with regard to vacations, salaries, environmental responsibility, and contributions to the community. If prices rise as a result, then Japanese industry will still be able to sell high-quality products at increased prices. What Japan must do now is attempt to move from "economic giant" to "standard-of-living giant," for which it will be necessary to overhaul the economic and social systems.

I strongly support Morita's conclusions, but he suggests that Japanese industry must compete with foreign industry on its terms, and to do that Japanese business methods must undergo reform. In such a light, the sort of world order that Morita himself is aiming to achieve through economic means appears unclear.

Both Kobayashi and Morita affirm the "standard-of-living giant" slogan recommended some years ago at cabinet level. I agree that this policy is important, since it represented the first time that Japan had made improvement of daily life a national goal. But if all that was implied is merely larger houses, more indoor plumbing, and a network of superhighways—that is, an improvement of the standard of living in terms of quantity alone—Japan will scarcely distinguish herself among the nations of the world. There is also the possibility that Third World politicians will criticize the idea of symbiosis as a means for Japan, and Japan alone, to attain these standards.

The idea that the goal of business is simply more business, that all profit is immediately reinvested in further economic expansion and more profit, is now acknowledged as one of the principal causes of Japan's "bubble economy" of recent years. Therefore, shouldn't the business world as a whole be engaging now in a serious discussion of a new world order with a truly symbiotic society as its goal?

Aid and Technology Transfer

If we will only recognize the symbiotic world order sanctioned by the Biodiversity Treaty in 1992, we cannot deny the oppressive universalism of technology and economic factors that have too long dominated the global community. As long as the developing nations seek to modernize after the model of Western culture, they have the sole potential of developing into a future market. Western manufactured goods can thus continue to be produced in ever-increasing quantities until the entire world has achieved a homogeneous modernization.

Economic assistance from developed to developing nations has for too long been regarded as pre-investment for market development. Yet all nations need not follow the Western-style path of modernization. Precisely because each pursues a unique path, diverse cultural identities are maintained in the world; so it is essential to rethink the universal application of classic technological and economic assistance, until now regarded as self-evident.

The very term "developing nation" will eventually lose its meaning, and the concept of economic assistance, in which rich *assist* poor, must be abandoned. A new kind of assistance program, which encompasses the "developed countries" as well, will become essential. If we accept the consequences of this new way of thinking, we may even reach the conclusion that Japan should be strategically concentrating economic aid on the United States. In order to realize a new symbiotic order of diverse cultures, money must be used *strategically*. I will discuss the reasons for this later, but what I mean by a strategy for the immediate future is to protect American identity by providing assistance to the U.S. automobile manufacturing industry.

It will be further necessary to change the very essence of technology transfer, through which the developed nations have, heretofore, passed on their technology without modification to developing nations. Is it necessarily a good idea, for example, to transfer even peaceful nuclear fission and fusion technology to India—where, as mentioned in chapter 2, the main source of fuel for cooking is dried cow dung—or to Africa? If indeed our goal is to create a symbiosis of diverse cultures, electricity and cow dung fuel must continue to exist in symbiosis.

Regional Identity

Likewise, if we build highways in every country of the world and make automobiles the universal mode of transportation, we probably cannot avoid destroying distinct traditional lifestyles. Isn't it possible to combine the most advanced technology of the developed nations with traditional technology in *each* "developing" nation? In order to provide a more concrete instance, let me relate my experience working in the Sahara desert. I was approached with the proposition of creating a desert city for a population of tens of thousands in Libya when a large reservoir of water was discovered several hundred meters below the surface of the North Sahara, near As-Sarir. The plan was to tap this underground deposit and use it to create farms.

When I first arrived at the site and looked to the horizon, all there was to see was the vast, empty desert. I thought: wouldn't it be wonderful if we could use the sand all around us as a building material? We would create a recycled city, born from the sands and which might someday even return to them again.

Grains of desert sand, unlike other varieties, are perfectly round. They are also finer than ordinary sand, and cannot be mixed successfully with cement. But after two years of work and with the cooperation of a desert-research center based in England, we were at last able to mold sand bricks from local material. In addition, we made plans for revising the most advanced mass-produced system kitchens and toilets to fit the lifestyle of the Bedouin inhabitants.

Owing to future maintenance concerns we decided not to install air-conditioning and heating but to rely instead on traditional "wind chimneys." A wind chimney is a tower within the house that helps to create an updraft inside by exploiting breezes or temperature differences. Though the desert surface undergoes drastic changes in temperature, the soil temperature from one to several meters below remains stable. A wind chimney brings cool air up from beneath the earth when it may be forty degrees outside, and when it is cold at night helps warm the floor, acting as a natural temperature equalizer.

Thus our experiment in desert planning was not simply to bring in the newest technology but to transform new technology and products to exist in symbiosis with the traditions and climate of the region, conforming with a lifestyle that forms the region's culture.

Preserving tradition by itself is a backward-looking approach, and quickly lapses into old-fashioned historicism. On the other hand, introducing a developed technology into such situations without modification results in the destruction of culture and lifestyle.

The technology of developed nations, and the economies they have fostered, are unavoidably being pushed toward an age of symbiosis that incorporates traditional regional identity, cultures, and lifestyles. In this important sense, the argument that business comes before culture, that cultural support for the arts depends first and foremost upon profit, no longer holds, even for the motive of business growth.

Shared Strategy for Business and Culture

I would like now to discuss yet another aspect of recent experience, relating to Japanese business as a whole. As everyone knows, excess Japanese capital has poured into the world, seeking new investment opportunities. I have often fielded questions from American and European business people and intellectuals regarding Japanese industry, which has secured property for development in Europe and America. When oil dollars began to purchase buildings and sites around the world, we Japanese saw only the goal of a quick investment return and imagined that sooner or later investors would withdraw. We all hoped that Japanese investment outside the country would be different, yet the emerging consensus is that our investments during "the bubble" have not proved much more solid than the oil dollar investment we denigrated.

From the perspective of friends in Europe and the United States, architecture and urban development serve to anchor a country's culture, and as such belong to a long-term general strategy that also encompasses business and technology. François Mitterand's "Grand Projets"—including the construction of the New Paris Opera, museums, the Grande Arche de la Défense, libraries, the Arab Cultural Research Center, and the renovations and additions to the Louvre—represented a grand strategy to assure that France in the twenty-first century would retain its status as an international center of art and culture. It is no longer true that a nation with a strong economy, advanced technology, and a large military force automatically commands the respect of other nations.

The fear of Japan whispered about in the world recently is not a simple phenomenon; its sources range from jealousy to complete misunderstanding. But frequently heard is that others have no idea what kind of nation the Japanese are seeking to create with their money and technology, or what kind of world order. Perhaps—unlike France, for example—Japan has no cultural goals and seeks only to expand profits. The very thought of an infinitely expanding giant economic machine is unnerving.

To become a world leader contributing to the construction of a new world order, a nation needs not only power but authority. Power is obtained through economic, technological, and military means, but authority is acquired through culture. In every country on earth, people look down on the nouveau riche who spend their time hustling after money and have little or no real interest in art or culture. The critical perception that "Japan has no face" is another way of saying that though Japan may be wealthy, it lacks cultural authority.

Sacred Zones: Indispensable for Symbiosis

The word "symbiosis" is likely to be of little interest among friends, or those outside a competitive context. Symbiosis as a new world order should really be used to describe the relationship we form between two essentially opposing—and mutually exclusive—elements. In this sense, it is completely different from Shichihei Yamamoto's Japanese-style "symbiosis" as imminent harmony.

The "harmony" that the Japanese are so fond of is a sort of peaceful compromise that avoids struggle, conflict, and competition. It is a concept our ancestors probably acquired in the communalism of agricultural society. There is also the term "coexistence," much used during the Cold War between the Soviet Union and the United States. I think this could be described as a situation in which neither party needed the other.

What I mean by "symbiosis" is a relationship of mutual need—while competition, opposition, and struggle continue. How can mutually opposing, different qualities and aims exist in symbiosis? A concept of sacred zones is, I believe, the key.

... In America, Too

Certainly, insofar as it is possible, commonly held rules are a good idea. No one, I think, would argue against free competition on a fair and agreed-upon basis. But, on the other hand, the fact that differences remain is not evil, nor is it irrational. The United States, for instance, would never seriously suggest that Iran should abandon Islam and Islamic customs.

Protecting the diversity of life means protecting the diversity of culture, and actively underwriting such diversity. A symbiotic order is an order in which we recognize others' differences—and their sacred zones—and compete on that basis. Economic activity can be objectively measured, but the same standards cannot be applied to culture, religion, or lifestyle.

I think that for Japan, the emperor system, rice cultivation, the sumo rank of *yokozuna* (grand champion), Kabuki, and the tea ceremony (with its *sukiya*-style buildings) are all sacred zones. Though the emperor system may be regarded as merely a symbol today, I believe the concept still plays an immeasurable role in stabilizing Japanese society. That is presumably the reason that the U.S. took positive steps to preserve the system after the war.

I mentioned rice earlier, and as long as rice is discussed purely as a foodstuff, I think it only natural to liberalize the market completely and allow the free import of U.S.-produced rice. But though it may be true that Japanese agriculture is gradually becoming a part-time occupation as the nation is increasingly urbanized, rice production is bound up with the very roots of Japanese culture in farming villages, festivals, folk songs, saké production, and the other aspects of history and lifestyle. The forestry industry, now in crisis, is supplemented by agricultural labor during fall and winter, as are lacquer work and other traditional crafts. This "culture of rice" does not accompany rice grown in California, which is a foodstuff pure and simple.

If sumo were simply a sport, no one would dispute that everything in it should be decided on the basis of matches won and lost. But from its inception sumo has been closely linked to the emperor system, and it has a strong traditional-cum-ceremonial aspect. If we ascribe special significance to the grand champion, who performs many of these ceremonies, is there anything wrong with regarding his rank as a sacred zone and requiring that he be Japanese? This is hardly racial discrimination by any interpretation.

My idea of sacred zones is fundamentally distinct from the doctrine of protectionism in trade, and it is important to note that America, too, has its sacred zones. Having adopted a dominant, universalist posture, this is hard for the United States to admit. For the sake of building the new symbiotic order, Japan needs to declare openly to the U.S. that it is right and proper to maintain sacred zones. Once Japan has helped America define and defend these, Japan will be better able to gain recognition of its own sacred zones. In my opinion, the automobile industry, baseball, and Hollywood are all sacred zones for the United States, as is the newer aerospace industry. American culture as we know it would not exist without these. All are rooted in the American lifestyle and are rightfully sources of pride for Americans.

If we argue solely from the perspective of economics, there is no reason why Japanese companies shouldn't buy Hollywood studios, become owners of major-league teams, or crush the U.S. auto industry. Japanese companies could always insist that they were *invited* to buy out American interests, or that U.S. consumers *prefer* Japanese cars. One of the rules of business is that a company can be sold at any time, and Japanese buyers have thus seen no problem with their acquisitions, even thinking, with some justification, that American owners should be grateful to find a buyer. But U.S. business leaders and the American people are two different things. Even the rules of business and technology are linked to a people's lifestyle and feelings.

Therefore, in addition to the need to bring Japanese industry closer into line with that of the West and to change the Japanese economic and social system as a whole, we need to recognize the cultural imperative not to invade the sacred zones of other cultures. When nations do business abroad, they must make efforts to preserve the unique local culture, participate in the life of great cities and smaller communities, and generally reinforce the connections between business and culture.

Even when two parties recognize each other's sacred zones, if they lack common rules, there is little chance to exist in symbiosis. If, however, they share at least certain rules and have the least desire to understand each other, they may be able to use that common ground to open a dialogue leading eventually to construction of a symbiotic relationship. The size of the arena of shared rules is never fixed. It is better to think of it as always changing, in response to the changing strengths of both parties and to global conditions. Symbiosis is a dynamic relationship always in flux. At times Japanese business style should be followed, and at other times the other nation's business protocol should be adopted. Through a process of trial and error, the arena of shared rules can be enlarged.

That is why Japanese companies ought not to become the sole owners or operators of foreign firms. Whenever possible, they should embark on, or expand, cooperative ventures. Yet the reason Japanese companies traditionally prefer to buy out other firms is that they regard it as a loss of face unless they have complete control. Nevertheless, through trial and error and repeated dialogue, and in the aim of deepening mutual understanding, we must change from a policy of outright purchase to one of participatory investment, from sole proprietorship to joint operations, from buying units of real estate outright to building a symbiotic relationship through participation in long-term urban redevelopment strategies. In any case, the new symbiotic order that is beginning will be different from the free competition we have known until now. It will prove without doubt a goal that requires painstaking effort, one fraught with challenging difficulties.

4

TRANSCENDING MODERNISM

Universalism of Industrial Process

Industrial products such as wristwatches, automobiles, and airplanes were great luxuries when first invented, but today most of us are able to buy anything from a watch to a personal computer. In architecture this same wave of industrialization gave birth to the International Style, those boxes of steel, glass, and concrete symbolizing the liberation of architecture from past modes through the use of new materials and revolutionary technologies; they created a universal model that has spread to all countries and cultures. For me, the International Style resembles Esperanto[1]—it sought to create a common architectural language for all humanity. But the model was, in fact, based on the values and ethos of Western civilization. Again, the analogy with Esperanto is clear, for Esperanto was a "universal" language based on Western examples.

By ignoring climate and culture, the International Style imposed a single style throughout the world. For example, as part of the process of modernization unfolding in the People's Republic of China, an all-glass hotel was constructed in Beijing a few years ago. But with Beijing's climate—cold in winter and hot in summer—the operating costs of an all-glass multistory structure are enormous. Such problems are typical of most buildings in the International Style. It is not enough to deliver the latest in building technology, for

The glass-clad Changcheng Fandian Hotel, Beijing.

if replacement elements and proper services aren't available, the new structure will soon be severely crippled: elevators stop running and spare parts for repair cannot be found.

When Toyota first decided to market its cars in the United States, it began by setting up a customer-service network of several hundred outlets; for without proper maintenance, sophisticated technology is reduced to uselessness. When high technologies are introduced to developing countries, they need to be adapted to culture and climate. Symbiosis between technology and local cultural tradition must be taken seriously.

It is certainly time to correct the mistaken Western notion that universalism is divinely ordained; we should abandon Esperanto-style ideals. Internationalism can best be achieved by deepening the understanding of our *own* language while engaging in exchange with other cultures. If Yukio Mishima or Yasunari Kawabata had conceived their classics like *The Temple of The Golden Pavilion* or *Snow Country* in Esperanto, these authors could scarcely have created the literary depth that we admire. It is precisely because they wrote in a richly suggestive vernacular that they achieved literature. But need we conclude that such works as might only have been written in

Japanese can, for that reason, be understood and appreciated only in Japan? Of course not, since readers worldwide enjoy Mishima and Kawabata, Jun'ichiro Tanizaki, Kobo Abe, and Kenzaburo Oe in translation. Through translation, twentieth-century Japanese literature has become known as a literature of international quality.

Thus, I hope to make perfectly clear that in rejecting universalism and internationalism, I do not champion a static traditionalism or narrow racialism. I believe instead that in the coming age the world's different regions will reexamine their individual traditions. At the international level, each region must confront other values and standards; while mutually influencing one another, each will strengthen its own distinctive culture. Rather than mere internationalism, I prefer to call this interculturalism.

Weaknesses of a Purebred Culture

As a culture matures, it becomes increasingly centripetal; conservative forces aimed at preserving purity come strongly into play. Dissonant, opposing, and heterogeneous elements are rejected, and the culture constructs its own internal hierarchy. In this process, the culture's identity is sharpened and refined. Such a refined, highly distinctive culture—a purebred culture, as it were—is surprisingly unstable, and this is particularly so when it has grown in tremendous leaps. Unlike a "mongrel culture," which contains heterogeneous elements, a purebred culture is unable to adapt to changes in its environment. One of the reasons European culture is undeniably on the wane is that, since classical times, Europeans have been excessively concerned with preserving the orthodoxy of their culture—excluding all the surrounding cultures of the Islamic world and Asia.

The weakness of the pure-blooded and the strength of the mongrel can be seen in business as well. If a company limits itself to a single product and concentrates entirely on production and sales strategies, it will acquire very sophisticated skills and know-how concerning that product. If the product is automobiles, for example, the company is likely to become an unchallenged giant in the industry. But if, due to external circumstances, the automotive industry as a whole falls upon hard times, the company will collapse—the victim of a revolution in transport, an upset in the balance of oil supply and demand, or trade friction.

In the past, coal mining was the leading industry in many outlying regions, such as Hokkaido and Kyushu, but now it is disappearing and taking the coal-mining towns with it. The textile industry, too, is on its way out as a major Japanese industry. A look at the present state of the former national railways system, the petrochemical industry, steel, and shipbuilding shows how technologies that are organized centripetally around a single product or service are susceptible to the passage of time. For all their size and strength, they deteriorate easily when conditions change.

To acquire the necessary flexibility and adaptability, many industries today are subdividing and diversifying. The companies Toray and Kanebo offer clear examples: originally textile manufacturers, their main products are now cosmetics, clothing, sporting goods, and pharmaceuticals. The breakup and privatization of the Japan National Railways is a further instance of the benefits of diversification.

Age of the Minor

The mongrel is able to assimilate heterogeneous, even opposing elements. Such an organization is youthful; but as it ages, it too begins to reject what is foreign to it. The key to the youth and life of a culture lies in whether the mainstream can still incorporate marginal elements. The reevaluation of the so-called minor elements—much talked about among French philosophers of the "new" school—should be taken as a warning to contemporary society. The subtitle of Gilles Deleuze[2] and Felix Guattari's[3] *Kafka* (1975) is "towards a minor literature," indicating the importance of this trend.

If only because the absolute subject contains plurality and free space within itself, we must respect minorities and heretics, thus encouraging a state of tension to subsist between the part and the whole. It has been said that a "simple conglomeration of individuals cannot be called a group. A group first comes into existence when heterogeneous elements assemble and exist together." Deleuze and Guattari make frequent reference to concepts of linkage and the rhizome, models of systems organized in neither a vertical nor a horizontal hierarchy, but displaying intersection and fluidity.

Liberation from all dialectic, dualism, and binomial opposition is what these philosophers seek. In order to transcend dualism, they offer new terms (insisting that these are not systematized sufficiently to rank as *concepts*): rhizome, multiplicity, and "machine." The rhizome is the antithesis of the tree, which, for Deleuze and Guattari, is a model of hierarchy. First we have the central trunk, from which branches sprout in order; a branch, for example, never sprouts a trunk. A rhizome, by contrast, is an interwoven complex that defies analysis: an intertwining of heterogeneous elements, unordered, without a center. It is dynamic and changing, producing nodules here and there as it meanders and twists back on itself. Deleuze and Guattari distinguish their "machine" from the unmoving rigid mechanism of modernism. Theirs is an assemblage of various independent and heterogeneous elements with a living, that is, fluid, existence.

I believe that the advent of an information society has provided us with the chance to deconstruct, and rebuild, the social "tree" structure of our present rigidly hierarchicalized industrial society. All the same, if we are not careful, the network of our information society may take shape as an ever more symmetrical "trunk," or centralized structure. The test in the years ahead will be whether we succeed in creating a fluid and living rhizome instead.

Incorporating "Noise" into Our Lifestyle

René Girard,[4] in his book *Mensonge Romantique et Verité Romanesque* (Deceit, Desire, and the Novel, 1961), says that when a structure is complete it begins to close itself off. The completion, or ripening, of a culture, society, or nation is followed by such a closure, and it becomes more and more difficult to assimilate things from outside.

The same is true of individuals. After constructing personal existence through adulthood, and then marrying, people's defensive instincts are naturally heightened. They select and reject information accordingly and build a closed structure around themselves. This structure corresponds to the lifestyle, personality, and society of the individual man or woman. In other words, as one matures one tends to close oneself off and, in the interest of avoiding danger, avoids intercourse with those heterogeneous elements necessary to achieve further maturity. But, according to Girard, the fundamental nature of human thought processes is differentiation—inevitably born of crisis—or what Girard terms "the theatrical factor."

In order to preserve both our physical and spiritual youth and to receive continued proof that we are alive, it is necessary that we incorporate heterogeneous elements—"noise"—into our lifestyle.

Girard's "scapegoat" theory is another aspect of the same phenomenon. According to Girard, the creation of a scapegoat—that is, the elimination of heterogeneous elements from the hierarchy, or structure of authority—is a means of preserving that hierarchy. For this reason, those heterogeneous elements ("noise") that shake the structure of authority and challenge its stability, are most important.

In "Necrosis," the second volume of his work *L'Esprit du Temps* (1976), the French sociologist Edgar Morin discusses the notions of crisis and event, citing the term "order from noise." The economist Jacques Attali has also written on this same topic in his article "L'Ordre par le Bruit" (Order from Noise), which appeared in the special 1976 issue of *Communication* devoted to the topic of crisis. Crisis and "noise" as defined by Morin are those elements opposing, or heterogeneous to, any system. This is not a heterogeneity that can be bracketed, absorbed, and harmonized in peaceable fashion; rather, it upsets the event or process, forcing it to a new level or a different dimension.

"Noise," in this sense, is related to a critique of Claude Lévi-Strauss's[5] now classical theory of Structuralism. The anthropologist Lévi-Strauss examined myths and family structures of peoples in various cultures, stressing and codifying the connections and relations between them. But his model rejected unknown elements and factors that remained outside his structures as theorized, or were otherwise difficult to incorporate—in other words, "noise."

To exclude "noise" from a society or culture is to send that society or culture on a path of decline. By contrast, in refusing to be bound by a single standard of values, by cleverly incorporating elements from other cultures into one's own, one is able to reconfirm one's own culture. This, I submit, will be the internationalism of the new age.

Japan is a small nation situated next to a giant one, China. The Japanese have always cultivated the ability to survive by incorporating the best elements of Chinese civilization. On the other hand, traditional farming villages throughout Japan were governed by a rigid communalism, and those who did not obey the rules of the village, or were in some way unique, were labeled strange or mad and, to maintain village order, were driven away. Outsiders were allowed to join the village unit only after careful scrutiny. A principal reason for Japan's survival is this dual structure, the fine balance the culture has maintained between a hermeticism underlying the social order and receptivity to new elements.

This remarkable sense of balance can be seen in the rapid alternation between "open" and "closed" in the years before the Meiji Restoration. Though Japan was technically closed to the outside world for several centuries, trade and communication with other countries nonetheless continued. Chinese publications—many of them Chinese translations of European works—afforded Japan a certain acquaintance with the West, and trade routes were never completely closed off.

Japan's problems began, instead, after the country was officially opened to the world, from the Meiji period onward. The race to modernize in the guise of complete Westernization resulted in a rejection of Japanese culture. This is *not* the same as incorporating Western culture into the Japanese as "noise." Since Meiji times, study abroad in the United States or Europe has been regarded as crucial for a complete education. Western food, architecture, and clothing have become the norm, and the Japanese have espoused Western values. This tendency to look exclusively to the West is still with us. To be recognized abroad, or to be active abroad, implies Europe or America. There is still little awareness of activity in the broader world that includes the regions of Islamic culture, China, Southeast Asia, Australia, central Europe, and Russia.

Japan must adopt a policy of placing these areas and cultures on a par with the West. Yet we must guard against lapsing into a provincial regionalism—that is, carrying out all intervention in such areas solely with local resources, refusing foreign capital investment and the help of outside specialists. Any new type of isolationism, or cultural exclusivism, can only result in decline.

We would do well to remember the case of Kyoto. While preserving Japan's ancient cultural traditions, the old capital became a pioneer innovator in a major public works project to supply water for industry and was the first Japanese city with streetcars—reaching out to talent from other cities in Japan and abroad to achieve these things. Kyoto is still able to preserve its traditions today precisely because it first took such positive and liberal steps, embracing the future with open arms. This is exactly what I would wish to suggest by incorporating "noise" into the established order.

This concept of "noise" has something in common with Masao Yamaguchi's notion of periphery. A culture that focuses only on the center may intensify its own purity, but its borders are fated to decline. Let us, then, direct our attention to the heterogeneous elements around us—strange, suspicious, quirky, idiosyncratic things. Let us be alert to these, cultivating alertness and magnanimity. Unless we bid a curt farewell to our distinct brand of communalism—the lifestyle of the farm village—that leads us to ostracize anyone with individual or special talent, Japan has no future.

Time-sharing in the Rabbit Hutch

The second guiding principle of the modern age—after the universalism of industrial process—is division of labor based on specialization. By analogy, the policy of segregation by "function" reaches an extreme form in the domain of physical planning with the determination of architectural and urban zoning. Society's "time, place, and occasion" rule is another form of division by function. Houses contain bedrooms for sleeping, dining rooms for eating, living rooms for entertainment, and halls to connect these separate facilities—this is a rule of modern residential design. And according to such a way of thinking, every home must have a considerable amount of space.

Japanese houses have been characterized as "rabbit hutches." Most are indeed small, but in the past this had a distinct advantage. Because of the versatility of tatami-floored rooms, the traditional Japanese house escaped a thoroughgoing division of space by function. The multipurpose tatami-floored room becomes a bedroom when you pull the *futon* mattresses out of the closet and spread them on the matting. When you place a low table in the center of the room, it becomes a dining room. Set out floor cushions here and there and you have a room to receive guests. Place a flower arrangement and hang a scroll in the *tokonoma*, and you have a tea room. By changing the signs of its decor, one room takes on many different meanings. This multipurpose space makes time-sharing possible, and in this way we triumph over the space limitations of a relatively small home.

This strategy of time-sharing also points the way to a possible transformation of the densely overpopulated city of Tokyo. The central business district is nearly one hundred percent utilized during the day, but from midnight to dawn it is a ghost town. Surely lockers and other systems could be devised that would make it possible for two businesses to use the same building around the clock. Hotels, for example, have nearly doubled their guest turnover and their profit by transforming themselves from mere places to sleep to centers for banquets, conferences, business meetings, places to nap during the day, and even sites for romantic assignations. Once we cease to regard a place or thing as wedded to a single function and adopt a flexible, time-sharing approach, we increase efficiency and require fewer facilities to meet a variety of needs. By restoring even a small degree of plurality to our present classification and segregation by function, we can accommodate the riches of a new lifestyle.

The startling rise in property prices in Tokyo in recent years is a major problem, although the post-bubble economy has put an end to this, at least temporarily. In chapter 16, I present a necessary plan for the complete reconstruction of the city. Rather than attempting to redevelop the present city by tearing it down and rebuilding it, I propose the construction of an artificial island in Tokyo Bay that I believe will restore the proper balance between demand for land and its supply. My plan involves cleaning up Tokyo Bay and preserving Tokyo's historic Shitamachi area, while restoring and replanting the old forests of Musashino in the city's western suburbs and digging new canals as firebreaks, in a symbiosis of development and restoration.

If the problems of land cost and the threat of fire were solved, I believe that Tokyo could become the most fascinating and futuristic metropolis on earth. One reason is that Tokyo is already a time-sharing city. There is no denying that houses in Tokyo are small; but the city itself provides every sort of "second home" conceivable, for even the most arcane tastes. Tokyoites may not be able to invite their friends or colleagues to their home for a party or dinner after work, but the city is filled with fine restaurants, bars, and clubs where they can entertain. A Tokyoite may not have a games room in his home, but he does not lack for mah-jong, pachinko, and billiard parlors, computer-game centers, and karaoke clubs. He may not have his own tennis court or pool, but there is no shortage of sports clubs, golf courses, driving ranges, and tennis courts throughout the city. These facilities take the place of one's own private living room, games room, pool, or tennis court; they are, in reality, second homes. Since they provide space efficiently, by the hour or other time unit, they are indeed time-sharing second homes.

Claims against Function

Systematic partitioning by function has not been restricted to the home but nowadays extends to urban space in general. In the Athens Declaration of CIAM (Congrès International d'Architecture Moderne) in 1933, the city was analyzed and divided into areas for work, living, and recreation, with transport facilities linking these different functions. Virtually all present systems of land-use planning and zoning, dividing the city into color-coded functional areas, are based on this way of thinking. But not everyone has assented to this functionalism, promulgated by Le Corbusier.

Jan Mukarovsky,[6] a member of the 1930s Structuralist group in Prague, criticized Le Corbusier's simple functionalism as follows: "Existence of the whole is the source of life-energy of all individual

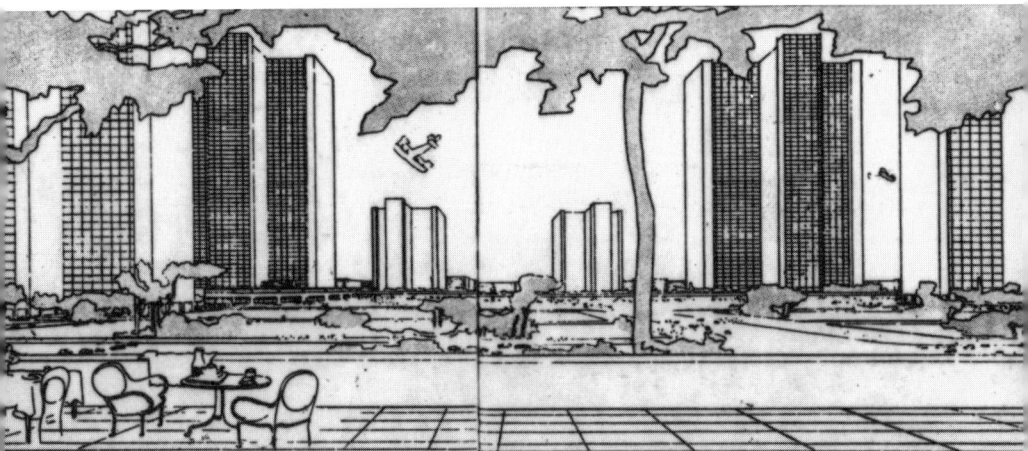

Were the "radiant" cities of Le Corbusier really so radiant?

functions, since no human action is limited to a simple function."
But with the increasing industrialization of society, segregation
based on functionalism has encircled the globe. Segregation of function is, above all, easy to grasp; like explaining a machine by describing its parts. In addition, functionalism proved a convenient weapon
for dismantling academic planning theory earlier this century. The
lions of modern planning rejected the condition of the city as they
found it, as a plurality of overlapping functions accumulated over
the ages seemed to them anti-modern. They made the isolation of
function and the provision of green spaces and fresh air their battle
cry and embraced Le Corbusier's notion of the Radiant City that
would sweep away the confusion of the past. The image of the city of
the future as a place of multistory buildings and huge empty plazas,
whose embodiment eventually spread to Brasilia and Chandigarh,
and all modern cities of the world, dates from that time.

This principle is evident in the zoning system that segregates residential from industrial areas, in the segregation of race and class (for
example, in Chinatown or Harlem, in New York City), and in the
designation of the city center as a business district and the suburbs
as residential areas. Social welfare policy is conceived along the same
lines. The handicapped and the elderly are accommodated in special
segregated facilities away from the center of the city and treated as

wards of the state, cut off from normal human relations with community and even family. It is crucial to retrieve and reclaim what has been sacrificed to the principles of modernism. The plenitude of existence, the essentially indivisible chaos of life, the complementary nature of functions, the intermediary zone lost to segregation, the ambiguity lost to clarity—all of these elements are missing from modernism and its architecture.

Aristotle on Hierarchy

To be sure, the functionalism by virtue of which every part and each space in the community maintains its isolated function is not just a product of modernism; it harks back to the very basis of Western rationalism and to Hellenic views on architecture and the layout of cities.

In his *Metaphysics*, Aristotle declared that "the primary elements of beauty are *taxis, symmetria,* and *horismmenon,* and that these may be expressed mathematically." *Taxis* is order or hierarchy. The word *symmetria* derives from *syn,* meaning common, and *metreo,* meaning measurement; therefore it means dividing an object into equal measures or quantities. *Horismmenon* means a limit. The philosophy of ancient Greece sought to lift man from chaos—through the exercise of reason in category, analysis, definition, and limit.

Categorization and analysis of nature by reason is a central attitude of Western culture in every age. The religious and mythological dualism that assumes good and evil—a God of light and an evil material world—is derived from this. Similarly, the philosophy of Descartes, which envisions all finite existence—dependent upon God's will—as divided into matter and spirit, and the philosophy of Kant, who distinguishes "the thing itself" from phenomena, and likewise freedom from necessity, are based on Western analytical dualism. This same philosophy has permeated the social structure, cities, and architecture of all industrialized nations. But how great is our loss as a result! The relentless pendulum swing between humanity and technology, science and religion, good and evil, the part and the whole, that has afflicted modern society, is a direct result of this unrelenting two-term opposition.

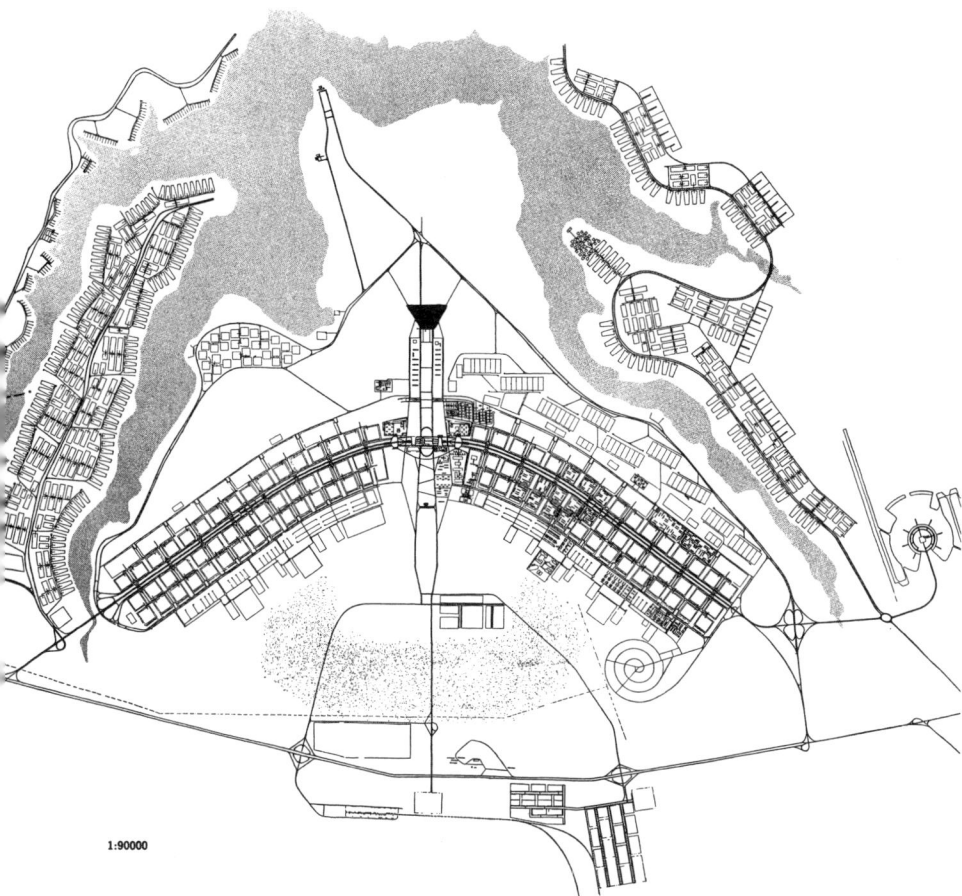

1:90000

Lúcio Costa: master plan of Brasilia (1956).

A Dynamic Pluralism that Incorporates Opposition

Even when we wish to refute dualism, we fall inevitably into the contradiction of a new opposition. In discussing the concept of symbiosis, too, we seem fated to produce yet another binomial paradigm in our attempt to transcend duality. This is without doubt the greatest weakness of the concept of symbiosis.

Maurice Merleau-Ponty's philosophy has been described as a philosophy of multivalence or ambiguity. Alphonse De Waelhens, in his foreword to Merleau-Ponty's *The Structure of Behavior* (*La Structure de Comportement*, 1941), contrasts Sartre with Merleau-Ponty: "In

the end, Sartre strengthened the Cartesian dualism of mind and matter, while Merleau-Ponty remained endlessly concerned with the
subtle connections between the two." One instance Merleau-Ponty
considered was that of a man confined to a prison cell. The pris-
oner's perception of a meal placed outside the cell changes drasti-
cally depending on whether or not his body can pass beyond the
bars. For the state of the body is the basis for the state of the mind
(*cogito*); that is, the mind can project itself outside the body and
remain out of synchronization with it.

Critics of such a notion—Jacques Lacan, for example—remind us
that to divide being into opposing matter and mind is already to fall
into Cartesian dualism. By the same reasoning, as long as arguments
for symbiosis resort to oppositions (such as symbiosis versus dualism), there can be no escape from a dualistic regression.

The concept of symbiosis is basically a dynamic pluralism. It
does not seek to reconcile two opposite concepts through dialectic,
nor does it follow Merleau-Ponty in searching for a unified principle
that transcends the two. At times symbiosis makes use of a binomial
opposition; at other times it recalls Merleau-Ponty's unified principle; and it can also be neither. It can best be described as a dynamic,
pluralistic principle capable of taking many different forms.

A Postmodernism to Assimilate Opposition

Man is flesh, man is spirit, man is a unity of flesh and spirit. Man
is something that is neither flesh nor spirit; as, for example, the consciousness referred to in the Buddhist philosophy of Consciousness-
Only, otherwise known as the *alaya* consciousness. The "*neither* flesh
nor spirit" here is an intermediary space, a central concept of the
philosophy of symbiosis. The intermediary space—that is neither—
assimilates both flesh and spirit, yet it is not a third element itself.

In intermediary space, we can postulate two elements in combinations of differing proportions; for example, flesh and spirit, in
ratios varying from 10:1 to 1:10. So, too, can an infinite number of
elements in a plural system be postulated. But, in fact, the concept
of intermediary space is easier to understand if we abandon any
notion of opposing elements, envisioning instead dynamic relations

between countless and freely combined proportions of flesh and spirit.

Deleuze and Guattari's rhizome contains this element of dynamic relationships. In the past, revolutionary philosophies have established their value and truth by refuting all previous philosophies. By creating a fresh opposition, they discredit and refute their predecessors. But the philosophy of symbiosis, while refuting the opposing element (be it philosophy, theory, or social system) that was previously the mainstream, also assimilates it. Modernism, for example, is the element that the philosophy of symbiosis must oppose most strongly. But rather than completely *rejecting* modernist trends, symbiosis must somehow absorb these.

Postmodern architecture, in the narrowest sense of the term (we might also call it "historicist" architecture), first made its appearance as a rejection of modern architecture but has fallen into the same old pattern of dualist opposition. Modern architecture—with its emphasis on function, rationality, and efficiency—called out for criticism. But a new horizon will only be discovered by a dynamic, free philosophy that assimilates modern architecture while criticizing it.

Japan's Identity in a New Nomadic World

The philosophy of symbiosis will be dynamic, free, and light; it is the philosophy of the nomads of the new age. In a society of settlers, people live at fixed sites within a certain territory, creating boundaries and neutral zones to avoid conflict. In such a society of mutually closed groups, peace means not violating the boundaries of others or interfering in their internal affairs. It is a world of coexistent protectionist societies. But nowadays we are a society of *homo movens*, which has learned the value of movement, exchange, and discovery. Our world transcends differences in ideology and culture, as well as levels of economic and technological development. A society of symbiosis is a pluralistic world where each person can display his or her own individuality; myriad different cultural spheres exist together. In such a situation, expression of national character, of a people's identity, assumes a new importance.

Imagine that in a part of the world peopled by nomadic tribes, an unknown band suddenly appears in the middle of the desert offering no sign of its intentions. Without a doubt, such people would be driven away as a band of brigands, or even demons. In the nomad's world, it is crucial to indicate who you are, why you have come, and that you mean no harm. Japan today is like a band of taciturn black-robed horsemen who suddenly appear in the desert, smiling slightly. There is nothing more unsettling. The group may be regarded as demonic. One of the reasons for "Japan-bashing" is the intimidating effect of this bizarre Japanese behavior.

The Japanese tradition that prizes silence and regards clever speakers as lacking in substance has produced a nation of determined artisans and silent, hairsplitting researchers and academicians. This has gone so far that an artist or scholar in Japan who happens to be articulate is regarded as a performer, and his achievements are suspect. We must put an end to this. Japan's educational system is far behind in teaching young people to express and explain themselves. Ambiguity is, indeed, a special and important characteristic of Japanese culture; but inability to express oneself has nothing to do with this.

Japan must present her culture more clearly to the peoples of the world and make clear the nation's goals: this is an urgent necessity. Our ultimate goal is surely a world in which many different cultures recognize one another's values. While opposing each other in their unique identities, these cultures also live in symbiosis.

Letting Go of the Pendulum

European history has long been marked by extreme swings of the pendulum between rationalism and nonrationalism. Following the Industrial Revolution, with its philosophy of mechanized production, the sudden appearance in England of William Morris's[7] Arts and Crafts Movement stressed craftsmanship and handwork. The universal popularity of Art Nouveau and *Jugendstil* design in Europe at the end of the nineteenth century, inspired by the curving lines of plants and other natural forms, was another reaction against the Industrial Revolution, one more pendulum swing. So, for example, was the architecture of Gaudí in Catalonia. At the beginning of the twentieth century, however, architects like Peter Behrens, Tony Garnier, and Auguste Perret advocated rationalism, and swung the pendulum back once more, culminating in the Bauhaus experiment.

Art nouveau incorporated the curvilinear forms of the plant world and sprang from the work of artisans (*Sources of Modern Architecture and Design*, Thames & Hudson, 1985).

Art nouveau stained glass (T. & H., 1985).

This pendulum phenomenon was imported into Japan. Those Japanese who advocated rapid growth and technology in the 1960s were suddenly opposed to it in the 1970s. Japanese journalism performed a sudden about-face and unleashed a zero-growth campaign, printing daily articles and editorials labeling all technology evil. A simple, ordinary life, lived at an easy rhythm, became the approved lifestyle. In the 1980s, Japan became ever more directly involved in the international community, and rapid growth was no longer a subject of debate; it became difficult even to maintain current rates of growth, faced with the vicious circle of oil-price shocks, the emerging economies of new nations, the high yen, trade friction, reduced government budgets, and a cooling-off of domestic demand. Now the most advanced technologies—such as biotechnology, new media, computer communications, and superconductors—are looked to in hopes of an economic upturn.

What we see here are two extremes: faith in the virtues of technology and, at the same time, rejection of its values. This dualistic pendulum phenomenon only confuses and unsettles our thinking; it produces few positive results. And the swings of the pendulum seem to be more violent in younger, less mature economies. When chauffeured by a bad driver, we are rocked back and forth by sudden acceleration and braking; a good driver makes these transitions smoothly and effortlessly. Indeed, to pursue the analogy, truly accomplished racetrack drivers have even mastered the technique of pressing the accelerator and the brake at the same time. The time has come, then, for the world to transcend dualism and leave these extreme swings of the pendulum behind us. Since human beings are by nature ambiguous, breaching constant contradiction and opposition—we have no biological grounds for disdaining or finding fault with what is intermediary.

Centralized Authority in an Industrial Age

After universalism and specialization, the last characteristic principle of the modern age is the elimination of social class to form a unified hierarchy. Part and whole are clearly distinguished, and the whole is valued over any part. In architectural terms this materializes as: 1) precedence of structural over interior concerns; 2) importance of infrastructure over substructure; and 3) superiority of public space to private space. All are examples of the whole dominating the part. So, for instance, since housing is merely a part of the city, it is only planned after the public spaces and facilities, including the squares and roadways that make up the city's infrastructure, are already in place. Housing is, therefore, secondary and subsidiary.

The same can be said with regard to works of architecture and the various spaces they comprise. Nor is this way of thinking restricted just to architecture or urban planning. Industrial society subscribes to the concentration of effort in the name of efficiency, with priority to large-scale science, large-scale technology, and large-scale industry. This industrial-based centralization has merely replaced the old feudal structure of centralization. Modernism's own hierarchy of levels, its insistence on the superiority of the macrostructure, reigns at the expense of plurality and variety among the parts, of humanity, and , finally, of any subtlety of perception. As we move into the information age, I predict the modern industrial structure will radically change. Small and medium-sized manufacturers will outstrip their huge rivals; service industries, rather than manufacturing, will become the leaders of industry.

Holon: Symbiosis of Part and Whole

There is already considerable interest across a wide range of fields in a nondualistic view of the part and the whole in the philosophy of symbiosis. One articulation of this view was offered by Arthur Koestler,[8] who formulated the concept of the *holon*. Koestler has coined the term Holon by combining the Greek root *holos*, meaning whole, and the suffix *on*, for "part" or "particle." The word refers simultaneously to the parts and to the whole. Koestler was a critic of reductionism. In reducing a phenomenon to its parts for analysis, he insists, the essence of the phenomenon—the harmonious sum of its parts—is inevitably lost, and the thing falsified. In his essay "The Tree and the Candle," in *Unity Through Diversity*, Koestler describes the properties of the Holon with reference to two examples. A burning candle serves as a metaphor for the concept of an open system, since the candle, while retaining its own basic form, takes oxygen from the atmosphere around it and in turn gives off moisture, carbon dioxide, and heat. He cites a tree as a unit of living hierarchy—an intermediate structure, so to say—because it embodies the whole system for all units smaller than itself but, at the same time, is only another unit in an even larger system, the forest.

Koestler points out that all biological and social structures, as well as human activities and linguistic systems, exhibit these two properties of openness *and* hierarchy. He calls this "open hierarchy" and regards it as the fundamental characteristic of the Holon.

Tokyo: Holon of Three Hundred Cities

In my book *Toshigaku Nyumon* (Introduction to City Planning, 1961), I called Tokyo an agglomeration of three hundred cities. I think that all larger cities may profitably be regarded as composed of smaller cities. We are accustomed to thinking of a city as an independent administrative unit with prescribed boundaries. But the simple act of tracing such a boundary does not insure unity. In fact, these smaller constituent cities each possess their own histories; physically they merge and separate, changing shape to accommodate local topography. If we concede that the metropolis is made up of independent areas, each with its own identity, linked to the others in fluid relationships, it is clear how Tokyo is an agglomeration of three hundred cities. When we have accepted this way of looking at things, we see that the smaller units that form the larger city need not be subjugated to the whole. Instead, the parts and the city in their entirety form a Holon.

A few years ago, I chaired a planning committee to establish criteria for scenic views in the city of Nagoya. The unique thing about the regulations we proposed was that we did not urge the creation of a unified view for the entire city but suggested instead that scenic views be designated in more than a hundred places throughout Nagoya. These locations were chosen as representing the cultural and natural life of the city, its inhabitants, and its environment; we called them Autonomous Scenic Zones. Each was a distinct expression of Nagoya and its lifestyle, and we encouraged variety in our selection. The concept was revolutionary if compared with the typical modernist approach, which would have been to establish universal standards and then apply these uniformly to all individual cases. Our work in Nagoya produced yet another Holon, that of the individual Autonomous Scenic Zones and the city taken as a whole.

State and City-State: A Revolutionary Concept

The Holon paradigm can also be applied to the relationship between the state and other self-governing bodies. When Prime Minister Masayoshi Ohira was still alive, I sat on his policy research council and had frequent opportunities to discuss various ideas with him. One day, he said to me suddenly, "Mr. Kurokawa, why not eliminate the prefectures entirely and just get by with the nation and its cities? In place of the prefectures, we could have a general communications agency." The prime minister's goal was to increase the autonomy of Japan's cities, in the direction of city-states. Our subsequent report was entitled "Plan for a National Garden City-State." Rather than a nation of garden cities, we were looking at a garden city-state at the national level. From the viewpoint of the hallowed concept of subordinating self-governing bodies, such as cities, to the state, this view of state and city-state as equal entities is indeed revolutionary and Holonic.

The philosophy of Holonism, wherever applied, is bound to exert a strong influence on theories of industrial and business organization as well as on architecture and artistic creation. The top-down method, where a general framework leads to a part-by-part breakdown of components, fails to give sufficient consideration to eventual details. On the other hand, there is no guarantee that the whole will be successfully integrated if we proceed from the bottom up, piling detail upon detail to arrive at a totality. The truly creative and Holonic approach is to equilibrate top-down and bottom-up approaches.

In my own design work, I begin with *macro* considerations, such as urban planning, the environment, and various social factors. At the same time, I start imagining and sketching very specific parts and details: the shape of door handles and curve of handrails, carpet patterns, furniture, and wall texture. This parallel approach—working simultaneously on the whole and the details—leads to a Holonic style of architecture. Non-Japanese architects and critics have described our work as a combination of bold spatial structure and eloquent, handcrafted details. This evaluation pleases me, particularly as it shows an appreciation of the Holonic relationship I have striven to create between part and whole.

Koestler's essay "Janus" is named after the twin-faced god of Roman mythology who, on the one hand, spurs humanity on to the various levels of the hierarchy but, on the other, urges a transcendent and whole reality. For in Koestler's part-and-whole there is the drive toward a symbiosis of man and God. Koestler distinguishes three levels of reality: sensual awareness, followed by conceptual awareness, and finally the mystical awareness of "oceanic feeling"—a world that transcends both sensory perceptions and concepts. Koestler claims that this oceanic feeling is similar to the synchronicity described by Carl Jung[9] and Wolfgang Pauli.[10] I interpret the idea of synchronicity, Janus-like, to mean the symbiosis of past, present, and future; Koestler, however, while referring to Jung and Pauli's synchronicity, enlarges it to include the symbiosis of body and spirit, consciousness and the unconscious, and man and God.

Merging Mysticism and Science

A continuity between religion and science has become increasingly apparent and, as the physicist David Bohm[11] has proclaimed, "Even life can be made from matter." An interesting discussion between Bohm and Renee Weber was included in Weber's book *The Holographic Paradigm and Other Paradoxes*. In their conversation, entitled "The Physicist and the Mystic—Is a Dialogue Between Them Possible?" they noted how, up to the present, physics has applied itself to discovering the unity of part and part, yet no trace of the unity of the part and the whole has been uncovered. For the first time, physics is broaching this issue.

We see here that the same problem that attracted Koestler is exercising the science of physics. Citing Einstein's remark that "the most beautiful of all things is God," Bohm and Weber claim that mysticism, once the province of religion and art, is beginning to evolve a point of contact with science. A new dynamism that transcends the dualistic categorization of science versus religion is making itself felt. The defeat of modernism is a common theme of our age; but Japan has the additional task of freeing itself from the ideology of Westernization. To Japan's inestimable advantage, it has a tradition of Buddhist thought giving voice to a philosophy of symbiosis that transcends the limits of dualism. This tradition, cultivated over long centuries, is inherent in Japan's culture and way of life.

Identity of Opposites

Daisetz Suzuki's[12] "identity of opposites" is the fundamental principle by which the part and the whole, or contradictory opposites, are revealed as existing in relation to each other. The *Vajracchedika Sutra* contains a verse that can be translated, "A is non-A, therefore it is called A." And this is the source of the philosophy of the identity of opposites:

The oriental individuum is not an independent individual as in the West. It contains no self-existent core, but exists by virtue of emptiness (*sunyata*), which transcends the individuum. Though the individuum and that which transcends the individuum are contradictory, they exist together without the loss of the individuum's identity. "Identity" (*soku*) means that two things are not different. "Non" means that two things are not the same.

The identity of opposites creates an ambiguity of meaning, a floating multivalence, through simultaneous affirmation and rejection at a conceptual level. The entities A and non-A are in fact a single entity. Since two contradictory entities are, thus, one, Suzuki calls the mutually embracing relationship of part and whole the philosophy of the identity of opposites. Human beings exist as a part of the universe; at the same time, the universe is enfolded in the consciousness of human beings. Zen teaches that the universe and humanity are mutually inclusive, and it is easy to find other expressions of this anti-dualism, or nondualism, in Asian thought.

In the world of the oriental individuum, the part and the whole are accorded equal value and the individual and the meta-individual exist together, neither losing its own nature or one contradicting the other. Nor is there an Aristotelian hierarchy in which the part is subjugated in its unity with the whole.

The Edo-period philosopher Miura Baien[13] devised a sympathetic philosophy of the unification of opposites, which he set forth in a trilogy: the discourses on metaphysics, corollaries, and morality. It has, moreover, been shown that this scholar invented the dialectic a half century before Hegel.[14] More important than any comparison with Hegel, however, is the recognition of Baien's inspiration in Asian thought, particularly Indian philosophy. His philosophy is typical of the Asian tradition in that it resolves dualism into monism and represents a symbiosis of analysis and unification, the part and the whole. In his dialectic, Miura Baien's philosophy indeed seems close to Hegel's; but it is clear from the name he used—the unification of opposites—that he ultimately sought a unified world whole. We can interpret this thought as a philosophy of apprehending all seeming opposites as a single continuum, a philosophy of the symbiosis of part and whole. We do not know whether Miura Baien ever studied the Buddhist philosophy of Consciousness-Only, but his thought bears a close resemblance to it. I personally am convinced that the philosophy of Consciousness-Only will be the source for the thought of the twenty-first century. While Western thinking has reached a dualist cul-de-sac, Buddhism and its philosophy of Consciousness-Only offers Japan a means to assume intellectual leadership in the new century.

5

THE PHILOSOPHY OF CONSCIOUSNESS-ONLY AND SYMBIOSIS

The *Alaya* Consciousness—Neither Matter nor Spirit

I named my tea room, my place for retreat and quiet thought, Yuishikian, or the "Hut of Consciousness-Only," in honor of the Buddhist philosophy of the same name. For me this is the key to a philosophy of symbiosis helping us transcend the dualism of modernism. The Consciousness-Only philosophy is a major pillar of Mahayana Buddhism, deeply rooted in Japan and occupying an exalted place within Buddhism as a whole.

The appearance of the Buddha wrought a great change on the world of Indian thought and religion. Prior to the Buddha, the concept of *samsara*, or transmigration, had been one of the central concepts of the Indian tradition: it was believed that all phenomena were bound to infinite repetition in the cyclical span of cosmic time. Another important feature of pre-Buddhist thought, as we know it from the Upanishads,[1] was the concept of the absolute self, *atman*, and its identity with the ultimate truth of the cosmos, or Brahman. The *atman* was condemned to pass through life after life, its fate decided by the good and evil deeds of the self.

The Buddha, however, denied the existence of this absolute self. He taught that no self-existing, integral, unchanging, and imperishable subject existed. Instead, a series of selves was born and extinguished from moment to moment. This was the revolutionary

Buddhist teaching of nonself (*anatman*), which radically challenged the doctrine of *samsara*.

It was the philosophy of Consciousness-Only that eventually reconciled the opposing notions of *samsara* and nonself. According to the teachings of Consciousness-Only, the subject that migrated was not a self but a consciousness—or, specifically, the *alaya*[2] consciousness. The *alaya* consciousness was part of the human subconscious, hence a source of inexhaustible possibilities and potentialities. The *alaya* consciousness contains the sources or seeds—known as *bija*—of all existence and every event.

As these seeds ripen and come into contact with causes and conditions, they appear as actual phenomena. At the same time, those phenomena produce instant feedback in the *alaya* consciousness. The *alaya* consciousness is the source both of all matter and spirit. In sharp contrast to Cartesian dualism—matter over against spirit—the philosophy of Consciousness-Only insists that both are manifestations of a certain primal existence. I see the *alaya* consciousness, neither matter nor spirit, as akin to DNA—a life code, a vital energy— and find it fascinating that the intuitions of religious philosophers of ancient India have reached across time to harmonize with the discoveries of modern science.

Good, Evil, and the Ethically Intermediate

The earliest Consciousness-Only teaching can be traced back to Nagarjuna.[3] Before Nagarjuna, Buddhist thought centered on the numerous *Prajnaparamita*, or Perfection of Wisdom, sutras. Thinkers of this persuasion are now sometimes referred to as *Madhyamikas*, or Those of the Middle View; and their philosophy was based on the concept of emptiness (*sunyata*), in which all phenomena were no more than names. The material world was a phantasmal thing, a parade of conventions and concepts without true existence. Nagarjuna revised and systematized this school of thought, rescuing the concept of emptiness from nihilism. In his *Mulamadhyamika Sastra*, he states, "I am not a nihilist. By rejecting both being and non-being, I illuminate the path to nirvana." Nagarjuna articulated his "unobstructed middle way" in the famous Eight Negations of the Middle

Way, and from his interpretation of the concept of emptiness originated a philosophy that might transcend Western dualism.

Some time after his death, in about A.D. 300, Nagarjuna's thought took shape as the *Sandhinirmocana Sutra*, regarded as the first scripture of the Consciousness-Only school. In the centuries that followed, three great Buddhist thinkers appeared who fully developed and firmly established the Consciousness-Only philosophy: Maitreya, Asanga, and Vasubhandu.[4] The central concept of the Consciousness-Only philosophy, the *alaya*, is described in the *Sandhinirmocana Sutra* as "the undefiled and ethically indeterminate consciousness that contains all seeds." Unlike Christianity, with its decisive distinction between good and evil, the Consciousness-Only philosophy recognizes three categories: good, evil, and the ethically indeterminate—an intermediary zone between the two.

A Creative, Indeterminate State

Many creative possibilities with potential for our own time are concealed in the vague category of the "ethically indeterminate." Increasingly, people are today forced to choose new systems of values. We often find ourselves in an ambiguous situation where a clear choice cannot be made. At least from the present perspective, action based on a simple "yes/no" dichotomy is no longer an adequate response to society's demands. I believe that a trichotomy, with a third, "neither-yes-nor-no" element, will be required. A state wherein a conclusion may or may not be reached—compared to either "yes" or "no," when thinking stops and becomes action—represents a truly creative state.

The principle of majority rule, the modus operandi of democracy, does not value vagueness. Owing to this, it encourages the suppression of thought. It forces us to vote either "yes" or "no," and the simple majority wins—even if the final count is, for example, fifty-one in favor and forty-nine opposed. But were an indeterminate category allowed, people could indicate that they wished to think the issue over further; and the results of such deliberation might well be the opposite of a premature "yes/no" vote. We can easily conceive of cases in which the best answer to an issue being voted was, for the time being, abstention. This inherent weakness in our majority rule system will become increasingly clear. How we meet the risk of ignoring the category of "neither-yes-nor-no," and deal with it in our social policies, is bound to become a major issue from now on.

The Buddhism nurtured in Japan over the centuries is mainly Mahayana Buddhism. As the core of Mahayana Buddhism, the philosophy of Consciousness-Only has made a deep impact on Japanese thought and culture. Its teachings are the key to transcending dualism.

Symbiosis of Life and Death

I was deeply impressed by the account of Susumu Hani,[5] the well-known Japanese film director, of his experiences in the African savannah and the blend of life and death he observed there.

In a television interview Susumu Hani explained that the animal realm is one of eating or being eaten. It was thoroughly natural to see a lion, for example, kill a giraffe and eat it. The giraffe cries out when it is killed, but only for a moment. The lion, having finished his meal, his hunger satisfied, quietly returns to the veldt, and other giraffes nearby go on grazing peacefully.

In contrast to this intimacy of life and death in the animal world, human beings are convinced that a single human life is the most important thing on earth, a thing of the greatest value. That belief reflects a rigorously dualistic view. The human fear of death is nearly hysterical when compared to other animals. Could it be that modernism has inflated this fear to the highest degree?

I saw in Hani's remarks a parallel with the Buddhist teaching of transmigration in which human beings, animals, plants, and even Buddhas are accorded life by a spirit transcending phenomenal life and death. The Buddhist teaching of impermanence means not only that all is vanity; it further suggests that since this is so, we must live in symbiosis in the cycle of that life. A time may be at hand when we human beings must arrive at an ethico-moral reconciliation: that very symbiosis of life and death. The philosophy of the West has taught us to view death as fearful and Hell as frightening, so we have denied death and pursued life with all our might. Death is dreaded as nothingness, nonbeing, or something even more terrifying. Perhaps it is time to take stock of our situation and once more look life and death—this purported dualism of human existence—in the face.

6

EDO: Pre-text for an Age of Symbiosis

Tradition and Change

A good deal has been published on the rich and varied culture of Edo[1] as the flowering of classical Japanese lifestyle. In the early 1960s, I predicted that Edo would be widely reappraised, and I studied the history of the city from a variety of perspectives. I have emphasized the importance of Edo's Shitamachi,[2] or "downtown" area; the value of streets and alleys as opposed to squares; the city's *sukiya*-style architecture in relation to its population density; the automatons of the Edo period; the philosophy of Miura Baien. I have collected and studied the woodblock prints of the last years of the Edo age, with special attention to the typically Edo-period color known as Rikyu grey.

In 1981, I designed the "Arts of Edo" exhibition at the Royal Academy,[3] London, and in my introductory talk at Oxford suggested that "the Edo period—or, more broadly, the three-century span of purely Japanese culture from the mid-sixteenth to the mid-nineteenth century—nurtures the roots of all that is Japan today." The major Japanese art traditions that survive—the way of tea (*sado*), flower arrangement (*ikebana*), the Noh and Kabuki dramas, *sukiya*-style architecture—all can be traced back to the latter half of the sixteenth century and all gained popular acceptance in the Edo period. They flourished until the so-called reforms of the Meiji period brought a wholesale rejection of everything associated with the past. Certainly the new government, but also the populace, sought to disassociate itself from the feudal past in the rush toward Westernization, even if that meant depreciating premodern life and culture.

With the opening of Japan to the West, Japanese architecture suddenly started copying Western architecture outright, and Japanese people took to wearing Western-style clothes. This seems to support the view that modern Japan begins from the Meiji period. We often hear that Japan rose from being a backward country to an advanced industrial state in a little over a hundred years—and that the leaders of today's developing nations should look to Japan as a model for their next hundred years of growth. Such formulas, however, overlook a number of important facts.

As is gradually becoming clear, the Edo period saw grand achievements in mass culture and was far more "modern" than has been appreciated. Ronald Dore notes in *Education in Tokugawa Japan* that by the end of the Edo period in 1868, forty-three percent of boys and ten percent of girls between the ages of six and thirteen attended school, a higher proportion than in England at the time. Edo was the largest city in the world, with a population of well over a million. In scientific scholarship, Yamagata Banto[4] proposed a theory of the solar system in his *Instead of Dreams* (*Yume no Shiro*, 1820), while Shizuki Tadao[5] translated John Keill's commentaries on Newton's *Principia* only very shortly after they had reached France. By the early nineteenth century, the cartographer Ino Tadataka[6] (1785–1818) had drawn accurate maps of the Japanese islands. Moreover, in the 1770s, the philosopher Miura Baien had set forth his dialectical system in three *Discourses on Metaphysics, Corollaries*, and *Morality*, predating Hegel's dialectic by fifty years. Most importantly, however, Edo society had already attained its own unique modernity, quite distinct from any European model. No doubt the speed with which Japan was able to assimilate Western ideas and practices in the Meiji period, like a blotter absorbing ink, related to the basically modern character of mature Edo society. Indeed, it is in the unique society of the Edo period that we should search for Japan's cultural roots.

Center of Popular Culture

Edo Japan, first and foremost, was a predominantly popular culture. In the eighth century, the total population of Japan was five million; a thousand years later, immediately prior to the Edo period, that figure had only just reached ten million. One hundred years into the Edo period the population had tripled, reaching thirty million by the time of shogun Tokugawa Yoshimune (1716–45). This in itself made for accelerated urbanization.

The world's largest metropolis, Edo was also home to the world's first mass popular culture. The vast shrine and temple complexes of earlier ages gave way to the popular architecture of *sukiya*-style tea rooms, Kabuki, Noh, and Joruri[7] theaters, as well as marvelous vernacular farmhouses and merchant town houses. As papermaking and woodblock printmaking techniques developed, a vast popular literature burst forth in the form of romances, humor, erotica, and several varieties of picture books mostly named after the color of their covers—"blue books," larger folios with little text, and more novelistic "yellow covers," also for adults, as well as "red books" and "black books" for children. Bookshops sprang up all over Edo.

High Population Density/Nonverbal Communication

A second important feature of Edo was its extremely high population density, which resulted in the cultivation of discretion and sensitivity. The average family had six members and lived in a home with a frontage of only *two* ken (about 3.6 meters). Under such circumstances, it was impossible for a married couple to have a private bedroom. Even in my own childhood I remember that my parents slept in the same room with one child, and my grandparents slept in an adjoining room with the other children. This was the norm in Japan.

In Tokyo today, with some 250 people per hectare, we speak of a high population density. But there were 688 people per hectare in old Edo. In a city so crowded, one loud voice can annoy scores of people. In Japanese we say, "The eyes are as eloquent as the lips," and we speak of "probing another's stomach." Silent communication of the eyes and the "stomach"—which is the Chinese and Japanese metaphorical equivalent of the heart, or breast, in the West—was a corollary of Edo's high population density.

In such a densely populated society, the slightest change in feeling or expression, gesture, or attitude, could have an impact on interpersonal relationships. Consequently a subtle and refined sensitivity was fostered, producing the psychological dramas of the Kabuki theater's *sewamono*, or domestic plays. The heightened sensitivity to materials that characterizes *sukiya*-style architecture can also be traced back to these roots. However, feudal society with its rigid class distinction, densely populated cities, and tight web of human relationships, did not permit the individual to expand his frame of reference and open his world to broader horizons. Instead, an intense concentration on and refinement of the internal world found expression in the human emotions of love, hate, and duty, in an extreme sensitivity to the changes of the four seasons, and in a love of plants and animals.

In modern city planning, high population density is regarded as undesirable. The ideal is thought to be single-family dwellings spread out at very low density among spacious parks and greenery. Yet I remain convinced that it is far more natural for human beings to live together in relatively dense population environments.

What are the best examples of the modern ideal of low-density urban populations? Take Canberra and Los Angeles, where the people of those cities are definitely not satisfied with their living environments. In Canberra, houses dot the open landscape at wide intervals. Is fruitful human interaction possible when you have to get in your car and drive to your nearest neighbor's home? And the high crime rate of Los Angeles—there being no way of knowing what has happened at one's next-door neighbor's house—makes it difficult to claim that such low-density urban environments are good.

Edo Rowhouse as Urban Model

Another trait of the Edo environment, attendant on its density, was its mixed, hybrid, pluralistic nature. The comic monologues of this period regale us with tales of colorful characters who lived in the rowhouses: a wise old sort, now retired; the stranger with a mysterious background; the quiet young couple, actually the daughter of a feudal lord and the head clerk of a great merchant, who have eloped together and are in hiding; the quack doctor; the hardworking carpenter with a large brood of children; and many other interesting characters, who shared the same lodgings in the typical Edo *nagaya*.

The Edo period is often thought of as an epoch of strict social castes, with little opportunity for people to move between them. But though externally these castes may have defined people's lives, internally a completely different principle was at work. The samurai class, for example, was actually very poor. The merchants, who were officially the lowest class, were in contrast relatively well off. Many of the merchant class were also leaders of the intellectual world, particularly in the study of Western science ("Dutch Learning," or *rangaku*). As a result, samurai had to swallow their pride and ask to be accepted as the disciples and pupils of these merchants. In other words, though an external class structure divided the populace into samurai, farmers, craftsmen, and merchants, other divisions cut across these groups: an economic class system, an intellectual class system, and an artistic class system. Social position was defined by the overlapping combination of all these relationships. There was nothing strange about a samurai setting up shop as an umbrella maker next door to a carpenter's shop, for example.

In fact, the present is, if anything, more class conscious than the Edo period as far as housing is concerned. When a public housing project is designed now, care is taken that all of the units should have a nearly equal amount of living space. Rent is calculated from the price of land and building costs by the so-called cost-price system. This ensures that people who move into the housing project are similar in social standing. For example, if the rent is just about right for a couple in their thirties with one child, the housing project is very likely to fill up with thousands, or tens of thousands, of couples in their thirties with a single child. The children that move in will all go to school at about the same time, and their fathers will all be at about the same step on the ladder of worldly success. The social environment of this housing project becomes, as a result, tremendously competitive. Which is more humane, the modern housing project or the Edo-period *nagaya*, populated by people of all ages, classes, and professions?

The separation of social classes in modern society results in exclusion of the weak. The modern housing project is not a suitable place for the elderly or handicapped. To avoid this unfortunate situation, I have always insisted that in designing public housing it is important to begin with a breakdown by percentage of the different types of projected inhabitants, ensuring that a wide variety of people will live together. We must start by determining the ideal percentages of couples in their thirties, forties, or sixties, handicapped people, and all other groups. Only then can the actual design and planning start.

For over twenty years I have continued to insist that if homes for the elderly are to be built at all, they should be located next to day-care centers. Then the elderly residents have a chance to play with the children, just as if they were their own grandchildren. The generations need to come into contact with each other. Some people think that because the elderly are not very active, homes for them should be located in quiet places in the midst of nature. This way of thinking reflects the coldness of modern society's functionalism and segregation, which values efficiency above all else.

On the outskirts of San Francisco I visited a retirement community—built quite some time ago—as part of survey I was conducting. The entire town was designed with the needs of the elderly in mind: because many older people have trouble walking, the area is flat and dwellings are all single-story. And because they tend to wake early, the dining hall opens at five a.m. for breakfast and the games room opens at six o'clock. At first glance it really does seem to be a town designed for the benefit of the elderly. But after breakfast, almost the entire population foregathers in the games room to play cards. This is indeed a strange sight. It bespeaks a society so harsh that there is no place in it for the elderly, who must be segregated from the real world. In the week I spent interviewing the people of this town, I learned that some sixty percent of the residents regarded their move there as a mistake. Living in an ordinary city is inconvenient and noisy, but at least there they could meet their grandchildren and other younger people. The residents' consensus was that they ought not to have come. But, in most cases the move had exhausted their life savings, and they were unable to escape.

The segregation of modern urban planning creates inhuman living environments like this one. In cities the world over, there is a conspicuous segregation by economic class. The high-density communities of Edo, in which different generations and classes lived together in symbiosis, offer us an important hint for urban planning of the future.

Symbiosis of Abstraction and Realism

The third characteristic of Edo-period culture is the importance of fantasy. The mysterious woodblock-print artist Sharaku,[8] for example, drew the features of actors in a frankly mannered fashion, yet his work does not lose its realism. In *shunga* pornographic prints, the male organ may be heroically proportioned, yet works in the picture—since the same level of realism and stylistic exaggeration applies in the rest of the print. The works of the Rinpa[9] school of artists—Koetsu, Sotatsu, Korin, and Kenzan, among others—are also strongly stylized structure, in sharp contrast to the concrete realism of Western contemporaries.

The combination of abstract and realistic techniques, pioneered in the West by Picasso, was already used to great effect by Japanese artists some four centuries earlier. Kabuki costumes and stylized *kumadori*[10] makeup also illustrate this characteristic abstracted realism. The leap from fantasy to abstraction is seen in other Edo-period arts as well, such as kimono patterns.

The importance of fantasy in Edo culture can also be seen in its attitude to nature. Edo was known as the city of blossoms—in part a metaphor for the city's brilliant and flourishing culture, as capital of the realm and seat of the shogunate; but the city was also extraordinary for the amount of greenery and flowers it cultivated. Though Edo lacked the public squares of Paris and the parks of London, the doorways and backyards of people's houses were lined with rows of bonsai, and in the summer, morning glory and flowering gourd vines climbed their façades. Flower markets were held most days of

Sharaku perfected symbiosis between the human physiognomy and abstraction in portrait of Ichikawa Ebizo (1795).

Kumadori, the makeup of a Kabuki actor

Symbiosis between fiction and reality: *Folding screen with red and white plum blossoms* by Korin. National Treasure.

Kimono pattern in Edo period: "crowded pine needles."

Kabuki actor wearing stripe-pattern kimono, Ichikawa Ebizo by Toshusai Sharaku.

the week, and peddlers hawked flowers and potted plants throughout the city.

The bonsai of Japan are not natural, but in each tiny tree we read a sign of nature. When the citizens of Edo looked at a bonsai pine they saw a hoary, thousand-year-old tree and heard the salt breezes of the seashore. I applied the emblematic quality of the bonsai in my design for the Roppongi Prince Hotel in Tokyo, planting a camphor tree at the center of the indoor poolside deck. The curve of the pool is itself a metaphor for the ocean. It is small, scarcely large enough to be of much use, but the sides are made of acrylic so people can watch the swimmers. It is like an image of the sea; the single tree I mentioned, like a bonsai, standing as a metaphor for the forest. With that tree, people can feel the coolness of shade in summer, and imagine the sighing of the wind through its branches.

Feudal lords resident in Edo were assigned official quarters on plots near the shogun's castle, and they also built private domains further from the center, incorporating large gardens. More informal *sukiya*-style architecture spread among the wealthier commoners, and with this a more highly stylized awareness of the garden evolved. Japanese gardens, of course, have a long history, dating from the palace-style gardens of the Heian period and including the sand-and-stone Zen gardens of the medieval era, but gardens first enjoyed broad-based popularity in the Edo period, exhibiting a high degree of abstraction and fantasy. If you want the ocean in your garden, you dig a pond and read it as the sea; if you want islands, you set a large rock or two in the pond. Nature in this fashion was man-made and fictitious in the context of the densely populated city of Edo. *Sukiya*-style architecture itself—or the tea house, built of wood, paper, and earth—is nothing more than a fantasy for viewing nature in this mode.

The androgyny of present-day pop idols was already notorious in Edo; this is another example of a culture of fictions. The beauties depicted by the mid-Edo-period woodblock-print artist Suzuki Harunobu[11] are as thin as Twiggy in her heyday. They are rejections of female physicality, androgynous presences that represent the exact opposite of a sex symbol like Marilyn Monroe. In Kabuki, the convention of men playing women's roles was exploited to present

Bonsai: needle juniper, 37 inches (94 cm).

The symbolism of *bonsai* at Roppongi Prince Hotel, Tokyo (1984), by Kisho Kurokawa.

Double Code: *Man Asks Woman to Step into His Room* by Suzuki Harunobu (woodblock print, Edo period).

Single Code: *Beauty Looking Back* by Hishikawa Moronobu (woodblock print, Edo period). ▶

woman as fantasy. The same impulse must have lead the geisha of the Fukugawa district of old Edo to adopt men's names. This type of inversion is a sophisticated part of the essence of an ambiguous culture. A culture that pursues a straightforward masculinity and femininity—where all men are John Wayne and all women are Marilyn Monroe—is based on straightforward physicality. This typifies the aesthetic of our own century, when the goal of human life is thought to be material welfare pure and simple. In contrast, a fictitiousness that allows men and women to exist in symbiosis is nowadays more and more sought after and will be pursued in the future. The feminization of men and masculinization of women—not to mention gay culture—are hardly signs of the collapse of civilization: they are the pulse of a new aesthetic consciousness.

Intentional Artlessness of *Sukiya*

The fourth remarkable trait of Edo culture was its extreme preoccupation with detail. The work of Kobayashi Rekisai,[12] a craftsman who specialized in making tiny models of everyday objects, transmits to us today this fascination. Kobayashi stood in a long line of superb craftsmen, stretching back to the Edo period. Among his many amazing works is a writing box only a few millimeters in size, yet painstakingly decorated with inlaid *maki-e* designs.

There are many other examples at hand: the famous and finely detailed Edo *komon* kimono patterns, miniature books, and Buddhist altars constructed as tiny miniatures. The architecture of the Edo period was similarly preoccupied with detail. The carvings that decorate the Toshogu shrine are an obvious example, and Edo-period castles, exemplified by Himeji, exhibit a far greater wealth of design detail than their Momoyama predecessors.

Sukiya-style architecture, when compared to the more palatial *shoin* style that preceded it, makes greater use of natural materials and a simplified, even rustic design. But aside from the question of sheer decorative detail, *sukiya*-style architecture shows great concern for the nature and proportions of the materials it uses. A naturally bent branch used in a *sukiya* -style decorative ensemble may at first seem an artless object that might be picked up anywhere, but in all likelihood that single branch was painstakingly selected from hundreds of naturally twisted specimens, especially chosen to *appear* artless and natural.

A fifth distinctive trait of Edo-age culture was its symbiosis of technology and humanity—what I call the notion of *karakuri*, or the automaton. In contrast to the West, where technology is opposed to humanity, technology in Japan was traditionally regarded as its extension, and existing in symbiosis. I shall come back to this point later in chapter 10.

Hybridism and Synthesis

The sixth trait of Edo culture was the development of a hybrid style of architecture. Carpenters of the Edo period freely combined the styles of all previous ages, inventing a uniquely hybrid mode. The Hiunkaku, or Flying Cloud Pavilion, of the Nishi Honganji temple in Kyoto is a masterpiece of the hybrid manner of the early Edo period. The *sukiya* style is a blend of the residential *shoin* style and the *soan*, or grass hut, variety of tea room architecture. The Jo-an of Oda Uraku is among the masterpieces of this hybrid tea architecture.

Another style that gained popularity in the Edo period was the so-called *gongen*,[13] or "avatar" style of architecture. The Toshogu shrine is the outstanding example of this, combining Buddhist and Shinto architectural vocabulary (the name reflects the belief that Shinto deities were avatars of the Buddhas and Bodhisattvas). The secret carpentry manual known as the "Transmission of Shrine Architecture" (*Jingu Soden*, handed down through the Kenninji lineage of carpenters) gives instructions for joining the main hall and worship hall of a Shinto shrine by a stone-floored zone, a combination of Buddhist and Shinto architectural ideas. Relatively early works such as the tombs of Daitokuin, Sugen'in, Gen'yuin, and Joken'in in Ueno, and the tomb of Bunshoin in Chiba can be regarded as precursors of this *gongen* style. By the mid-Edo period, full-blown examples abound: Yushima Tenmangu, Kanda Myojin, Kamakura Hachimangu, Nezu Gongen, Kameido Tenmangu, and Tomioka Hachiman shrines.

Japanese culture has always maintained a skillful synthesis of

Kanda Myojin shrine, Tokyo, example of the Gongen style.

diverse influences, and a hybrid style of architecture is hardly an anomaly in Japanese history. But this hybridization reached a peak during the Edo period, an era of architectural experimentation, when design and construction methods were given great importance. This tradition culminated in a complete syncretism of styles from the late Edo through the Meiji periods: Tsukiji Hotel, the First National Bank, Mitsuigumi Headquarters at Nihonbashi, all in Tokyo, as well as foreign merchants' houses in Yokohama. Master carpenters of that time incorporated Western styles into their work, and produced buildings with a naive yet creative blending of East and West.

From what photographs appear to show, the arch of the gate of

Mixed styles in the Edo period: Yushima Tenmangu (above) and Nezu Gongen shrines, both in Tokyo.

The Tsukiji Hotel (at right), a representative example of the highly regarded *wayo setchu* (quasi-Western) style.

Yukichi Fukuzawa—here portrayed on Japan's ¥10,000 banknote—a reformer who said, "Edo is my sworn enemy."

Tsukiji Hotel, for example, suggests Islamic architecture. The building itself is a dramatic combination of the diverse and hybrid—crisscross lath and plaster outer walls, bell-shaped and round windows in the tower, a hipped Western-style roof, a weathercock, a red-lacquered sash, and frame construction—and clearly surpasses in verve any of the *imitations* of Western architecture produced in Japan from the mid-Meiji period onward. This is because the hotel was designed before Japan had internalized Western values; the charm of Tsukiji Hotel lay in the collision of two different cultures and their *symbiotic* synthesis.

Unfortunately, due to the Meiji government's determined policy of Westernization, epitomized by the otherwise *enlightened* views of leaders such as Yukichi Fukuzawa[14] (famous for his remark, "Edo is my sworn enemy"), the value of such hybrid architecture was ignored. The Meiji period rejected the symbiotic culture of the Edo period as backward and chaotic; the age of modernization and "pure" Westernization had begun.

For over twenty years I have been working to recreate the aura of a hybrid architecture, most of which has been lost to us. The richest source of documentation is the woodblock prints of the period, especially the Yokohama and so-called "Civilization" (*kaika*) prints. From the last years of the Edo period on into early Meiji, representations of foreigners and their customs were popular. These lively prints depicted the new government policy of "civilization and enlightenment" and showed such scenes as Western ships, steam locomotives, foreign dress and accessories, and foreigners disporting in the brothels and gay quarters. The hybrid architecture of the age was also a popular subject, and many such buildings are shown.

Yokohama prints and Civilization prints were produced for a period of only about twenty years, spanning the last decade of the Edo period and the first decade of Meiji. Some eighty percent were created between 1860 and 1865. In 1868, the final year of the old regime and the first year of Meiji, Tokyo's harbor was opened to foreign ships, and popular interest began to shift from Yokohama to Tokyo. In general, the Yokohama prints depicted scenes in and around Yokohama, and the Civilization prints were views of Tokyo. As for the hybrid architecture of this period (now practically gone, yet faithfully recorded in the prints of both locales), I should like to be able to reproduce the symbiotic dynamism of its aesthetic in my own work, attempting to discover a true postmodern style intended to overcome the limits of the modern.

The journey of a *daimyo* to Edo (detail) by Odagiri Shunko (Edo period).

Centralization *and* Decentralization

The seventh, and last, special characteristic of Edo culture is the symbiosis of part and whole under the centralized shogunate and decentralized fief governments. The shogunate determined national policy; it was a centralized administrative system with enormous power. But from the mid-Edo period on, the shogunate (in financial difficulties, partly on account of the enormous expense incurred in the construction of the Toshogu shrine at Nikko) encouraged each of the fiefs to build up its own economy. The Satsuma fief in Kyushu developed cut-glass wares, Nagasaki encouraged the manufacture of blown glass; Ako was known for its salt production, Kanazawa for its Kutani ceramics, and Wajima for its lacquer ware. Wakayama also produced lacquer ware, and Ibaraki *yuki tsumugi* cloth; Oita manufactured a special kind of tatami matting, and Tosa supplied camphor. All of these were fief-administered local industries.

In education, too, each fief had its own system of village schools and academies. In addition, specialized private institutes were established to teach Western studies, neo-Confucianism, military strategy, and poetry, as well as various practical skills. The pinnacle of these local systems was the Shoheiko Academy in Edo, the official institu-

tion of the shogunate. But since the Meiji Restoration, Japan's educational system has gradually become increasingly centralized and standardized. The reevaluation of Japanese education initiated by the Nakasone administration (1982–87) included reforms to reintroduce more freedom and individuality, but in fact we could learn a great deal simply by looking back at the educational system of the Edo period.

The shogunate's policy of requiring feudal lords to shuttle back and forth between their fiefs and Edo contributed greatly to the development of a communication and transportation infrastructure up and down the country; but as the fiefs were never absorbed into the central government, each retained its own independence and vitality. This precedent can guide us today: it shows that we are not forced to make a choice between centralization and decentralization; we can have both, as in the ideal model offered by Edo. The strength of this model can be illustrated abroad both in the workings of the French geopolity and in the dynamic urban grid of the Federal Republic of Germany, especially now that it has been decided to restore Berlin as the capital.

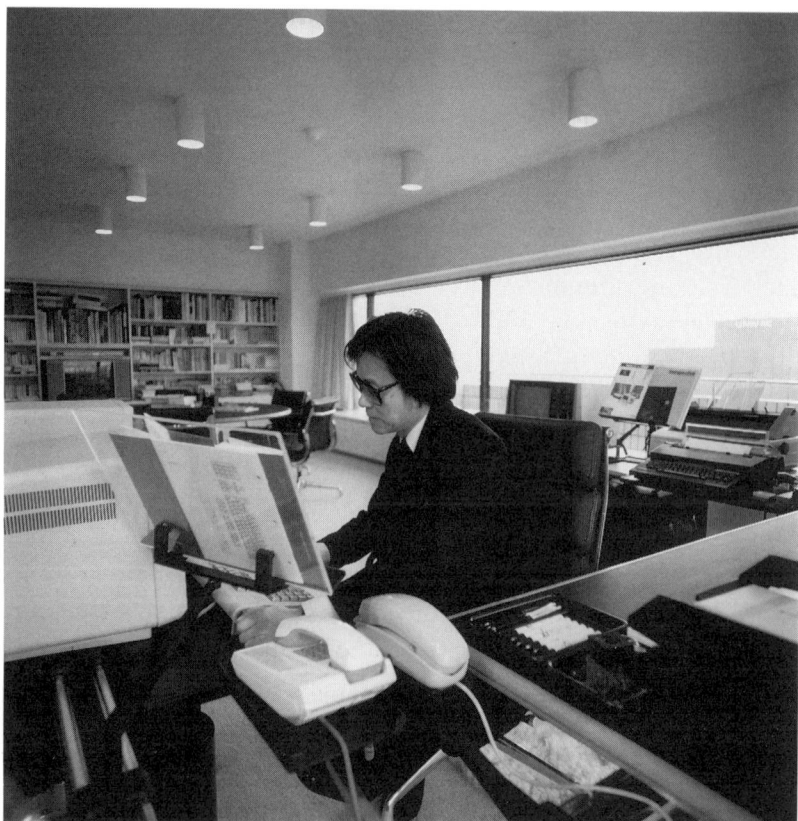

Kisho Kurokawa's study, adjacent to his Yuishikian tea room, exemplifies symbiosis between advanced technology and tradition.

7

HANASUKI:
Aesthetic of Symbiosis

Recreating Kobori Enshu in the Yuishikian

At home in Tokyo, I enjoy a lifestyle in which an advanced technology exists in symbiosis with tradition. My apartment is perched on the eleventh floor. Next to my study, with its IBM computer, I have constructed a traditional Japanese tea room,[1] which I have named Yuishikian—the Hut of Consciousness-Only. My personal computer is part of a communication network organized by a friend, Richard Farson, founder of the Western Behavioral Sciences Institute in La Jolla, California. It is directly linked over the Venus P satellite network to some fifty men and women in the worlds of scholarship, politics, and finance (1980). Yuishikian, on the other hand, is my place to retreat and think—and, with the hospitality of the tea ceremony, to receive and entertain guests and friends from Japan and abroad.

Yuishikian is the recreation of a particular tea room that once existed but has disappeared; it represents a formative and crucial, yet nearly forgotten, model of Japanese aesthetics. This model is profoundly linked to the basic principles of the Japanese aesthetic, *wabi* and *sabi*.[2] But all this will be discussed in greater detail further on; I shall first of all describe the tea room that served as the model for my Yuishikian.

This particular tea room was built at Takimotobo, a residence for

Yuishikian (Hut of Consciousness-Only) tea room, Tokyo.

Buddhist monks constructed at the Iwashimizu Hachimangu shrine in Kyoto by the scholar-monk Shokado Shojo.[3] Shojo's tea room was, in turn, a reconstruction of an earlier tea room, the Kan'unken,[4] built in the first decades of the seventeenth century but destroyed by fire in 1773. Shojo studied the tea ceremony under the great tea master Kobori Enshu,[5] and his Kan'unken was an exact replica of Enshu's Shosuitei, the tea room in the latter's Fushimi residence. Both consist of four standard mats and one *daime*-sized[6] mat. My Yuishikian, then, is a recreation of Kobori Enshu's most representative tea room, the Shosuitei at Kobori's Fushimi residence. I spent seventeen years reproducing this tea room. Why did it take so long?

Originally, tea rooms were constructed of materials that could be found easily and near at hand. Rare and expensive materials were

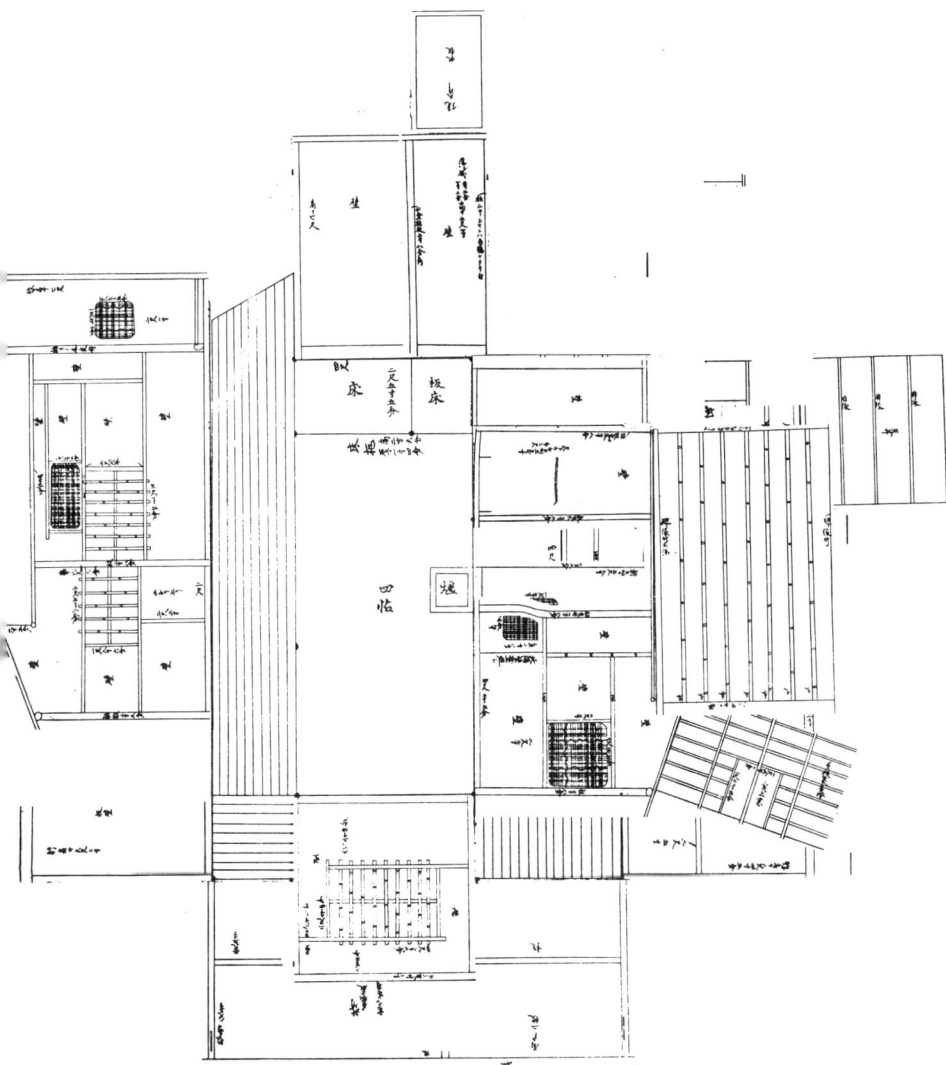

Plan of the Kan'un-ken, a replica of Enshu's Shosuitei.

avoided. A trunk or branch from a nearby grove of trees, and a stone discovered along the roadside, might be included in the final design. As a result, the tea room appears not to have been designed, but assembled through a process of natural accretion. Yet of course the aesthetic perceptions of the tea masters were at work in the selection

guests' entrance
(*nijiri-guchi*)

hearth

host's entrance

tokonoma alcove

host's entrance

tokonoma alcove

hearth

guests' entrance
(*nijiri-guchi*)

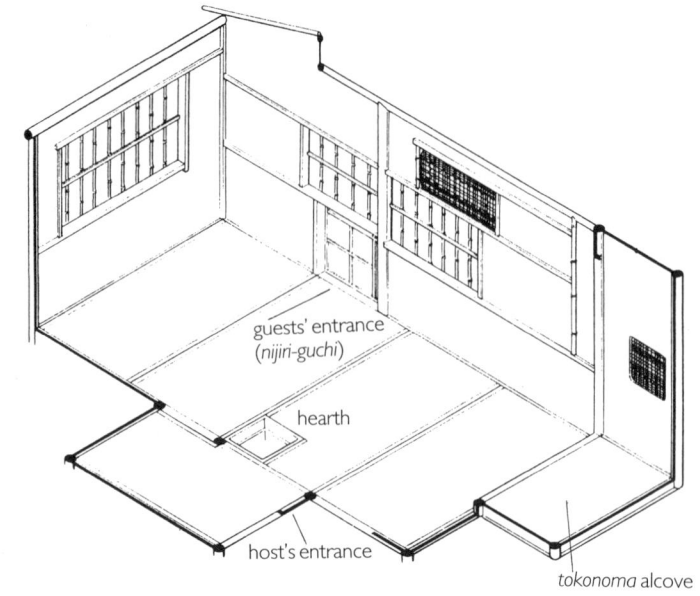

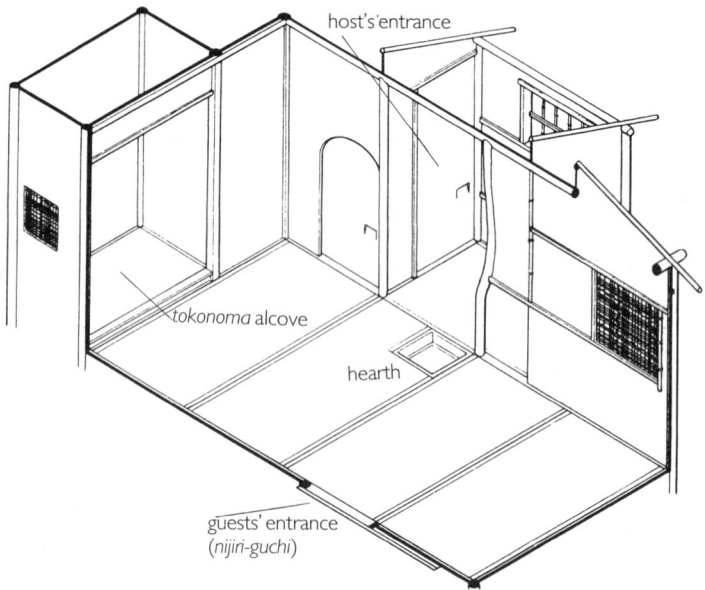

Complementary isometric diagrams of Kobori Enshu's four mat
daime tea room (Shosuitei) at his Fushimi residence, Kyoto.

process. Their ability to discover the beauty of commonplace objects, unremarkable to the average person, was crucial. And they possessed the skill to incorporate these objects into the design of a tea room. Though tea rooms of the age of Kan'unken and Shosuitei did not employ rare or luxurious materials, obviously many problems arise when one undertakes to reproduce the same tea room some three hundred years later.

Tea-room plans provide a detailed account of the original structures. In the eighteenth-century plans I worked from, not only are materials and dimensions noted, but the way in which natural timbers bend and twist, and the details of finish are all clearly recorded. Yet when one actually attempts reconstruction, one finds that crucial information is still missing. The challenge is to acquire that information in the process of construction.

To clarify the missing details, I studied diaries and accounts of tea ceremonies held in this tea room. In his *Matsuya Kaiki* (1741),[7] Matsuya Hisayoshi describes a tea ceremony that he attended at Enshu's Shosuitei. In addition to a detailed account of the tea utensils and the food and sweets served, he also describes the tea room. His remarks gave certain details not provided by the extant plans.

I knew from the plan that the tea room had a basketwork ceiling with a bamboo frame, but the material from which the ceiling was woven was not identified. According to *Matsuya Kaiki*, it was made of reeds. The plan told me that the *tokonoma* post was made of *kunogi*. It took some time to identify this wood. Was it a sort of tree that no longer existed? Or was it now known by a different name? Was *kuno* an orthographic mistake for *kuri*, or chestnut? I considered various possibilities, but in the end an acquaintance in Kyoto who is familiar with ancient manuscripts told me that *kunogi* was a dialect variation of *kunugi*—a kind of oak.

According to the plan, the back and sides of the *tokonoma* were papered with antique paper, but what sort of paper? I looked for a model to the Jo-an[8] tea room. This was designed by Oda Uraku,[9] and its *tokonoma* was papered with the leaves of old almanacs. Searching for almanacs from the early decades of the seventeenth century, I haunted rare book and antique shops. It took over ten years to acquire enough paper for my *tokonoma* walls. In one place in the tea room, a gently curving log is called for, and I had to pester my carpenter to go searching in the mountains for just the right shape; it took more than ten years to find it.

The height at which a flower container is hung from a decorative hook or nail in the tea room is quite important as well; but this was not indicated in the plan, and it was no mean feat to determine the authentic height. A plan called "Enshu's Four and One *Daime*-sized Mat Tea Room at Fushimi Roku Jizo," by a certain Ensai (otherwise unknown), tells us that the hook should be three *shaku*, two *bu*, and five *rin* (about 91 cm) from the floor. But, when we tried hanging it at this height, it seemed inappropriately low. I checked the source again and found that some regard the note on this plan an orthographic mistake for three *shaku*, two *sun*, and five *bu* (about 98 cm). Still, even this height seemed far too low and so out of harmony with the tea room as a whole that on this particular detail I made an exception and followed the example of the Yuin teahouse, setting the decorative hook at three *shaku*, seven *sun* (about 112 cm).

Following this process of careful consideration of historical sources and inspection of available materials, and relying on the skills of the mere handful of tea-room carpenters to be found in all Japan, it took me seventeen years to complete Yuishikian. And since there is no space in central Tokyo to build a tea room, I constructed it as a rooftop garden to my apartment—harmonizing it with the rest of the garden area—so that, when completed, my Yuishikian nested among the apartment buildings of the central city.

Why did I take so much trouble to recreate this particular tea room with such painstaking accuracy? Notably, in order to create an exemplar of the aesthetic vision I call *hanasuki*.

Wabi Implies Splendor *and* Simplicity

I offer the term *hanasuki* in place of *wabisuki*, as I believe that *wabi* as a concept has come to be interpreted in too narrow and one-dimensional a fashion. Traditionally, *wabi* has been thought of as silence as opposed to loquacity; darkness as opposed to light; simplicity as opposed to complexity; spareness as opposed to decoration;

monochrome as opposed to color; the grass hut, not the aristocrat's palace. Even in school texts, *wabi* is defined as an aesthetic of nothingness.

But isn't the true and essential Japanese aesthetic one in which silence and loquacity, darkness and light, simplicity and complexity, spareness and decoration, monochrome and polychrome, the grass hut and the aristocrat's palace exist in symbiosis? In *wabi* a superbly decorative principle, a special splendor, is to be found—like the undertaste in fine cuisine, that lingers and perfumes each subtle dish.

Nanbo Sokei[10] found the essence of Takeno Joo's[11] tea ceremony in Fujiwara no Teika's poem in the *Shin Kokin Shu*:

> I gaze afar
> And ask for neither cherry flowers
> Nor crimson leaves;
> The inlet with its grass-thatched huts
> Clustered in the growing autumn dusk.

The blossoms of spring and the red leaves of autumn are a metaphor for the gorgeous *daisu*-style tea ceremony of the aristocrat's mansion. When we gaze deeply at such splendor in nature, we arrive at a realm where "not a single thing exists"—the rush-thatched cottage on the shore. Those who do not first know the blossoms and the leaves can never live in the thatched hut. Only because we gaze and gaze at the blossoms and leaves can we spy out the thatched hut. This is to be regarded as the essence of tea.

What Nanbo was saying is that only one who knows the splendor and gorgeous beauty of the blossoms of spring and the red leaves of autumn can appreciate the *wabi* of the roughly thatched hut on a lonely beach. This is not an aesthetic of nothingness by any means. It is a doubly coded aesthetic, in which we are asked to gaze at the roughly thatched hut while mentally *recalling* the gorgeous flowers and leaves. It is an ambiguous, symbiotic aesthetic that simultaneously embraces splendor and simplicity.

Murata Juko,[12] known for his pursuit of the most severe state of Zen, says in *Yamanoue Soji Ki*:[13] "Juko described his ideal as a splendid steed tethered to a grass hut." *Wabi* is not simply a grass hut; it is the scene of a beautifully caparisoned, powerful horse tied to a humble, elegantly modest straw hut. The goal of this aesthetic is ambiguously encoded: two symbols simultaneously contradict and overlap.

Splendor of *Wabi*

The twentieth-century novelist Jun'ichiro Tanizaki wrote in his essay *In'ei Raisan* (In Praise of Shadows):[14]

> Sometimes a superb piece of black lacquer ware, decorated perhaps with flecks of silver and gold—a box or a desk or a set of shelves—will seem to me unsettlingly garish and altogether vulgar. But render pitch black the void in which these stand, and light them not with the rays of the sun or electricity but rather a single lantern or candle: suddenly those garish objects turn somber, refined, dignified. Artisans of old, when they finished their works in lacquer and decorated them in sparkling patterns, must surely have had in mind dark rooms and sought to turn to good effect what feeble light there was. Their extravagant use of gold, too, I should imagine, came of understanding how it gleams forth from out of the darkness and reflects the lamplight.

We see here that Tanizaki is by no means merely praising shadow for its own sake. His aesthetic, too, is doubly coded—the absolute opposition between gorgeous golden decoration and shadows of the night. In his dramatic phrase "the brocade of the night itself," we detect the lineage of an aesthetic of *wabi* that is very far indeed from a philosophy of nothingness.

The ambiguity of this aesthetic of *wabi* is even more pronounced in the related term *sabi*, propounded by the haiku poet Matsuo Basho.[15] Mukai Kyorai,[16] Basho's leading disciple in poetry, described the master's technique of versification as "unchanging flux"; this symbiosis of "flux," or impermanence and changeableness, with an "unchanging" quality that transcends the flow of time and achieves eternal existence, lies at the core of Basho's idea of *sabi*. Kyorai writes in the treatise known as the *Kyorai Sho* that:

Matsuo Basho, haiku poet who popularized the term *sabi*.

Sabi is the color of a verse; it does not mean a sad and lonely verse. It is like an aged warrior who arrays himself in his gorgeous armor and throws himself into battle. Or, though he dons brocade robes and serves at a banquet, he is still old. It is the combination of a flower-bearer and an aged servant.

In other words, the mere withered, sad state of old age is not *sabi*. Variously, *sabi* is the sight of the old man in his glorious armor, fighting bravely; or seated at a splendid banquet in his fine raiment. The aesthetic of *sabi* is produced in the contradiction of two symbiotically existing elements, the splendid brocades and the old man's subdued appearance.

Thus, the interpretation of these two core principles of traditional Japanese aesthetics, *wabi* and *sabi*, as spare, restrained, and anti-decorative concepts is badly misconstrued. In an effort to restore the present vulgarized and corrupt version of *wabi* to its original sense, I have invented a new term: *hanasuki*.

Zeami,[17] who raised the art of the Noh theater to perfection, wrote in works such as *Fushi Kaden* and *Kakyo* that *hana*—the term literally signifies "flower"—is the life of Noh. The aesthetic of *hana* implies the symbiosis of heterogeneous elements, of disparate moods or feelings. In *Fushi Kaden*, Zeami instructed the actor who portrays a demon to perform in an amusing way, combining the qualities of frightfulness and enjoyment. In the role of an old man, the actor should don the mask and costume of an old person and "portray an old man while still possessing the flower." When one performs Noh during the day, he tells us, he must act with the dark energy of night inside himself. Zeami's aesthetic is a characteristically Japanese embodiment of symbiosis that has much in common with the original meaning of *wabi*. Indeed, I am convinced that Zeami's "flower" aesthetic is identical with the true meaning of *wabi*.

Yuishikian, an Example of *Hanasuki*

Yuishikian, which I conceived as an emblem of *hanasuki*, has twelve windows and is an extremely bright tea room. Kobori Enshu endorsed tea rooms with many windows: the eight-windowed Konjiin tea room at Nanzenji was a favorite. My twelve windows can be regarded as a sort of stage lighting: by opening and closing different windows from season to season, the host's mat can be illuminated in a variety of ways. If I leave the door to the garden open, that view with all its light is part of the tea room interior as well.

In front of the *daime*-sized host's mat the four long mats are arranged in a row. This simple yet bold positioning emphasizes the theatricality of the host's mat. The *tokonoma* is framed by a white juniper post on one side and the *kunugi* oak, with a bark resembling red pine, on the other. The juniper is roughly finished in a square cross-section by hand-chiseling four corners, while retaining the bark on its four sides. The bark has also been left on the oak post, which disappears into the upper wall. Combining materials with such a range of expression produces considerable dynamism.

The roof and the window placement add variety to the design, making Yuishikian a highly decorative tea room. At the same time, I did not sacrifice the simplicity and calm that are characteristic of tea-room architecture. This is what makes Yuishikian a model of *hanasuki*.

Articulating *Wabi*

Why has the idea of *wabi* changed so that we are forced to invent a new term, *hanasuki*, to convey its original meaning? I can offer two answers to this question. The first goes back to the confrontation between the great tea master Sen no Rikyu[18] and his master, the feudal warlord Toyotomi Hideyoshi (1536–98). Hideyoshi has been described as the son of a farmer, or possibly of a foot soldier. Whichever he may have been, he had little time to acquire learning or polish in the years of his rise from so humble a station to the position of ruler of all Japan. Even had he been blessed with the time and opportunity, he apparently lacked by nature a sensitivity to the arts and learning.

Sen no Rikyu served Hideyoshi as an artist-in-residence and his teacher in the art of tea. In their relationship we can detect the conflict between authority and art, ruler and creator. Though Hideyoshi was the supreme ruler of all Japan and brooked no opposition from anyone, in tea ceremony matters Rikyu was his superior. Given Hideyoshi's nature, he most likely resented this great man of the world of art, a realm even Hideyoshi could not rule. After hearing Rikyu speak on *wabi* tea, with its notable emphasis on simplicity and humility, Hideyoshi asked Rikyu to design a tea room entirely papered in gold leaf, as if to taunt his master. And, in fact, he actually held a tea ceremony in such a room.

I believe that Rikyu was forced to articulate an extreme form of *wabi* as an antidote to Hideyoshi's ostentation and that he pursued this radical *wabi* as rigorously as a Zen monk pursues the way of enlightenment—in the context of this struggle between ruler and artist. Such were the particular circumstances that led Rikyu to develop *wabi* into an aesthetic of nothingness, of death.

Sen no Rikyu.

Hideyoshi Toyotomi. Important Cultural Property.

Ennan by Furuta Oribe shows symbiosis between simplicity and fertility, silence and loquaciousness.

In this contest between politics and art, Rikyu may at first seem the loser: Hideyoshi eventually drove him to ritual suicide. But in the struggle, Rikyu refined and distilled his aesthetic ideal to a nearly inconceivable extreme of simplicity: a tea room of one-and-a-half mats. Rikyu was a genius, the supreme arbiter of the aesthetic of *wabi* tea. But a more balanced concept of *wabi*, or of *hanasuki*, can be detected in the tea ceremony practiced by Rikyu's disciples.

His leading disciple[19] was Furuta Oribe.[20] The simple addition of a single mat to Oribe's three-mat *daime* tea room, Ennan,[21] results in the four-and-a-three-quarters mat tea room by Enshu. Furuta's tea room, then, is one of the sources of Yuishikian. In the deep eaves over the earthen area by the corner entrance, the displaced external post construction, and the abundance of windows—including a small floor-level latticework portal staggered with another higher portal and a flower-viewing window—Furuta's design displays a wealth of detailing. It testifies to a sensitivity attuned to the symbiotic interplay of simplicity and grandeur, silence and drama: a skylight is cut through the roof of the entrance to offer a view of nearby Mount Atago.

A second important follower of Rikyu was Oda Uraku. His Jo-an tea room is also a classic example of inventive and original *hanasuki*:

The Jo'an hermitage by Oda Uraku, a good example of *hanasuki*. Window in the open entrance (at left) is round, a truly a bold departure. National Treasure.

Round window of the
Jo'an hermitage.

a round window is boldly cut through the sleeve wall at the left end
of the main façade; and a triangular floorboard inset beside the
tokonoma brings a fresh new touch to the three-and-a-half-mat plan,
not to mention the decorativeness of the arched, cut-out wooden
hearth partition, old calendar pages pasted around the base of the
walls, and the bright atmosphere created by the row of waist-high
windows.

Finally, when we consider Yuishikian's model—the Shosuitei tea
room designed by Enshu (Oribe's disciple)—we reach the unavoid-
able conclusion that Rikyu could not have taught only simplicity and
spareness.

Bruno Taut at Katsura Detached Palace

The reason, therefore, that the traditional interpretation of *wabi*
has been restrictive, as well as somewhat shallow, is to be found in
Rikyu's articulation of the concept in so extreme a form, as an antidote
to Hideyoshi's ostentation. I also believe that the problem may be
traced to the encounters of Bruno Taut and Walter Gropius[22] with the
Katsura Detached Palace and their well-publicized responses to it.

The attention of Japanese architects was first drawn to their own
tradition by the remarks of these Europeans, who praised Katsura

Katsura Detached Palace, Kyoto (seventeenth century).

and the Grand Ise Shrine[23] as prototypes of modern architecture, perhaps with insufficient explanation. Japanese architects meekly followed their lead; they accepted the judgment that their native aesthetic tradition was one of nothingness, silence, and simplicity. But it is essential to note how the judgments Taut and Gropius passed on these works of Japanese architecture were made entirely from within the modernist context.

The modern architectural aesthetic was born from industrialization and mass production; its straight, spare, nondecorative line is

Katsura: decorative metal fittings on staggered shelves in Chu Shoin (above) and wainscoting in Shokintei arbor.

that of the mass product. Taut, and later Gropius, read Katsura Palace as an icon, an ideal reflection of modernist principles. But they overlooked several important features of the princely villa: the decorative metalwork of the staggered shelves in the first room of the Chu Shoin; the dramatic checked pattern of the *tokonoma* of the first room in the Shokintei arbor; the side window of the *tokonoma* of the

Ise Shrine, Mie Prefecture (photograph 1986).

Toshogu shrine, Nikko (seventeenth century).

second room of the New Shoin; the round window in the transom of the Shoiken retainers' quarters; the velvet baseboard wall covering and the elegant door-pulls of those same quarters. These details are astonishing in their richness, and they stand out even more sharply, embedded as they are within a space so pure and simple.

We can now see how one-dimensional was the appreciation of Katsura Palace by Taut and Gropius. Their rejection of the contemporary Toshogu shrine[24] at Nikko as an example of the inferior taste of the shoguns is further evidence of their failure to grasp the totality of Japanese aesthetic tradition. The shrine at Nikko must have seemed to these modernists somehow extreme. Yet only when such opposites are placed side by side can Japanese architecture of that age be appreciated in its wholeness. What understanding is there to be had by rejecting one and interpreting the other in a selective and self-serving manner? Perhaps this is just another manifestation of the theme of expediency at the core of modern architectural theory.

Ancient Japanese earthen pot from the Jomon era (ca. 10,000–300 B.C.).

Pottery from the Yayoi era (ca. 300 B.C.–300 A.D.).

As the late sculptor Taro Okamoto[25] has suggested, the Japanese tradition embraces two aesthetic currents existing together in symbiosis. One is bold and dramatic, the other a simple, nondecorative, and extremely refined beauty. He traced the first to the ancient Jomon era and the second to the subsequent Yayoi period.[26] There is nothing strange about the fact that both Toshogu shrine and the Katsura Palace were of the same Edo period, nor are there the least grounds for dismissing the former as an embarrassing lapse in taste by the Tokugawa shoguns. The vigorous, even violent decorative impulse of Jomon culture reached a climax in the gorgeous castle architecture of the Azuchi-Momoyama period (1568–1600), which continues to nourish Japanese culture to the present day.

There are certainly those who believe they have discerned the depth of Japan's aesthetic tradition when they visit the temples of Kyoto, with their unadorned, unfinished wood. But we must not forget that when Todaiji[27] and Toshodaiji[28] were first built, their pillars were painted crimson and their rafters glowed vermilion, gold, and green. They were a rainbow of rich primary colors. Except for certain Zen monasteries, the temples of Japan were in general as colorful as

Hall of the Great Buddha, Todaiji temple, Nara.

the Toshogu shrine is today. I regard the policy *not* to restore those colors as they faded naturally and to accept their new, quieter, but very different beauty, as an indication of the range of Japanese aesthetic sensitivity. Our asserting Japan's symbiotic aesthetic is not only a reaffirmation of traditional beliefs, but also a key to the sensitivity of what will surely replace Modernism as the aesthetic of the twenty-first century.

8

RIKYU GREY: Art of Ambiguity

The Quality of Rikyu Grey

Unlike concepts, sensations are hard to identify and explain. But this is fitting—for in trying to analyze sensation, we only betray its spontaneity and inherent naturalness. "Rikyu grey" represents an aesthetic of ambivalent, or multiple, meaning. My interest in it began nearly forty years ago when, with a group of friends, I had started the Metabolism movement based on our growing dissatisfaction with functionalism. Function as an architectural criterion achieved several goals, but it also resulted in overarticulated and concretized spaces. In that process, the nebulous and undifferentiated spaces that naturally exist between demarcated areas were ignored. Spaces embodying more than a single meaning were virtually eliminated in so-called functional building design.

My investigation of Rikyu grey was originally published as an essay in a special issue of *Japan Architect* in September, 1977, and republished in the same year as part of a book, *Gurei no bunka* (The Culture of Grey). The term Rikyu grey, as Isamu Kurita has suggested has no clear origin; and it is used here as a marker expressing the multiple meanings or ambiguity of Japanese space. As I will show, an analogous aesthetic sense pervaded sixteenth-century Mannerism and the subsequent Baroque movement in the West—and, more recently, the shifting codes of today's "camp" taste.

Masayoshi Nishida notes that Rikyu grey (Rikyu *nezumi*) appeared in the *Choandoki* (Annals of Choando)—a book of tea written in 1640 by Kubo Gondaifu Toshinari, priest of the Kasuga Shrine in Nara—and he cites the following passage:

> After Soeki [Sen no Rikyu] was summoned by Hide-yoshi to be his teacher of tea, all ceremonial tea came to follow his style. Soeki disliked whatever was ornate or gorgeous and he wrote numerous satirical verses admonishing people to follow the principle of *wabi* (rustic simplicity). "Change your collar cloth," said he; "wear a fresh sash of charcoal gray cotton (*sumizome*) cloth and a new pair of socks; carry a new fan. To serve your guests at dinner, lentil soup and shrimp in vinegar sauce is quite enough."

Ever since, this charcoal-gray color has remained popular, and dark gray twilled cotton cloth was widely imported from China. The dark grey color of this cloth is what came to be known as Rikyu grey.

Whereas until this time grey had been considered a vile color conjuring up the image of rats or ashes, upon becoming known as Rikyu grey it was better appreciated. In the mid-Edo era it gained tremendous popularity—along with brown and indigo—as the embodiment of the aesthetic ideal of *iki*. *Iki* in this period is a complex concept but may be conveniently described as "richness in sobriety." As the cult of tea spread beyond the upper classes to be practiced in the homes of ordinary people, so did the taste for grey. People took pleasure in coining names—Fukagawa grey, silver grey, indigo grey, raddish grey, lavender grey, grape grey, brown grey, dove grey, and lentil grey—whose perceived variations of tone had great appeal throughout the period. This taste prevailed in Edo culture from the Genroku age beginning in 1688 and lasted for the duration of the eighteenth century.

Toru Haga has written of the An'ei and Tenmei years (1722–1781) that modes in kimono fabric preferred by women included *kabeshijira* and *akebono shobiri*. *Akebono shobori* is a faint bluish-purple pattern like the essence of morning glories, while *kabeshijira* is a very delicate, finely woven silk pattern that appears pure white but in shifting light reveals a subtle raised motif.

Gen Itasaka has compared the change in taste during the Edo period to the transition between the styles of the woodblock print artists Moronobu[1] and Harunobu. Moronobu's women are pleasantly plump beauties with round faces, and ample bosoms and hips. Harunobu's women (see page 126) are less sensual, androgynous figures with slender faces and delicate, willowy silhouettes. This trend is of particular interest because it suggests the progressive denial of the generous voluptuousness that symbolized the prosperity and material abundance of pre-modern Japan up until Genroku. The An'ei/Tenmei aesthetic, on the other hand, was characterized by a nonsensual, eccentric, and nonphysical beauty, expressing the spirit of an age of more refined ambiguity and a sophisticated rhetoric.

In his *Beauty in Japan* Masayoshi Nishida explains Rikyu grey as a "colorless, nonsensual hue produced by combining various colors until they cancel each other out." *Rikyuiro* was a dark grey-green, or ash, color with a greenish tint; Rikyu grey is grey with a hint of *Rikyuiro* . Possibly, through the aesthetic of Rikyu grey, Sen no Rikyu was deliberately attempting to inspire a flattened world frozen in time and space.

Two-Dimensionalization of Space

In the grey of twilight, the spatial qualities of the city of Kyoto, Japan's most traditional community, are at their best. Roof tiles and plaster walls dissolve into shades of grey, and all sense of perspective and three-dimensionality is obscured. This dramatic effect, in which a three-dimensional world shifts into a two-dimensional plane, is impossible to experience in any city in Western Europe. The spatial arrangement of Western cities and buildings is superbly three-dimensional, thanks to discoveries made in the Renaissance period. Towers, monuments, and public squares form fixed perspectival nodes indispensable for apprehending urban space. Western cities thus yield their most dramatic effects under strong, bright sun which enhances their three-dimensional qualities and aspect.

The spatial composition of Katsura Detached Place is similar to a drawing in a picture scroll where the axonometric vision scans to dissolve building façades and street spaces into mere surfaces. Like a garden of meandering walks among hills and a lake, it refuses any single, fixed point of perspective. It is a two-dimensional world without a vanishing point and in the grey of twilight the most dramatic effects of this two-dimensionality are felt. At the root of Japanese aesthetic consciousness—be it in painting, music, drama or even in buildings and cities—is this two-dimension frontality. It is a quality of timeless nonsensuality, the continuum in which contradictory elements coexist; and at the same time it dissolves disperateness. Rikyu grey, or the "philosophy of grey," shares and mediates all these concepts.

By contrast, Western architecture is architecture of stone and sun-hardened brick—physical, substantial, and three-dimensional. Therefore, its space is like a container with openings made in it. This technique is all the more suited to be characterized by perspective, three-dimensionality, and distinct shadows.

Structures in Japanese architecture, especially as illustrated by the *shoin* and *sukiya* traditions from Rikyu's tea rooms to Katsura Detached Palace, are created of natural materials which impart none of the impression of a physical body carved out to form space. Rather like a stage flat, each vertical plane retains own viewpoint—a virtual image which goes beyond mere substance. In the sense that such architecture incorporates *ku* (Japanese for *sunyata*, the Sanskrit term for the relativity of existence and non-existence, '*ku*' is the first character in the term *kukan*, or space), it remains an architecture of two-dimensionality.

In Japan, until the early modern period, architectural drawings were merely rough sketches with written instructions. In the *Shomei* (A Guide to Carpentry) of the Hirauchi family, and also in the records of the Kora family, there are numerous detailed building plans for temples. Among those in the Kora family records are plans for Daitokuin, Kyoto, including detailed frontal views, floor plans, cross-sectional drawings, and sketches of ornament. Whereas Western European architects often drew bird's-eye views or three-dimensional renderings, Japanese master builders produced only plane or

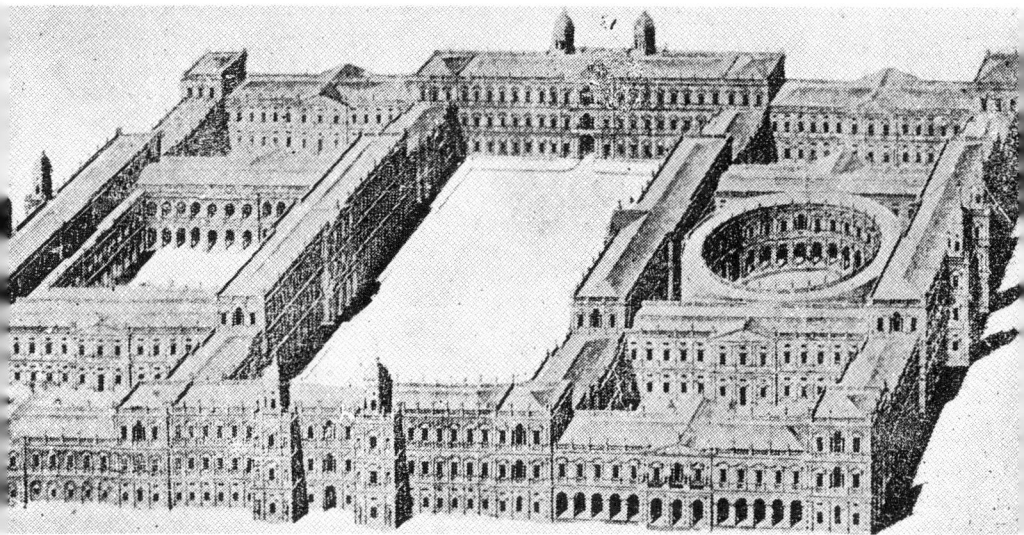

Axonometric drawing of Western palace complex.

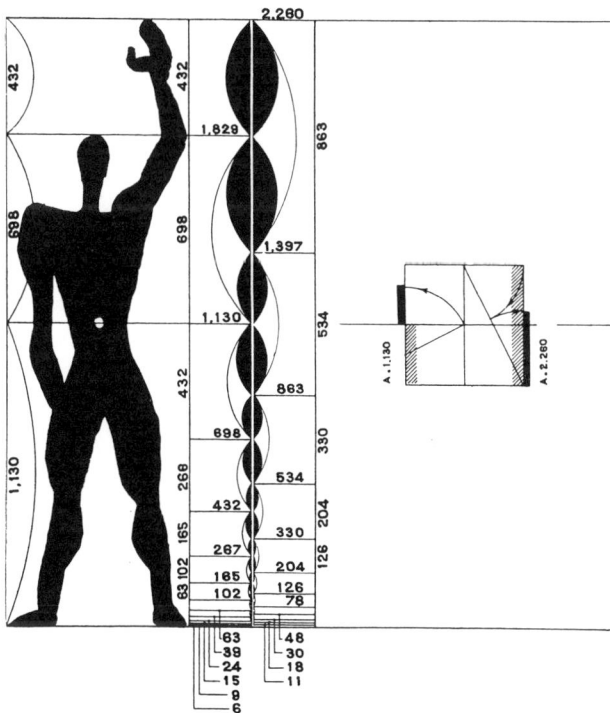

Le Corbusier's "modulor" system of proportions based on the human figure.

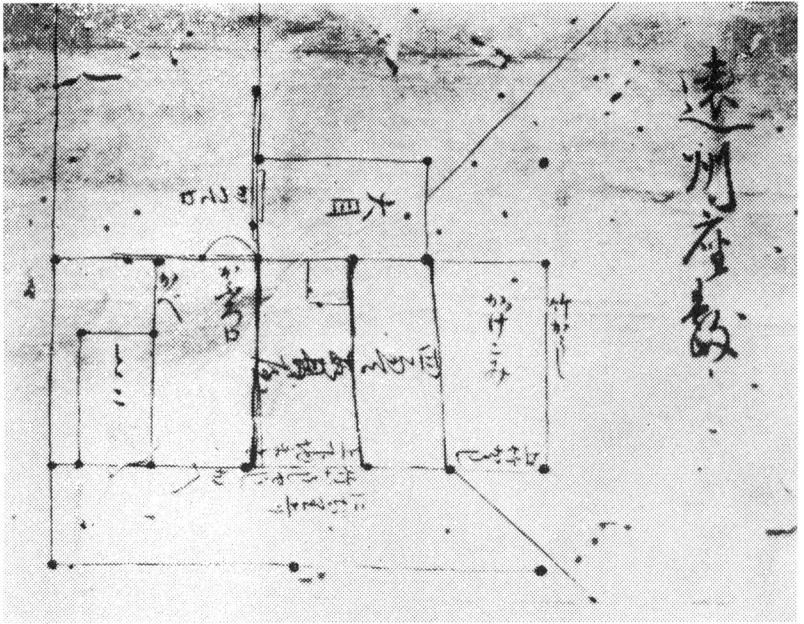

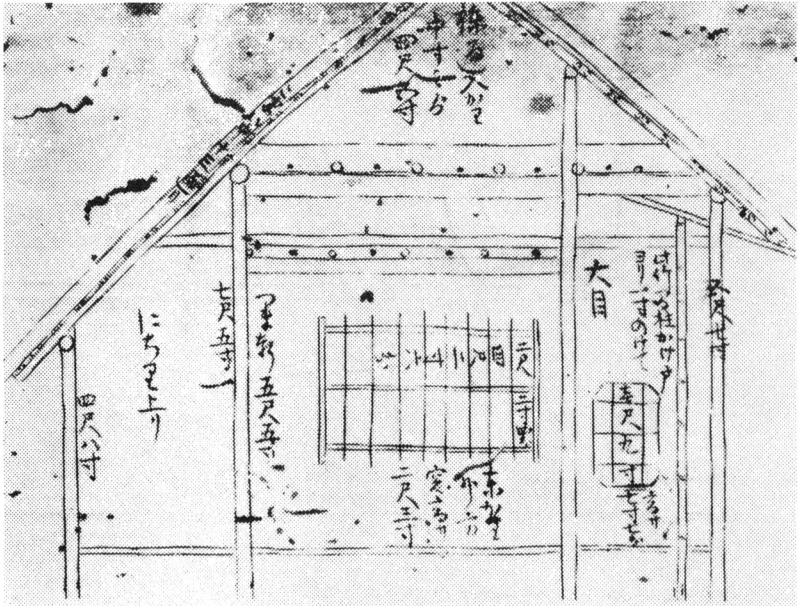

Japanese architectural drawings emphasize surface and plan.

frontal views. This practice, too, suggests the unique treatment of Japanese architecture as an unfolding diagram.

Another indication is Nambo Soeki's *Namporoku*, which records Rikyu's ideas about tea ceremony rooms.

> As I have said many times, the deepest meaning in tea is to be found in the simple, rustic tea hut. In the most formal *daisu* ceremony, the prescribed rules must be observed because that is customary. In the simple hut, through it conforms outwardly to the formal measurements, you can break away from these, discard technique, revert to the innocent and empty mind—going beyond customs and rules, beyond worldly cares.

"Break away from formal measurements / discard technique / revert to the innocent and empty mind." These are notions in complete contrast to the techniques of Western architecture, which extend from the Greek and Roman orders to the modular buildings of Le Corbusier.

The tea room that Rikyu envisioned as "breaking away from formal measurement" and "discarding technique" went beyond the four-mat style to a single mat room. He attempted to defeat the narrowness of physical space by creating a detached, nonsensual, spiritual locus. By Western standards, the height of the ceiling, the windows, and the low entrance *nijiri-guchi* are ridiculously small, almost inhuman. Heterogeneous design elements such as circular windows, unplaned alcove support pillars, and various kinds of ceiling materials and apertures may seem about to clash with each other yet coexist harmoniously. From the point of view of Western architectural hierarchy, this is no doubt difficult to understand.

But in Japanese architecture, including tea room design, each of the traditional elements—such as ceilings, alcoves, and walls—is autonomous; that is, all exist as independent planes in a two dimensional world. They resist any three-dimensional relationship. There are many examples, such as two opposite walls where the windows are placed with total disregard to conformity in size, height, or other measurements. This is, in fact, a technique used on purpose to maintain and emphasize two-dimensionality. In any case, Rikyu grey likewise affords a medium in which three-dimensional (that is, volumetric, sculptural, or substantial) space of unified meaning submits a single dimensional, field of multiple meaning.

The first time I incorporated the aesthetic of Rikyu grey into my own designs was in the Ishikawa Pension Hall (Kanazawa, 1977) and in the National Ethnological Museum (Osaka, 1975). The exteriors of both are clad in Rikyu grey tiles, and all the various aluminum and stainless–steel construction details, from the rounded edge of

Kisho Kurokawa: Ishikawa Pension Hall (1977).

Kisho Kurokawa: National Ethnography Museum, Osaka (1975), two views. ▶

the aluminum die-cast eaves to the granite and Angora stone facings, are uniformly in hues of light or charcoal grey. However, I do not wish to mislead the reader into thinking that the sensation of Rikyu grey works only as color. Buildings may either resist or express the force of gravity—in contrast to this, grey can create a detached, drifting sense, as in the streets of Kyoto at twilight. This is but one technique of blotting out the materiality of structure and materials, rendering space autonomous as well as ambiguous—in short, dramatizing it.

What the Ishikawa Hall and the Ethnological Museum share is a deliberate combination of mutually antagonistic, heterogeneous elements and materials, and my intention was to create through these a sense of detachment and coexistence. Thus, in the Ishikawa building, we created an almost mystic serenity by employing grey aluminum paneling on both walls and ceiling.

The *Soku* Form and Nonaction: Collision and Rebound

This technique of bringing together different domains and spatial dimensions can be found in various other aspects of Japanese culture. Fujiwara no Teika[2] (1162–1241), the court poet mentioned earlier, writes in his *Guhisho* (A Private Sketchbook) about the *soku* form, the poetic sequence in court poetry in which verses are seemingly unrelated in imagery and rhetorical technique.

Virtue is rarely ascribed to *shinku*, where the stanzas are closely related in theme. *Shinku* poems are too predictable for the Japanese sensibility; the poem develops as would a plant, from root to branch and leaf; they express only the ordinary, never the unusual or exotic. Each stanza of *soku* is complete—yet, joined in sequence, they produce a strange and unique effect. That is why Lord Tsunenobu praised *soku* technique. In the following stanza, for instance,

Yu sareba	As evening falls,
Nobe no akikaze	From along the moors the autumn wind
Mi ni shimite	Blows chill into the heart
Uzura naku nari	And the quails raise their plaintive cry
Fukakusa no sato.	In the deep grass of Fukakusa village.

two separate images of loneliness are recalled. Somehow their juxtaposition expresses the same nonsensuality represented by Rikyu grey or by the multiplicity of *sunyata*.

The same effect is achieved on the stage by the *senuhima* (nonaction) of the Noh drama, as described by Zeami in his treatise entitled *Kakyo*, from which the following is an extract:

> Sometimes spectators of the Noh say, "The moments of 'non-action' are the most enjoyable." This is an art which the actor keeps secret. Dancing and singing, movements, and the different types of miming are all acts performed by the body. Moments of "non-action" occur in between. When we ask why such moments without action are enjoyable, we find that our pleasure is due to the underlying spiritual strength of the actor which unremittingly holds the attention. Far from relaxing when the dancing or singing come to an end, or at intervals between the dialogue and the different types of mime, he maintains an unwavering inner strength. This inner strength will faintly be revealed, bringing enjoyment. However, it is undesirable for the actor to allow this inner strength to be obvious. If obvious, it becomes an act, and is no longer "non-action." The actions before and after an interval of "non-action" must be given continuity by a state of mindlessness in which the actor conceals his intent even from himself. This, then, is the faculty of moving audiences, by linking one's artistic powers to a single mind.

The silence and stillness in the interval between the action of the Noh drama must be performed with utmost care. *Senuhima* represents the same quality that I have mentioned in connection with *sunyata* and or in my definition of Rikyu grey. The *senuhima*, or moment when the expression of one mind communicates with another, is a transitional, complex, silent space replete with meaning. Yet the concepts of *sunyata*, Rikyu grey, and *senuhima* each represent distinct areas of meaning. Naturally, I am well aware that it is out of the question to discuss these on the same level—but in order to pursue my point about the nature of the intermediary, I have searched every corner for contexts that will illustrate my own theory of space.

Rikyu Grey *Is* Early Baroque

In the West, baroque and "camp" exhibit similarities with the aethetic principles of Rikyu grey. In his book on the baroque, Eugenio D'ors states that when conflicting intentions are bound together in a single motion, the resulting style is by definition baroque. According to this thesis, "baroque" implies vacillation. It is the simultaneous wish to affirm and reject; an attempt to fly while being pulled downward by the force of gravity. From this same contradictory impulse the column was born, for its structure is what could be described as a paradox of inspiration. The spirit of the early Baroque age, according to D'ors, can be represented by raising the arm while simultaneously trying to lower it.

He goes on to say that the actions of Christ in a painting on the post-Resurection theme *Noli me tangere* in the Prado is a virtual formula for the baroque. The picture by Correggio, the mentor of many instinctively baroque masters, shows Mary Magdalene at the feet of Christ, who rejects her while at the same time drawing her to him. He is telling her *not to touch* him even as he stretches his hand out to her. D'ors remarks that as Christ instructs this woman in the way to heaven, he abandons her to tears and desperation on earth. And Mary Magdalene, too, is a vacillating creature; in the very act of repentance, she succumbs to profane love. She remains earthbound while attempting to follow Christ. D'ors argues that this is the reality and essence of the eternally feminine and that as well qualifies a style: the Baroque.

I have singled out Baroque from the ages of Western culture not through any desire to analyze particular works of art, but because Rikyu grey can be seen via D'ors's analysis of the baroque phenomenon as multipolar and continuous. Even though the Baroque age was scientifically and technologically more advanced than the Renaissance, probably at no other time have there been such efforts to express human spirituality and sentiment. It seems to me that this was the one time in Western history that rationality and irrationality coexisted—a nondualistic spiritual world was actually achieved.

Of course, even this baroque impulse scarcely fulfills the aesthetic goals I seek to demonstrate. Mannerism, a word which came to mean "affectation" or "superficial imitation," was the pejorative name given by seventeenth-century critics to artists of the late sixteenth century. The term "baroque" likewise derives from the criticism of an aesthetic which strayed from the strict rules of the Greco-Roman tradition.

Antedating Della Porta's[3] façade of the Gesù (1584, completed

Della Porta: façade of the Gesù, Rome (late sixteenth century).

Bernini: *Ecstasy of Saint Teresa* (1646), altar of the Cornaro Chapel, S. Maria della Vittoria, Rome.

"Rikyu grey" in Western culture: symbiosis between reason and irrationality, between the soaring mind and gravity. Ambiguity lies at the very heart of baroque, Rikyu grey, and even "camp."

Gaudí: Church of Sagrada Familia, Barcelona (late nineteenth century, uncompleted).

in the transition between the Mannerist and Baroque periods) is the ambiguous balance of the Palazzo Massimi (begun about 1535) by Baldassare Peruzzi.[4] A painter possibly corresponding in style was the Frenchman, Nicolas Poussin[5] (1594–1665). D'ors calls him "an artist of rational passion," and indeed his version of the baroque was an equilibrium brimming with tension between intellect and emotion. Thus, Poussin's *A Poet's Inspiration* is a superior example of motion in stillness. Bernini's *Ecstasy of St Teresa*, El Greco's *Adoration of the Shepherds*, Domenico Tintoretto's *Goddess of Good Fortune Banishing Vices*, and Gaudí's *Sagrada Familia* similarly demonstrate a serene equilibrium between a rational and irrational spirit, as well as the qualities of nonsensuality and ambiguity unique to baroque art. However, when this state of tension reaches the decorative extreme of the interior of the Sta. Agnese church by Borromini in Piazza Navona, it is too fantastic and no longer has anything to do with Rikyu grey.

Confrontation and Harmony

Few other instances express the sensation and aesthetic of Rikyu grey (and its almost baroque complexity) better than the interior of the Yodomi no seki tea room at Saioin in Kyoto. From the curved lines and white hues of the entrance to the tea room itself, from the *mizuya* (preparation room) to the fit of the rounded edges—all is diverse, yet superbly harmonized—serene, yet dynamic. It was the baroque which finally broke up the classical orders in Western architecture by employing dramatic curved elements; but I consider the interior of the Yodomi no seki more baroque even than the façade of the Gesù in Rome by Giacomo della Porta, which is considered the archetype of early baroque architecture in Italy.

There are other examples of the ways heterogeneous elements can be handled, such as in the built-in waiting benches at Katsura Detached Place. Naturally bent timbers are used for supports and pillars, and these are eccentrically placed, without influencing the rest of the structure in any way. In other words, they create their own dramatic spaces where confrontation and harmony coexist.

The Toshogu Shrine is usually cited an as example of Japanese

Yodomi no seki (about 1685) by Fujimura Yoken, Saioin, Komyoji, Kyoto.

"baroque" but it does not exemplify the baroque (or Mannerist) aspect of Rikyu grey. The "baroque" essence to which I refer is represented by the mutual resistance and harmony of weight and drift, stillness and movement, straight and curved lines. A further example of this is the Hiunkaku (Fleeting Cloud Pavilion) of the Nishi Honganji Temple, Kyoto, a structure said to be the only remaining part of Hideyoshi's Jurakudai Palace. This asymmetrical three-story garden pavilion demonstrates an amazing heterogeneity of straight and curved lines coexisting in an overall appearance of great tranquillity. This, again, is precisely the same sensation as Rikyu grey, as well as a further early example of "baroque" aesthetics.

Hiunkaku (Fleeting Cloud Pavilion) at Nishi Honganji temple, Kyoto (early Edo).

Ambiguity and Double Meaning at the Periphery

It was Herbert Read[6] who said that ambiguity in English prose is achieved through metaphor. William Empson[7] in his *Seven types of Ambiguity* (1930) takes examples from Shakespeare, Chaucer, and Milton to explain the complex and alternating meanings of poetic language. He shows how single words or grammatical structures can simultaneously create quite different impressions in the reader.

However, as Masao Yamaguchi[8] has pointed out in *Double Meaning in Culture* (1981), sensitivity is produced in the marginal areas of double meaning in art and culture. Because those marginal areas are so diverse, various kinds of sensitivity are able to thrive: images not ordinarily defined in everyday life, contradictory elements and images (or symbols) which have not yet been given words, appear ceaselessly, proliferate, and achieve a new integration. However, such sensitivity is not nurtured in a world of logical consistency.

According to Yamaguchi, the basic motif of the folklorist Kunio Yanagida's[9] approach sprang from the dual meaning contained in marginal zones of Japanese culture. Yanagida discusses many such phenomena, for example: the guardian gods of travelers at the roadsides; the outcasts who lived on the edges of settlements at the boundary between wilderness and cultivated land; Hashihime, a schizophrenic border goddess who might kill men in cold blood if angry but, when pleased, could also bestow rare and precious treasures.

In the West, ambivalence and ambiguity are tolerated only in discussions of some special "spirit of the age" or the quality of some new art. The baroque spirit and Empson's analysis of Shakespeare and Chaucer are examples of this rare phenomenon. Masao Yamaguchi explains the marginal qualities of a given culture by saying that these emerge when, on the fringes of the those concentric circles that make up the pattern of any culture, attempts are made to adopt heterogeneous elements. From the point of view of Western logical conformism, which assumes cultural forms to be something homogeneous and stable, anything on the fringes of that culture is potentially threatening, representing vandalism and heresy. In this sense, D'ors's theory of the baroque is illuminating.

Our World as Double: Buber and Van Eyck

My purpose in rehabilitating the term Rikyu grey while simultaneously evoking the baroque aesthetic is to open a way for a dialogue with world culture, now that the age of uniform standards is drawing to a close. Some notable pioneers in this regard have been the architects Aldo van Eyck,[10] Louis Kahn,[11] and James Stirling.[12] The Dutchman Aldo van Eyck, who participated in the Tokyo Design Conference in 1960, is known for his theory of dual phenomena. Against the traditional Western European belief that houses and cities represent disparate dimensions of a hierarchy, Van Eyck's new order, or "Twin Phenomenon," was based on a revival of the Albertian idea that a city is a large residence and a residence is a city in miniature. A representative work of Van Eyck's is his celebrated Amsterdam Orphanage (today the Berlage Institute) in which modular units of space combined to form a dramatic whole, leaving unaware of the basic units. In some places floor level varies; in others building units merge into larger spaces; and lighting also causes the units to melt into the whole—all concrete examples of Van Eyck's theory.

The influence of the Twin Phenomenon concept was substantial, but of special interest to me was Van Eyck's reference to the philosophy of Martin Buber, explained in *Ich und Du* (1923). In his *Über das Dialogische Prinzip I*, Buber compared the relation between *I* and *things* (*ich* and *es*) and the *I* and *you* (*ich* and *du)*. He remarks that, for human beings, the world is double in that it conforms to dual human attitudes. He says that the "I" in the basic I-you relation is different from the "I" in I-it. I encounter you, because you turn towards me and approach. But the direct relation between you and me is further shaped by my action. In this way, such a relationship entails both choosing and being chosen; it is simultaneously active and passive. I have not succeeding in concentrating and dissolving myself completely by way of this formula, but the positing of you could not have happened without me. "I" become I in relation to you, and, by becoming "I," am able to describe you. Buber further says that the realm of it (*es*) exists in a complex of time and space whereas the realm of you does not. When the relational phenomena have passed, the individual "you" must become an "it," but individual "its," by moving into relational phenomena, can merge into a single "you." Buber's logic of the I and you has plainly transcended Western logical consistency and approaches Buddhist philosophy. But this is only natural, for this Hebrew scholar quotes copiously from the Buddhist sutras.

Double Meaning as Built

The idea proposed by Aldo van Eyck was, then, a Buddhist, non-Western theory of ambiguity that had not till then formed any part of the philosophy of modern architecture. Yet, as Charles Jencks[13] pointed out years ago in his book *Modern Movements in Architecture* (1973), issues of ambivalent or multiple meaning form the most important points of departure in contemporary art, architecture, and culture.

The Leicester University College of Engineering building (1964), by the late British architect James Stirling, is a bold structure of glass and brick. It is built of traditional English materials, but the treatment of its projecting glass façade, the glass roof components tilted at an angle of forty-five degrees, and the cubical configuration create its dramatic effect. Two contrastive building materials are treated in an ordinary manner, yet the effect is one of intense tension and symbiosis. The building seems to suggest an integration of two entirely contradictory ways of thinking, the articulation—yet encasing—of space. Stirling later clarified this approach in the Faculty of History building at Cambridge University (1968). The glass facing on the faculty office section slants at a forty-five degree angle, attaining the ambiguous expression of a taut spatial envelope but, at the same time, a tense resistance to the articulation of the underlying structure. Moreover, the Leicester building incorporates a whole range of architectural images—from traditional English factory detailing to hints of aerospace engineering—yet all these come across as very strongly controlled. In this, it might even be said to recall the intellectuality of Poussin's *A Poet's Inspiration*.

The buildings of the celebrated American architect Louis Kahn afford rare examples of intelligent and dramatic space created by elaborate articulation, and non-articulation, in the same designs. His Salk Biological Research Institute (1965) at La Jolla, California, plays on the articulation of bearing and core structures, but creating an extremely controlled effect of symbiosis which counters any possible disjunctive effects. This building stands in the lineage of the University of Pennsylvania's Richards Medical Research Institute, the work that earned Kahn world renown as an architect.

In his Kimbell Art Gallery (1973) at Fort Worth, Texas, space was articulated into a world of sophistication and diversity. The utterly dissimilar materials—concrete, travertine, and lead roofing—create a sense of antagonism and yet tranquillity, of motion in stillness.As *Architectural Forum* wrote in its mid-summer issue of 1972:

Aldo van Eyck: Amsterdam Orphanage (1960, architect's model).

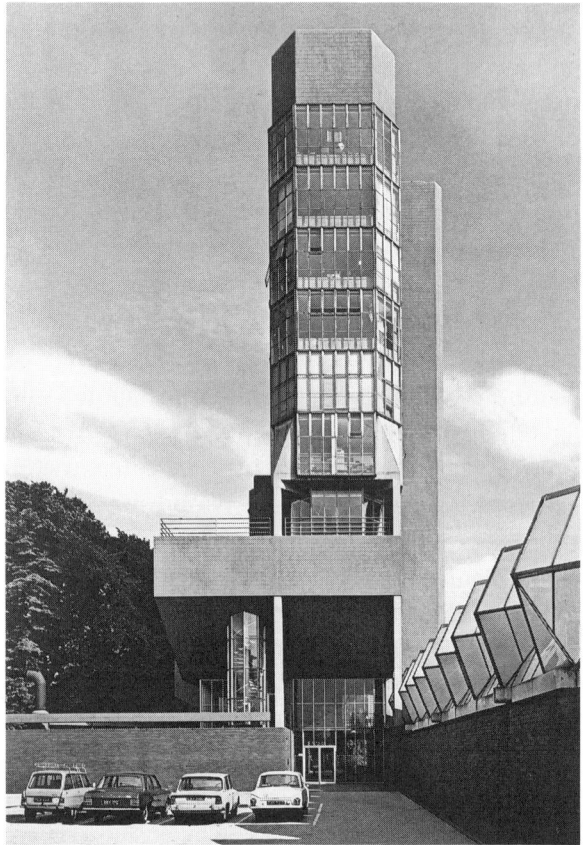

Stirling and Gowan: Leicester University College of Engineering (1964).

Louis Kahn: Kimbell Art Museum, Ft. Worth (1972).

Louis Kahn: Indian Institute of Management, Ahmedabad (1974).

The mind of Louis Kahn is a cross between a gaslight
and a laser beam.
It is a mind full of connections, respecting the past, perceiving the future emerging from it.
... It is mind ever searching for tranquillity amidst turbu-
lence, and for continuity amidst contradiction.
... To amass harmony in the service of man.

In spite of rationalism, the quality of multiple meaning in space
appeared early in the history of modern architecture. In a presentation sketch for his "House for an Art Lover" (1901), the Scot C.R.
Mackintosh[14] had already achieved a feeling of "unstable stability"
created by the subtle use of curved and straight lines. At about the
same time, Otto Wagner's[15] Vienna Post Office Savings Bank—
though its architect declared art to be dictated only by necessity—
affords spaces of a similar and wonderfully ambiguous stamp.

"Camp"

Susan Sontag, in her "Notes on Camp" (1964), claims that the
history of camp can be traced back to such Mannerist artists as Pontormo, Rosso, and Caravaggio,[16] or to the curiously lit paintings of
the Frenchman Georges de La Tour. In the field of literature the
movement has its roots in in the sixteenth century in the high-flown
expression of John Lyly and the Euphuists, in music with Pergolese
and Mozart and in the Baroquists—and, later, in the poetry of Ruskin
and Tennyson. Art Nouveau is also a source, and the tradition
includes a whole range of works, from the weirdly beautiful *Sagrada
Familia* by Gaudí down to von Sternberg's movie, starring Marlene
Dietrich, *The Devil is a Woman* (1935). The aesthetic of camp, which
turns its back on ordinary notions of good taste, warns us away from
the staleness in modern architecture. For Modernism has degener-
ated-because of a too serious and steadfast adherence to convention.

Mannerist painters often attempted to heighten sensual effects
through the subjective and unstable device of shot colors. Pontormo,
in his portrait *Dugolino Martelli*, communicates a tension which
barely arrests the inherent instability of the painted surface. The

same sensation informs his epoch-making *Madonna and Child with Saints* (1518) in S. Michele Visdomini, Florence. Mannerist painters, while employing Michelangelo's technique of *contrapposto*, tried to break the artistic bonds of the Renaissance and reintroduce a more cerebral atmosphere by creating forms in which sensation and intelligence could merge. Chiaroscuro lighting is one of the hallmarks of this school, as exemplified in Caravaggio's *Palmist* . The technique creates an overall dramatic effect with a subtle balance of instability.

Camp rejoices in an abundant, and exaggerated, display of the complexity of human nature and space. It is expressed at once by the urban pastorale, discussed by Empson in his *Seven Types of Ambiguity*, mentioned above, and by the disquietingly androgynous quality of Greta Garbo's physical perfection. For devotees of camp, Marilyn Monroe and Jane Mansfield are too feminine to be meaningful.

Greta Garbo was always herself, and her poor acting only heightened the effect of her beauty. As Jean Genet pointed out in *Notre Dame des Fleurs* (1944), to extract polysemy from a culture, artistic preference must not stop merely at good taste for its own sake but must have a sense of what bad taste is. In other words, camp is sensitivity to double meaning wherever a two-way interpretation is likely, or even possible.

In the twentieth century functionalism brought forth internationally comprehensible and readable forms and new criteria for "good design." Now, however, we have come full circle to a contradictory world increasingly confused by the unbearably logical consistency of so-called good design. Thus, I submit that the time has come to venture into the frontier of the spirit which, so to speak, stretches broadly on all sides at the fringes of our established rules and standards. The core of the human spirit is not easily divisible; it is endowed with bountiful meanings and the power of suggestion—and at the same time with tranquility, the world of Rikyu grey.

9

INTERMEDIARY SPACES

Engawa: **Symbiosis of Interior and Exterior Space**

One might say that the difference between Western space and spaces in Japan is that the former is discrete and the latter are continuous. Western architecture is designed to "conquer" nature, thus the significance of the wall, dividing exterior from interior. Japanese space, by contrast, seeks to encompass building and nature, to unite them as equal partners. The wall as divider between outside and inside did not evolve in Japan, as I have already mentioned, partly because of a difference in basic materials: Japan is a culture of wood and the West a culture of stone or brick. In addition, Japanese builders have long made a conscious effort to integrate inside and outside.

The *shoin* and *sukiya* styles afford an unobstructed interpenetration of interior and exterior—a symbiosis with the world of nature, where house and garden are one. Even in the country house where I spent the war years, for example, we always opened the sliding exterior doors at the first light of morning, no matter how cold it was—whether the garden was filled with snow or the fragrance of flowers. In the West we perceive the window as a frame, with nature as the painting it frames, or as something "out there." An important feature of the Japanese house, by contrast, is the *engawa*.

The *engawa* is a sort of veranda running around the house as a projecting platform on stilts and protected by the eaves. It serves as

The *engawa*, or veranda, an intermediary space that is both indoors and outdoors.

an exterior corridor, mediating between inside and outside. While it protects the interior from wind, rain, and the strong rays of the summer sun, it can also be a place to entertain guests and offers an entrance from the garden to the house. The *engawa* takes on a variety of functions not specified in the conventional Western plan with its series of rooms linked by hallways.

The *engawa* is interior space beneath the eaves; but, at the same time, it is part of the exterior space of the garden. In our old country house, formal guests would be received in the guest room, but local merchants and neighborhood friends would come calling to the *engawa*, sit down and have a cup of tea and chat. Thus the way of receiving guests was distinguished spatially according to the significance and role of each.

My notion of intermediary space is linked to the idea of reintroducing this kind of communication among people, unobstructed by any dualistic inside/outside separation. I have identified a range of architectural details—the space beneath the eaves, or *engawa*, corridors, and lattice doors among them—as intermediary. Let us now look at the ambivalence and multivalence which boundaries and peripheral spaces afford in the context of the city.

I first stressed this theme in the theory of Metabolism. Just as emptiness in Buddhist philosophy is a perfectly real, if intangible entity, intermediary elements and spaces need not necessarily take physical form. Looking at the traditional Japanese street space, one realizes that an intermediary element or zone is not always a physical place, like a public square.

The Square vs. the Street

Traditionally there have never been plazas or squares in Eastern cities. Their functions have been performed by streets.

As shown by the Vedic scriptures, four types of city design were conceived in ancient India. These were called Dandaka, Nandyavarta, Padmake, and Swastika, all characterized by lattices of straight streets. The models ranged in scale from 1200 by 1200 meters to 7500 by 7500 meters, with two-thirds of the total space devoted to farming. Homestead units varied from 7.2 by 4.8 meters to 12 by 9.6 meters, with a courtyard providing shelter for livestock. The first step in town planning was to bisect the site using a sundial. A trunk road was built along this north-south line and was called the Rajabata, or King's Road. A crossing road was named the Mahakara, or boulevard. These two roads formed the basic skeleton of the town.

These ideal town schemes had no plazas or squares. Public build-

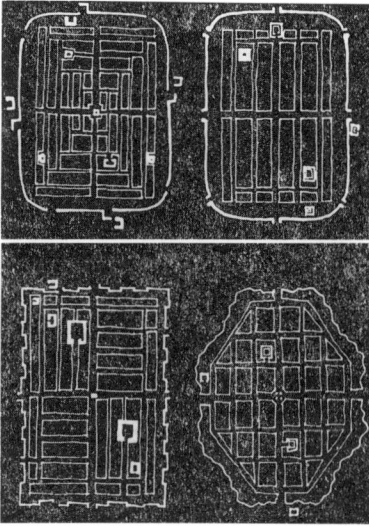

Four ideal cities from the Vedic scriptures.

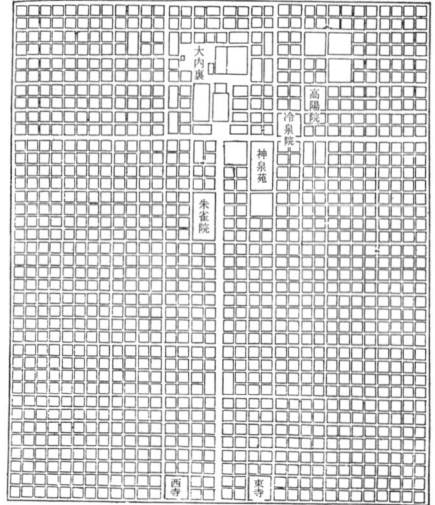

The ancient capital of Heian had no plazas or urban center (open spaces are imperial grounds).

ings and temples were erected along the Rajabata and Mahakara, and a linden tree was planted at their intersection. The tree was believed to be mother of the sun, moon, and stars—a symbol of the mystical powers governing the universe. But it was not a nucleus for the citizens' daily activities. Social space was provided by the two roads, the Rajabata, which might be called the "Sun road" since the sun shone on it throughout the day, and the Mahakara, a ready passage for breezes and hence the "Wind road." We may imagine the Sun road was a lively place, filled with people after the long rainy seasons, enjoying the good weather once again. On hot humid nights, many must have moved their beds onto the Wind road, watching the stars in the night sky before a breeze lulled them to sleep.

In addition to domestic functions, the Sun road and the Wind road were used for festive parades, while religious processions were held on the Mangarabichi, or Fortune road, on the periphery of the town. So, urban spaces for religious rites and for demonstrations of power were on the same streets as those where people led their lives.

This was generally true of Japanese cities also, with their wooden houses offering easy access. The ancient capital of Kyoto, previously called Heian, had an elaborate latticed pattern of streets and avenues. But here, too, there was no plaza. The temples and public buildings were built along boulevards instead of being concentrated in the center when they might have enclosed a public square or provided a nucleus for the city.

One possible reason for this arrangement was its convenience for festivals, which in the East mostly took the form of processions rather than mass assemblies. The major streets in Kyoto, however, did not function as part of the community life of the ordinary people. They were intended for the nobles in horse-drawn carriages and for festive processions—a showcase for the power of the rulers and aristocrats. They were lined by the houses of wealthy citizens, an arrangement designed to bind the inhabitants to the city through rites and a display of power.

Minor roads, alleys, or passages, on the other hand, were an integral part of the populace's lifestyle. Alleys threading among typical town houses with narrow entrances, such as in the Nishijin weavers' district in Kyoto, were communal roads, not traffic arteries. Major streets marked boundaries of different districts or communities, while minor roads wove through each smaller district. Houses lining a minor road formed a closely related neighborhood. These minor roads are barely three meters wide. Façades with lattice windows made the houses more a part of the street than a shelter from its activities. On summer evenings these roads were crowded with people seeking relief from the heat. People chatted together over the lattice windows, and the rooms facing the road occasionally doubled as shops. While major streets were for formalities, festivals and demonstrations, minor roads formed communal areas for the townspeople.

A similar lack of squares or plazas applies to the castle towns that thrived in Japan from the Middle Ages to the Edo period. These towns evolved around a castle—nucleus of the town and the residence of the local ruler—but the town's vitality sprang not from the castle but from a network of streets running through sections inhabited by commoners. From a distance the highway appeared to lead straight to the castle, or symbol of the town, but inside the town was a labyrinth. Temples were established along the highway beyond the town, while craftsmen and merchants—such as carpenters, shoemakers, ironsmiths, tailors, and dealers in silver or silk—were given quarters inside the town. The sections for blacksmiths and gunsmiths were situated down from the prevailing wind because of the smoke produced. Horse traders were required to live at the edge of the town by the highway. Palanquin stages were erected at the entrances to the town.

The main street was frequently the scene of festive processions. Fairs were held along it to promote the development of the town. During the *Bon* season in late summer, the time when ancestral spirits are believed to return to their earthly homes, large crowds turned out on the temple-lined roads.

As evidenced by the use of the word *tsuji* ("streetcorner" or, broadly, "street") in such combinations as *tsuji giri* ("armed street robbery"), *tsuji seppo* ("street preaching"), *tsuji fuda* ("street bulletin board"), and *tsuji uranai* ("street fortune-telling"), streets in Japanese towns served not only as a passage for traffic but also as space for communal life.

The approach to the Konpira Shrine in Shikoku offers a typical example of such dual functions. It passes through a town with souvenir stores usually crowded with visiting pilgrims and is lined with rows of stone lanterns, pine trees, and stone walls. At places this approach road becomes a complex where nature, architecture, and traffic all meet. Some sections are paved in cobblestones, and there are also long, steep flights of stone steps. All is blended to make the street lively and enjoyable.

The street has been put to particular religious use in the approach to the Grand Shrine of Ise, dedicated to Amaterasu Omikami (the Sun goddess), the highest deity of Shinto. These shrines are the best of the nation's native architectural tradition. Sacred trees and sacred rocks are set at key points along the path, which from time to time

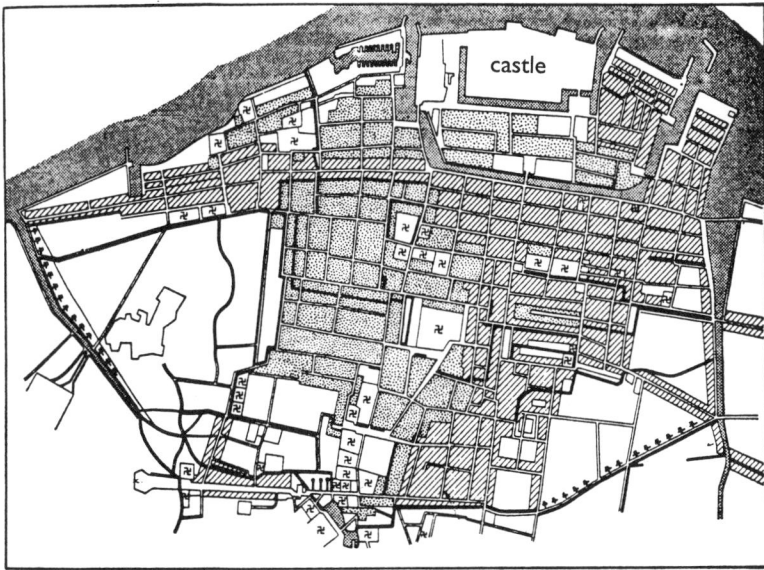
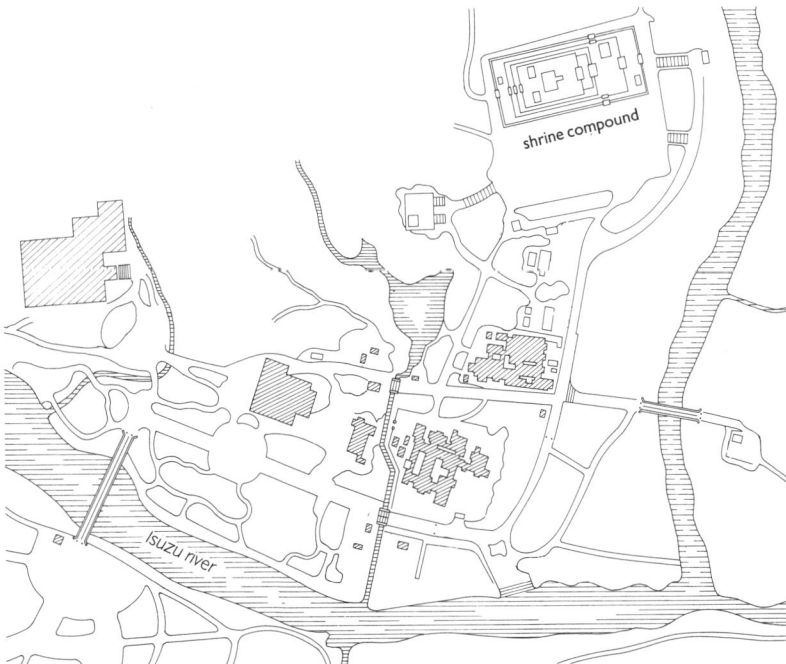

Japan's streets are *loci* of symbiosis, connecting and expanding individualized spaces.
Castle town of Takamatsu (above), and Ise Shrine compound and site.

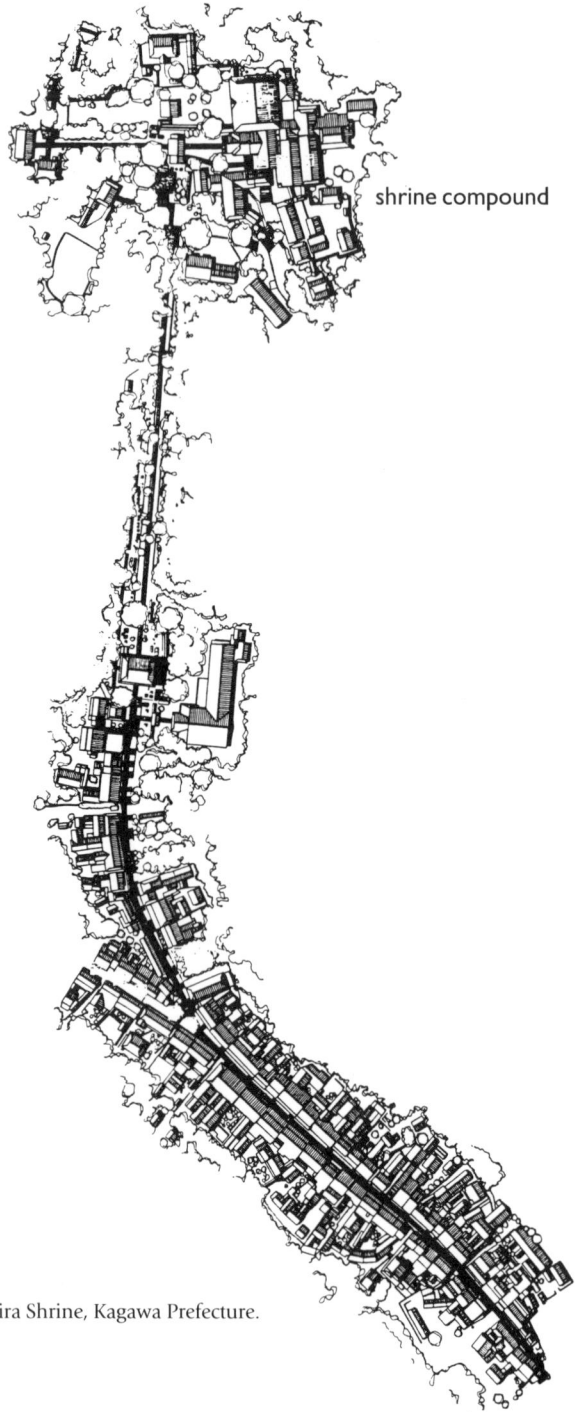

shrine compound

Approach to Kotohira Shrine, Kagawa Prefecture.

crosses bridges and follows streams. As a result, even the sounds heard along the way inspire in the worshipper a growing serenity, and serve as psychological preparation for prayer at the shrine—an effect apparently intended by the original builders. The arrangement means that the operative confines of the shrine extend all the way to the Isuzu River, starting point of the approach.

Were there ever streets which fulfilled such dual functions in the West? The ancient Greek *polis* of Miletus in Asia Minor—known to history as the first planned town—was laid out on a grid but differed in two fundamental ways from more truly Oriental cities. One is the

Four patterns of ideal Renaissance cities, all with central plazas and radiating streets.

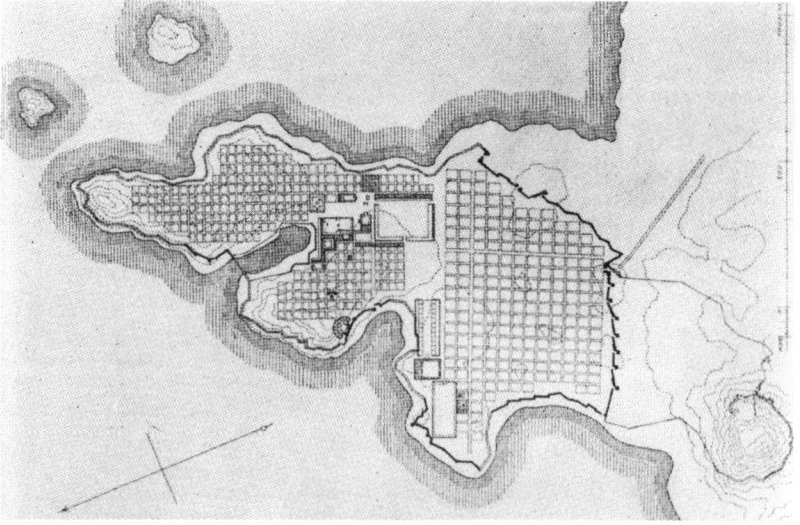

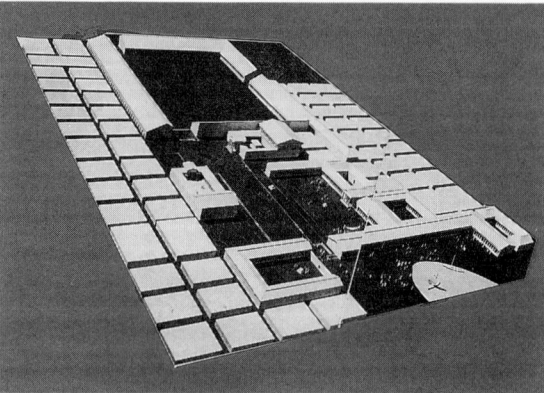

The West, lacking "streets,"
instead had plazas. Plan
and reconstruction of the
ancient Greek city of
Miletus and its *agora*, or
plaza.

manner in which public buildings were arranged. In the East placement of temples and public buildings along processional streets enabled these roads to function as public spaces and link individual dwellings to the community, while the Greek *polis* had a central, gravitational public area called the *agora*.

The *agora* was a place for markets and political meetings, and fortune-tellers and prostitutes solicited custom there, with robbers lurking in the shadows at night. The orthogonal streets were connected to this central space by colonnades. The *agora*, therefore, was a vehicle relating the lives of individual inhabitants to the city and infusing a community consciousness.

The other difference concerns the relationship between houses and the street outside. In Miletus the rooms of houses opened onto a courtyard which played a central role in family life and was used for socializing. Thick walls separated the house from the road, with only a few small windows. This structure was rigidly closed to the outside, unlike Japanese houses which consist mainly of post and beam structures more or less open to the street. A ditch, one to two meters wide, made of stone and running at the back of the houses, was presumably filled with refuse and rainwater on wet days.

A fragmentation of spaces according to function was already evident in Miletus: private spaces, an atrium for family and neighbors, a road with provision for drainage; roads for traffic; a public space in the center of the *polis*. These were the rudiments of functional order. The separation between architecture and infrastructural space had already begun during the later Greek period.

Plazas and squares in feudal cities during the Middle Ages took on a more pronounced character as places for the exhibition of power and religious rites. Street patterns become more centralized, culminating in a radial arrangement where all roads converged at the ruler's palace.

The emergence of more such plazas and squares in the West had to wait until merchants gained social importance and towns underwent major general improvements in living standards. Countless neighborhood squares were then created, while the monumental central square was retained intact. This was an attempt to relate the

A representative Western plaza, old print of Berlin.

lives of individuals to the city insofar as possible, but nothing near the East's communal and more flexible street pattern developed in the West. This difference is largely attributable to different ways of thinking in East and West.

Symbiosis of the Street

This East-West difference is amply illustrated in Japanese urban space, based as it is on the open structure of our wooden houses. In the ancient capital of Heiankyo (present-day Kyoto), for example, there were—as already discussed—no squares. Temples, shrines, and public facilities were set along the roads. Without a central plaza or core, the capital was a diverse checkerboard of streets divided into broad avenues and narrower lanes. The broad avenues with their aristocratic dwellings were the thoroughfares along which the ox carts of the nobility were drawn, and down which the many festivals and processions paraded. These avenues were the framework that linked the citizens to their city both ceremonially and in terms of secular authority. In contrast, the small streets, like those still to be seen weaving in and out among the houses of the townsmen in Kyoto's Nishijin district, formed the actual arena of city life. The avenues divided the city into major districts; the streets were the warp and weft of those districts.

Areas on both sides of one street would be known by a single name—for example, the smiths' district, or the armorers' district—and make up one interrelated unit. According to Kazuhiko Yamori, author of *Toshizu no Rekishi* (History of City Plans), this type of Japanese urban space developed from the latter half of the ninth to the tenth centuries. Before that time, the street was like a river, separating or encircling communities—in other words, an obstacle. In early Heian, the square residential blocks bounded by streets were called *machi*, and later on these were divided into four equal parts, or *cho*. Eventually, however, the *cho* on opposite sides of an intersecting street were united into a single unit, a system completed by the military dictator Toyotomi Hideyoshi in the late sixteenth century. This process of reconfiguration was conceived against the historical back-

Lattice of a *machiya* house.

drop of the disbanding of the medieval guilds¹ and the establishment of a freer market economy. Over the succeeding centuries,
these changes led to the development of the Kyoto-style town house
(*machiya*), with the street as community core. The *machiya* facing
each other across the intersecting street evolved architectural features
to exploit the social and commercial possibilities of this new common space. In addition to lattice doors and windows, architectural
benches and horseguards (*komayose*) further emphasized the continuity along these streets of open-structured wooden façades. The lattices of the *machiya* accorded an appropriate degree of openness
while simultaneously guarding the privacy of residents. The street
space was neither totally public nor private but an intermediary
zone, fulfilling the same function as the *engawa* between house and
garden.

Thus the street has traditionally played an important, if intangible, role in Japanese society. Since the enactment of a new system of
urban districts in 1962, however, Japanese cities have come to be
divided according to a system of districts and wards. In imitation of
the West, areas surrounded by streets are once more the units of
urban space. These have been renamed for the convenience of com-
puterized record-keeping, and the old *cho* and their names are disappearing. Wonderful old historical names such as Kajimachi (Smithies
District), Teppocho (Armorers District), Bakurocho (Horsegrooms
District), and Tenmacho (Post-horse District) have been replaced by
bland abstractions, such as Heiwa (Peace), Midori (Greenery), Kibo
(Hope), and Hibari (Lark). I am currently serving as vice-president
of the Zenkoku Chimei Hozon Renmei (Society for the Preservation
of Japanese Placenames) in order to revoke, or revise, that 1962
statute, for I am convinced this new system of districts will condemn
our old communities built around their streets to destruction.

An Inviting Street Architecture

The function of the street in the contemporary city continues to
be of vital importance—and revival of the street as it once existed in
Asian cities is more urgent than ever. I do not, of course, oppose
streets designated for automobile traffic. Looking at the present state

of our streets, in which passenger cars, trucks, and bicycles are crowded dangerously together, I am convinced that alternative systems of commercial intra-city transport *must* be developed, and that the urban motorway system of bypass loops and belts must be improved. At the same time, however, it is important to build, or retain, city streets that also function as living space.

All over Japan today there is an interest in rendering the city a scenic place, and the preservation movement continues to make increasing headway. But even in cities like Kyoto or Kanazawa, where so many historic buildings remain, there are not nearly enough streets along which we may enjoy a safe and pleasant walk. Pedestrianizing is one answer—but we need not restrict ourselves to a system of streets exclusive to either cars or people. Experiments that allow vehicles to share the streets are feasible. In mixed residential and commercial districts, for example, road humps can be installed to slow traffic and trees planted in islands in the road. Architecturally interesting, arcadelike streets can be built. All of these are methods of restoring the originally ambivalent, multivalent nature of street space. Today, when most urban space is rigorously divided into public and private, restoring to streets their nature as an extension of communal living space might make our cities more habitable and interesting.

As early as 1962 I referred to my design for the Nishijin Labor Center in Kyoto as an "architecture of the street," since it aimed to create a new street space to compensate for the loss of those streets usurped by automobiles. Similarly, the lobby of the Japan Red Cross Society headquarters in Tokyo is a more purely architectural example of the interpenetration of interior and exterior spaces within a single building, creating an overlapping, multivalent intermediary zone. The thirty-meter *engawa*-like space beneath the roof of the Fukuoka Bank Head Office performs the same function, recalling the aims of the Kyoto Project at a more purely urban scale. Finally, the Daido Seimei Company's office in Tokyo attempts an architectural recreation of the traditional *machi* on both sides of a streetlike space in the central business district of Japan's largest city.

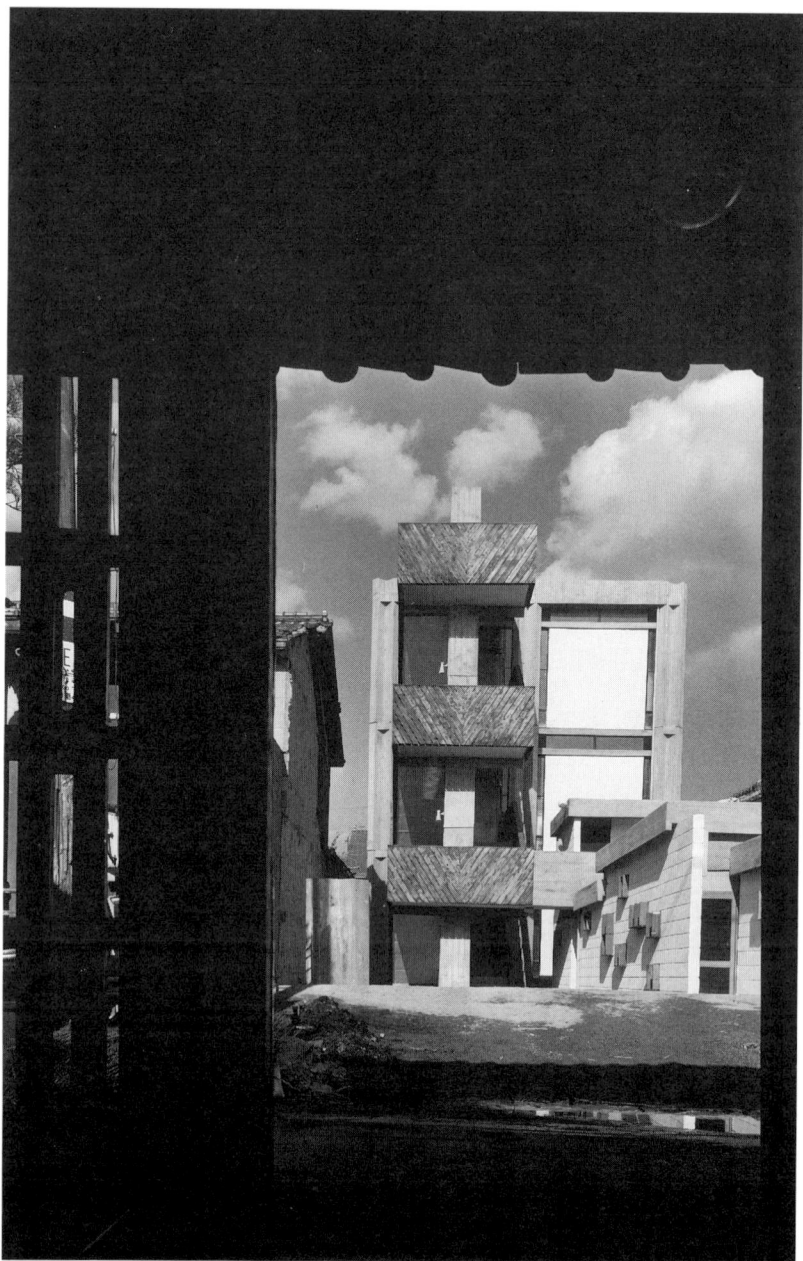

Kisho Kurokawa: Nishijin Labor Center, Kyoto (1962). "Street architecture" affording symbiosis between inside and outside (above, and next two pages).

Kisho Kurokawa: Japan Red Cross Society foyer, Tokyo (1977). ▶

Spatial and Temporal Relations between Opposites

Whether in architecture and town planning, or in daily life, the concepts of intermediary space and ambiguity are vital keys to implementing the philosophy of symbiosis. In the West, one seeks to transcend dualism through the dialectical method of resolving opposites on a higher level. The two opposites are either unified, or one of the two is negated, and rejected. Symbiosis, instead, creates a dynamic relationship between contradictory elements while allowing them to remain opposed. A relationship between two such elements or issues can be achieved by interpolating a spatial distance (neutral zone) or a temporal space (cooling-off period) between them.

In Western society, neutral zones and cooling-off periods have historically been regarded as negative or a means of last resort. In the contractual society of the West, decisions are bound by legal agreement; ambiguity and intermediary zones are avoided. Contemporary America is a typical contractual society; perhaps mutual trust is only possible within the rules of a contract, since the nation is a vast conglomeration of so many different ethnic and cultural groups. It is impossible to carry on business in America without lawyers, and situations that most Japanese would regard as easily solved by a little discussion often evolve into courtroom proceedings. In contrast, many projects in Japan are undertaken on the basis of verbal promises. Except in the most extreme circumstances, acquaintances or companies in a supplier-customer relationship seldom carry grievances to court.

Trust, in Japan, means trust without contracts. When a problem arises it is settled by making mutual adjustments. For such a procedure to work there must be room—in other words, ambiguity and intermediary space—for adjustment. The more determined two parties are to draw up a contract providing for every future risk and contingency, the more inflexible their positions will become. Perhaps in the process a certain peace of mind will be assured, but real understanding and desire to deepen the relationship in future will be much less likely.

The limits of attempting to control all transactions by the West-

◄ Kisho Kurokawa: Daido Seimei
Tokyo Building (1978).

ern contractual system are increasingly apparent—particularly in an international age, when diverse nations, enterprises, and individuals are living in peace though poised in relationships of benefit and harm, profit and loss.

Cities with Squares, Cities with Streets

From the most ancient civilizations until the Middle Ages, space was the realm of the gods. It was habitually constructed and explained by means of symbols, myths, and ceremonies. The pre-modern era began with the disclosure of the real nature of these inner gods. After Leonardo da Vinci dissected the human anatomy and Newton the universe, the mythological spatial order perpetuated by Scholasticism was dispelled and space came to be defined in terms of substance and functional relationships. For Leonardo, human beings consisted of bodily organs and their functions; for Newton, the universe comprised the celestial bodies and gravitation.

The age of CIAM seems still to belong to the phase of Newtonian physics. Like Leonardo or Newton, Le Corbusier dissected cities; he categorized their essence as living space, working space, and recreational space, joining these conceptually by an infrastructural network of transport links. By all appearances, now, we are beginning to inhabit a new world—a world of Riemannian space.[2] The German mathematician G. F. B. Riemann (1826–66) created a new calculus, superseding that of Liebniz and Newton, as well as a new geometry that provided the first definitions of manifold and curvature. Those in-between spaces which Newtonian physics saw only as emptiness today are recognized as substantial space by non-Euclidean, or Riemannian, geometry.

In the dawning information society, is there anything with the character of Riemannian space?

Let us consider Tokyo as an example of a modern city. Several million people commute daily from the outskirts of the city to the center, amounting to a round trip averaging some three hours daily. According to the thinking of CIAM, real commuting times were not very meaningful. But in reality, this journey time—roughly one-eighth of an office worker's day—cannot simply be written off. We no longer live in small communities in which one can just disregard time required for transport and circulation.

According to a survey conducted by Japan's national radio corporation, the proportion of each day that city residents spend going from one place to another can be expected to increase. This time needs to be considered an important part of our lives, not merely a means. In other words, trains and cars, and the very streets themselves, must be treated as living spaces in a new sense in the coming age. We can no longer afford to view transport simply as movement from one substantial space to another, as Le Corbusier seems to have done.

The significance of urban streets ought to be examined with care, as East and West hold fundamentally different perceptions. To simplify somewhat, Western cities have traditionally lacked livable streets, but have adopted squares in their place; Eastern cities, meanwhile, lacking squares, have adopted streets instead. In European cities, social life centers around the square, just as residences surround central courtyards. As can be seen in ancient cities, such as Athens, streets have the function of connecting these squares. In the majority of cases, the buildings lining those streets were of closed design with small windows so that people could discard garbage or peer out. But any architectural interpenetration of building and street spaces was rare indeed. As such streets were designed to link squares, a short walk straight down any one of them would invariably lead into a square. Although these plazas tended to knit together all aspects of urban life, the streets themselves were simply pathways directing urban flow. This tradition survives all too clearly in modern city planning theory, which regards streets not as living spaces, but merely a means devoid of substance.

This is an enigma. As noted, the Vedic planning ideal of ancient India long incorporated a unique method of urban design featuring a "street of Sun" and "street of Wind." Instead of mere aspects of circulation, our forebears considered streets to be places of life linked to climate.

Let us also consider the layout of Kyoto.

The roads of Kyoto consist of wider avenues (*oji*) and narrower streets (*koji*). The *koji* pass through the centers of the *machi*, or districts. In other modern cities, such districts are simple blocks delimited by streets, but in Kyoto, a *koji* forms the center of its district. Formerly, such streets actually played a more significant role as everyday living spaces than as transport routes.

The *machiya*, or Kyoto-style town residence that lines both sides of a narrow street, itself less than three meters wide, utilized lattices called *garari* to create semiopen spaces facing the street, thus exploiting the openness of wooden construction technique. On summer nights, these streets filled with people enjoying the cooler air out of doors, who could be seen chatting with those within through the lattices. When the lattices were taken away in the daytime, the *machiya* served as stores. Such were the loci in which residents lived out their lives, places that linked people's daily existence to the city as extensions of their livelihood.

In Eastern cities, streets are the social spaces linking more personal domains, or spaces of association. This arrangement recognizes the significance of perambulation and the value of all that is acted out in this medium. To give an example that illustrates this difference, the festivals of Asia were—and are—typified by processions, while European parades were generally more secular; in the West religious assemblies were frequently static gatherings of many people in a large square in front of a church. The peripatetic modes of urban tradition in Asia suggest a structure that should prove effective for the highly mobile humanity of the dawning information age.

Toward an Architecture of the Street

The lives of individuals come to trace very wide-ranging paths in the course of a twenty-four-hour period, paths that can be construed as living spaces. Thus, the integration of the totality of such paths can be considered the living space of a city. As it becomes increasingly possible to document this, the issue of trajectories is likely to become a major theme of urban planning. I use the term "architecture of the street" to describe various historical examples suggesting that Japan's traditional buildings were often far ahead of the rest of the world in this regard. One such instance is the unique layout of

Buddhist temple corridors, organically linking an entire complex of separate structures: temple gate, main hall, lecture hall, treasury, belfry, and priest's quarters. Although these individual functional elements were of different sizes and shapes, the method of joining them by means of a corridor, or "architectural promenade," was based on a clear notion of spatial organization and flow generating a solemn architectural beauty. A different example is the treatment of a humble garden path as a space redesigned for strolling.

The approach at Kotohira Shrine in Shikoku yields a further illustration. As one proceeds uphill, one experiences a "space of expectation" upon nearing the final objective: one can note the changing scenery, stop to rest briefly along the way, and then move on, looking to left and right. Thus, the approach itself affords a superb architectural experience.

As mentioned, the approach to the celebrated Ise Shrine bears similar examination. There is the stark white of the path as one crosses over the Isuzu River, the sound of one's own steps on the pebbles, the near architectural effect of trees lining both sides of the way, the sacred trees located here and there, and finally the shrine itself. The very street is an experiential space in which the worshippers can participate. Despite its lack of a roof, it may be termed "architectural."

The arrangement of corridors about the Japanese-style room is based on an approach differing greatly from Europe. In the Japanese design, as it evolved over the centuries, the corridor serves as a condenser, linking the veranda and the garden as well as the rooms themselves. Each room is open to the garden via the corridor, but is also joined to the next room in a quite sophisticated way. With the corridor as medium, the building can even be enlarged creatively to form a unique space. The corridor can be interpreted not merely as a means of circulation—but also as an independent space between the garden's vistas and personal indoor spaces.

Jane Jacobs's Thesis: Complementary Functions of the Street

Jane Jacobs, the American intellectual and critic, published a book entitled *Death and Life of Great American Cities* in 1961. This book, which greatly shocked the American planning establishment, is a clinical indictment of U.S. urban redevelopment since World War II. Jacobs concluded that one major fault is the neglect of streets.

I have referred to the spatial use of streets as an important aspect of Eastern, as contrasted with Western, cities. However, the custom of looking upon streets as living space is certainly not unique to Asia; in the cities of medieval and Renaissance Europe, residents created their own forms of street life. Jacobs has only praise for this approach, presenting a minute analysis of street-based life in latter-day American cities.

In postwar U.S. city planning, Jacobs complained that all functions were separate. Children's play spaces were arranged as neighborhood parks, local playgrounds, or sports areas for older and younger children. There is an order, or ranking, based on size. The design concept was to distribute these evenly throughout a community. However, when children are forced to play only at widely scattered sites distant from their homes, a separate environment for children is created that leads to numerous accidents. Children may be injured without anyone being aware of it, and there are occasional kidnappings. Moreover, adults use these places for corrupt activities at night, and delinquents develop a tendency to fight in the parks, play areas, and random spaces under highways that have been designated according to city plans. These locations become dangerous mainly because they are separate from ordinary living spaces.

In the past, children did most of their playing in streets, and streets with little traffic were ideal. Children drew on the tarmac with chalk, and openings in fences provided acceptable play routes. By its very existence, the city itself was a *locus* for play for all alike, both children and adults. The children actually learned about the city through such play. Of course, streets were never an entirely comfortable playing space for children. There were no jungle gyms or sandboxes, and the available spaces were too small. As a result, children once in a while climbed on fences and fell, while others tore their clothing trying to creep through holes in the fences. Still, the children learned about the city through all this.

Meanwhile, since children played in the midst of the adults' routine activities, they were always within sight. According to Jacobs, the

Kurokawa's response to Jane Jacobs's proposal, the Andersen Memorial Hall (top) and Central Lodge (bottom). National Children's Park in Yokohama (both demolished). ▶

children were safe under the watchful eyes of people in the streets. I, too, find the lack of such integration a major flaw of planning, which to date has ignored the obvious fact that distinct separations of a city's functions prevents any complementarity.

This does not apply only to the issue of children's play spaces. Jane Jacobs points out that communication generally takes place in the streets. Leaving a key with a neighbor when one plans to be away for a short time is a street scenario. Similarly, the milkman was always the first to notice some unusual event or occurrence. Street activity allows us to assist one another and complement each other's lives—guaranteeing interdependence as well as privacy.

Blending Functions and Uses

Jacobs cited mixed functions and uses as another role of city streets. In post–World War II planning, sharp divisions were drawn between parks, residential districts, and industrial zones, joined only by roads. Evidently, infrastructural roads serve as little more than channels for travel with a clearly defined objective, such as an outing to a park from a residential district, or the quotidian return from workplace to home. If roads are mere channels, of course, people take the most efficient vehicular routes—rarely those teeming with life.

In contrast, a survey to determine which roads in large American cities were most favored by inhabitants suggested that people prefer roads with a mixture of complex, diverse uses. Such a road might have an elementary school, a market, a bookstore, and a bar—as well as a church and housing—and would be animated with life around the clock. Early in the morning, housewives get up and sweep the spaces around their homes. The milkman passes by, or used to. After a while, working people, each dressed in his or her own style, hurry off to work. The morning rush continues for some time, until housewives, finally free to take a break, go out into the streets to chat with neighbors or to send the kids off to school. Toddlers are playing in doorways. After lunch, older children begin returning from school, and in the evening, adults return from work. At night, the bars come alive. From morning to night, or even twenty-four hours a day, the street is filled with activity. Crime cannot occur in such a place, and

A street procession as part of traditional downtown festival.

children rarely meet with serious accidents. Human relationships function smoothly.

The situation is different in urban spaces with clear-cut functional divisions. The Marunouchi district of Tokyo, an area composed almost exclusively of office buildings, is one example. The streets suddenly fill with workers during the morning rush hour, at lunch time, and again at evening. However, these flows of pedestrians have limited purposes: getting to the office, returning home, or reaching a restaurant. The roads in such areas are simply channels, and have no other practical significance. These districts become quiet and deserted in the evening, changing to real "empty space," where only cats stray in total darkness. Roads like these, lacking around-the-clock activity, attract crime and alienate their users.

The demand for street spaces that permit a mix of uses and functions is bound to augment in an information-based society. In future large cities will function as information centers, and street space will be the core element. When people gather and circulate, there are encounters, festivals, and experiences. At times, people even go into crowded streets to seek mental solitude and to "escape." From such diversity, people select their own values and discover their goals. Information is generated, exchanged, and multiplied. An important key in determining the quality of future cities will be the issue of how these spaces of diversity will be given shape.

Semipublic Spaces: A Sense of Shared Space and Solidarity

The Daido Seimei Company's Tokyo building is located in Nihonbashi in downtown Tokyo, a district divided into smallish superblocks. These create the bland atmosphere of a street of office buildings, however; the neighborhood lacks any of the charm of a shopping area. The Tokyu and Takashimaya department stores are located nearby, and what is needed is a network of pedestrian walkways.

Our original concept for the building was to add a street passing from the main avenue to the street behind. In any case, Daido Seimei was eager to create more points of contact with the public and to incorporate this idea as part of its corporate image. I became involved in the planning of this project after our firm designed the

Daido Seimei building in Sapporo. In that instance as well, the focus of our design was to make contact with the public for a firm whose business is life insurance. Since there is heavy snowfall in Sapporo, a square would serve no purpose in winter. Instead, the third floor and a mezzanine below that were opened to the public as a miniature botanical-garden terrace and a gallery with a small café, resulting in the designation of a new semipublic space, albeit a small one. Panel heaters were installed in the open mid-air garden on the third floor—which features plants native to Hokkaido—to prevent the ground from freezing in winter. Local artists may also use the gallery for exhibitions.

Semipublic spaces are one aspect of the intermediary space issue I have been pursuing for many years through streets and green spaces, and which I also refer to as "intermediate" elements or "Rikyu grey" spaces. The excessive segregation of public and private spaces may be one reason that cities are today so alienating. Interestingly, the history of modernization has also been a history of individual property rights. Land and space have become more tightly defined as either publicly or privately owned, with increasingly minute subdivision. Similarly, the postwar emphasis on home ownership has shut people into confined spaces supposedly with an image of "home," producing a concern within society to improve the quality of that space. This rush to private ownership by individuals and the closed character of the resulting spaces have been the principal factors in the separation of cities into public and private domains—with little ground in between.

In cities, people are rarely able to enjoy the peaceful experience of life in an interval between sharply divided public and private spaces, nor are they able to experience the dramatic interpenetration of public and private realms. Nevertheless, I believe that cities are basically places where space is shared and feelings of solidarity arise, although these feelings may be coincidental and short-lived. With this in mind, incorporating public space into private spaces, and adding a personal character to public areas, creates semipublic space as an intermediary zone in which the two intermingle, coexist, and influence one another.

My attachment to semipublic space as an intermediary zone has remained constant, beginning with the street space at the Nishijin Labor Center at Kyoto in 1962 and continuing to the space under the eaves of the head office of the Fukuoka Bank and the off-street space of the Daido Seimei Tokyo Building.

Street Spaces Incorporating a Sense of Nature

The basic points of my book *Toshi Dezain* (Urban Design, 1964) were the reconsideration of CIAM's functionalist view of cities, and comparative urban studies of East and West, including a reevaluation of the unique features of a Japanese culture grounded in Buddhist thought. The foundation of my thinking at that time coincides with concepts I still pursue today—intermediary zones, the issues of ambiguity and marginality, multivalent[3] and ambivalent qualities, Rikyu grey, and the culture of grey. My book was also a testament against the functionalism, rationalism, and Western dualism pursued by CIAM, in particular since World War II.

I shall not pretend to negate the role that rationalism has played in Japan's modernization, nor do I intend to deny the prevalence of functionalist architecture. However, the problems of intermediary zones and marginality have been more or less explicitly dropped from the discourse regarding multivalent space in architecture and cities. The re-evaluation of street space as one kind of intermediary zone is the work of gleaning, one by one, those qualities of space overlooked in the process of modernization.

One need not pretend that the characteristic street space of Heiankyo existed at the time the city was first built. However, the grid-shaped street system, which disposed public facilities in a scattered manner, did include a mechanism that allowed for the later qualitative development of street space. As I mentioned earlier, Hideyoshi promoted quality of street spaces by dividing the *machi* of that time into four equal parts called *cho*. Subsequently, the *machi* was redefined as a pair of *cho* facing each other across a street. Because of this change, the street as common space developed as a semipublic, intermediary zone, penetrating the houses on both sides. Of course, the birth of modern commerce following the dismantling of craft unions, or *za*, and the flourishing of the *chonin* culture among the townspeople, cannot be overlooked as having further contributed to the quality of urban space.

The quality of street space was further articulated in the handling of the eaves, lattices, lattice windows, push-up shutters, *komayose* (or horseguards), and the dooryard gardens of houses lining both sides of the street. In other words, the boundary between street and building remained in flux, reflecting the inhabitants' lives; the intermediary space thus formed took on the character of a stage where dramas unfold. Openings were provided where the morning sun might stream in, while the darkness of evening would begin with the advance of late afternoon. Behind the entry, where the sun shone only briefly, the greenery of bonsai trees provided a more concentrated natural ambiance. Shrines to the god of harvests, the offices of local medical doctors, and such were all set along the streets, contributing to their quality as architectural space.

In the street space of the Tokyo Daido Seimei building, stores similarly add a sense of life, and the office entrance has been made

Street space at the Daido Seimei Tokyo Building (Daido Life Insurance Company, 1978). Axonometric drawing.

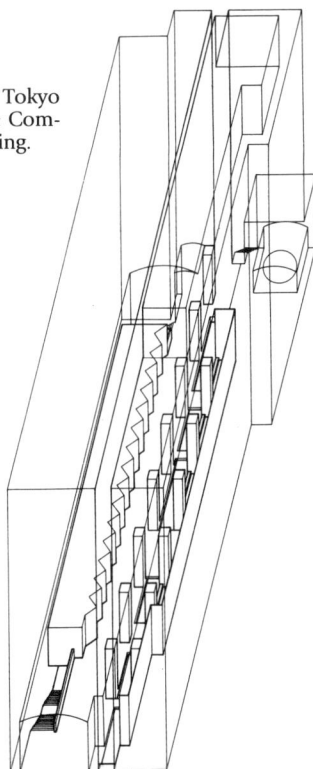

to resemble the approach to a *machiya* residence. An artificial brooklet flows along the street, and plants are being cultivated. (All the same, I had wanted the latter to resemble more closely the bonsai along a street of *machiya* houses, and would have preferred that the benches along the brooklet replicate the traditional benches found in such streets.) The actual structure is completely divided in two, a main office space and a subordinate facility core. The bridge connecting the two parts was given an accordion form, similar to that of railway carriage connection, to accommodate the shifts that an earthquake might cause. Dividing the building thus resulted in the creation of an opening within the city. Compared with our headquarters for the Japan Red Cross Society, this division in two of the Daido Seimei building was a more dramatic means of introducing a sense of nature—including light, rain, and occasional snow—into the street space.

Architecture of the Street: Creating Intermediary Space

My interest in marginality, or intermediary space, began with comparative urban studies of West and the East, particulary Japan. The site of my first project, the Nishijin Labor Center in an older part of Kyoto, gave me the opportunity to contrast the historical structure of Heiankyo with the present-day city. At that time, around 1961, I was just beginning to conceive my book entitled *Toshi Dezain*, and I had already begun to examine the differences between the plazas of the West and Japanese street space.

With the Nishijin Labor Center project, I emphasized "street space" that, although outside the space contained in the building, interacted with the space inside. From another angle, this intermediary space also connected the building with the city outside. At the time, I described the results as "architecture of the street" and "fulfilment of the relational concept."

In explaining urban spaces, Le Corbusier used the three concepts of *working space, living space*, and *recreational space*, as well as the relational concept of transport linking these spaces. In modern urban planning theory, functions have been abstracted and isolated as independent entities. Meanwhile, the relational concept of transport

Intermediary space at the Fukuoka Bank
Head Office (1975), viewed from street
(above) and from atrium.

217

has distanced infrastructural concepts from spatial understanding. I surmised that CIAM's concept of urban spatial composition had originated in a fundamental East-West difference in the hierarchy of urban spaces. Hence, my statement in *Toshi Dezain* that "the West has no streets and the East has no plazas."

The West has treated the plaza as a medium for fusing the spaces contained within individual buildings and so creating urban space. The plazas serving thus at every level—including residences, neighborhoods, communities, and whole cities—have taken the form and scale of courtyards or patios, neighborhood plazas, district plazas, and city plazas. Naturally, this hierarchy of plazas has given rise to a hierarchy of urban spaces, a spatial organization in which the role of the street is accorded subsidiary rank. Certainly, in this light, there is nothing unnatural about Le Corbusier's relegation of streets to a functional concept. I have described the streets designed by the Greek architect, Pikionis as marvelous spaces. Likewise, I am aware that the streets of small Italian cities of the Renaissance period, like those of Urbino, were richly varied, producing architecturally attractive spaces. And we are aware that the streets of Miletus were laid out in the lattice pattern also seen in Kyoto.

However, these street spaces are decidedly different from those of Japan, particularly Japanese street space from the fifteenth to nineteenth centuries. This difference lies in their lack of an interpenetrating structure in which the outer wall of the unitary space of the building interacts with the street. This may be due to a historical difference in the use of materials—masonry versus wood.

However, a more fundamental difference with the East can be seen in the Western concept of strictly segregating private and public spaces, and making the interior independent of the exterior and even of defending it from exterior influence. Although the streets of ancient Athens were laid out in a grid pattern, the only factors that merged individual living spaces with the city were the patio, the neighborhood plaza, and the agora, or marketplace. I stress the term "Eastern" in addressing the West because we know that the notion of street space as an intermediary region also existed in the ideal city plans of the Vedas. The philosophy of *sunya*, or "emptiness"—the origin of the common term *ma*, or interval—is found in the *Churon* of Nagarjuna (a second-century philosopher of southern India) as well as in the Consciousness-Only philosophy of Bazbandu (a fourth-century philosopher of northern India). Therefore, the existence of street spaces as intermediary regions in the ideal cities of India is not at all unexpected.

In Heiankyo, places were described by one of several units: *jo*, *bo*, *machi*, *gyo*, or *mon*. The *machi* unit was a block of houses delineated by streets. In the latter half of the ninth century, places began also to be designated as *koji*, or minor streets. However, the latter were used for convenience by residents when they began to build connected structures, and not in official documents.

Later, in the early 1200s (Kamakura period), the expressions *tsura* (cheek) and *omote* (face) came into use. *Tsura* that faced each other on both sides of a street formed a single *omote* in combination, which came to be called a "two-sided *cho*" and, at last, a *machi*. Clearly, the adoption of *koji* street names in medieval times had set the stage for this arrangement.

Toyotomi Hideyoshi (1536–98) undertook the Tensho land division, a wholesale reorganization that established dispersed communities comprising public facilities, temples and shrines, mansions for court nobility and military families, tradesmen, and so on. An important condition was the transfer of land from individual landowners to a collective, whose members assumed joint ownership. The earlier *Chishi Musata* tax revolt of 1532 related to the establishment of a collective taxation scheme among general householder tradesmen. Tax nonpayment was at last sanctioned in 1591, the nineteenth year of the Tensho era, when Hideyoshi permanently exempted streets from taxation. Much can be attributed to Hideyoshi's urban planning, notably his introduction of shared ownership of street space and establishment of communities straddling both sides of a street. However, an essential premise for developing the *machiya* system of commerce (urban residences with stores facing the street), establishing town meetings, and promoting the organization of combined *cho* districts was the economic and cultural activity of the tradespeople themselves. In any case, it seems safe to say that, from the Muromachi age to the early Edo period, the conceptual grid plan of Heiankyo, based originally on Tang-dynasty modes, gradually gave way to a more characteristically Japanese urban space centered around street space as an intermediary region.

The Philosophy and Beauty of Intermediary Space: Edo and Miura Baien

I hold that the seeds of Japan's modernization were planted from the Muromachi period to the Edo period. Moreover, I believe that the aesthetic consciousness of our nation, which we now consider traditional, also has its origins in this era.

I have searched for the origin of the Japanese aesthetic consciousness and views on art in the discourse on "Rikyu grey" recorded in *Choandoki*. Likewise, by evoking the image of the Edo-period woodcarver Hidari Jingoro, whose biography is far from clear, I sought to discover the new mass cultural phenomena of the times. Much like the present day, the early Edo period saw a tripling of the population[4] over the preceding one hundred years, and unusual changes were occurring prior to an eventual period of population stagnation. This was an age of urbanization during which modern commerce made headway and division of labor was taking form.

Nor was this so-called feudal period an age of stability enforced through regional divisions; instead, within the framework of the shogunate and the policy of seclusion, the people actually gained increased mobility. The culture of travel (pilgrimages) became established, and an intermediate human confraternity called the *ko* flourished spontaneously. Supposedly, for example, 70 percent of all households participated in these *ko* that organized the flow of pilgrims to various shrines.

At that time, as at present, opposition and friction abounded. The more densely populated and diverse a society becomes, the more effort must be expended to create intermediary regions between opposing parties and to integrate different elements arising on the fringes of society. I firmly believe that, in conjunction with the philosophy of emptiness, Buddhism encompasses a philosophy of three-dimensionalism, or multidimensionalism, that may be con-

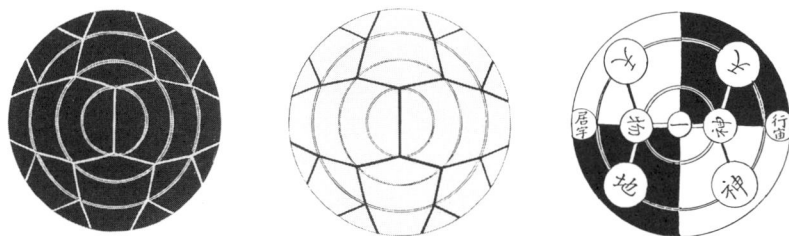

Schematic drawings by Miura Baien (Edo period).

trasted with Western dualism or rationalism. This is related to the *Sokuhi no Ronri* (logic of *sokuhi*) of Daisetsu Suzuki, which joins mutually opposing elements. *Hankangoitsu*, a work by the Edo-period philosopher Miura Baien, presages this view.

Gengo (begun in 1752), Baien's most important work, is structured in sections corresponding to heaven, earth, and humanity. Interestingly, this resembles the tripartite structure used in divination. In my book *Toshi Dezain*, mentioned above, I had already identified the philosophy of symbiosis as the desirable future philosophy of built form, or "space." I argued that Oriental philosophy deserved wider attention in order to correct Western dualism and the functional isolationism of modern architecture in the first half of the twentieth century. Now, thirty years later, my basic stance remains unchanged.

My interest in the Edo period is certainly not a new one—Baien's works *Kengo, Kango*, and especially *Gengo* are, indeed, well worth studying. Baien's work was previously considered to be treatises on logic. Since he wrote half a century before Hegel, he is sometimes called the world's earliest modern philosopher and dialectician. However, I find comparison of Baien's philosophy with Nagarjuna's *Churon* to be a better way to discover its nature as a truly Eastern philosophy. The following epitomization is found in *Taga Sumisato-kun ni Kotafuru Sho* (In Answer to Taga Sumisato), which Baien wrote as a central argument of *Gengo*:

> The fundamental principles of the universe are shadow and light, which are opposites, yet the result of their opposition is unity. Thus was formed the universe.

Because opposition produces unity, I both invert and unify elements to elucidate their essential aspects. Reason reveals that one is two, and two is one.

"Two" indicates that even distinctions show reason, and "one" indicates that diverse elements become one and the juncture between the two disappears. Inversion and unification are the methods of reasoning. Without inversion and unification, one cannot perceive the truth of shadow and light...

The universe, or heaven and earth, is essentially spirit and substance. Since spirit constitutes heaven and substance constitutes earth, one thing creates one universe and ten thousand things create ten thousand universes. The ancients spoke of countless aspects of the confused worlds, in which various substances are not distinguished. In such worlds, some things are countless in number. This is the secondary, unending phase. In other words, if the universe is so disordered and muddled, many substances must appear to exist. However, elements with shape are one, and elements without shape are one. There is nothing else.

Elements with shape are called "substance," while elements without shape are called "spirit." Since elements without substance cannot be seen or touched, the ancients misunderstood these to be empty, or nothingness. Of course, it is possible to consider these as empty elements lacking the substance and reality of earth, or lacking substance in contrast to the earth's substance. However, to judge them as mere nothingness and emptiness is a serious mistake.

If such nothingness or true emptiness were actually the case, then there would be no sun, moon, or stars, and neither I nor substance would exist. The sun, moon, and stars already exist in the heavens, while I and substance already exist on the earth. This "emptiness" is not nonexistent; it does indeed exist. Pointing to a substance and claiming that it does not exist is a twisted and distorted way of speaking. Therefore, the earth is reality and has substance. The visible substance of earth includes mountains and plains, lakes and oceans. The invisible emptiness of the heavens includes the sun and moon, clouds and rain. Considering this point carefully, one can determine that invisible spirit fills both the substance of the earth and the emptiness of the heavens, leaving not the smallest gap. Relating this fact to the human body, the body is substance much like the earth, and the spirit generated as our human body temperature can be compared to the heavens. One cannot say that the warmth of the body does not exist simply because it has no shape. The basis and manifestation of this warmth is the dynamic, divine ability of the human body. If it must be named, it could be called "heart."

Baien began writing *Gengo* in the mid eighteenth century at the age of thirty. He worked for twenty-three years to complete this massive work of more than 100,000 words. It was not printed in its entirety until 1912, the first year of the Taisho period, 124 years after Baien's death. Although any attempt to summarize Baien's philosophy in a few ideas would be ill-advised, his notion of *Hankan Goitsu*—which sees matter and spirit as unified and interpenetrating qualities, envisioning invisible spirit as substance filled with meaning—should be taken seriously both as Eastern philosophy and as a doctrine of intermediary region. In this way, it is similar to the ancient philosophy of "emptiness" integrating existence and nothingness, and the more recent concept of part and whole, as found in Suzuki's *Sokuhi no Ronri*.

The issue of intermediary regions can be approached from a variety of angles. "Rikyu grey" is consciousness of a certain beauty, or the aesthetic of ambivalent and multivalent intermediary regions. My *Chukantai Ron* concept was a spatial notion giving weight to a third, or intermediary, region in response to dualism. This argument is related to the categorization of semipublic and shared spaces as intermediary regions between public and private. The concept of emptiness is the philosophical origin of "intermediary region," which includes the concept of *ma*, or intervals, as the word is commonly used. This was an important point of view, related to the issue of boundary regions arising in the gaps between the spatial units of buildings, and the issue of the qualities of functionally interpreted spaces. In Japanese thinking regarding architecture, vagueness of spaces, the interpenetration of interior and exterior spaces combining opposing and contradictory elements, and the multivalent nature of space all originate in "emptiness." Other extensions of this are to be found in Zeami's concept of *Senuhima* or the Buddhist term *en*.

As mentioned, some of the buildings I have designed with these issues in mind are the Fukuoka Bank Head Office, the Japan Red Cross Society Headquarters, the Ishikawa Pension Hall, and the National Ethnography Museum in Osaka. My views on human movement, from *Homo movens* to the study of pilgrimage confraternities in the Edo period, and on travel, temporary residence, and nomadism, have all derived from an effort to discover the spontaneous intermediate human groupings lacking in the Western community concept of settled residence. *Sokuhi no Ronri* posits the new view that the part equals the whole, a viewpoint that the Western hierarchy of individuals and society—or parts and whole—does not countenance. This contains a premonition of the shift from tree system to lattice system, shedding light on new regionalisms and grassroots movements. A major characteristic of the street space is that it concentrates and contains all these viewpoints in the concept of intermediary region. The element lacking in modern architecture in the first half of the twentieth century is the concept of such an intermediary space and those issues arising at the margins or boundary.

The challenge of contemporary architecture is, I believe, to capture the qualities of intermediary regions in actual built spaces.

A Discontinuous Continuum

Among Japanese, mildly ambiguous forms of communication,

or body language, such as verbal promise and the nonverbal communication called *haragei*, may not be altogether effective. Yet there is a crucial need to instigate a new system of interpersonal transactions in which some allowance for adjustment is overlaid on the Western contractual system in current use. Such allowances could be found in those keys to my philosophy of symbiosis, intermediary space, and ambiguity.

In Japan, as elsewhere, we still say that we *undertake* (literally, accept and carry) an architectural project or other contractual obligation. This term may imply rather more than the obligations actually specified in the contract. So, whereas non-Japanese construction firms regard their relationship with the client as finished once the work specified in the contract is done, in Japan we tend to feel a moral responsibility to look after the building we have created throughout its life. After a typhoon, for example, the contractor will frequently get in touch—even though the building may have been standing for decades—to enquire whether it has been damaged and to enquire as to any needed repair work. This way of thinking applies not only to the construction industry but to most human relationships, and reflects an atmosphere of trust.

The concept of *ma*, or interval, is strongly rooted in Japanese life and the arts, as well as in traditional architecture. One who hasn't grasped the concept of *ma* and is difficult to get along with, a social inept, is called "a person lacking *ma* " (*ma no nuketa hito*, or *manuke*). *Ma* indicates both spatial distance (a neutral zone) and temporal distance (a cooling-off period). Those who properly gauge their words are effective speakers and create a deep impression. When two sides are in fierce opposition, it is often surprisingly easy to adjust conflicting claims by declaring a *ma*—that is, a cooling-off period or moratorium.

In writing Chinese ideographs, the space between the lines is more important than the lines themselves. This space is not nothingness; it means, or speaks, as much as the lines. *Ma* is also important in folk songs and Noh chants. The *engawa* is a space, or *ma*, inserted between nature and building, exterior and interior. This type of intermediary zone functions as a *ma* permitting two opposing elements to exist in symbiosis. Intermediate space makes possible a discontinuous continuum, so to speak, enabling a plurality of opposing elements to coexist in a dynamic, ever-changing relationship. The nature of intermediary space lies in its ambiguity and multivalence. It does not force opposing elements into compromise or harmony, but provides the key to a living symbiosis.

Sacred Zones for All Nations and Peoples

As mentioned in the beginning of this book, the theme of the 1979 Aspen International Design Conference was "Japan and the Japanese," and I had suggested "Rice" as one of the important sub-themes for the event. The thrust of my argument was that California rice is indeed food, but for the Japanese "rice" is more than that; it is their culture. Since the conference I have continued to argue that rice is culture, and I have opposed the liberalization of foreign rice imports into Japan.

I can sum up my reason for this view in a phrase: the concept of "sacred zones." I have said again and again that the philosophy of symbiosis destroys all dualisms. Yet in doing so it in no way resembles the "coexistence" of the United States and the Soviet Union during the Cold War, nor can it be compared to the synthesis of thesis-and-antithesis in dialectical materialism. And it is not, of course, the haphazard mingling or temporary compromise of different elements.

The most important feature of the philosophy of symbiosis is the concept of intermediary spaces and sacred zones. I have discussed intermediary spaces at length, yet, basically, the term refers to a zone tentatively established between two opposing elements; it is a third area which belongs to neither. When such a space is set between two opposing, rationalized extremes, the ambiguous elements purposefully excluded in the process of sharpening a two-term distinction can be recouped.

There are many intermediary spaces in our world, zones which have been forgotten, discarded, ignored, or dismissed because they do not belong to the main, opposing currents. Many of the concepts that I have here investigated as premises of the philosophy of sym-

Spring rice-planting in Japan.

Scene typifying the Japanese rural landscape of rice paddies and fields.

biosis can be grouped under the heading of intermediary space: street space; concepts of ambiguity, ambivalence, and multivalence; Rikyu grey; *ma*, or interval, and several others.

An intermediary zone is brought into being when two unlike and opposing elements continue to exist independently, yet each extends some part of itself toward a mediating space. Even if each element offers, for example, only 10 percent of itself to the intermediary zone, a third, partially shared region is created. This is not a theory of domination, in which the stronger of the two opposing elements rules the weaker. Rather, it is an attempt to discover common patterns and features *without* erasing the opposition between elements.

The most fundamental principle of the philosophy of symbiosis is that there is *always* an intermediary space shared between extremes: cultures however disparate, ideologies however opposing. It is that which distinguishes the philosophy of symbiosis from coexistence and compromise, from all dualism, from dialectical materialism, and from tripartite philosophical models.

The philosophy of symbiosis also possesses a fundamentally new idea—that of sacred zones. As I noted earlier, I continue to oppose the liberalization of rice imports to Japan, and my main reason partakes of this notion. Each country, people, culture, company, and individual has its own sacred zones. Up to now, the sacred zones of religion and cultural tradition have been taboo. The cow is sacred in India; the pig is taboo in Islamic culture. In modern times, such taboo, or sacred, zones have been declared irrational and unscientific and are considered signs of a lack of development. They have been excised from our lives with the sharp knives of science and economics. The rules of dominant countries are proclaimed as universal, and the sacred zones of weaker countries have been declared *irrational*—"nontariff trade barriers."

Recognizing the Other's Sacred Zone

In the Structural Impediments Initiative forum (SII),[5] the Japan-U.S. institutional negotiation framework, Japanese customs such as intragroup trading, consensus price-setting, and rice policy have come under attack from the United States as incompatible with international rules. The philosophy of symbiosis, by contrast, seeks to chart the respective sacred zones of different cultures.

As times change, today these sacred zones may disappear or alter. Therefore, each country must proclaim which are the most important and essential. Sacred zones are linked to the lifestyle and national pride of a country. They have strong roots in cultural traditions and are intimately linked to religion and language. To return to the example of rice, America's California-grown rice has been improved in quality and taste. Some varieties are even rather better tasting than the average rice available in Japan. When we consider that Californian rice costs a fraction of the price of Japanese rice, it's only normal to wonder why it shouldn't be imported. But, as already stated, this argument treats "rice" as if it were only a foodstuff.

If all the rice in California were suddenly to vanish, California would be little changed by the fact, nor would American lifestyle or national pride be damaged. But what would happen were rice growing to disappear from Japan? The traditional Japanese countryside with its pattern of groves surrounding homes and shrines, its forested village hills, its paddies and fields—the most characteristic Japanese landscapes—would all disappear. The production of Japanese saké, a work of art in itself, would cease, as would many crafts, folk songs, and festivals; and the regional cultural traditions transmitted with those festivals would all perish.

Thus, if rice culture were to disappear from Japan, a large part of the Japanese cultural heritage would disappear with it. This is the reason why I have opposed liberalization of rice imports for well over a decade. The Japanese government and the farmers' associations, too, argue that Japan must protect its food supply by being agriculturally self-sufficient. But as long as Japan argues with America on the premise that rice is mere food, Japan has no hope of winning.

Intermediary Spaces and Sacred Zones Build New Horizons

The worlds of Kabuki and the tea ceremony, with their hereditary lineages; *sukiya* architecture, with its traditional techniques; and Sumo, which is not so much a sport as a meeting of the emperor sys-

Kabuki performance and audience (scroll, Edo period).

Woodblock print depicting Sumo wrestling (Katsukawa Shunsho, Edo period).

tem and rice culture—these are all typical sacred zones of Japanese culture.

Because America and Europe champion a modern rationalist ethos, they are reluctant to admit sacred zones within their own cultures; embarrassed perhaps to acknowledge such nonrational elements. In modern times, we tend to believe that if we cannot understand others one hundred percent, it is because we haven't tried hard enough. The human race has suffered greatly through this notion that we must understand one another completely. It is one of the great illusions of our age that we believe we can do so. Even between lovers or marriage partners, the woman has her own sacred zones and the man his. Additionally, every individual naturally possesses his or her own pride, individuality, and sensibilities as a human being. This is the premise of symbiotic relationship. The sacred zone is respected precisely because it encompasses the ineffable.

Above all, the philosophy of symbiosis seeks to create an intermediary space between two opposing elements. This space marks common or shared elements tentatively established between the two; yet it may, in the future, be forcefully appropriated or rejected by one of the two. In that sense, the intermediary space is necessarily dynamic, vague, tentative, ambivalent, and multivalent.

However, symbiosis does not altogether deny universalism, common rules, or the ethos of modernism. It rests simply on the assumption that between every pair of opposing elements, there are likewise common terms, common rules, and universal values. While the universalism of modernism demands one hundred percent shared elements and full mutual understanding, symbiosis recognizes only a proportional sharing; this is the prophecy I have made throughout my life for the twenty-first century. Anyhow, the basic difference between a machine and life is the capacity for waste, play, and ambiguity in the living organism. The necessity of sacred zones and intermediary space is the very proof of living beings.

The essential distinction between machines and life is that the latter makes allowance for intermediary regions of "unproductive" activity. The presence of sacred zones and intermediary regions demonstrates that an organism is alive. Since the origins of the philosophy of symbiosis lie in the theory of sacred zones and intermediary regions, I believe this philosophy brings into focus the horizon of a new world that clearly differs from the past and its philosophies.

10

MAN AND NATURE

"Temporary Shelters" Blending with Nature

Buddhism teaches the impermanence of all forms. People, animals, plants, the rest of nature, and the Buddhas themselves are always changing, ever migrating within the chain of life. As human beings existing within that ever-changing process of transmigration, we must awaken to the ephemeral nature of life. In that context our ideal should be not to conquer nature, nor to hunt our fellow animals, but rather to live as a part of nature, and in accordance with its rules.

From ancient times the Japanese have built their homes as if they were temporary shelters and adopted a lifestyle of symbiosis with nature based on the doctrine of impermanence. Yoshida Kenko,[1] the author of *Tsurezuregusa* (Essays in Idleness), says:

A house, I know, is but a temporary abode, but how delightful it is to find one that has harmonious proportions and a pleasant atmosphere. One feels somehow that even moonlight, when it shines into the quiet domicile of a person of taste, is more affecting than elsewhere. A house, though it may not be in the current fashion or elaborately decorated, will appeal to us by its unassuming beauty; a grove of trees with an indefinably ancient look; a garden where plants, growing of their own accord, have a special charm; a veranda and an open-work wooden fence of interesting construction; and a few personal effects left carelessly lying about, giving the place an air of having been lived in. A house which multitudes of workmen have polished with every care, where strange and rare Chinese and Japanese furnishings are displayed, and even the grass and trees of the garden have been trained unnaturally, is ugly to look at and most depressing. How could anyone live for long in such a place? Even a casual glance will suggest how likely such a house is to turn in a moment to smoke.

Since the home is no more than a temporary shelter, one should not take too many pains in decorating it; even when it has grown old and worn, it is better to leave it as it is and harmonize with it. In the *Nanpo Roku*, Sen no Rikyu is quoted as advocating a simple, natural life: "Lodgings that keep the rain out and enough food to keep us from starving—this is sufficiency."

Japanese culture is a culture of wood. We have consistently replaced wooden structural elements in our homes and whole buildings as they age or decay. In addition, many buildings are destroyed by nature's violence, in typhoons, earthquakes, and floods, and we Japanese have been forced to rebuild after each natural or man-made disaster. Perhaps the perception of buildings as no more than temporary is due to these circumstances as well.

Until modern times water in Japan was not controlled as at present, by reinforcing banks and dikes in every area with stones and concrete. In fact, the approach was just the opposite. A weak place was always built into a dike or bank where an overflow or flood would do the least damage. This is a natural principle akin to that of the collarbone, which acts as a defense of the neck and back bones by breaking in their place.

We recently dismantled the house that my grandfather and father had lived in for many years, in the countryside of Aichi Prefecture. It was a rush-thatched house thought to date from the mid-Edo period. It survived the Nobi earthquake in 1891, but had suffered damage on several occasions, and each time it was repaired it had been added to and partly refurbished. Even so, investigation showed that some of its timbers were from the Edo period and had been planed with the characteristic Edo-period tool, the *chona*, instead of an ordinary plane. The reed thatching, too, had been changed on alternating sides of the roof, once every two to four years.

All this suggests how much work is involved in the upkeep of a wooden house. But the visual appeal of such natural materials as wood, tatami mats, and Japanese paper, and even their pleasant smells, are valued by the Japanese—accustomed to an environment intimately linked to nature. In fact, Japanese houses seem to exhibit a stronger tendency to merge with nature than to stand in opposition to it. Perhaps we can accept the eventual degeneration and collapse of buildings and dikes more easily because we see this as a part of the rhythm of nature.

Insect Sounds—Midway between Noise and Music

Another important feature of the Japanese house is its openness. The characteristic post-and-beam construction produces a building with no structural need for walls. If the sliding paper doors and outer rain-doors are opened, the house attains a complete openness, with the *engawa* providing an intermediary space between interior and garden. Japanese architecture even incorporates surrounding scenery and nearby mountains into its gardens, through the technique known as "borrowed landscape," or *shakkei*. Living hedges, for example, are often used to encircle a home. Unlike a solid wall, a hedge, or *ikegaki*, doesn't completely block out the outside. While it protects the residents' privacy, it is also continuous with the surrounding natural environment, offering a Japanese type of semi-seclusion.

The word *ne* (roughly translated as sound, but slightly different in meaning, as we shall see) is another key to explaining the continuity that the Japanese feel with nature. *Ne*, however, describes aural rather than visual continuity. The word for music in Japanese, *ongaku*, means to enjoy sound (*on* is another way to pronounce *ne*, and *gaku* means to enjoy). *Neiro,* or sound color, means the nature or quality of sound. When things don't work out well and we are reduced to desperate straits, we "raise a cry" (*ne o ageru*).

In Japanese homes and restaurants, we occasionally still maintain the custom of keeping insects in cages so that guests can listen to their sounds and be reminded of the season. To the Japanese, insect sounds are not mere noise; they are the *ne* of insects, a natural music. The single word *ne* comprises the music created by human beings and the music of nature; insect sounds, an intermediary zone between mere sound and music, are further evidence that the Japanese prefer to live in friendship with nature, linked intimately to it.

The West, Conqueror and Domesticator of Nature

In contrast to Japanese building, European architecture seems to oppose nature, emphasizing its own independence and separateness. European cities separated themselves from nature by building fortified walls. The stone walls of houses separate inside from outside, their solidity often emphasized by small windows and doors. In the European view, human beings conquer, tame, and utilize nature. Renaissance and Baroque gardens, for example, are quite artificial and geometric, mostly comprising lawns like huge green carpets. We can perceive them as highly idealized visions of nature; to stroll through them is to feel man's victory over nature, its domestication.

What a contrast this presents to the traditional Japanese garden, which attempts to create a *simulacre* of nature in the form of an abstraction. The main pleasure to be had comes not from walking around in the garden but from entering an imaginary world whilst quietly gazing at it. Of course, many famous Japanese gardens also allow for perambulation, but the path is usually limited to a sharply circumscribed area; even those built specifically for strolling through are designed with various stops along the walk for viewing the garden.

From Selling Forests to Sharing Their Benefits

In their attitude toward forests, Japanese and Europeans also show striking differences. Many European forests are crisscrossed by public paths and have man-made clearings and facilities for rambles;

in other words, they are a tamed version of nature. They are largely a mixture of broadleaf deciduous and evergreen trees; undergrowth is not a barrier to access and there is plenty of sunlight. Woodlands may even be incorporated into city life as a man-made green space. Many European children's tales, such as the exploits of Robin Hood, reflect life in the forest as a friendly place.

In Japan, on the other hand, forests consist mostly of evergreen conifers. The grounds is damp and thickly covered with brush—not to mention snakes, centipedes, and other insects. Most Japanese forests are in the mountains and therefore inaccessible. As a result, from ancient times there has been a strong tendency in Japan to worship mountains themselves, in an animist sense. They were regarded as sacred, the dwelling place of spirits; or possibly a gravesite, the preserve of great serpents. The only human being who would live there was a hermit or a defeated warrior in hiding. Forests were not a part of life's daily activities; for looking at from afar, nature was a spiritual support. This Japanese relationship with nature has remained fundamentally unchanged to the present day. The mountains ringing Japanese cities are not incorporated into urban living space; they exist in symbiosis with the city as "borrowed landscape." Japanese do not enter the forest of their own volition as Europeans do. In fact, this is a major problem where the preservation of nature in Japan is concerned. Since the Japanese have little direct relationship with nature in their daily lives, they have scant awareness of the need to protect the natural environment. The traditional Japanese attitude of symbiosis with nature contradicts more up-to-date thinking about our natural environment; because of this the natural environment in Japan is very much under threat.

In international market terms, Japanese timber forests are no longer successful commercial ventures. This has resulted in a severe shortage of forestry products in Japan, and pushed Japanese forestry to the brink of financial disaster. At the same time, a number of cities are undergoing the same sudden expansion that Tokyo has experienced. Large residential suburbs are growing up around these cities, made possible by wide-scale conversion of farm and forest land into housing developments.

Artifically created garden at the palace of Versailles, outside Paris.

We no longer see such phenomena in Europe, because Europeans are accustomed to good husbandry of the natural environment. Since they are better acquainted with nature, they feel more strongly about defending it. In the future, we Japanese will have to move beyond our abstract spiritual feeling for wilderness and link forests with urban space, so that they can be properly utilized. To do that, the Japanese will have to change their thinking about re-forestation and the timber industry. Up to now, trees that grow quickly and sell at a high price—namely, evergreens such as cedar, cypress, and pine—have been given priority. Now we must designate zones for planting deciduous trees and create sunnier forests that can also serve as leisure areas. We must restore the symbiosis of humanity and nature in daily life by changing our strategy on a national scale from one of forests for sale to forests for sharing.

The parks of Frankfurt and Düsseldorf abound with birds, squirrels, and all kinds of insects. The symbiosis of the people of these cities with nature—all within a stone's throw of underground stations and motorways—is an impressive sight. The same is now desperately needed in Japan.

By way of illustration, the mayor of Hakuba village told me that, although this small heartland community has been selected to host the Winter Olympics in 1998, the villagers do not want the natural environment to be destroyed. He asked our office to propose a scenic landscape ordinance for balanced development. We conducted a questionnaire survey among residents and were somewhat surprised to discover that many village residents desired a nature park. Although 98 percent of Hakuba is forested mountain area, its residents wanted a park because all these forests were of Japanese cedar or cypress, so there were no forests of broadleaf trees where they could take their children for walks. In other words, there were no forests for people.

Clearly, be it in Germany or in central Japan, symbiosis is required between population centers and forests, that is symbiosis between life and nature.

◄ Gardens at Shugakuin Detached Palace, Kyoto.

Agriculture, Forestry, and Fishery in Symbiosis

I use the term *seiboku*, or "life trees," to refer to trees for land-scaping and leisure as opposed to trees used for timber. I have even suggested that the Ministry of Agriculture, Forestry, and Fisheries promote a "life-tree industry," since rural Japan is gradually becoming urbanized, and there is an increasing shortfall of trees for urban afforestation. The new Pacific national development axis will intersect forested, mountainous regions, such as those in Wakayama, in anticipation of the establishment of such a life-tree industry.

If just one-quarter of Japan's forests could be replanted as deciduous forests, fishery along the Japanese coast would almost certainly be revitalized. This is an instance of the symbiosis that should be respected between forests and ocean. Japan is an archipelago and as such might be expected to become one of the world's greatest inshore fishing grounds. This has not occurred, however, simply because agriculture, forestry, and fishery are all primary industries somehow seen now as outdated. There is little interest in Japan to increase involvement in fishery at present.

The Western notion of progress holds that production industries belong to a former age, and that humanity necessarily advances by progressing to tertiary industry. This is not at all acceptable in my view. In the twenty-first century, primary, secondary, and tertiary industries powered by the information explosion need to coexist in balanced symbiosis. Environmental technology industries would of course be included. However, if the latter serve simply to maintain the environment in an attractive state, they will doubtless have little growth potential. But if multimedia and environmental technology are dynamically linked to agriculture, forestry, and fishery, substantial expansion will result. Japan must re-evaluate its own resources in light of this potential interrelationship, and the same applies to Asia as a whole.

Concerning agriculture in Japan, the confused reaction to Thai rice imported in 1994 (to compensate for inadequate domestic supplies) revealed that Japanese consider the word "rice" to refer only to high-quality, short-grain rice. Clearly, no other kind of rice was acceptable to the Japanese consumer. For some time I have maintained that, to Japanese, rice *is* culture and even art. This view was amply confirmed during the 1994 shortage. Since the Japanese consume rice as a form of art, they are willing to pay greatly inflated prices for it. Inexpensive rice imported from abroad has no market potential beyond what may be required for animal feed and sweets manufacture.

A more serious problem is the decreasing acreage now allotted to agriculture owing to the negative perception that "agriculture has no future." This is simply preposterous. The rice-cultivation issue apart, agriculture is inseparable from Japan's traditional pastoral landscapes and an irreplaceable part of Japan's culture. Rice farming is the theme of many folk songs, festivals, and other customs. *Wajima-nuri*, a traditional lacquerware, began as a source of work for farmers in the slack season, during which peasants have also tended the mountains and periodically thinned the forests. Agriculture, forestry, and local cottage industries thus existed in symbiosis. For such reasons, if agriculture diminishes, forestry will also suffer, and if forestry is discontinued, fishery will come to an end—as I shall show. Although agriculture, forestry, and fishery function symbiotically and are inseparable, they have in modern times been administered vertically as separate, unrelated realms. The consequences of this misguided approach are now being felt.

Symbiosis between Forests and Oceans

Environmental technology encompasses a variety of elements. For example, many kinds of fertilizer may be used to nourish trees, but the best fertilizer is produced by the tree itself. Deciduous trees lose their leaves in winter, and the fallen leaves furnish vital humus. The cycles of nature can be exploited more effectively if deciduous tree-farming is combined with agriculture and livestock-raising. For instance, sophisticated technologies have already been developed to produce new fertilizers from the wastes resulting from these activities.

The symbiosis between forests and oceans is particularly important. Rain penetrates the humus formed by fallen leaves and flows along rivers to the sea. Recent research reveals that this affords an unmatched source of nutrition for shellfish. In Japan, broadleaf trees are now being planted in proximity to oyster beds so that forests have, in fact, become the food of oysters.

Where upward currents of deep seawater spread nitrogen, phosphorous, iron, and other nutrient salts and metal ions having reached into the ocean from forest soils, large numbers of plant plankton flourish at depths of up to 30 meters—the depth to which sunlight penetrates the water. In the resulting food chain, the plant plankton are eaten by animal plankton, which are in turn eaten by small fish. The result is a vast fishing ground.

Areas where forest nutrients wash into the water and are dispersed by upward currents of deep ocean water represent only about one-tenth of one percent of the ocean's surface, yet some 50 million tons of fish are caught a year in this combined area. Since the world's total annual catch is about 100 million tons, one-half of the catch is apparently taken from just one-tenth of one percent of the world's oceans. Such discoveries have made fisheries in Hokkaido and elsewhere more aware of the importance of forests, and the authorities are beginning to plant more trees. However, not just any kind of tree will do; Japanese cedar and cypress are virtually useless from the standpoint of symbiosis between forests and oceans. Nevertheless, most Japanese forests are now Japanese cedar and cypress. Although in the past cultivators were aware that deciduous, broadleaf trees were good for marine fisheries, such trees were not considered desirable in a forestry business based largely on the production of timber for construction. As has been evident in Nagasaki and elsewhere, the shallow root systems of Japanese cedar and cypress result in landslides following even light rains, further reducing the number of fish.

Rice as a Sacred Zone

I made brief mention above of rice as a "sacred zone" for the Japanese. Here, I will explain this in more detail. I became particularly interested in Japanese rice cultivation in 1975. Four years later, I became more specifically involved in this field. As I have mentioned, I chaired an international symposium in Aspen, Colorado, on the theme of "Japan and the Japanese." Many Japanese and American specialists from the public and private sectors attended, and the event was expected to be highly influential. I focused in particular on Japanese rice cultivation as the strategy of this international symposium. Of course, the rice issue was not then as prominent a theme as it is now.

Around the same time, I had the opportunity to converse with Seiji Tsutsumi[2] on television, and I pursued the theme of "rice as sacred zone."

Since those two talks in the late 1970s, I have consistently dealt with the question of rice as culture, not only as food, in my considerations of rice as a sacred zone. For example, even if California-grown rice tastes as good as Japanese rice and can be sold more cheaply, it is "rice as food," and not "rice as culture." If that "rice as food" is placed on the same store shelves as Japanese rice, and a debate follows about ensuring food security, Japan will be criticized for its selfishness and protectionism. In protecting Japanese rice cultivation, the cultural stance of "rice as culture" is necessary.

What exactly is meant by the concept of 'rice as culture'? First, it is the status and role of rice paddies in traditional Japanese scenery. When Japanese are asked about the rural scenes dearest to their hearts, almost all will mention rice paddies and forested mountains. However, these rice paddies and forested mountains are now facing their greatest crisis.

Over the past decade, I have traveled around Japan to investigate the state of rice paddies and forested mountains, starting with the Noto Peninsula. My impressions have only been deepened through these investigations.

Agriculture, Forestry, and Traditional Culture

Farming has become a sideline for almost all modern-day Japanese farmers, as young people in particular prefer corporate jobs. Agriculture as such has thus already begun to collapse. Nevertheless, the traditional Japanese landscape of rice paddies has managed to survive. Ironically, this is a result of urbanization. In Oita Prefecture, for example, Oita City has become a hub where young people gather from surrounding rural areas. Such provincial cities nevertheless are underpopulated and rarely grow sufficiently to absorb the land set aside for their expansion. Thanks to this phenomenon, rice paddies and mountains remain on the outskirts of such provincial cities, and there is still time to save them in these areas.

Another consideration is the traditional practice of supplementing agriculture with seasonal jobs. For example, the application of undercoating for *Wajima-nuri*, a traditional laquerwork craft of the Noto Peninsula, has been a farming sideline for many generations. This venerable craft would very likely decline and disappear if agriculture were to cease on the Noto Peninsula.

The same can be said of forestry. Due to rapid market liberalization, Japanese foresters are being inundated by inexpensive timber imported from Canada, Malaysia, Brazil, and other countries. Since forestry in Japan focuses on timber for building construction, both private and national forests consist mostly of Japanese cedar and cypress, as has been noted. However, American cypress is priced well below Japanese cypress, hence its new popularity. National forests, being subsidized, are somehow still holding their own, but privately owned forests face a serious crisis brought on by insufficient funds even for the essential forest-management tasks, thinning out trees and removing lower branches.

In the past, farmers would normally cut unneeded trees to fill their time in the slack season, and the wood thus gathered was used in traditional industries such as *shiitake* mushroom cultivation and charcoal-making. These are closely connected to forestry and have helped to keep mountain villages economically viable. Nonetheless, if farming should disappear, the labor pool employed in forestry will go with it. Thus, the future is uncertain for farm villages and forests alike.

If rice cultivation in Japan should eventually cease, Japanese saké breweries will also suffer considerably, as sake brewing requires good water and the highest quality rice. Moreover, Japanese saké is not being produced in the U.S. Some might feel that whiskey and wine production would suffice for the twenty-first century, but I hope to see saké remain a characteristic commodity, with much the same status as French wines and Scotch whiskey.

The local celebrations we call *matsuri*, or festivals, originated in the culture of rice cultivation. Many folk songs were sung by farmers as they planted the rice fields, and most of these songs are passed on not by professional singers, but only by farmers. In agricultural communities all over Japan, there are unique customs, such as a very old form of Noh theater in Yamagata Prefecture called Kurokawa Noh. This singular type of Noh is performed in the winter snow by farmers, who have maintained this art form for several hundred years.

In the U.S., if California rice were to disappear, this would constitute little more than the disappearance of one kind of "agribusiness." But the disappearance of Japanese rice would place forestry, traditional crafts, and a whole related culture in jeopardy as well as signaling an end to Japan's traditional rural scenery. This difference seems important.

Respect for Sacred Zones as the Crux of Globalization

Following the end of ideological opposition perpetuated by the Cold War, cultural differences surfaced everywhere. In the first Japanese edition of *Philosophy of Symbiosis*, in 1987, I predicted that cultural supremacy would gradually collapse as the twenty-first century approached—yielding a symbiosis among diverse cultures. A number of ethnic minority groups coexisted in the former Soviet Union, but they were forbidden to use their native languages and instead were educated in Russian. Such brazenly supremacist attitudes have often characterized the twentieth century, giving rise to tragic incidents like those being lived out Yugoslavia today. I believe that in the long term, even the rights of China's non-Han ethnic groups will be restored. If by political and diplomatic efforts we could eventually attain full mutual understanding, there would be no need even to speak of something like "symbiosis." The reality of political and economic conflict makes a discussion of symbiosis necessary.

In addition to human examples, animals threatened with extinction must be protected, such as the Japanese crested ibis (not to mention others already extinct, such as the Japanese otter), instead of being abandoned with remarks to the effect that "it can't be helped, because that's free competition." Some would say, "Why preserve the Japanese crested ibis? There are ibises in other countries, and there are other birds similar to ibises, so it doesn't matter if one becomes extinct." This view is tantamount to saying, "There are strong cultures and weak cultures. It can't be helped if the weak ones perish while the strong survive, because that is natural selection." This misconstrues the tenets of Darwinist evolutionism and natural selection.

Such simplifications may be acceptable in the areas of economics and technology, but not in those regarding culture. Culture, much like a gene pool, is a cumulative, historical achievement. At a level beyond that of any relative merits they might possess, unique local cultures exist as they are, in their native locale. No matter how poor an ethnic group, no matter how low its corresponding GNP, a culture characteristic of a particular ethnic locality cannot be ignored by the rest of the world. The richness human society achieves in the symbiosis between different cultures, like the richness afforded the global environment by the existence of various life forms, must not be neglected. Although some may feel that it came too late, Japan nonetheless finally passed an Endangered Wild Plant Species Preservation Act in April 1995. Similarly, but on a far greater scale, the Bio-Diversity Treaty signed in Brazil in 1994 marked a momentous event. This signaled the historic beginning of a revision of the tide of neo-Darwinist evolutionism.

Meanwhile, the world is evolving as an increasingly borderless and global community—a trend creating in turn the need to reestablish areas for global competition. It no longer seems likely that the melting pot of universality will merge everything, as once believed by rationalists and modernists in the recent past. So each country will need to maintain "sacred zones" that will not be sacrificed under any circumstances, as their loss would signify the end of ethnic pride and identity. These sacred zones *must* be respected. Only through mutual respect can globalization pursue a smooth course while evolving areas for mutual competition.

Protection of Sacred Zones in Other Countries

Besides rice cultivation, Japanese sacred zones include the emperor system, sumo wrestling and its grand champion rank, Kabuki, and the tea ceremony. Sumo began as a ritual of the imperial family during the eighth century, in the era of Emperor Shomu. As time passed, this imperial household event took on the character of a sport and eventually became sumo wrestling in its current form. Until a wrestler reaches the rank of *yokozuna*, or grand champion, sumo can be viewed fundamentally as sport. Wrestlers win or lose according to impartial rules, and they rise consistently through the ranks as they win. Sumo is not without its ceremonial remnant, however, as the rank of grand champion is believed to carry with it unique responsibilities. The grand champion preserves the peace of the land—praying for good harvests and peace while enacting traditional ceremonies. This aspect of the sport cannot be ignored, since the grand champion must be able to perform such rites and must be someone, therefore, who possesses Japanese nationality.

Kabuki is similar. Even if an American studied in the National Theater and became a highly proficient performer, he could not inherit one of the traditional stage names, such as Kichiemon Nakamura. However unfair this appears, it cannot be helped. Like the arts of the tea ceremony, Japanese dance, and flower arrangement, Kabuki follows the *iemoto*, or school head, system, and its traditions are protected by being passed down through the generations. The name and concept of Kichiemon Nakamura exists only by virtue of this system.

A parallel situation obtains in the United States. It applies to Hollywood films, Broadway musicals, the automobile industry, baseball, jazz, and the cowboy lifestyle, which encompasses country-and-western music. Thus, in 1994, I happened to go to a baseball game in Chicago. General Schwarzkopf, hero of the Gulf War, threw out the first ball for the White Sox. For Americans, the sport of baseball is such a sacred zone that a war hero, or even the president, must throw out the first ball. So, no matter how rich a foreigner may be, it is not acceptable to buy into major league baseball or the Hollywood movie industry.

Paradoxically, the U.S. is far from being aware of its own sacred zones. On the contrary, the message it sends to the world is that every field is level and open. Emotionally, Americans cannot easily tolerate Japan's encroachment on its automobile or entertainment industries, but as an ideal, priority is given to the concept of a "level" playing field. This creates a zone of tension for universalism and the notion of the U.S. as a superpower.

In addition, American CEOs sometimes allow their very businesses to become objects of speculation. For instance, they buy and sell film companies in a surprisingly casual way. When I spoke about sacred zones with Akio Morita of Sony, he told me, "That can't be right, because it was Columbia that approached me and asked me to buy." The same thing seems to have happened when Nintendo bought into U.S. major league baseball. However true it may be that the American side requested these purchases, the fact that Japanese companies went ahead with the deal irked the American public. In the U.S., as well, business decisions and public sentiment should be accorded some degree of thought and coordination.

Henry Kissinger once wrote to me regarding the philosophy of symbiosis and my idea of sacred zones. He wrote, "I have always been unable to accept the explanations of bureaucrats or those related to government. But now I can participate in discussions more positively in light of your views." Zybgniew Brzezinsky also wrote to express a similar reaction after reading the English edition of my *Philosophy of Symbiosis*.

To take yet another example, I once asked Keizo Saji of Suntory why we Japanese make such products as wine, as doing so infringes on a sacred zone of the French. In addition, Japanese sometimes win *chanson* contests and international competitions in French cooking. When the French see this, they tend to feel that Japanese are odd. Evidently, by refining one's technique, one can take first place in the world of *chanson* or French cuisine. But why is it necessary to make the effort? The Japanese might be perceived as less curious if they adopted a stance of respecting the sacred zones of *chanson* and French cuisine out of deference to that culture.

My concept of rice as a sacred zone is not protectionist, or intended to defend "rice as food." Rather, it is a proposal on the issue of how to build a new world order. Although this may seem extreme, it is related to my recent proposal that Japan should donate ¥1 trillion in overseas development aid to the U.S. automobile industry. Indeed, the clear-cut division between developing countries as poor, and developed countries as rich, can no longer be maintained. In that light there should be nothing odd about Japan providing "aid" to the U.S. The recovery of the U.S. automobile industry would restore the world's greatest pool of consumers, and all would eventually reap the benefits. By the same token, the U.S. could be expected to provide support should Japan's electronics, automobile, household appliance, or other major industry falter and trigger a crisis in Japan. Approaches like these to a new symbiotic world order will increasingly be accepted as necessary and appropriate.

Garden City of Helicopter Commuters

The symbiosis of man and nature involves more than just trees, birds, animals, and insects: whatever is manufactured by human beings also becomes, as time passes, part of nature. We must recognize not only man-made lakes, canals, and forests, but even our cities and our technology, as a part of nature. The dualism that insists that what God made is nature, and what human beings have produced is artificial and, therefore, opposed to nature, no longer holds.

The previous generation of Japanese city dwellers were largely people who had been born in the country and migrated to the city. Their memories of the countryside were still strong and dear to them; it was only natural that they viewed the city as being in opposition to nature. But today some 80 percent of all Japanese are born in cities. Just as naturally, most children born and now raised in the city have neither memories nor experience of nature. Ask some children where dragonflies and beetles or other insects come from; they're likely to answer "the pet shop at the department store." It is hardly surprising that we have raised a generation which experiences the city as a part of nature, concrete as a kind of earth.

I believe that the twenty-first century will see a dynamic symbiosis of the city with nature, such as that hinted at by Susan Sontag in her "urban pastorale" or by Frank Lloyd Wright's futuristic vision of

Broadacre City crisscrossed by commuters' helicopters. In both we see a move away from city or nature, to city and nature in symbiosis. Edo, for example, was in fact already a thoroughly artificial city. Noboru Kawazoe, in his book *Tokyo no Genfukei* (The Original Tokyo), relates that though Edo was a city without official green space, it was nevertheless dotted with plant markets; its citizens cultivated their own bonsai trees; and the streets and alleys were filled with the blooms of morning glories and flowering gourds. The citizens of Edo were thus well able to nurture a rich, metaphorical conception of nature through their artificially grown bonsai and potted plants.

The city of the future where people will live in symbiosis with technology, animals, birds, and insects—together with window gardens, bonsai, and man-made forests—is near at hand.

Forests and Canals: Secret to Urban Disaster Preparedness

In this section, I would like to discuss the symbiosis between human beings and nature from the standpoint of disaster prevention.

At 5:46 on the morning of January 17, 1995, a powerful earthquake struck Japan near Kobe, with its seismic center in southern Hyogo Prefecture. This major earthquake, which killed over 5,000 people and caused more damage than a minor war, disproved several myths held by the Japanese—who had succumbed to a false sense of peacetime security, notably in three areas. In the first place, this earthquake struck the Kansai region of western Japan. Second, it was of unprecedented scale, and it occurred almost directly beneath a city. Third, the effects of the disaster spread, resulting in secondary and tertiary disasters.

Until this Great Hanshin Earthquake, it was known that a violent earth movement could occur anywhere in the Japanese archipelago, but a major earthquake was thought unlikely in the Kansai region; certain other regions were believed more prone to a major quake. Seismology, like most sciences, bases its predictions on statistics. Scientists imagined that regions having escaped major quakes in the past were statistically unlikely to be hit. The Building Standards Act (1950) was written and passed on the strength of this hypothesis.

In fact, Japanese earthquake data goes back only as far as the

Collapsed freeway, Kobe, after the Great Hanshin Earthquake (1995).

Great Kanto Earthquake of 1923. Naturally, documents confirm that major quakes occurred before this date, but information on their force is sketchy and inaccurate; true magnitudes and intensities are unknown. Since the Great Kanto Earthquake struck beyond the range of a seismometer set up at Hongo, on the campus of the University of Tokyo, its damage had also to be estimated on the basis of incomplete records and the precise extent of the earthquake has

Aftermath of the Great Kanto Earthquake (1923).

never been firmly established. Nevertheless, detailed information was available concerning the epicenter and the types of damage that resulted, and buildings standards were devised to ensure that new construction could withstand a shock of equivalent magnitude.

What Kind of Earthquake Was the Great Kanto Earthquake?

The epicenter of the Great Kanto Earthquake was near the southernmost tip of Kanagawa Prefecture, about fifty kilometers from Tokyo. Although no precise data exists on the strength of the earthquake, damage estimates and various reports suggest that it was a 0.3G/300 gal-class temblor. (The "G" refers here to the acceleration of gravity, indicating variation from stasis until the occurrence of actual vibration. A G is a unit of acceleration corresponding to 1000 gal) Designing a building with proper earthquake resistance is impossible given no more than a standard of seismic intensity 7, which would result in visible faults and cracks in the ground. Designing an earthquake-proof structure is difficult even when the magnitude is also known. To provide some point of reference, the acceleration of the earth's gravity is 980 gals.

Magnitude, normally expressed as M and commonly mentioned in media reports, refers to the common logarithm of the greatest amplitude (measured in microns) recorded by a seismometer of certain specifications, with a magnification of 2,800 times, located 100 kilometers from a quake's epicenter. Although often used, this unit is difficult to understand. Still, it provides an international unit for comparing earthquakes in different regions of the world. By way of comparison, the Great Kanto Earthquake is thought to have had a magnitude of 7.9.

Seismic intensity is another familiar term. Those seismic intensities regularly announced by the National Meteorological Agency are based on physical perceptions of observers located at meteorological observation stations, so the same earthquake could be perceived differently in areas with different ground conditions. Therefore, the agency has now begun to determine seismic intensity in some locations by means of mechanical observation. The agency's seismic intensity scale is correlated to gals as follows:

Seismic intensity 1 / minor
Seismic intensity 2 / light (can be felt by all)
Seismic intensity 3 / weak
Seismic intensity 4 / medium (items fall from shelves) 25-80 gals
Seismic intensity 5 / strong (cracks appear in walls, grave markers topple, and chimneys and stone walls are damaged) 80-250- gals
Seismic intensity 6 / violent (up to 30 percent of two-story wood-frame houses collapse; many persons are unable to remain standing) 250-400 gals
Seismic intensity 7 / extremely violent (more than 30 percent of two-story wood-frame houses collapse; landslides and cracks in the earth appear; faults and the like become apparent) more than 400 gals

Although the Kanto Earthquake is understood to have reached 300 gals, it is really only known that the seismic energy of the earthquake—centered elsewhere—was transmitted to Tokyo at 300 gals. Thus efforts have been made to design buildings in Tokyo capable of withstanding 300 gals, or equivalent to another Great Kanto Earthquake. However, if an earthquake of this scale were to hit Tokyo directly instead of first striking southern Kanagawa Prefecture, all buildings constructed to withstand another such earthquake would be at risk. Moreover, it has recently been suggested that the Great Kanto Earthquake was more powerful than previously believed. As precise records are lacking, however, this would be difficult to confirm.

The Great Hanshin Earthquake struck Kobe in the very midst of this debate, reaching 900 gals in some areas. Because the Building Standards Act is based on the 300 gals estimate of the Great Kanto Earthquake, the occurrence of a 900 gal earthquake—an astounding threefold increase—came as a terrible shock to me personally, and I wondered how this could be dealt with.

For the first time since the Great Kanto Earthquake, a major earthquake had occurred with its seismic center close to a large city. Although the Niigata Earthquake (1964) and the earthquake under the sea off Miyagi Prefecture (1978) were major temblors, they occurred under the ocean floor several kilometers offshore. In journalism, the term "direct-hit earthquake" is used to describe an inland earthquake with its epicenter directly beneath a city. The possibility of such an earthquake had been discussed many times in rather sensational terms, because danger would be extreme even if the earthquake were relatively small. Tragically, our worst fears of a direct-hit earthquake have now become reality. Japan had no previous record or experience of such an earthquake, which in the event occurred under northern Awaji Island, almost at the center of Kobe.

Suitability of New Earthquake-Proofing Standards

Small earthquakes sometimes occur while we architects and engineers are meeting in hotels or similar structures. We often try to guess the location and scale of the earthquake, and are usually right on the mark. That is because one first has a slight perception of an earthquake, and then feels the stronger vibrations.

The slight vibrations felt first are initial motions known as P-waves. The stronger waves, known as S-waves, arrive later. P-waves are propagated at about 1.7 times the speed of S waves. The distance to the epicenter can be determined by the Omori Formula, which measures the duration of the preliminary tremor, or the interval between the S-wave and the P-wave.

In past earthquakes, a P-wave was always felt initially, and after a brief interval (following the preliminary tremor), the S-wave would arrive. The vertical vibration from the epicenter, which is felt directly, is faint. As the horizontal vibrations that then travel along the earth's surface are stronger, scientists place more emphasis on measuring the horizontal vibrations when determining an earthquake's scale. In a direct-hit earthquake, however, vertical and horizontal vibrations occur simultaneously, exerting tremendous force on buildings. Tellingly, many survivors of the Kobe earthquake voiced similar impressions, describing the strike as completely different from previous earthquakes they had experienced. Confirming this phenomenon, survivors gave descriptions such as "My body was tossed almost to the ceiling in an instant, and then I was shaken around," or "It was as if an airplane had crashed in the next room."

The Urban Building Law (1923)[3] remained unchanged until the postwar Building Standards Act was passed in 1950, but even then the reference to the Great Kanto Earthquake remained. A partial revision of the act in 1970 included no major revisions concerning antiseismic countermeasures. In a major revision in 1980, a true earthquake-proof design law was incorporated, based on the findings of a study group having investigated the recent San Francisco Earthquake. This set of regulations, containing much more effective parameters, is now referred to as "the new earthquake-proofing standards." Virtually no building constructed according to these new rules—that is, any large building constructed after 1980—suffered major damage in the Great Hanshin Earthquake of 1995.

Kobe Port Island is the site of super high-rise hotels, concert halls, and housing situated on reclaimed land. The entirety of these were constructed since the new antiseismic standards went into effect, and all exhibited splendid earthquake resistance. Beneath such structures, piles were of course driven. Although severe ground liquefaction occurred, the buildings themselves suffered little effective damage beyond broken glass.

For this reason, some specialists believe that our newest standards are sufficient for the future. Others, however, submit that Japan's earthquake-proofing standards, though thought to be the world's strictest, should be humbly reappraised. Most of those advocating tougher antiseismic standards are structural engineers who lay major stress on the damage caused by vertical vibrations from the recent direct-hit earthquake.

The Safety vs. Economy Paradox

In the current socio-economic climate, maintaining a balance between building safety and costs is necessary. The following illustration is intended to explain this.

Some years ago, a social engineering research institute where I serve as director was studying the development of a new aircraft, which was to be designed with a particular emphasis on safety. We investigated whether a system could be developed that would protect nearly all passengers in the event of a crash, and we determined that this was indeed possible. The assembled specialists agreed that, technically, this would *not* be difficult to achieve. Each passenger would don a flight suit, and all passenger seats could be ejected, like the seats of a fighter place, upon the pilot's command in an emergency, enabling passengers to float to earth by parachute. At the same time, food, water, radio devices, a rubber boat, a tent, and the like were to be released. Both passengers and their emergency survival kits could descend by parachute onto land or water.

The purpose of our study was not to perfect such a system, as a similar one already functioned satisfactorily in fighter aircraft. What we achieved was to determine that the costs of realizing such a system would be unreasonably high. Airfare between Japan and the U.S. would reach ¥12 million to ¥20 million per passenger. Such an aircraft would be technically, but not economically, feasible.

Society weighs safety and fiscal factors to ensure some sort of balance. Similarly, in the field of architecture, the design and construction of buildings capable of withstanding an earthquake three times the scale of the Great Kanto Earthquake is technically possible. Yet, were building standards to be modified in this aim, supporting columns would occupy greater space, rooms would be smaller, and construction costs would soar. This might be acceptable for public buildings or for extremely wealthy clients, but if offices, rental housing, and other commercial structures were to adopt such standards, production costs would quickly prove unmanageable.

Land prices are already far higher in Tokyo than in New York or London, and construction costs double. Even executives receiving some of the world's highest salaries lack a sense of plenty and comfort in their lives, owing to the exaggerated cost of living. If construction safety standards were further strengthened, ordinary living costs would rise to new heights, and decreased international competitiveness would result. Clearly we must increase the earthquake resistance of buildings to the highest levels possible while carefully examining the extent to which such a change is practical.

Econocentrism and the Computer

The introduction of antiseismic construction standards through the Earthquake-Proof Design Law, constituting a major revision of the Building Standards Act in 1980, represents an important advance. Nevertheless, safety can vary widely depending on the degree of tolerance permitted in instances of real application. The policy of most builders has been to follow the new earthquake-proofing standards, but to shave as close as possible in order to save money, since large earthquakes occur rarely. Thus, when we architects design buildings that barely comply with antiseismic standards, builders commend us for our "inexpensive and outstanding designs." Clearly, Japan's bias toward econocentrism intervenes even in design.

Computer-aided design easily allows us to satisfy earthquake-proofing standards at the barest minimum level. In the Meiji period, well before the age of computers, a few architects, such as the "elder statesman of Japanese architecture," Kingo Tatsuno, willingly designed preposterously thick columns. Consequently, it is sometimes suggested half-seriously that late Meiji-period buildings are actually stronger than modern ones. While architects of a hundred years ago used their intuition to provide some leeway, computers now perform hyper-accurate calculations and can even simulate wind-tunnel tests. We can now determine the required minimum with extreme precision and design our buildings accordingly. But, in fact, superseding the earthquake-proofing standards by 10 to 20 percent in public facilities and the like would be desirable. Furthermore, there is more to such calculation than meets the eye. An especially troublesome aspect of earthquakes is that the degree of acceleration, as well as the frequency and strength of vibration, differ among the first, second, or twentieth floors of a building. Furthermore, even among like buildings, earthquake damage can vary widely depending on the quality of the supporting ground. Although two-story wooden buildings with tile roofs generally present the greatest risk, this is not true in all cases. Every structure has its own characteristic frequency of vibration, but high-rise buildings are more likely to resonate with slow ground vibrations. The Great Hanshin Earthquake registered especially strong horizontal vibrations with long frequencies of one to two seconds. When a building's characteristic frequency of vibration coincides with such horizontal vibration, the result is horrendous damage. The major damage to buildings and suspension bridges in Kobe in 1995 seems to point to the misfortune of these structures' characteristic frequencies of vibration coinciding with those of the earthquake, resulting in the direct transfer of shock waves.

Japan's antiseismic standards have to date been based primarily on inferences about the Great Kanto Earthquake. Therefore, standards for the Kanto, or greater Tokyo, region are stricter than for the great cities of western Japan. The recent Hanshin earthquake has shown unmistakably that such regional distinctions are inappropriate. It is a lesson that must not be overlooked.

Should a Major Earthquake Strike Tokyo

I once ran a simulation of a revisitation of the Great Kanto Earthquake at 6:30 P.M., with a wind speed of three meters per second. The simulation suggested that fires would break out simultaneously in 860 locations, which exceeds the firefighting capacity of equipment in Tokyo and its neighboring communities. Up to 250,000 persons would die—20 percent quake related and 80 percent from fire—while upwards of 750,000 people would be injured. This contrasts with the fact that nearly 80 percent of those killed in the Kobe region in 1995 were crushed to death when buildings collapsed in the first stage of the disaster, a typical scenario in a major direct-hit earthquake. The effects of a direct-hit earthquake on Tokyo would far exceed my estimates.

The simulation also revealed that Tokyo harbors various substances and materials that would release toxic gases in a fire. These include chemicals stocked in factories and labs, construction materials that contain toxic substances, and mobile loads in tank trucks. If all these were set fire to, Tokyo would choke—even if actual deaths from burning could be minimized. An accurate determination of the likely number of deaths is scarcely possible at present.

In the Great Hanshin Earthquake, the phenomenon did not occur in which cars catch fire and explode, igniting a chain of fire along major roads, as little traffic was on the roads in the early morning. If a major earthquake were to occur in Tokyo or elsewhere during rush hour, however, automobile fires could spread on an enormous scale. A similar chain of injury would apply in the case of railroads carrying passengers and freight, as the damage from derailments and overturned cars would be appalling.

Each district of Tokyo has a designated emergency refuge area. If the neighborhood surrounding the refuge began to burn all at once, however, fire would consume all the oxygen in the area, resulting in mass suffocation. In designing residences and other structures, I am sometimes asked to include a fireproof concrete room that would serve as a refuge for all the building's occupants in an emergency. If surrounding rooms exploded, however, the occupants would surely perish from oxygen deprivation unless they had an auxiliary supply. We must consider whether this might not happen in emergency refuge areas as well.

In the Great Kanto Earthquake, a terrible tragedy occurred at a clothing factory called Honjo Hifukusho. The quake struck at noon, and the 40,000 people taking refuge in the factory had all been incinerated four hours later—in that day's worst single disaster. Fire had encircled the buildings, and sparks ignited household goods and clothing that evacuees had loaded onto large wagons. Equally deadly, however, when fire breaks out suddenly over a wide area, is the suctioning away of air at speeds exceeding those commonly associated with typhoons, so that all at once the oxygen supply is insufficient.

The worst single disaster of the Great Kanto Earthquake occurred at a clothing factory in Honjo, Tokyo.

Japan's Fixation on Escape

The basic impulse in Japan is to escape should an earthquake or fire occur. In contrast, citizens' disaster prevention regulations in Switzerland require all community residents to cooperate in fighting any emergency. Anyone fleeing the scene of a disaster is subject to punishment.

The original purpose of this legislation was to organize civil defense in case of insurrection or nuclear war, but it now applies to civil disasters as well, and citizens' disaster corps are established in each locality. Underground shelters were built and supplied with food, water, medical supplies, firefighting equipment, gas masks, and other survival goods, as well as weapons, including machine guns. When a major fire or the like occurs, everyone works together. Should efforts fail, the leader declares that all must take refuge in the underground shelter. The Swiss undergo compulsory military training, so that all males know how to handle weapons, and many are trained regularly in firefighting.

The Swiss approach is apparent in building design as well. For example, fire doors in Japan open outward, so that people can escape in case of fire. Fire doors are then closed so that the fire cannot spread, even if one room or a whole floor burns completely. Swiss fire doors, however, open inward so that if a fire breaks out, people can rush from other floors to the origin of the fire and extinguish it together. In Japan, fire shutters in a number of buildings close automatically when a fire breaks out, so any attempt to extinguish a fire might actually put one at considerable risk.

The view that people ought to escape first, leaving the field to professional firefighters and the police, results only in larger secondary and tertiary disasters, and should be reconsidered. As I watched TV coverage of the Great Hanshin Earthquake, I was moved to tears by the pathetic sight of the hands of persons pinned under a collapsed building. The hands—of a mother and child—were moving, showing that they had survived, but there was no way to extricate them from the weight of the massive columns, concrete, and debris that pinned them down. Chain saws, hammers, crowbars, and the like might have made it possible to save them, but no such tools were available, and the mother and child were lost. I could not bear to watch as people on the street lamented, "Without tools, we can do nothing. It's impossible to free them with our bare hands."

For some time, I have maintained that security comprises four domains: military security, economic security, security from environmental deterioration and disasters, and cultural security. I believe that real security can only be achieved by integrating these four sectors. In addition to conventional areas of concern, which largely take into account only military strife, there are other areas of exposure whose importance will grow, including security from global financial instability, such as the recent Mexican crisis; security from environmental crises and ozone depletion and the erosion of tropical rain forests; security from cultural crises and religious strife; and security from disasters, such as earthquakes, typhoons, and fires. The Great Hanshin Earthquake suggests that the security of people's lives should be considered in a more integrated manner.

Kobe's Recovery—the Broader Perspective

Ironically, the aftermath of the Great Hanshin Earthquake has provided reassurance in one area, which is the relative lack of damage to new buildings, even those constructed on reclaimed land. This may come as a surprise, as news coverage focused heavily on liquefaction of artificial land, the deplorable state of power and energy supplies, and damage to harbor facilities resulting in the closure of Kobe Port.

Nonetheless, those buildings newly constructed on reclaimed land did not suffer significant damage. No deaths occurred at Kansai International Airport or on Port Island, and buildings in such locations were only slightly damaged. Ground liquefaction did, of course, occur and port facilities were thrown into disarray, but the attention given these problems obscured the fact that damage to buildings on reclaimed land was minimal. Only power and energy lines and harbor facilities there were hit, and this is rather heartening when we consider the ongoing restoration of Kobe.

In the wake of the Great Hanshin Earthquake, Japan is obliged to rebuild Kobe as a safe and secure city to avoid incurring global censure. Following the Great Kanto Earthquake, at a time when Japan had not yet risen from the ranks of developing nations, the country took proper, if somewhat ineffective, city planning measures and produced quite an attractive city until the devastation of World War II. Japan is now the world's second economic power; to honor the memories of those who perished in 1995, we must rebuild a safe, comfortable, attractive city that Japan can show to the rest of the world with pride.

In the area of national development planning as well, prompt action is required to expand Japan's single prioritized national axis. For the past thirty years, I have continued to demand that Japan create two or three such axes, like those I proposed in 1961. Because Japan is a long, narrow archipelago, a chain of highways, high-speed train lines, and the like was first laid down the natural center of the country, from Hokkaido to Kyushu, passing through all major cities.

However, the recent Kobe earthquake revealed that this single prioritized axis is insufficient to support and service the entire coun-

Earthquake resistance of buildings on reclaimed land: Kansai International Airport (above) and Port Island, Kobe.

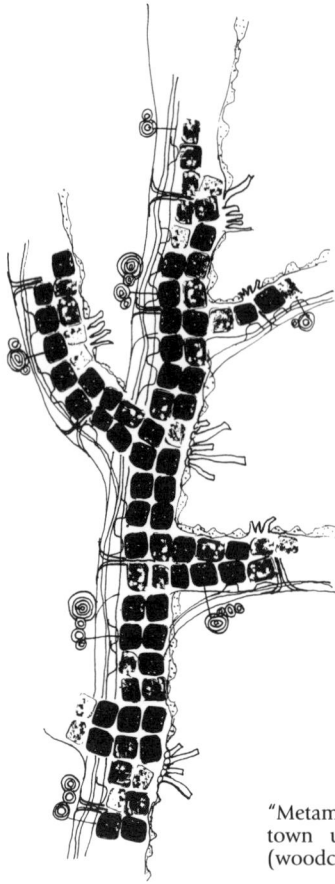

"Metamorphosis 65": scheme of town units and infrastructure (woodcut, from author's sketch).

try. Thus, in 1995, the mass of evacuees, rescuers, and emergency supplies clogged all infrastructures concentrated in this narrow band, bringing traffic to a standstill. Kobe is located at the natural juncture between eastern Japan and western Japan, and the breakdown of this axis paralyzed Japan's industry and its very economy. Because such disasters can so easily affect economic activities, the national land development plan should be revised in the light of this to integrate a broader perspective. Traffic jams of the kind experienced around Kobe could be eliminated with a new Pacific axis running from Kyushu through Shikoku to the Kii Peninsula, and a Sea of Japan axis extending along that coast. Bypasses and loops could connect these to the existing infrastructural axis.

Moreover, the culture of large cities alone will not be enough to ensure survival in the coming century. To guarantee our future, we must create new fishery, farming, forestry, and environmental industries that make use of oceans, forests, and other natural elements; establish new research centers and living environments integrated with nature; and reexamine the quality and emphasis of industry. Prioritized axes crossing natural areas, in addition to those serving major cities, will be needed to maintain the support industries of the twenty-first century.

A new economic and industrial region has begun to extend from the Tokyo area to the Tohoku region, and even further north to parts of Hokkaido. This poses a danger of excessive concentration in eastern Japan. Although Kansai International Airport has now opened in western Japan, its benefits are not sufficient to correct this imbalance. The hinterlands around Tokyo, including Saitama, Chiba, Kanagawa, Tochigi, Yamanashi, and Shizuoka—and more broadly Niigata and Hokkaido—continue to expand. Because East Japan is so powerful, Japan will soon lean too far to the east unless a counterbalancing economic sphere of comparable strength is nurtured in the Kansai. To accomplish this, a West Japan economic sphere linking the Chubu and Kinki regions with Chugoku, Shikoku, and Kyushu should be created. This can be effected by building a second prioritized axis of development in the west to stimulate distribution and economic development. This Pacific axis will also significantly aid the recovery and reconstruction of Kobe.

Tokyo: Protection with Forests and Canals

When I simulated the events that would occur if an earthquake on the scale of the Great Kanto Earthquake were to hit Tokyo again, I concluded that there are only two ways to reduce the number of casualties—trees and water, in the form of forests and canals.

Miniature forests of evergreens could easily be established within residential districts. These would form small parks, ranging from 200 *tsubo* to 500, or even 1,000 *tsubo* in area (1 *tsubo* equals two tatami, or about 3.3 square meters.) They would be densely planted with trees that are especially effective at stopping fire, such as *mokkoku*

(*Theaceae*). Creating preferably 7,000—or at least 3,000—of these parks within the city of Tokyo, scattered throughout residential areas with their high proportions of wooden buildings, would greatly prevent the spread of fire. Although I considered experimental data on divers means of fire prevention, including digging ditches and widening roads, I determined that the most effective would be these small, dense forests of evergreens. Even in the absence of a major earthquake or fire, they would afford restful, green oases in the city.

Watercourses, or canals, are another effective means of preventing the spread of fire. When a fire runs up against a body of water at least seventy meters wide, there is a high probability that it will cease to burn; therefore, as illustrated here, two seventy-meter canals could be dug to form an outer and an inner ring west of the city. Avenues of trees for fire prevention should be planted along both banks of the canals, so that even if the estimated 860 fires of my computer-simulated earthquake broke out simultaneously within the inner ring, the double ring of canals would halt the fire—reducing deaths by half.

This proposal was presented as "Tokyo Plan 2025," published in book form in 1988, and received a very favorable press. However, most interest was concentrated on my concept of creating an island in Tokyo Bay, and the canal proposal was less noticed. However, this scheme originated with the two enormous canals and 3,000 mini-forests as earthquake countermeasures for Tokyo. The main reasons for the island proposal were sludge removal to improve water quality and provision of land for tree nurseries and as an eventual assets exchange.

Land prices in Tokyo are among the highest in the world, and whether the land for forests and watercourses could even be afforded is uncertain. Even if ample funds were budgeted for this purpose, few landowners would be willing to sell, as real estate sale involves high capital gains taxes under the current tax system. As an alternative, the concept of a "new capital island" was proposed. Plots of equal value on the new island would be exchanged for any land appropriated for earthquake countermeasures, thus avoiding the necessity to pay taxes and satisfying landowners with reclaimed land

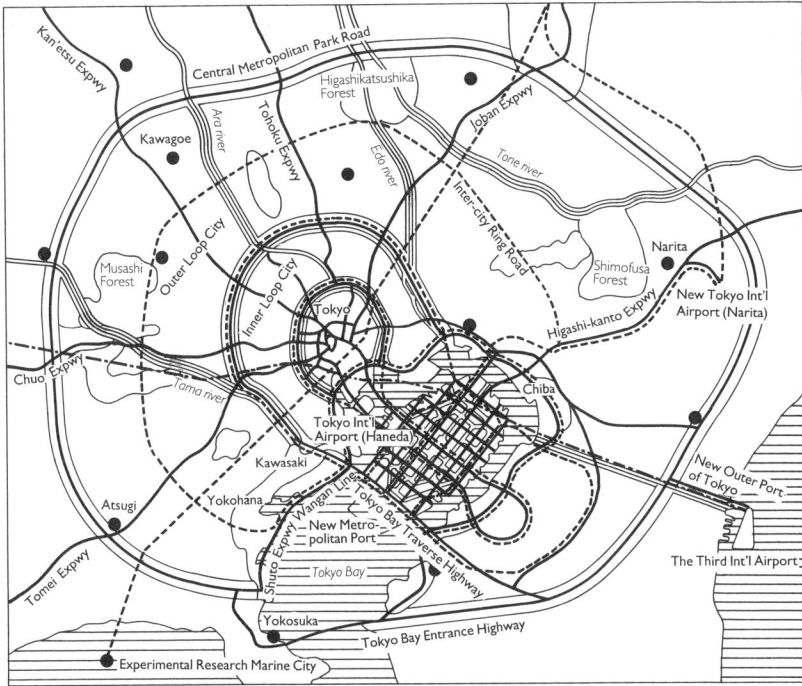

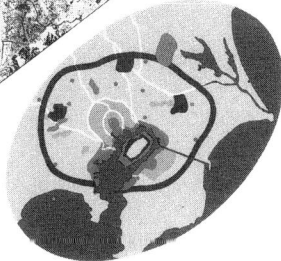

Concept drawing of "Tokyo Plan 2025"
(top) and photomontage (bottom).

that might be expected to appreciate over time. Artificial islands have already been proposed for intelligent buildings, teleports, and the transfer of government offices; however, in my scheme, greater weight is placed on individual housing units for salaried employees. The land would first be designated as reimbursement for disaster prevention measures in Tokyo; in addition, low-cost housing would be made available as exchange, or sold. This would attract large numbers of people from Tokyo's central wards to the island, at least partly resolving the housing problem at the same time.

A further proposal of Tokyo Plan 2025 was to create three large forests in the suburbs of Tokyo as emergency refuges. However, this was also obscured at the time by attention given to the artificial island development. Three forests are shown on the drawing, each of which is as large as the area of Tokyo within the Yamanote line. The goal was to restore the vast Musashino forest of the central Kanto Plain and to maintain it for future generations.

Only forests and canals can be effective in a major earthquake or fire, and there are no other conceivable substitutes. I would like to repropose this plan for Kobe too. Since Kobe is likewise a coastal city, construction of canals would be simplified. In fact, canals once existed in both Tokyo and Kobe—used to move coal and other goods—but were later filled in. The smaller town of Amagasaki, in contrast, maintained its canals to serve its many factories and the like. I am currently involved in city planning there that will make use of these.

Watching rescue efforts following the Great Hanshin Earthquake, I was shocked that fire engines could often reach the site of fires but could not fight them, because no water was available. Had canals been kept or restored, water would have been available for firefighting and boats could also have been used for evacuation and rescue efforts. And, in more tranquil times, residents could still appreciate the pleasant streets along their banks. Another lesson from the recent earthquake was that normal roads often become impassable as fire engines try to negotiate the same roads being used to evacuate residents. For this reason as well, it is important to re-establish watercourses.

Specifically, the former yards of Kobe Steel and similar industrial sites should be purchased and used provisionally to begin replotting and constructing a new city. Earthquake victims could have been allowed to reside there while redevelopment of damaged areas of the city progressed. Since a planning scheme with canals and forests is already underway in Amagasaki, another tactic would be to go ahead with this first and transfer the earthquake victims to Amagasaki. As in Tokyo in 1923, the complex negotiations regarding the sites of collapsed houses have not been well coordinated, while replacing the electrical, gas, water, and other facilities remains a complex problem. Therefore, infrastructural solutions, including a more efficient road network, cannot really be planned yet, and we must acknowledge that all these issues will require time.

Planting Forests and Building Reservoirs at Schools

During this process, it is essential to reequip public facilities with means to respond to primary and secondary disasters. At minimum, reservoirs and emergency refuges need to be provided in every neighborhood. I believe that schools are best suited for this role. Most schools already possess fireproof buildings and substantial grounds. If trees were planted closely around the perimeters of school grounds, they could serve as safe emergency refuges. We might also note that being surrounded by trees produces a stabilizing psychological effect. In addition, since the space beneath schools is rarely utilized, underground rooms could be built here and stocked with food supplies, radio equipment, survival kits, water tanks, and any further items vital in an emergency. With firefighting paraphernalia and emergency toilets also provided beneath schoolgrounds, preparations would be complete.

Announcing that people might take refuge at schools during times of disaster would prevent the confusion of searching for emergency refuges. During a recent earthquake in Los Angeles, radio communications linking elementary schools proved a powerful asset. In the Great Hanshin Earthquake as well, many people sought shelter in schools, which however did not maintain sufficient telephones lines to meet demand. Elementary schools are closely integrated with the local community under the existing school district system, so the probability that people would seek refuge at a school during an emergency is high. Unquestionably, equipment and supplies should be prepared for this eventuality.

As part of their disaster preparedness, cities such as Tokyo must determine how best to restrict traffic on highways and other main roads in an emergency. If a major disaster again occurred in Tokyo, cars would doubtlessly clog the highways, creating huge traffic jams, just as happened after the Hanshin disaster. There, as the victims tried to flee, relatives and friends attempted to travel inbound to offer help. These opposing traffic flows caused chaos as fire engines, ambulances, and police vehicles tried to navigate traffic jams. Had decisions been taken in advance about the emergency use of roads and regular training drills conducted, the situation might have been quite different. To give a simplified example, all lanes of the Tomei Expressway might be used only for inbound travel to Tokyo, while the Chuo Expressway could be assigned for travel outbound from the beleaguered capital.

Creation of a New Nature

Environmental policy must go beyond the preservation of Japan's existing forests to include the planting of new forests in cities like Tokyo. As in the environmental protection and historic preservation movements of Europe and the United States, the first step has to be taken by dedicated individuals. Whether it be to preserve cityscape, historic buildings, or the enviroment, any such movement starts with committed people's contributions, however small, and from there develops into a national cause.

In Japan, however such action tends to percolate from the top down, with a committee of so-called experts calling for the preservation of nature or cultural monuments and making a loud protest against "development." But those same experts either make no effort to raise the funds needed or they demand to appropriate the farm and forest land surrounding cities. But farms are places for growing rice and vegetables; and forests are the sources of timber and wood products. Now, when these very industries are in trouble and losing money, it is irresponsible to insist that farms and forests be "preserved"—unless some form of economic assistance is forthcoming.

We cannot simply rely on the natural environment left to us by our forebears. In exchange for improving valuable existing sites, we must also work to create new, man-made nature to bequeath to our descendants. In Tokyo, the vast tract of forest attached to Meiji Shrine offers a good example. This apparently primeval forest was actually planted only seventy-five years ago. Here we have a vision of the forest not as a holy site or dwelling place of spirits, but as part of the living space of the city.

In the development plan for Tokyo that I will describe in detail in chapter 16, I have proposed the creation of three such forests, each of ten thousand hectares. Reminiscent of the Musashino forest, which once covered much of the Kanto Plain around the present city, these would be mixed woodlands of deciduous trees combining in function and feeling two traditional types of woodland: the sacred grove, which surrounded the Shinto shrine of each village in old Japan, and the village wood, planted around homes in farm communities to protect them from the ravages of typhoons.

The same approach may also be relevant to the symbiosis of private and communal space in the urban environment. Today the city is divided between private property, owned by individuals or firms, and roads, parks, and the like built and maintained with public funds. But at one time there was also in Japan an intermediary zone between public and private, namely communal space. In agricultural communities, rights to water and common grazing were a communal asset shared equally by all villagers. And as we have seen in Kyoto, the street was a kind of communal domain administered by the *chogumi*, or district organization. In Edo urban districts, houses were instead packed together along the narrow frontages of a four-sided block. This layout left an open space behind the houses, at the center, which was called the *kaisho*, or meeting place, and this, too, was a type of communal property.

The city of Nagoya was endowed with a unique scheme during the Edo period. Each district was, as elsewhere, divided into long, narrow lots facing the main streets. But in the empty area behind the houses a temple or a graveyard was built, with a single path leading from it out to the street. This pathway was called the *kansho*, or idle place, and was yet another traditional version of communal space.

Nowadays, if we take one step off our own property, we are on land administered by the city or prefecture: so we have no incentive to maintain it. When it becomes untidy we may call the local authority and complain, but we are hardly likely to clean it up ourselves. In the days of communal space, however, everyone cooperated to keep the shared area tidy; and it was also a place where children could play without parents worrying about their safety. Such communal spaces were intermediary zones between private and public property.

The activities of the National Trust of Great Britain in preserving the environment, especially the coastline, and administering private estates on behalf of the public can also be interpreted as a defense of communal property. In Japan, too, a Japanese version of the National Trust now exists, while a grassroots movement to preserve the primeval forest at Shiretoko in Hokkaido is also encouraging.

In the renovation and redevelopment of our cities in the twenty-first century, we shall have to revive communal property—as an intermediary between private and public—in many different forms. This will be linked to the creation of natural environments within the city as little pockets of nature, or even spaces under the eaves of a building. Or, as I looked to do in the Fukuoka Bank Head Office, the space in question might be private property opened to the public. We must employ a variety of means to assure this.

In the past, "borrowing" landscape was one means of achieving symbiosis with nature. The Shugakuin Detached Palace offers a celebrated example of this technique of incorporating distant views into one's own visual orbit. The technique was effective as long as population density was relatively low and a rich natural landscape still survived near urban areas. But today, we can scarcely all borrow nature. For instance, in resort areas, many people enjoy nature's beauty but forget what an ugly sight their own vacation home is. The true technique of borrowed landscape is mindful that we are also part of the landscape and that someone else may be looking. We must be as concerned with the landscape we "lend" as the one we borrow.

11

PHILOSOPHY OF THE *KARAKURI*: Symbiosis between Humanity and Technology

A Tea Room in the Space Shuttle

In the Western world, technology and humanity are generally thought of as opposing one another. We find this view of humanity as having become alienated and estranged in Jean-Jacques Rousseau's[1] call for a "return to nature." Yet today, no one looking objectively at the contribution of technological progress to our daily lives would wish to reject it.

Ours is no longer a dualistic choice between technology and humanity. The challenge facing us today is how to articulate a philosophy able to humanize technology. In Tokyo, as I mentioned, my study with its IBM computer opens onto my tea room, Yuishikian—without the least dissonance. "A Tea Room in the Space Shuttle" is the slogan I have devised to express the symbiosis of humanity and technology. The space shuttle in orbit does not by itself represent mature technology. Only when we launch a space shuttle that includes a human space, such as represented by the tea room, will technology contribute real enjoyment and pleasure to human life.

For the Japanese, technology was first seen as an extension of humanity. The notion of mankind and technology in symbiosis goes back to Edo, in the form of a fascination with automata, or *karakuri*. Hosokawa Yorinao's *Illustrated Miscellany of Automata (Karakuri zui)* was published in 1796, followed in 1815 by Tagaya Kanchuzen's

Instructional Illustrated Catalogue of Automata (*Karakuri kinmo kagami-gusa*). In the same period, Takeda Ominoshojo's automated-puppet plays were popular in Osaka, and the master carpenter Hasegawa Kanbei invented various mechanical stage devices for the Kabuki theater and introduced a new sense of spectacle and excitement to the popular stage.

Hosokawa's *Automata* includes a diagram of a prototype of today's robot: the tea-carrying doll (*chahakobi ningyo*). If the host, seated opposite his guest, places a cup of tea in the doll's hands, it carries the cup of tea to the guest. The guest takes the cup from the doll, and it stops. After drinking the tea, the guest sets the cup back in the doll's hands. It turns around and returns to the host with the empty cup. The mechanism inside the tea-carrying doll comprises a spring made from whalebone and a complex system of interlocking gears. The doll is modeled as an adorable child, rather than a machinelike robot. In the Edo period, the technology of the automaton device was hidden instead of externally displayed, affording spectators a sense of wonder and mystery. Machines did not take on independent identities but mirrored human beings.

Examples of mechanistically inspired *karakuri* architecture include the suspended central pillar in several pagodas and the helix structures of "snail-shell" towers, or *sazaedo*. The five-story pagodas at the Yanaka Kannoji, built in 1627, and Nikko, built in 1823, both have central pillars that hang from above without actually touching the ground, and support nothing. Their purpose is to lower the center of gravity of the entire structure, thus stabilizing it. Such towers also include the Sansodo at Rakanji, built in 1780, and the Sazaedo at Seishuji in Aizu Wakamatsu, built in 1796. The outer walls rise and fall in a helix structure—suggesting the Buddhist idea of transmigration through one birth after another—expressing continuous ascent and descent.

Technology in Japan was thus made pleasurable and attractive through humanization, in contrast to the brutally exposed mechanisms of the West.

Tea-carrying robotic doll reproduced from the instructions below.

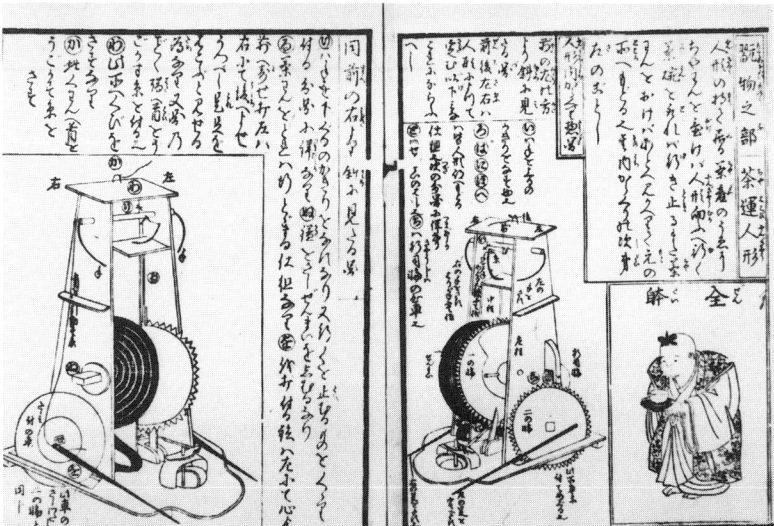

Diagrams and instructions for robotic doll, Edo period (Hosokawa Yorinao, *Karakuri Zui*, 1796).

"*Karakuri* architecture": snailshell pagoda, or *sazaedo*.

Biomation and the Limits of Medical Technology

Dr. Kazuhiko Atsumi attracted attention nearly a generation ago by implanting a mechanical heart into a goat and keeping the animal alive for 344 days. He coined the word "biomation" to signify the application of technology to biology in the coming century:

> The development of technology has led to the replacement of human labor by that of the machine—in other words, automation. The labor accomplished by machines has gradually evolved from physical labor—as in the steam engine, automobile, conveyor belt, telegraph, telephone, typewriter, and copy machine—to mental

labor, accomplished by computers and other examples of so-called artificial intelligence. The end result has been the widespread dissemination of information technology, contributing in turn to the evolution of an information society. At the same time, however, this information society has resulted in standardization, homogenization, and alienation. To resolve this, we must learn from the subtle behavior of living organisms and from software applications. In other words, a cross-fertilization between automation technology and the "*bio*" of living things will give birth to the technology of a new human society. I call this hybrid procedure *biomation*. The age of biomation will be an age of humanity, freedom, multiplicity, individuality, art, leisure, and now health and medicinet....

Since John von Neumann's work on automata after World War II, computers have greatly increased in speed until they now rival the processes of human thought. In the post-machine age, human beings and machines will grow even closer in their behavior; and, in certain areas, the borders between the two will be eliminated to create a new symbiosis. For example, today some people live with a pacemaker. Artificial limbs now approach human limbs in complexity. Implants of devices to bolster, or replace, human biological function are bound to increase.

The reverse possibility also exists: human beings might one day constitute part of a machine. A recent science fiction film, for example, portrayed a plasma production plant in which thousands of comatose humans produced blood that was then trucked away for use by others. Despite our revulsion at such an idea, it may become technologically feasible in the near future. If such things should happen, or even before they happen, a tremendous debate could arise: should we permit this? And if so, are we to think of these comatose persons as human beings or machines?

With the progress of medicine and biotechnology, new and complicated issues of bio-ethics arise daily. One approach is to distinguish between parts of the body that replace themselves and others that do not. Human hair, for example, is used in thermometers. Hair is undeniably a part of the human body, but since it "grows back" such use is acceptable. Blood too regenerates itself. To a certain extent, skin and certain other substances are also renewable, and in fact are already transplanted more or less freely.

If we pursue this line of reasoning, we eventually come to the brain, which controls the activity recognized as the core of human personality. As long as the brain remains healthy, an individual is himself; all other parts of the body are, so to speak, expendable. The brain no longer functions in terminally comatose patients; nor do they display will, thoughts, or feelings. We can regard this as a limiting case, in which only those replaceable parts of the body continue to live. Of course we should respect a person's right to die with dignity, but if there is no chance brain function can be restored (and agreement has been previously expressed), it might be acceptable to use that person's body to generate blood for others. It becomes, in the end, a matter of individual choice.

Boundaries: Life and Death, Man and Machine

I once visited a German hospital where about twenty children suffering from hydrocephalus were being cared for. Hydrocephalus can enlarge the skull to nearly a meter in circumference. The children were all suspended from the ceiling, head down. They could not survive in any other position; if they tried to stand, the weight of their heads would break their necks, and, lying down, their heads might be shaken by some vibration, again causing death. Still, such patients can live for some time if hung by their feet. The hospital was making every effort to keep them alive, in the hope that a miraculous treatment might be discovered that would cure them. The children smiled at me on my visit. Though their skulls were enormously enlarged, the features were normal in size and seemed pulled together in the middle of their faces. But in spite of their smiles I asked myself if these children who, even upside down, would survive a few years at most, were full human beings, and whether or not they were happy. Yet clearly the humanist position is to recognize that every person, no matter how weak, has a right to live and deserves our assistance.

In practice, most people—if asked about this issue—would be in doubt. For example, millions die of starvation in Africa every year. If every Japanese were to donate 10 percent of his annual income to relieving starvation in Africa, all could be saved. But no one actually does this. AIDS provides another example. Some people insist on AIDS patients' rights and say we mustn't discriminate against them, while others maintain they should be quarantined. By defending the rights of the AIDS patient we incur the risk that the fatal disease will spread to others, as the price of the belief that human life has no meaning unless guaranteed to all. As a result, we must admit that AIDS will continue to spread. Compassion is an extremely **expensive** proposition, and an inefficient one at that; but no doubt we shall choose the way of living in symbiosis with the weak and ill, even if it lacks efficiency and contradicts eugenic notions.

Advances in science and technology have blurred the previously clear-cut boundaries between life and death, man and machine—meanwhile, humanity awaits a new ethical agenda. The issue of some sort of symbiosis between mankind and technology, including the complex problems discussed here, becomes ever more pressing as we approach the new century.

An End to Hierarchy and Anthropocentrism

Clearly an issue we must now face is the development of a new way of thinking about life and death, and a corresponding way of living. Industrial society—and, paradoxically, modernism—have placed a higher value on life than ever before in human history. This excessive appreciation of human life is greatly mistaken on two counts.

First, it assigns special value to *human* life at the expense of all other life. Just as, for philosophical idealists, God once represented absolute existence, now humankind has assumed this role. The resultant anthropocentric hierarchy sets human life at the center and all other life on the periphery. As such, it is natural that this attitude has come under attack from the science of ecology. But we cannot return the Earth to the time when life first appeared on the planet. In nature, selection operates, and the weak risk extinction. Yet if our criticism of anthropocentrism is driven by nothing more than an excessive faith in ecology, we fall once more into the trap of dualism.

Humankind cannot live without consuming other living things. My teacher Benkyo Shiio, in his Buddhist teachings of symbiosis, described the human condition, the fact that we must assimilate other organisms to live, as a relationship based on mutuality. The Buddha, human beings, animals, plants, and the stone by the side of the road all exist symbiotically in a vast life cycle, living and giving each other life in symbiosis. Quite simply, human beings consume other life forms as vegetables and meat, fish and rice; and, when we die, we become in turn food for these same plants and animals.

The inorganic stone by the roadside also preserves human life. We should neither regard our life as more important than any other form, nor suggest a return to an ecology of a "pre-human" age. Life and death are only conceivable from the standpoint of *all* forms of life. A lifestyle based on *awareness* that we are kept in life by other life forms is the philosophy of symbiosis, and we must not merely regard these as sources of food and raw material.

Human Existence in the Intermediary Zone

The second common error is to regard man as unique and separate from all other organisms. Careful thought recognizes that human beings are not made up of opposing elements, matter and spirit. Our bodies are populated by a variety of organisms, including different viruses and bacteria—and all sorts of inorganic substances, largely necessary to sustain life. A human being is a symbiotic complex made up of a plurality of living things in dynamic relationship with one another.

In contrast, the modernist view is that we are an unadulterated organism composed of matter and spirit. This abstract model of human life has come to be accepted along with a concept of health-as-progress, or the unending approach to a purer human state. The invasion of any other form of life is called disease and that form is repelled as an enemy, or attacker, by classic Western medicine. To eliminate this invader, a typical Western procedure is surgery—the cutting away of the disease producer and the "invaded" tissue with it.

Recently, other methods of treatment are gaining attention, including holistic medicine, which seeks to encourage the body's natural defenses and to enlist mental and spiritual energies to assist the body. The techniques of traditional Chinese medicine are also being investigated, but the belief that a healthy organism is one from which all foreign bodies and other life forms have been purged is a strong one.

An excessive affirmation of life may reflect an absolute terror of death. In the present age there is greater fear of sickness and death than of war. As Susan Sontag has explained, sickness, especially such incurable sicknesses as cancer and AIDS, has become an unwonted metaphor for death. Fear of it has thrown society into anxiety and people try to avoid the thought of it. To enjoy life, they banish death from their awareness, denying its reality. But from birth we are half-healthy, half-sick. There is no human perfect from birth, who harbors no contamination and never experiences physical weakness. All human beings have some physical imperfection, large or small, and live in symbiosis with other organisms.

Sickness is none other than the collapse of that symbiotic balance—a change leading to death. All humans live in the intermediary zone between full life and the annihilation of death. The future science of medicine will no doubt learn to recognize and accept that intermediary state of symbiotic balance which includes disease organisms. The philosophy of symbiosis offers the acceptance, so to speak, of "a coexistence between life and death."

12

FROM POSTMODERNISM TO SYMBIOSIS

Single-coded Modernism

As I have shown in chapter 4 and elsewhere, the day-to-day usefulness of modernism has reached an end. Modernism sprang from the pursuit of desires fostered by a material civilization, and the technology that made possible such advances has begun to turn against humanity. Environmental pollution, for example, shows us the unfriendly face of technology, and we see that, even should the human race find a way to survive the practical effects of the modernist creed, it would not afford a very desirable existence.

This has led to a reconsideration of the modern period, industrial society, material civilization, and modernism as a complex of aims, and to a search for a new philosophy in harmony with present-day Postmodern issues. The quest for a new art, culture, and society—a new state of knowledge—has become increasingly evident. The French philosopher Jean-François Lyotard,[1] in his *Post-Modern Condition: A Report on Knowledge* (*La condition postmoderne,* 1979) explained the term postmodernism:

> We call the present state of knowledge of our highly advanced society "Post-modern." This term is widely used by American sociologists and critics at present ... for the state of a culture having been transformed by a

sweeping revision of the rules of the game, beginning in the late nineteenth century, in the fields of science, literature, and art.

For architecture, the American critic Charles Jencks had suggested even earlier six defining principles in his *Language of Post-Modern Architecture* (1977). The first of these dealt with an architecture that speaks on at least two levels simultaneously. A sign on the freeway, for example, reading "Exit 5 mi." has only a single signification; it would no longer function if it could be read in different ways. If laws or government documents have more than one reading, they cannot serve their respective purposes. They are designed to have, insofar as possible, only one interpretation, clear to all.

Documents of that sort, unsurprisingly, do not make for interesting reading. This is the nature of what is called a single code. Novels, however, can be read in many different ways, though they are written with words from the same language as single-code documents. The reader uses his imagination to find meanings beyond the literal, enriching the story with his own experience—that is one of the pleasures of fiction. The more room for the reader to participate imaginatively, the richer the literary quality of the work. In semantics, language that can be read in two or more ways is said to be based on a double code. Or, to borrow Jencks's term, we could call such forms "multivalent."

To take another example, an artist who paints in a realist manner but whose work fails to move the spectator might be called at best an inspired sign painter. However, even among realists and superrealists, there are those, such as Andrew Wyeth, who by most are respected as artists—and those who aren't. This is the difference between an artist able to endow his work with a capacity for multivalent reading, and another who cannot.

Silence Transcended

Modern society was above all a single-code society, and Modern architecture was largely an unreadable language of steel, glass, and concrete—that valued convenience and functionality but from which no narrative could be deduced. Its most representative work is,

Lakeshore Drive Apartments by Mies van der Rohe, Chicago (1951)—example of modern "silent" architecture.

arguably, the Lake Shore Drive Apartments in Chicago by Ludwig Mies van der Rohe, completed in 1951. Widely regarded as a masterpiece of modernism, these two high-rise, luxury apartment towers present a *ne plus ultra* of abstraction, a silent architecture abjuring all historical, symbolic, and narrative quality. The only way to read the work is as an icon of modern architecture.

At its founding by Le Corbusier, Mies van der Rohe, and their contemporaries, the modern movement was important as a rebellion against the status quo. The French Académie des Beaux-Arts, for example, concentrated entirely on the teaching of historical styles and dominated the world of architecture. No architect daring to stray from this historicism, much less challenge it, could hope to find employment. The founders of the new movement declared their independence of academic methods and their opposition to all historical styles and decoration.

But the avant-garde role of modern architecture has long since terminated. The *academy* long ago lost its authority to the orthodoxy of modern architecture itself. As a visitor at Sydney University in the summer of 1984, I was warned that postmodernism was taboo in the Department of Architecture—the faculty regarded it as a blight. That is how I realized modern architecture had begun to exercise the same unbending, rigid authority as that of the old Beaux-Arts. I do not totally reject the modern by any means. My own work always makes use of what I regard as the positive aspects of modern architecture. But when I see how rigid this has become, how it has lost all flexibility, I am forced to ally myself with those who attack the weaknesses of the modernist orthodoxy, in both architecture and society.

Modern architecture appeared at a time when abstraction was believed to be more advanced and avant-garde than representational art. Modern architecture was appreciated for its abstraction, just as were the painting and sculpture of the age. There is something to be said for the superiority of abstract art over concrete representation. After all, while other animals can only respond to direct, concrete stimuli, humanity alone can indeed process intellectual abstractions. But the abstraction of modernism is a byproduct obtained through industrialization; it is only accidental. That is why it has ended up as a single-coded—or "silent"—architecture, lacking, as the late neo-Marxist philosopher Louis Althusser put it, an epistemology.

When we walk through the streets of an Italian Renaissance city—Florence, for example—the experience of just strolling along is highly enjoyable. Each building speaks to us, each sculpture engages us in conversation. We can read the streets, just as we read a novel. The city as a whole is a work of literature, and we can browse through it as we walk.

Unfortunately, cities built since the advent of modernism are quite the opposite: they disturb and exhaust us. No tourists flock to Brasilia or Canberra, and young couples don't stroll hand in hand through the bleak banking and business district near the once famous Kasumigaseki Building in central Tokyo. It is in this sense that Jencks offered his first definition of the postmodern as "architecture that 'speaks' to us on at least two levels."

His second definition of postmodernism is a hybrid architecture, mixing historicist themes with contemporary life, and high art with

The Uffizi, Florence, with replica of Michelangelo's *David* in foreground.

popular culture. One example of this process has been the use of elements from the popular cultures of Las Vegas—or Hollywood—to enliven contemporary architecture. To discover the charm and interest even in such paradigms of "bad taste" is one of the strategies of postmodern architecture. Modern architecture scorned Las Vegas as vulgar and, like modern literature and abstract art, made no attempt to hide its elite point of view. Postmodern architecture, however, has set itself the task of destroying the boundary separating high art from popular art.

Thirdly, Jencks sees postmodern architecture as being intentionally schizophrenic. The term schizophrenia, of course, describes the illness in which a person is possessed of two conflicting mental states at the same time, but postmodernism uses it to refer to a healthy person who intentionally behaves in such a way—yet another sort of hybridism.

The fourth Jencksian definition of the postmodern is an architecture possessing a language. In other words, to be read in a multivalent vein, it *must* have an architectural language; while the fifth definition proposes that it is also an architecture "rich in metaphor, new and embracing rather than exclusive." Finally, postmodern architecture is "an architecture that responds to the multiplicity of the city." It must be based on a reading of the plurality of the city's values and its overwhelming complexity.

Value-added Nature of Information Society

I would like now to rework these definitions of the postmodern into my own argument, point by point, in the context of present-day culture. To begin with, the economies of the developed countries have already moved from heavy industry to research-and-development, education, publishing, and broadcasting—the activities of an information society—together with service industries, and the banking and financial sector. This is a major transformation of society from an industrial to a nonindustrial base.

In industrial society, the production of things was paramount; quantity is preferable to quality, and the important thing is to produce goods of standard quality in great quantity at the lowest price possible. But in an information society, the added value attached to goods plays a major role. We see a shift to producing goods that are well designed. Even the old "star" products—automobiles and electrical appliances—must take note of the value-added factor of design, which now accounts for a fair proportion of the cost of the finished product.

Japan was once an important silk-producing nation, specializing in the spinning of silk thread and exporting large quantities of raw silk. Yet it is inconceivable that Japan should be a silk exporter now. Japanese wages have risen to the highest in the world and it is impossible to make a profit by producing raw materials. Now Korea, China, and Taiwan are the raw-silk producers, while Japan designs silk fabrics and sells them to foreign markets. The products of designers such as Issey Miyake[2] and Rei Kawakubo,[3] with the value of their designs added, are sent out into the world.

The cost of the raw materials of a garment designed by Issey

Miyake makes up less than 10 percent of its retail price. With Miyake's value-added design, however, it becomes a high-priced item. The fields of education, publishing, and broadcasting are based, too, not on hard costs but on "soft" costs. The hotel industry is another example: four-star and five-star ratings are determined by such value-added features as quality of service, restaurants, and room decor.

In this evolution of an information society, we look to city planning and architecture for more than mere beauty, strength, and convenience. It is not enough to regard postmodernism as an artistic and literary movement that has influenced architecture and urban planning. The production base of our society is itself changing profoundly, and as we evolve from an industrial to an information society, the defining traits of postmodernism emerge as just a part of this great transformation.

Personalization and Narrative

In the modern age much was made of "humanism," as the slogan of industrial society. Humanism was the dispensation that permitted and excused unchecked development. But in the postmodern age, this concept of an idealized, abstracted humanity must be jettisoned.

What, in truth, does it mean to design with such a notion of humanity in mind? There are no abstract human beings—only men and women, old people, middle-aged people, young people, children—individuals of both sexes and different ages. There are Japanese, Americans, and British—individual citizens of different countries; and if we pursue this line of reasoning to its extreme, there is "person A" and there is "person B."

You can search the world in vain for the abstracted, *average* human being—the "humanity" that has served so long as the subject of modernism—for it is no more than an icon. In this age, however, we must build cities and produce buildings and homes for the actual "person A"—a man, a woman, or an elderly person—for individuals, with their own identities and personalities. This is the task of bringing human beings down from their pedestal of ideal abstraction, returning them to the milieu of private life.

Let us enter a Gothic cathedral: this cathedral is a work of architecture inspired by devotion to God. When we lift our eyes, light pouring through the stained-glass windows falls on our heads. The music of the organ also cascades down on us from above. In that imposing space we sink to our knees in submission, we repent, and we pray that we may draw nearer to God. Such is the medieval paradigm.

Basing itself on the Renaissance, the achievement of modern architecture has been to create a humanist architecture that replaces God with man—a mighty, faceless, ideal image of humanity. Since such architecture is vowed to be an abstraction of humanity, the individual knows no peace or comfort in its superhuman scale but only a crushing alienation.

As the role of government has grown with the rise of a modern industrial society, public spaces in cities have been enlarged in the name of the general welfare. The lobbies and halls of public buildings are enormous spaces with no place for anyone to make himself comfortable. To reach a normal environment, where they can laugh and cry, people have to rush back to their own homes. In other words, the city denies any possibility of private life. But in the postmodern age, architecture and the city will restore private life to its rightful place, in many different forms. For example: narrow streets that one can walk along alone; pocket parks just the right size for a couple to squeeze into, hand in hand; a bench set under a single tree; space with the excitement of a maze; special places, restaurants, or shops that seem to say you are the only one who knows where they are; places that are so frightening you never dare to return; places that come alive at night; a little hidden corner where you can lose yourself in your own thoughts. By incorporating such core images of private life into the city and its public spaces, we will be able to make our cities more complex and interesting.

The reason that the old *shitamachi* area around Asakusa is so interesting—and the crowded, twisted, up-and-down, ever-changing back streets of Harajuku and Akasaka so much fun—is that they have achieved a good combination of public and private living space. In the cities and buildings before modernism, we find a mix of the frightening, fascinating, and reassuring. In old Edo, there were "haunted houses" (*obakeyashiki*) where you could go for a good scare, there were frightening old streets that people used for tests of courage; and night was different from day: a dark, mysterious time when spirits reigned. But modern city planners tear down haunted houses, destroy the mazes, and banish a city of night that might satisfy our curiosity. Now night is inferior to day, little more than a diluted version of it. We need to recapture the symbiosis of cities of day and of night.

Repersonalizing is just this: restoring interest, surprise, and stimulation to our tedious urban environments, so that people can weave their own stories from them. Much is made of the present as an age of private enterprise. But such enterprise has a greater role than simply to reduce the role of government by shifting an increased part of the financial burden onto the private sector. Private enterprise can do much to recreate the fascinating city of "night"—the city of private, novel spaces in contrast to the banal domain of the daylight city.

Ruled by an Invisible Icon

The premodern age was an age of central authority. The presence of the king or ruler (or, in his place, a vast bureaucracy) was always felt at the center—from which all rules, and lines of sight, radiated. In the urban design of the premodern age, and that of the Renaissance in particular, a square or plaza occupied the center with streets radiating out from it. Standing in a square in Rome, or Paris, and looking down one of those streets, we see buildings of equal height neatly lining both sides, extending off into the distance in a dramatic demonstration of the law of perspective. Our lines of sight extend into infinity from the central square, symbol of authority.

If the premodern age was an age of a transcendent code, then the modern is an age liberated from codes. Michel Foucault[4] has proposed Jeremy Bentham's Panopticon as a model for the premodern age. Thus, in the premodern age the instructor always stood at the front of the class, and all his pupils faced him. In the modern age, this authority figure no longer exists, but the pupils still feel his gaze

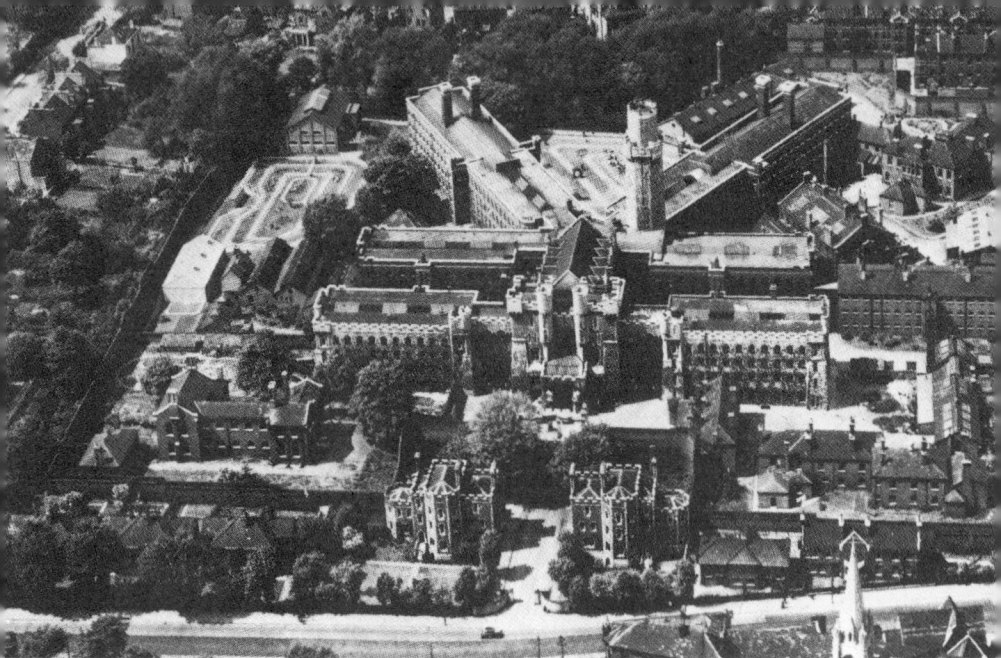

Holloway Prison, London (aerial view) and plan of Pentonville Prison, London (from *The Builder*, 1847), both based plan on Bentham's panopticon model (*Victorian Architecture*, Thames & Hudson, 1985).

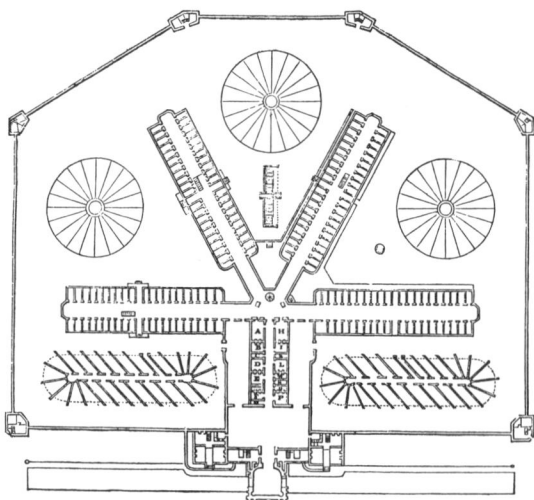

on their backs. The contemporary reality is that—while the authority figure is gone—each of us is ruled by his icon inside ourselves. For example, when driving a car and observing the rules of the road, we may say we do this because the rules exist; but our obedience can also be taken as an example of rule by an invisible authority.

The rule of the icon manifests itself everywhere as self-control and self-discipline. The International Style was an icon of this sort; although an architect who refuses to design according to its modern aesthetic will no longer be punished by society, architects have until recently been possessed by an internal fear of liberating themselves from the obsession that all must design in the International Style.

In the postmodern age the spell of the teacher's gaze on our backs will be broken: following Foucault I call this the age of the "third classroom." In the first classroom, the teacher stands in front. In the second classroom, we feel the teacher looking at us from behind. In the third classroom, there is no teacher, either real or perceived, at front or back. Initially it may seem a confused age, and there are those who seek to restore hierarchy and order. But a new age cannot be forced to bloom through political or moral coercion. In the end, no one will wish to return to an order of the past.

Diachronicity and Synchronicity

When a school of minnows changes direction, the action is not initiated by any chosen leader. Instead, a single fish takes the lead by making the first move, and the rest follow as if sharing a single mind. Seemingly, any fish can act as leader at any moment, yet the school as a whole does not lose its dynamism.

In our leaderless situation the concepts of diachronicity and synchronicity are about to become important. For contemporary architecture cut itself off from the past and set the future far ahead; in spatial issues, all regarded the West as leader and all other cultures as inferior or less advanced. But my own philosophy of architecture is to introduce diachronicity and synchronicity into urban space, thus relativizing notions of space and time.

How are we to conceptualize past, present, and future with regard to architecture? In Giambattista Piranesi's[5] *Imaginary Prisons* (Carceri d'Invenzione, ca.1743), there is neither present nor future; in the *Città Nuova* drawings created around 1914 by Italian Futurist Antonio Sant'Elia,[6] there is no past or present. Modern society is of the present, with no real interest in past or future. That is why modern architecture rejected the history and tradition of the past, along with its symbols and decorative language. At the same time, it rejected

Unité d' Habitation by Le Corbusier, Marseilles
(1952)—an icon of ideal human society.

the future as unknowable: Modernism could only conceive of the future as an extension of present trends.

All that was required was that architecture rationally serve present functions and the demands of our society. Le Corbusier's Unité d'Habitation apartment complex outside Marseilles (1945–52) and Mies van der Rohe's Lake Shore Drive Apartments were both examples of postwar offerings to the icon of an ideal society. Modern architecture conceived of time as a pyramid of three layers: the past a base on which the present stratum rests with the future as pinnacle. In this model, past and future are only articulated in terms of the present. For me, instead, architecture seems a maturation process, metabolizing from past to present and on into the future.

Time is not a linear function, nor does it have the hierarchical structure of a pyramid or a tree. It is an interwoven network, a rhizome. The term "rhizome," as used by Deleuze and Guattari, represents a model in which there is no clear hierarchy, unlike the pyramid or the tree with its trunk and branches. A rhizome never ossifies—it is a series of relationships forever dynamically re-forming and regrouping.

If past, present, and future are conceived of after such a model, we can consider ourselves at an equal distance from all times and freely engage in relationships with any period. No longer do we feel close only to the present, while past and future are distant. This relativity of time is what is meant by diachronicity. Synchronicity, on the other hand, is the relativity of space. Lévi-Strauss demonstrated the mutual relatedness of all cultures and thereby relativized the status of Western culture, which had long been accorded absolute superiority. Structuralism gave the cultures of Western Europe, America, Africa, the Islamic countries, and Asia all equal validity, with each set at an equal distance from the others. In the age of the "third classroom," time and space are relativized in this way. As a result, we are able to weave different ages—past, present, and future—and different cultural values—those, say, of Western Europe, Japan, and Islam—into a single work, or building, so that they exist in symbiosis.

Sacred, Profane—and Pleasure—in the City

A major feature of the postmodern era is the elimination of dualism and binomial hypotheses. The boundaries between such apparent opposites as flesh and spirit, religion and science, artifice and nature, technology and humanity, pure literature and popular literature, seriousness and irony, work and play, and life and death will gradually become fuzzy; from the intermediary space between these pairs of opposing poles new domains of creativity will assert themselves. The postmodern sensitivity will bridge the spiritual and the material, the sacred and the profane. Things seemingly contradictory at first glance will turn out to be compatible, even all of a piece, like the Klein bottle. And from this situation a new set of values will arise.

Roger Caillois,[7] in *Man and the Sacred* (*L'Homme et le sacré*, 1939), proposes the inclusion of a third term in the traditional dualism of sacred and profane: pleasure. The sacred corresponds to the "first classroom" situation where the king, or authority, claiming to be sacred, looks down over the people. The profane corresponds to the "second classroom" and modernism, the age of the masses, of mass production, of an Esperanto-like universality, of Heidegger's[8] *das Mann*—man as an ordinary person. Ordinariness is the value that modernism has lauded, in rejecting variety and difference; its paradigm is metaphorical "domesticity."

Pleasure is the "third classroom," the postmodern age, which resists the separation of sacred from profane. In architecture, for example, the neighborhood police boxes (*koban*) of Japan are designed in a multiplicity of shapes and styles: in brick, with onion turrets, or other curious shapes—the very thought of the familiar policeman glaring out of them is a delightful image. This will help transform the city into a blend of the sacred and the profane—authority and lightheartedness.

In the world of intellect, the New Philosophy broaches difficult concepts with the flippancy of the comic strip, once again blending sacred and profane. Deleuze and Guattari write: "Be the Pink Panther and your loves will be like the wasp and the orchid, the cat and the baboon." In the past, philosophy restricted itself to a rigorous and hermetic language of its own, but here we see the contamination of philosophical investigation by everyday words and images of a mass sensibility, while the authors place themselves at an equal distance from both languages. This, too, is an example of the rhizome; the authority of dualism is already crumbling.

From Association to "Bisociation"

The postmodern age will produce conviviality—another way of expressing Zeami's *hana*—or pleasure, novelty, and enjoyment. Modernism allied itself with a type of purism that elevated function as the highest good while rejecting play, ease, interest, and pleasure as extraneous elements. From the Renaissance to the end of the baroque age, decoration was regarded as an important element in architecture. The rejection of decoration began only with modernism, and this is why it is today a style that can no longer be read. Postmodernism recognizes the value of variety and the worth of hybrid styles, acknowledging that Western values are not the only legitimate ones. An infinity of cultures exists around the globe.

As Western-style rationalism comes to be recognized as just another regional culture, English and French, for example, may be heard as no more than local languages. In the postmodern age, we will be forced to attend to the divergence among cultures worldwide and encourage different cultural identities to live in symbiosis. In architecture, this has already lead to a reappraisal, uniting elements from different cultures in a new hybrid style. Such will no longer be criticized as the product of compromise, "neither fish nor fowl," but seen as a positive expression of multivalent energy. My high regard for the architecture of the late Edo and early Meiji periods—the Tsukiji Hotel and the Mitsuigumi House—is due to their being early instances of this creative, hybrid style.

The concept of the whole is about to implode; part and whole will exist in symbiosis in the age of the postmodern. The modern era was a Hegelian age—an industrial age, in which the concept of the nation and the monolithic scientific-industrial complex was formulated. The post-modern age, instead, will be a utopia after the fashion of Charles Fourier's[9] phalanxes, or cooperative communities. It will be a federative and cooperative world in which small groups take the initiative. Arthur Koestler calls this a move away from "association," with its nuance of rough and ready competition among groups barely cognizant of their mutual differences, to "*bisociation*," a more delicately balanced relationship that consciously tolerates a certain degree of mutual opposition.

SOHO Society

Koestler remarks: "The essence of creativity is to be found in the integration, on a new plane, of two previously unrelated structures of consciousness." Association entails a relation between two parties with some connection to each other, but bisociation is the collision of two completely unconnected entities. Naturally, tension, resistance, and a tremendous stimulus result, in which Koestler discerns a new creative spirit. Koestler designated the Janus-like relationship between part and whole with the acronym SOHO, meaning "self-regulating open hierarchic order." The nineteenth-century trend toward specialization prefigures Koestler's thought in its concern with the part. But the notion of feedback inherent in a "self-regulating" component is quite distinct from that earlier line of thought. The shared observation-and-management style of the "third classroom" can be identified in this self-regulation, which, indeed, has led me to dub my own notion of a society based on shared-management goals "a SOHO society."

In short, the postmodern world will be one where equal value is accorded the whole and the individual—industry and the worker. It will be a society of the type rejected by modernism, and thus to some extent inefficient. According to modernist logic, in order to maximize its efficiency society must be both unified and organized. Thus, whatever ideals may have been professed hitherto, and however much capitalist societies claim to value the individual, in reality the trend has been to cede priority to the whole. The significant challenge of postmodernism will be whether it can achieve a society of symbiosis in which the part, or the individual, is valued as greatly as the whole.

My own holistic approach in architecture, as outlined, is to design details, such as door handles, at the same time I am producing sketches for the whole building. I thus design both part and whole simultaneously. By contrast, most architects first settle on the overall configuration of the work and then proceed to think about the shape and dimensions of the rooms, while door handles are barely even considered.

In conventional city planning, too, roads, parks, public spaces, and other major facilities are first decided on, and somewhere toward the end of the process attention is given to the houses meant to line the roads. That, however, is misguided. We cannot create new cities unless we consider the city and its houses together, according them equal value. True creativity flows from conceiving part and whole together.

Toward an "Exchange of Symbols"

The materialism of the modern age valued things in terms of their function and utility; parts of things without any apparent function were rated frivolous. I do not reject the principle of function per se, nor will it be rejected in the post-modern era, because functionalism was never limited to modernism. Edward Robert de Zurko,[10] in his book *Origins of Functionalist Theory* (1957), traces it to Aristotle and the Augustan architect/engineer Vitruvius, on through Saint Augustine in the fourth century, Saint Thomas Aquinas in the medieval period, and the Renaissance architects Leon Battista Alberti,[11] Leonardo da Vinci, and Andrea Palladio.[12] Functionalism has been advocated by such Enlightenment figures as Claude-Nicolas Ledoux,[13] Lessing,[14] Goethe, and Schinkel,[15] and later on Horatio Greenough[16] and Louis Sullivan.[17] From there the baton was picked up by Modern architecture, and it will just as surely be passed to the postmodernists.

The essence of the problem is not functionalism, but rather that one-sided overdependence on the intellect underlying Western culture. Intellect is valued far above emotion; rationality, the essence and ultimate form of humanity. Rationalism has played a decisive role in industrial society, but it has also led us to disdain and devalue the importance of consciousness, spiritual phenomena, and emotion. In the postmodern age, the material and the mental, the functional and the emotional, the beautiful and the terrifying, analysis and synthesis will have to exist in symbiosis.

Jean Baudrillard[18] has used the bold term "death of the economy" to describe the new age, which will be an age of the exchange of symbols. In any mass consumer society great quantities of goods and currency are exchanged: manufactured products are bought and discarded in a spiraling cycle. In an information society it is not goods but symbols, information, and signs which are consumed. Baudrillard, in his *Symbolic Exchange and Death* (*L'échange symbolique et la mort*, 1976) offers a radical criticism of this ideology of production. In modern society, goods and the economics of production have, through long association, become indistinguishable. He suggests that we are moving away from an age of the accumulation of value-and-meaning to an age of *la poétique*, in which all excess is pared away in an "exchange of symbols." Poetry can be thought of as the creation of evanescence, and the contemporary age is one in which an aura is created from signs that possess no particular meaning. A piano that has never been used, a clock that does not tell the time, a chair that can't be sat on, weapons that cannot be fired—our lives are filled with these artifacts of symbolic exchange, or what Baudrillard calls *simulacres*.

Simulacre as Symbiosis of Sanity and Madness

This "age of symbolic exchange" will effect great changes in human relationships. Even among friends, information that someone possesses but is not available through the mass media, will be extremely valuable. In search of new information, people will form and dissolve relationships, or join special interest groups. A person bearing a wonderful tale yesterday will be dismissed out of hand if he tries it on you again today: his information will have already been consumed and is valueless. Compared to the lukewarm relationships of the modern age, the pleasures, stimulation, and joys of life will be intense. But, each of us will need his own gyroscope to seek out an independent lifestyle. In that sense, it will also be a most challenging time. Each person will have to select his own information. Instead of an easygoing, hedonistic mass society, great demands will be exercised on our powers of discrimination. On television, news shows, debates, and other "hard" programming will proliferate.

The key word in the age of symbolic exchange will be *simulacre*. According to Baudrillard, "A *simulacre* is a construct of atmosphere, or a system delineated out of the extraordinary." The film director Yoshimitsu Morita has made a film titled *No Yo na Mono* (Something Like It)—whose title precisely defines *simulacre*. In another of Morita's films, *Kazuko Geemu* (Family Game), the family automobile acts as a *simulacre*. Whenever a problem arises, the hero, with a wink, calls his wife or the son's tutor out to the car in its underground parking garage to have a talk. His car is not something to drive; he uses it as a private room—a reflection of Japan's housing crunch. The hero also uses the automobile as a space he can control, where he is able to regain intimacy and take the initiative in his life. Here the car has already been transformed from a vehicle into "something like a car."

Consider the sale at a tremendously high price of a Rolls-Royce that once belonged to the Beatles. It was precisely because it carried the cultural cachet of having been their possession, not because of its functional value, that it sold for an enormous figure.

In the future we will live in a world surrounded by *simulacres*: "things like" other things. The Japanese have a long tradition of appreciating objects for their background and context, as well as their function. This is their sensitivity to *ki*, or auralike energy. The Chinese character *ki* (also pronounced *ke*) appears in words such as *kehai* (presence or seeming), *fun'iki* (mood), and *kibun* (feeling or condition). It refers to a cultural value attached to, arising from, or surrounding an object. *Ki* is also used to point to the irrational, the religious, the transcendent. Through the notion of *ki*, a corridor is opened linking a symbiosis of function and aura—material and spiritual concerns—with the symbiosis of sanity and madness, science and religion.

La Poétique: Deconstruction Beyond Meaning

The theory of symbolic exchange is linked with the linguist Ferdinand de Saussure's[19] theory of *la poétique*, the symbolic function of language which he revealed by using anagrams to decipher poetry. According to Baudrillard, "*La poétique* is a symbolic exchange from which, ultimately, nothing is left over, a reverberating interplay of structural elements." Language reverberates within the bounds of the poem or of poetic form in general, and then perishes of its own accord. Whereas the role of literature and philosophy is to point to a subject, such as a transcendent God, and make "meaningful" statements about it, in poetry, such meaning is completely extinguished.

Let us try to situate this concept with regard to architecture. Creation of unequivocal meaning becomes the task of a certain type of design project, one with a strong, clear "narrative" quality. Examples are frequently met with in the former socialist countries in those one-dimensional, aggressive attempts to consecrate a whole city district to a mythologized Lenin, with symbolic statues and streets named for heroes of the revolution. But this monumentality is already a thing of the past.

Though I have specified how our living environments, including cities and architecture, entail a narrative, with many and diverse readings, I nonetheless believe that this "novel," when deconstructed, ought to be akin to a poem that expresses, finally, nothing. As Baudrillard writes, "*La poétique* as the exchange of symbols brings into play a meticulously limited vocabulary. The goal is to totally exhaust these signs."

Fuzzy Logic: The Science of Ambiguity

In the modern age, vagueness and the "irrational" were either rejected or forced into a dualistic mold. We were continually faced with a choice between exterior and interior, public and private, eternity and the moment, good and evil. But at last the truly ambiguous nature of human existence is reemerging.

We now know that the human brain, especially the frontal lobe, is more creative than analytical—with a high tolerance of ambiguity. The more we learn about ourselves, the more we discover humankind to be an ambiguous form of existence that, in many respects, confounds analysis.

Modernism was greatly mistaken in assigning this ambiguity to the notion that science is not yet sufficiently advanced to solve all mysteries. Human beings are not made solely of components intended to be taken apart and analyzed. Ambiguity is also essential to human makeup. Shuhei Aida,[20] a professor at Denki Tsushin College in Tokyo, comments on this from an engineering perspective in his book *Aimai kara no Hasso* (Thinking from Ambiguity):

> The dictum "I think, therefore I am" is famous as a philosophical expression of human essence. The wellspring of the "ambiguity" of human beings is thought, which depends upon the activity of the brain. The brain is a miracle of nature, constituted of a tremendous number of cell groups, yielding a mass of tissue able to perform infinitely various functions. The brain processes not only physical stimuli such as sound, light, and heat but feeling and emotion as well. It exercises a subtle

control over our emotive and physical makeup. The brain's information processing and transmission of instructions are carried out by electric impulses. Therefore, when "I" think, impulses within the brain flash different patterns, are directed in a certain order, and take shape as thoughts and images.

In each person's brain is an independent environment: a language, props, and a stage, as it were, and every day a grand drama unfolds there, directed by thought and intellect. The body is not only a tool or device for implementing one's thoughts and will, for it is also that which makes the self possible. Here lies the special character of the human being as union of brain and body, where "ambiguous" engineering originates.

Lotti Asker Zadeh, of the Department of Electrical Engineering at the University of California, has for some time now advocated what he calls "fuzzy logic." If we think about it, the language, colors, forms, and sounds that surround us all signal ambiguous information. There is room for judging, interpreting, and understanding all these data, and in the residual margin of ambiguity we somehow reach agreement. This is of course why words can mislead—or various colors and shapes convey different images to different subjects. Traditional engineering tried to eliminate this margin of ambiguity. Fuzzy logic, however, attempts to harness ambiguous information for engineering purposes. Its advocates seek, for example, to build a fuzzy computer and software that can steer an automobile by remote control.

This ambiguity, the intermediary zone that cannot be explained by dualistic logic, is an essential element in the postmodern age of symbiosis. We find a new image of humanity in the "moratorium human-being," a concept articulated by Keigo Okonogi of Keio University Medical School in his *Moratoriamu Ningen no Jidai* (The Age of Moratorium Man). This moratorium person is one who remains uncommitted, so to say, unfinished, with no rigid self-definition or social role—a human being as potential, an ambiguous human-being-in-waiting.

Nonlinear, the Fractal, and "Implicated Order"

Ambiguity has nowadays achieved major status as a theme in both science and philosophy. In his book *The New Scientific Spirit* (1934), Gaston Bachelard[21] had already focused on such qualities:

> If the modern age sought an all-encompassing truth, the new age will seek relative truths. If the modern age was the age of Euclid, the new age will be one that merges the Euclidian and non-Euclidian. If the modern age was one of rejection or contradiction, the new age shall combine rejection and contradiction. In mathematics, the present Euclidian realm will be pushed into a non-Euclidian realm. In physics, if the modern age is a Newtonian realm, the new age will be non-Newtonian. In science, if the modern age is that of Lavoisier, we shall witness a move toward a non-Lavoisieran science. In logic, if the modern age spans Aristotle through Kant, the new age will be non-Aristotelian and non-Kantian. And, in contrast to the age of Modernism, in the age that awaits us all these negations will encompass and embrace their opposites—in other words, the ideas and beliefs of their predecessors.

Up to now, progress and revolution in Europe have occurred through rejection of the status quo, an about-face reversal; but Bachelard announced the new age to be one in which the status quo would be at once rejected and embraced, a time of symbiosis of old and new. This Bachelard called the new "science of negation."

From that perspective, Japan's Meiji Restoration may come in for reevaluation. Though at one time pronounced ambiguous and incomplete in comparison with Western-style revolutions, it did not reject all tradition but sought to carry tradition into a new realm. This Japanese aptitude for continual revision and gradual reform is well adapted to Bachelard's new age.

In mathematics, Benoît Mandelbrot's fractal geometry[22] and non-linear analytic geometry are supplanting the Bourbakian axiomatic mathematics and the older Newtonian world view. Nonlinear analytic geometry served to explain phenomena such as wind currents and tornadoes, previously regarded as nonmathematical and without structure. Fractal geometry, now, treats the "nested structures" found in nature, revealing chaos within order and order within chaos. Ilya Prigogine's dispersal theory and Hermann Haken's synergetics are able to describe states of chaos where order and anti-order exist together.

Traditional science was limited to simple phenomena possessing a clear order, ignoring the disordered and chaotic. Post-modern science will study order *and* disorder, pursuing the relations between them. In a return to a Leibnitzian view of the world, the previously ignored realm of disorder will live in symbiosis with order in each branch of learning, thanks to the new realm of chaos theory. Leibnitz declared that the whole exists in the part, a view that has much in common with Koestler's Holon formulation.

As a postmodern science with its notions of ambiguity advances and develops, Christian civilization will receive a great shock. Christianity taught that nature and man are both creations of God, but for postmodern science, each of us possesses within ourselves the power to recreate nature. This would appear to herald the irrevocable death of God. Postmodern science, then, is approaching the Buddhist teaching that all organic and inorganic existence is inhabited by Buddha nature.

Following his encounter with the Indian philosopher Krishna murti,[23] the logician and physicist David Bohm began to develop a unique new version of physics. For Bohm every part of the natural world contains an "implicated order" embracing all aspects of existence. He quotes Spinoza's remark that "Mind is incorporated in matter, and in that sense matter is all-embracing. Matter is an extension of God." Bohm goes on to say:

> In classical physics, matter is regarded as exclusively material, a mechanical form of existence. There was no room for mind, feeling, or soul in this model. But in the new physics, there can be no true separation between inhabitants of the same zone. The mind is born from matter.

From this revolutionary new position, Bohm, for instance, advocates holistic medicine.[24] Conventional medicine has treated the body as if it were only matter, but our spiritual and physical functions are interrelated. In Japan, our word for sickness is "afflicted energy" (*byoki*); traditional Oriental medicine has long regarded mind and body as a unit in an ancient tradition of holism.

In this chapter, we have examined several defining characteristics of postmodernism understood as a new current transcending modernism. To sum these up, I propose to accept the postmodern phenomenon in its entirety as a manifestation of the philosophy of symbiosis.

13

TOWARD THE EVOCATION OF MEANING THROUGH SYMBIOSIS

The Name of the Rose

The title of Umberto Eco's powerful novel is taken from a hexameter composed in Latin by a twelfth-century Benedictine scholarmonk, quoted at the end of the book: *"Stat rosa pristina nomine / Nomina nuda terminus"* (The name of the rose is given by God; our roses are roses without names). This is Eco's contemporary, semiological challenge to the greatest philosophical controversy of the Middle Ages, the debate concerning the existence of universal natures. The work is set in a northern Italian monastery in the fourteenth century. A Franciscan monk, William of Baskerville, arrives there with his pupil, Adso, to investigate a strange series of murders that has occurred. As the two make their inquiries, they learn that hidden in the monastery library there is a labyrinth, where the second, lost half of Aristotle's *Poetics* is kept. Aristotle's work is said to teach that laughter is the remedy that prevents our becoming slaves to universal truth. This is a powerful rebuttal of the doctrine that universal natures do exist—as well as Plato's doctrine of ideas and the Scholastic philosophy that was the handmaiden of medieval theology.

The meaning of *catholic* is, of course, *universal*. The Catholic Church is not simply a congregation of believers but itself a universal and, therefore, sovereign institution that exists prior to, and beyond, its members. And without this abstract notion, the concepts of original sin, as well as salvation through Christ, are inconceivable.

The English Scholastic philosopher William of Ockham, on the other hand, proposed that universals exist only as terms—signs that stand for and refer to individual existences. Eco's name for his leading character, William of Baskerville, is a pastiche of William of Ockham and the Baskervilles of the famous Sherlock Holmes tale. Here we can discern the hand of Eco the semiologist, with his conviction that "meaning" is nothing but words (or signs) evoking further words (more signs), and that interpretations merely generate interpretations. In addition, Eco sprinkles his novel with references to Thomas Aquinas,[1] Roger Bacon,[2] Meister Eckhart,[3] and Sir Arthur Conan Doyle,[4] as well as citations from or references to ecclesiastical architecture, philosophy, politics, alchemy, and many other fields of art and learning.

A look at the layout of the monastery depicted in the novel reminds us that the church, though set in the midst of the complex, is not the center of the novel's action. The main events take place in the *aedificium*, a large castlelike structure located on the periphery. The scriptorium, where the story reaches its climax, is also at the periphery, in the heart of the library housing the second volume of

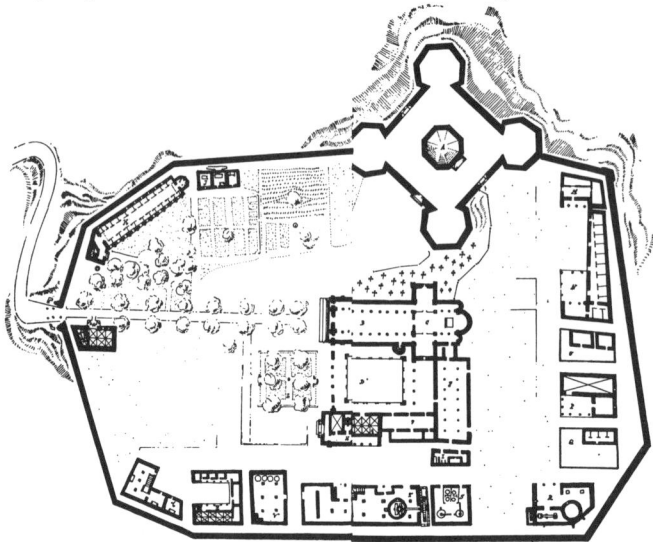

Layout of the monastery in *The Name of the Rose* by Umberto Eco.

Aristotle's *Poetics*. It is an octagonal, twelve-story tower with sixty flights of steps joined in labyrinthine fashion. The stairs lead to a wall with a secret door in it, disguised as a distorted, fairground-type mirror and moved by a hidden spring mechanism. The number eight of the octagonal labyrinth representing the universe is a multivalent symbol: it refers to the eighth day after the universe had been created; to the final day of judgment; and also to the stages in the sequential development of Eco's plot.

I begin this chapter with Eco's *Name of the Rose*, since it masterfully evokes the most pressing contemporary issues, not just in literature, but also those common to philosophy, architecture, art, and technology. The world depicted in this novel is the world to come—whether we call it postmodern, "modern-next," or whatever.

Epistemology and Meta-statement

From Greek and Roman times to the modern period, architects have tried to answer the question "What is architecture?" The epistemological quest for knowledge of being and the nature of existence has formed the central issue of Western metaphysics from the time of Aristotle, through Plato, Descartes, Hegel, and the thinkers of the modern age. This presupposes a single, "true" notion of existence that can be described in terms of *logos*, or reason. By the same token, what might be called the epistemology of architecture has presupposed a single universal "architecture," logically comprehensible to people of every nationality and culture. So, too, does the epistemology of modern architecture posit an ideal image—the International Style, a "universal" transcending all differences in culture.

What system of values produced this universalization? Clearly, that of industrial society, based on the pursuit of material comfort; more broadly, the values of Western man. Here we have something similar to the invention of Esperanto. However, do we not—as already discussed—enjoy a more richly creative world when Arthur Miller writes in English, Dostoyevsky in Russian, and Yukio Mishima in Japanese? Then, via translation and interpretation, we are moved by our readings of different cultures.

Yet the notion of the universal persists. The Cartesian linguist

Noam Chomsky postulates "deep structure," or universal grammar, beneath the surface of the various world languages. Some theorists go so far as to hypothesize an analogous meta-level structure common to the heterogeneous cultures of the world, whence a single, unified notion of existence can be extracted. But this metalinguistic theory of culture is restricted to the context of modernism, and has been fiercely attacked by postmodernists.

For example, J.-M. Benoît in *La révolution structurale* (1975) criticized Chomsky: "... the concept of a universal grammar is nothing but the extreme generalization of a particular notion specific to Western culture. This concept is challenged by our experience of the relativity of all cultures." The Cartesian definition of substance demands that reality be reduced to an unchanging unit, which is the very reason why Chomsky, with his theory of deep structure as a universal grammar, calls himself a Cartesian linguist.

Such transcendent meta-theories, like the notion of architecture with a capital "A," have for some time been a target of postmodern criticism. Lyotard, in his *La condition postmoderne* (1979), has remarked:

> As long as science refuses to limit itself to expression of a simple functional regularity and aims to pursue truth, it must legitimize its own rules of operation. In other words, a statement that legitimizes the status of science is required, and that statement goes by the name of philosophy. When such meta-statement is based forthrightly on some grand scheme—dialectic of mind, decipherment of meaning, rational man, or the liberation of the proletariat and creation of wealth—as a way of legitimizing itself, we call the results based on those schemes or stories "modern." At the risk of greatly oversimplifying the matter, postmodernism amounts, first and foremost, to the distrust of all such meta-schema.

If we can say once again, by analogy, that modern architecture has posited a universal icon based on Western culture, we may call this a meta-statement, on the order of architecture with a capital "A."

Tokyo Tradition: Toward an Ontology

Culture and tradition are scarcely confined to what is tangible. Lifestyle, customs, aesthetic sensibilities, and ideas are indivisible aspects of a broader culture and tradition. Japanese culture, in particular, lays a special emphasis on mental, spiritual, and aesthetic sensibilities, far more than on physical objects and forms. Thus, even Tokyo itself seems at first a modern metropolis without nationality; but actually the city contains pronounced Japanese characteristics and elements.

For me, an architecture based on the philosophy of symbiosis must first be rooted in one's own history and culture, then endeavor to incorporate themes from other cultures. Since no single, universal architectural iconography is known, architects must first of all express their own culture. At the same time, they must meet other cultures head on, engage in dialogue, and, through symbiosis, create a new architecture at once local and global.

The history of modernism in the West reflects the control and manipulation of nature by *logos*. The modern city was created by suppressing nature; and modernization meant that such cities as had expanded naturally had to be replanned. Architecture, too, was seen as a way of asserting human rationality, the means of subjugating a nature considered exterior to human existence. Modern man is a being whose interior nature—his spontaneity and sensitivity—is sacrificed to reason. Thus, reason, science, technology, and economics outweigh culture, art, literature, and thought. To challenge modernism is to attack Western rationalism as a whole, and postmodern architecture has yet to achieve this essential conquest of Western dominance.

The essential transformation of the postmodern age has been heralded as a change from epistemology to ontology. In his *Sein und Zeit* (1927), Martin Heidegger wrote, "The epistemological question has been whether we can properly describe being. In contrast, ontology asks what the nature of existence is." While the question "What is architecture?" was epistemological, in seeking to distinguish a universal and ideal image, ontology poses the question "What is the meaning of architecture?" Ontology is linked to semantics; neither seeks out a single, "true" order in the form of, say, the International

Facades of typical *machiya* houses in Kyoto contributed to design of Kurokawa's Saitama Prefectural Museum of Modern Art, Urawa (1982).

Bracketing of five-story pagoda at Kairyuoji temple, Nara (eighth century). National Treasure. This detail influenced interior of Kurokawa's Kojimachi Wacoal Building (1984, left).

Karamon gate at Tokugenji temple, Yurakuen (left), and detail of National Bunraku Theater, Osaka (1983–94), by Kisho Kurokawa.

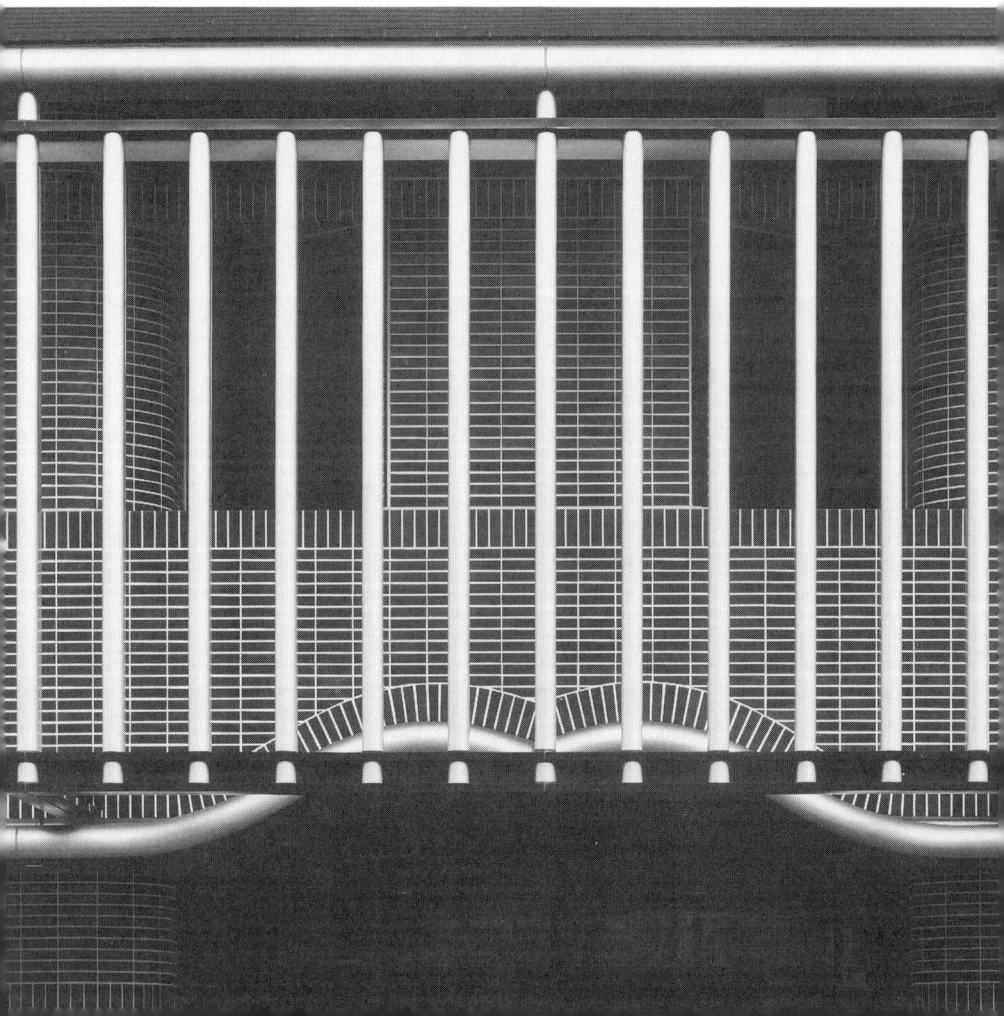

Style, but rather the evocation of *meaning* through architecture. Such disciplines, far from positing a single, ideal image of a truth transcending time, see the very differences that arise in the unfolding of time and history as able to produce meaning.

"Noise" and Multivalence in the Postmodern City

It is easy to predict how postmodern architecture might evolve as an architecture of minor, heterogeneous cultures or an architecture of deconstruction, seeking to reintroduce "noise"—one that sets itself off-center. In this sense, the postmodern is often an architecture of *mélange*, with tendencies toward hybridization—but opposed to any simple mix of historical styles. Rather, it is a conglomeration of many different value systems. As the ontological question suggests, architecture that embraces heterogeneous elements will allow for the evocation of a wide range of meanings. The collision of different cultures and their blending as "noise" will create a new culture.

Eco's *Name of the Rose* is rich in quotation, metaphor, and sign. But who would call this bestselling novel a hybrid pastiche, lacking imagination? All its materials are extracted from the culture, religion, and philosophy of the Middle Ages. For Eco, medieval Europe served as a *pre-text* to transcend modernism. Indeed, our methods are similar, as I have chosen Japan's Edo period as my own *pre-text*. My own reason for focusing on Edo-period culture is that Edo was the largest city in the world, and produced a popular culture whose unique character prefigures my philosophy of symbiosis. At any rate, the decision of which historical signs to quote and how to incorporate them is for any artist the creative process itself. This is the fundamental difference between imitation and hybridization.

Modern architecture regarded the abstract purity of steel, glass, and concrete as universals; quotation and symbiosis of heterogeneous elements were rejected as impure. Today, however, few would deny that a city in which historical buildings are preserved and exist alongside contemporary works of architecture in symbiosis is preferable to the abstract, utopic cities of Le Corbusier or Oscar Niemeyer. We can no longer dismiss this postmodern city in which history and the future exist in symbiosis as hybrid. Nor, however, can we assume

Hokusai's *Great Wave Off Kanagawa* (woodblock print, Edo period).

that all ten million readers of Eco's *Name of the Rose* comprehended each of the author's quotations, references, and clues, for there are numerous ways of understanding such a work. This multivalence and ambiguity are destined to replace the universal in all fields and contexts; such is the essence of the new age, in which we shall vanquish and transcend the logocentrism of modernism.

Exclusion of the Heterogeneous

We have noted how modern architecture, as an epistemology, is deeply rooted in Western dominance and *logos*. In order to move on to postmodern architecture, which poses ontological and semantic demands in an attempt to recreate meaning, how shall we transform our methods of architectural design? The basis of modern design was an ideal image (an "order" of sorts), singular and universal, known as the International Style. It was articulated by analysis, structure, and organization, always pursued in accordance with the principles of logic. The results were expressed in terms of a universal synthesis that triumphed over intuition. Heterogeneous elements were excluded from this design process; connection, clarification, and denotation were paramount.

Glass wall of Saitama Prefectural ▶
Museum of Modern Art, Urawa
(1982), by Kisho Kurokawa.

Further detail of Kurokawa's Saitama Museum of 1982, suggesting "Edo as pre-text."

Yet, we have also seen how dualism and mutual opposition are inherent in Western metaphysics and *logos*: reason and sensitivity, body and spirit, necessity and freedom. In the history of architecture as well, the opposition of reason and sensitivity manifests itself in a pendulum phenomenon. The industrial revolution was followed by the Arts and Crafts Movement, succeeded in turn by Art Nouveau and *Jugendstil*. In their wake came the Rationalism of Peter Behrens and Tony Garnier; and, on the heels of expressionism and futurism, modern architecture emerged under the banner of functionalism. This pattern of action and reaction has had more than one unfortunate effect.

In a modern architecture dominated by reason, revolts of sensitivity by such architects as Alvar Aalto, Frank Lloyd Wright, Hans Scharoun, Paolo Soleri, and Bruce Goff have been regarded as exceptional. Such men are declared geniuses and thereby excluded from the mainstream. Yet their revolt of spontaneity and sensitivity against the rule of reason is also a feature of the modern age. With the advent of a new age, these heroic advocates of sensitivity and spontaneity are unlikely to be credited with a role in modernism's defeat.

Order, the only *a priori* criterion of the "correct" in architecture, is now unnecessary: *Relativity* by M. C. Escher, 1981 (© 1997 Cordon Art-Baan-Holland. All rights reserved), and interior of Kurokawa's Roppongi Prince Hotel, Tokyo (1984).

Will=Text: Meaning Replaces Syntheses

My own ambition as an architect, as I have repeatedly said, is to overthrow Western dominance and logos. My aims are linked with expressions of will in a battle line drawn across a variety of fronts—in literature, philosophy, art, and other areas. The philosophy of symbiosis is the present expression of my will, previously articulated as Metabolism and "metamorphosis," and it enables me to pursue an architecture of meaning. The philosophy of symbiosis is not another metaphysics; I believe it is more accurate to see it as the *text* of a movement.

An architect's text, or philosophy, is rooted in that person's biography and culture. The architects of the modern age sought internationalism—a universal transcendence of their own personalities and regional characteristics. Postmodern architects, on the other hand, must set out to express different wills, deriving from their own history and culture. A keen sensitivity to differences in history, period, and culture will allow meaning to reemerge.

Whereas the ultimate goal of modern architecture was to achieve a synthesis, postmodern architecture will invoke meaning. As concerns methodology, symbolization will replace analysis, deconstruction will supplant structure, relativity will replace organization, quotation will override the logic of forms. Mediation will displace synthesis; transformation, adaptation; nuance, clarification; and connotation, denotation. At the same time, we can expect both reason and intuition to prevail. The effectiveness of symbolization, deconstruction, relativity, quotation, mediation, transformation, nuance, and connotation as techniques will, however, depend greatly on a keen sensitivity to differences among ages, cultures, and other elements.

The philosophy of symbiosis is a *text* for the deconstruction of metaphysics, *logos*, and Western dominance. It arose out of the Indian Buddhist philosophy of Consciousness-Only and Japanese Mahayana Buddhism. In other words, this expression of my will is jointly rooted in my personal identity and in Japanese culture. I do not look at tradition as restricted to the transmission of tangible artifacts; it also transmits such intangibles as lifestyles, customs, thought, and aesthetic sensibility. While we can certainly instill a sense of Japanese culture into contemporary architectural expression using high-tech materials, it is equally possible to insinuate very traditional Japanese modes of awareness, including absence of a center, open-endedness, asymmetry, the expression of *sukiya* or other detail, and disjunction.

Such aspects of Japanese aesthetics appear as a certain sense of balance, that is *not* in the form of a system but rather as separate elements. We might also refer more vaguely to aura, mood, or feeling. The essence of Japanese sensibility is described in the philosophy of symbiosis—a text emphasizing both the special nature of Japanese culture and the overthrow of the modernist paradigm. Mood, feeling, and atmosphere amount to a symbolic order without established structure.

Meaning Brought into Being by Relationships

It is through a spectrum of dynamic, intersecting relationships, and juxtapositions—the link between a single sign and its referent; the way the content of the sign changes when quoted; the existence of a mediating space between different elements; the relation of parts to a whole—that mood, feeling, and atmosphere are created. In architecture, the meaning produced by the individual elements of the design, and by their relationships and disjunctions, should be multivalent and ambiguous. When meaning creates such a feeling or atmosphere, architecture may be said to approach poetic creation.

To regard architecture as no more than actual space, a stacking up of bricks one atop the other, is to accept the old models of the pyramid and the tree. The alternative is to consider all elements of architecture as signs, among which new meanings and atmospheres are constantly being created. When each element of the completed work of architecture—pillars, ceilings, walls, stairways, window, skylights, rooms, entrances, open spaces, furniture, lighting, door handles, the treatment of walls—is readable as quotation, transformation, nuance, connotation, symbolization, and mediation, then the solid, substantial structure, or stack of bricks, is already deconstructed. Another way to characterize the discovery of meaning in the inter-

Details of Japanese *torii* at Itsukushima Shrine, Hiroshima Prefecture (above), and Nagoya Municipal Museum of Modern Art (1987, facing) by Kisho Kurokawa—the Japanese aesthetic of *ma* (interval).

mediary space between elements is to say that we extract meaning by setting elements in relation to each other. Pillar and wall, which hitherto have only had meaning as structural elements, can be *de*constructed to allow for an independent symbolic existence.

The four bamboo poles temporarily set up at the Shinto-style ground-breaking ceremony observed in Japan before commencing any construction job have this nonmaterial connotation. Their physical nature as bamboo poles disappears in connoting the symbolic aura of the place for the descent of the gods. In his work *Le Système des Objets* (1978), Baudrillard wrote of enclosed space:

> Space, too, has a fictional connotation. All forms are relativized as they pass through space. A spacious room has a natural effect. It breathes. When there is a lack of space, the atmosphere is destroyed because our breath is robbed by the things crowded into it. Perhaps we should read a reflection of the moral principles of separation and division in this distribution of space. This would be a reversal of the traditional connotation of space as a plenary, existing substance.

◄ The generation of meaning transcends past, present, and future: sunken garden at Nagoya Municipal Museum of Modern Art (1987) by Kisho Kurokawa.

The space referred to is the vacant space between objects, called in Japanese *ma*, or "in-between space." It is wholly natural in the sense of being outside existence, hence savage and pulsating. Unlike a pile of bricks, it does not have the connotation of solidity or actuality, but of emptiness or nothingness.

Atmosphere is evoked via the grid of relationships that link thing to thing. Baudrillard's theory of architecture brilliantly stands the epistemology of modern architecture on its head, transforming it as an ontology. If the pyramid and the tree are paradigms of modernist hierarchy, the models of postmodern order are the semilattice structure and, especially, the rhizome of Deleuze and Guattari. The rhizome represents the principle of union and difference—a manifold in which relations may be established at any number of points. It is completely different from the tree, that model of a unidirectional, frozen hierarchy. The concept of the semilattice resembles the rhizome's multiplicity. It, too, is an open-ended order in which diverse points continually evoke meaning in their relations. Julia Kristeva[5] describes this type of ontological relationship as a *"polylogue"*—that condition in which "many different logics, many different selves, exist in different places and at different times." It is "an active, parallel order of things that arise in the process of evoking meaning."

Most significantly, the evocation of meaning is never realized via an established hierarchy, but is an active state brought into being by relationships.

Building for an Information Society

Our present information society transcends economic and technological evolutionary stages, as well as differences of ideology, enabling the entire world to move forward at the same time. Information-related industries include: multimedia broadcasting, publishing, finance, research, education, tourism, design, fashion, trade, transport, and food, as well as leisure and service sectors. What these industries have in common is their independence of any production or assembly process—instead, they generate information, added value, and culture itself.

While industrial society aimed at universality and homogeneity, information society will increasingly seek multiplicity. Universal, homogenized data offers reduced value; in order to establish their own identities, people will wish to distinguish themselves from others. In this manner society and culture will tend toward an infinite diversity; nor will architecture prove an exception. The differentiation, or the "differencing," of architecture will be achieved in the evocation of new and various meanings.

It would be mistaken to regard the postmodern as merely chaotic and transitional, since new meanings *are* the manifestation of the architecture of the information age. Differences will be nurtured by concern for relationships, or by Heidegger's "care" (*Sorge*), requiring a keen sensitivity as prerequisite. The information society is fostering transglobal relationships in real time through travel and communication. Different languages and cultures are brought directly to our homes via television and other media, furnishing possibilities of multivalent meaning unthinkable in the age of Western dominance.

In Search of Pluralism

Roland Barthes, in his *Mythologies* (1957), referred to all this as the "age of the power of meaning." Since information society evokes meaning through differences, we will see a shift from the hard "syndigmatic" linear thinking of modernism in a style of denotation to softer "paradigmatic" nonlinear thinking as connotation. Barthes saw such a move toward connotation as a mythological function. Theodor Adorno, the influential German philosopher, also pointed to the importance of mythological function (mimesis) in contemporary society. In his *Aesthetische Theorie*, he spoke of this as "reasoning harmony."

The objective rationalism of Galileo, Newton, and Descartes may be epitomized in the technique of perspective drawing, used in architecture and the visual arts. Perspective, which reduces the entire world to a single, visible point, is a kind of Medusa's head, turning all who look on it to stone. In single-point perspective, not only is the viewer himself eliminated from the picture, but everything beyond his cone of vision is rejected.

We must henceforward try to shift the point of vision so that it

Tea arbor—old and new: Nagoya Municipal Museum of Modern Art (1987, below) by Kisho Kurokawa, and traditional example.

better reveals the relationships among *all* things. A point of view in which the world and its people might be seen from the perspective of things is probably also necessary. This would imply a view of the infinitely varied whole. By analogy, modern man, who has depended too much on his eyes to view the world, cannot understand why a person from a "primitive" tribe doesn't wear clothes. The "primitive" man answers: "My entire body is my face."

Recently, measurement theory in quantum physics has revealed how even the unique and "true" measurement available to scientists is nothing more than an arbitrarily selected state. This selection, in and of itself, causes instantaneous collapse of the quantum-wave function, rendering a single state perceptible—that is, measurable. In fact, it has further been hypothesized that all possible states exist at the same time, overlapping one another. This is known as the Copenhagen Interpretation. Similarly, an architectural image revealed through reason alone, and established solely from the point of view of the visible—equivalent to the single, correct measurement made by science—is actually no more than a partial glimpse of a rhizome-like multiplicity.

Without a doubt, architecture of the information age will shift from a paradigm of self-enclosure to one of open-endedness, from the whole to the part, from hierarchy to deconstruction, and from centeredness to non-centeredness. As model, it will take the freedom and unique diversity of all humankind, the symbiosis of different cultures, and a profoundly pluralistic ideal of society and culture.

History Made Manifest in the Hiroshima City Museum of Contemporary Art

The hill of Hijiyama rises in the midst of urban Hiroshima but is said to have once been an island in Hiroshima Bay. It was chosen as the site for a new cultural symbol of the contemporary city—as distinct from the Hiroshima Peace Center, erected after World War II to signify "no more Hiroshimas." Following completion of the master plan for the Hijiyama complex a decade ago, work proceeded in stages, as roads, an observatory, the park area, and the Blue Sky Library were built. The Hiroshima City Museum of Contemporary

Hijiyama, new symbol of Hiroshima, with City Museum of Contemporary Art (1988) by Kisho Kurokawa at its summit.

Art is situated on the ridge of the hill, just off axis from the library. With the eventual addition of a natural history museum and a museum of local history, the Hijiyama complex will fully represent the new Hiroshima.

Our design for the Hiroshima City Museum of Contemporary Art (1986) is based on my philosophy of symbiosis. The building was carefully situated on the ridge of Hijiyama hill in order to preserve as much of the wooded slopes as possible. Then, to keep the height of the building from exceeding that of the surrounding trees, part of the exhibition space was set underground, so that some 60 percent of the total floor space is below grade. A number of intermediary zones between the work and its natural setting have been incorporated on the building's exterior—circular approach plaza with a colonnade, open patio, external corridor, stone garden, and sculpted stone stairway—thus facilitating the symbiosis of architecture and nature. The facing materials graduate from the natural stone foundations to roughly finished stone, polished stone, tile, and aluminum paneling; symbolically speaking—from earth to sky, from ground to the universe, from the past to the future—all is in symbiosis. I have been using this mode of composition for nearly a decade, for example at Melbourne Central and the Okinawa Prefectural Government Headquarters (both completed in 1986).

The overall profile of the museum is based on a series of linked gable roofs. It is a work of architecture articulated like a village or a group of dwellings: we might call this the symbiosis of part and whole. It has permitted a scale that does not overpower the natural setting. These gable roofs are a quotation of Edo-period earthen-walled storehouses, but the use of a contemporary material like aluminum transforms that historical sign and imbues it with ambiguity. Such is the efficacy of connotation. The central approach plaza is a quotation from an ideal Western city, yet there is no fountain or work of sculpture at its center—a reference to the Japanese empty-center concept, or absence of center. The roof of the colonnade ringing the central plaza is cut away at the front, in the direction facing the city, connoting the site of the atomic bombing, and the pillars of the colonnade rise, so to speak, from stones exposed by the blast. Like the *roji*, a path or garden leading to a tea room, this approach plaza has no definite function, yet it is an important area in the evocation of the meanings of the symbiosis of history and the present, and of heterogeneous cultures.

A Henry Moore arch[6] is set in the outdoor sculpture garden at the foot of the steps to the plaza, and in the axonometric drawing at least, this suggests a viewfinder automatically leading the eye to the site of the atomic blast. The approach plaza also acts as an intermediary zone between the permanent exhibition space on the one hand and galleries for special exhibitions on the other, in the form of an anular colonnade. The exterior stair giving lateral access to the

City Museum of Modern Art, Hiroshima (1988): symbiosis of Western concepts with traditional Japanese aesthetic consciousness, and play with "the present" (this double page, and next two pages).

museum is a work of sculpture created by Bukichi Inoue, a new experiment in the symbiosis of architecture and sculpture. The Hiroshima City Museum of Contemporary Art is the first in Japan to unite contemporary works of architectural, industrial, and graphic design in the same collection. In 1988, for example, it exhibited architectural models and plans by Le Corbusier in its possession. The museum continues to pursue a unique collections policy, including works which it has commissioned from some eighty Japanese and foreign artists on the theme of Hiroshima. I believe it will prove a museum of international caliber in the years to come.

Symbiosis of History with the Present

The theme of the design for the Honjin Memorial Museum of Art (Komatsu, Ishikawa Prefecture, 1989) is symbiosis of history and the present. As in the Hiroshima City Museum of Contemporary Art, I have quoted the Edo-period storehouse as a metaphor. The pure geometric form of the circle is here flattened somewhat, and a complex, fissured space devised.

The square moat and lattice-style fence surrounding the building are a modern manifestation of the ancient Chinese theory that the Heavens are round and the Earth is square. The moat signifies that this district was the site of a moated castle. The interior features a simple two-story open space, but even this is bare and unfinished, and with its wedge-shaped skylight it expresses the absence of a center and rejection of a universalizing, pure geometry. By emphasizing asymmetrical forms, the work subtly challenges the centrality of *logos* and the West.

The basic theme for my prize-winning plan for the New Osaka Prefectural Headquarters Complex (nominated competition, 1989) is the symbiosis of past and future. A reconstruction of Osaka Castle is located on the same site—its moat, stone walls, and principal tower quoted as historical allusions. While other competitors included twin high-rise towers, one for the administrative headquarters and the other for the police headquarters, my plan has only one—the administrative headquarters. The rest of the structure keeps medium or low height, in an attempt to maintain balance with

Osaka Castle. Administrative, police, and prefectural assembly blocks, the governor's mansion, a family court, assembly representatives' lodging, and a cultural hall are all planned for the ten-hectare site. A geometry of domes, vaults, four-sided pyramids, triangular roofs, and patios has been employed symbolically to distinguish these different architectural forms. The tall administrative block will rise in three tiers in allusion to the form of Hideyoshi's *tenshu*.

Symbiosis of Heterogeneous Elements

Fukuoka Seaside Momochi (1988) first served as an exhibition for the work of eight architects, but was planned as an eventual multipurpose structure housing a branch of the Fukuoka Bank, a bookstore, and an information center. It allows these various units to function individually, while permitting each to express its own unique form, and so to establish a fluid, composite whole.

The exterior is faced with water-polished stone above a gentle natural stone embankment: the trusses of the central glass spire are made of wood, and natural light enters from clerestories and skylights; all are metaphors for nature. Signs of traditional Japanese architecture are quoted in the designs of windows and lattices. The light tower and curving walls connote European culture. The exterior is designed to be complex and to create an intermediary space leading visitors toward the interior, so that they may experience the symbiosis of inside and outside that characterizes traditional Japanese design.

The Shibuya Higashi T Building (1987) is a mini–office tower in the midst of Tokyo. The narrow foyer is filled with different signs: a screen of folding metal, a polyurethane screen alluding to lacquerware, an unfinished concrete wall, and granite facing all exist in synthesis. Here is the symbiosis of past and future, West and East. Though the work is a simple cube, a wedge-shaped segment of glass curtaining with a strong lightning-bolt patterning of aluminum rises the full height of the structure—serving to reject the universal by casting the building off-center. The roof, like the severed cross-section of an aircraft wing, alludes to flight, defying the building's gravity.

Traditional Japanese and European architecture in symbiosis at Fukuoka Seaside Momochi (1988) by Kisho Kurokawa.

◀ Kisho Kurokawa: Honjin Memorial Museum of Art, Komatsu (1989): history and modernity in symbiosis within the metaphor of the Edo storehouse.

Kisho Kurokawa: Shibuya Higashi T Building, Tokyo (1987).

The methodology all these designs have in common is the philosophy of symbiosis—my expression of will. Each presents its challenge to the dominance of the West, the *logos*, dualism, and the universal.

In contrast to the methodology of modern architecture—analysis, hierarchy, organization, synthesis, adaptation, clarification, and denotation—the processes I have espoused are symbolization, deconstruction, relativity, quotation, mediation, transformation, nuance, and connotation.

With regard to these strategies, the signs quoted in all these designs are "free" elements, and anyone reading them is free to adopt his, or her, own method of interpretation. There is no one accurate reading of any sign; the object of such tactics is to permit the various signs to combine freely and participate in the evocation of meaning. A certain *poétique*—an atmosphere of discrete narratives in symbiosis—is my continuing goal.

14

ABSTRACTION RENDERED SYMBOLIC

Abstract Symbolism and the Grande Arche

La Défense, at the western end of the Louvre-Concorde-Étoile axis in Paris, is an area that the French government devoted considerable energy to redeveloping as a second city center from the 1960s. The master plan is typical of plans for urban centers at that time—with parking below an artificially raised pedestrian deck surmounted by a forest of skyscrapers, the whole surrounded by a freeway loop. A second redevelopment of this area began in 1989, as a project to commemorate the bicentennial of the French Revolution. The late President Mitterand's strategy called for the construction of an international communications center, which later took form as the Grande Arche, built to symbolize the twenty-first century. This was intended to house an agency to promote the "North-South" dialogue in international relations.

After the elections, the international communications center was abandoned in the face of opposition from Jacques Chirac. But the Grande Arche was completed and at present the offices of the World Human Rights Fund are located in the roof atop the Arche. Soon after announcing its second renewal scheme, the government decided on participation of the private sector in expansion of the area beyond the highway that encircles La Défense. I was invited by the private developer SARI to present a redevelopment plan for the area

Grande Arche at La Défense, Paris, designed by the Danish architect Sprekelsen.

adjoining the Grande Arche complex. SARI decided to preserve the giant shell-roof exhibition hall designed by Bernard Zehrfuss and renovate it in the context of what they called Informat. This was to be a city within-the-walls, including shopping facilities and a hotel. In the area immediately adjacent to the Grande Arche, Jean-Pierre Buffi designed a group of low office buildings. A cylindrical super-skyscraper four hundred meters high, or Limitless Tower, by Jean Nouvel and our Pacific Tower were to be built west of La Défense, on a site extending to the Valmy district.

The role I envisioned for the Pacific Tower was to be a supporting player to the Grande Arche and to emphasize the function of the Arche as a landmark. As one of the jury members who selected the Grande Arche design, I was happy to have this opportunity. Pacific Tower also served to connect La Défense to Valmy by a pedestrian bridge, making it another gateway to the Défense district. Spreckelsen, architect of the Grande Arche, said that part of the inspiration for his design came from my Fukuoka Bank Head Office (completed 1975). Indeed, the initial scheme for our building was quite similar to the Grande Arche. While inheriting the highly abstract tradition of modern architecture, the Grande Arche is also a symbolic quotation of the Arc de Triomphe farther east. Together with I. M. Pei's glass pyramid still farther eastward along the same axis at the Louvre, it is a notable example of what I call Abstract Symbolism.

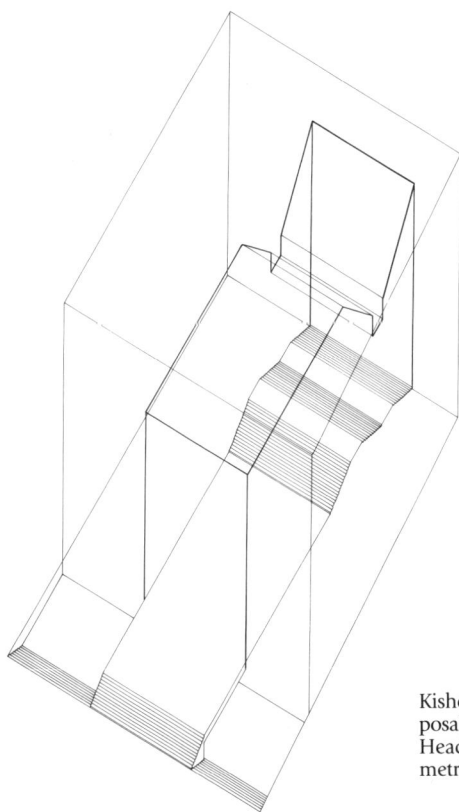

Kisho Kurokawa: first proposal for the Fukuoka Bank Head Office (1975), axonometric drawing.

Meanwhile, Pacific Tower assumed the crescent-shaped volume of a right cylindrical segment hollowed into a sort of gateway, partly in response to the shape of the site and the adjacent freeway. The west façade is a flat curtain wall, oblique to the main axis of La Défense and designed not to block the vista from the Grande Arche. Viewed from the front, the inner faces of the gate are flanged at different angles, creating an intermediate space similar to that of the Fukuoka Bank Head Office, yet intentionally asymmetrical. The space beneath the "eaves" (the intermediary space) will be used for outdoor concerts and theatrical performances.

Abstraction: Legacy of Modern Architecture

The salient feature of the twentieth century, the age of modernism, is abstraction. Abstract art movements that arose in the early twentieth century include Cubism (1907), Orphism (1912), Supermatism (1913), Constructivism (1914), De Stijl (1917), and Purism (1918). Cézanne, who precedes all of these, sought to discover the universal laws that transcend mere accidents of representation. He limited the depiction of any form of nature to with only three geometrical figures—the cone, the cylinder, and the sphere. The great Romanian sculptor Brancusi, who created "Mademoiselle Pogany" (1912) and "L'Oiseau dans l'espace" (1928), went so far as to declare that truth lies not in the outer form of an object but in its inner essence.

Piet Mondrian, who founded the De Stijl group with the architect Jacobus Johannes Pieter Oud and others, believed the arts should be based on a mathematical simplicity. In "Home, Street, and City" (1926), he writes, "In order for our living environments to possess a pure and, therefore, healthy and practical beauty, we must insure that they do not merely reflect our petty, selfish emotions. For that, we desire a new aesthetics, based on relations between pure color and line. The reason is that only through such relations of pure structural elements can pure beauty be created."

Le Corbusier called the home "a machine for living," Eisenstein declared the film to be a machine, and Marinetti said the same of poetry. The propensity for abstraction in the twentieth century was created from the longing for a future that would be produced by the

Constantin Brancusi: *Sleeping Muse* (1910).

machine or, in other words, an industrial society. The International Style that architecture targeted was conceived of as a universal style spread throughout the world by industrial products.

The twentieth century has been governed by Eurocentrism as well as Logocentrism, not forgetting the universalism of Christianity, and Catholicism in particular. Even if we are forced to recognize that postmodernism has of late lapsed into a narrowly historicist eclecticism, this does not imply that modernism could have continued as it was, without revision, into the twenty-first century. We must clarify what part of the legacy of modern architecture is worth preserving and what must be revised, or discarded. For example, Jacques Derrida's theory of deconstruction is a philosophical doctrine, not a method of formative expression. My philosophy of symbiosis proposes the symbiosis of different cultures—a symbiosis of *logos* and emotions, and diversity. The legacy we should preserve from modernism and modern architecture is, I believe, abstraction. But here we are faced with a dilemma. If by abstraction we mean the universal, that is, an abstraction born of Platonic geometry, the problem arises of how we may ensure a symbiosis of abstraction with regional trends, or diversity.

The Universe and Abstract Geometry

The answer to the query of whether abstraction is, indeed, the special spiritual—or aesthetic—characteristic of the twentieth century is a qualified "yes." But ancient humankind also possessed the tools of abstraction, in the concept of mimesis and the mythological notion of geometry as divine order. Without a knowledge of geometry and practical skills in surveying, the Great Pyramids of Giza could never have built. The first pyramid is a tomb for the fourth-dynasty king Khufu, while the second and third pyramids are for Khafre and Menkure. They are symbols of the power of these pharaohs who caused them to be built; other than this, they have no significance.

Why, then, were the pyramids built in the form of a pure geometrical figure? Almost certainly because the ancients perceived the absolute order of the sacred Universe in purely geometrical terms. We may deduce this from the strong attachment to geometry and geometrical forms everywhere in the world and in all periods.

The *Huanianzi,* a text from the early Han dynasty of China, states that "the Heavens are round and the Earth is square." This cosmological belief continued to influence Chinese city design and architectural forms in later ages. Chinese architecture is based on two types of building: the *tang* (hall) and the *dian* (palace). The basic form of *dian* is a combination of round and square shapes, with conical and pyramidal roofs. The Qiniandian at the Heavenly Altar (Tiantang) in Beijing (1540) is a surviving example of this style.

Round and rectangular geometrical forms are found in the Buddhist cosmology represented by Mount Sumeru as well as in the *mandala.* The Tower of Babel was a spiral, and the tower of Samara, near Mosul, is thought to be an ancient example of the minaret, but it is also a perfect example of spiral geometrical form. The hemispherical dome of the Pantheon in Rome, and occulus at its summit, are tributes to Platonic geometry and to the spirit of the classical age.

According to an essay in E. H. Gombrich's *Symbolic Images* (1972), the injunction "He Who Has Not Mastered Geometry Need Not

Large spiral tower at Samarra (848–52), present-day Iraq.

Enter Here" surmounted the entrance to Plato's Academy. The rules of geometry were codified first by Euclid, then again by science. The Platonic world order has been passed down to us by Christianity, without the slightest incongruity.

Tetsuo Ito, in his book *The Forest and the Ellipse*, traces the origin of the ellipse to the early sixteenth century, when the astronomer Johannes Kepler discovered the elliptical orbit of stars in 1609. This "new" geometrical shape helps to distinguish the forms of Baroque architecture from those of the Renaissance, which had sought to express harmony with God.

The Zen monk Sengai (1750–1837) produced a famous ink painting of a circle, square, and triangle, expressing not only a view of the universe but the truth of Zen. Presaging the work of the somewhat later astronomer Yoshio Shunzo, the Edo-period scholar Miura Baien developed a philosophy of unifying opposites, which he expressed using geometrical figures. And Le Corbusier, in his *Esprit Nouveau*, explains classical architecture as "the lesson of Rome"—in terms of the geometry of cylinders, pyramids, cubes, and spheres.

Elementary forms in a Zen painting by Sengai (Edo period).

Traditional iconographical interpretation, which reads meaning in diagrams and symbols, is once again attracting attention.

Style for the Twenty-first Century

If there is to be a new architectural style for the twenty-first century, it will probably be Abstract Symbolism. Recently, an exhibition of my work and a lecture series was sponsored by the Royal Academy in London. The titles of the lectures were "Abstract Interrelation" and "Abstract Symbolism." I have long referred to the twentieth century as the age of the machine. In the 1960s, I predicted that as we approached the twenty-first century, architecture would undergo a paradigm shift from the age of the machine to an age of life principle. All of the concepts I then discussed—Metabolism, metamorphosis, and symbiosis—are among the most fundamental principles of life. *Topos* and interrelation are other important such concepts. Abstract symbolism—linked to this concept of interrelation—will be the key to opening up a new horizon in architecture.

As already noted, abstract forms and geometrical figures have existed from ancient times, linked to the cosmologies of the different cultures they appeared in. Yet each age has given different meanings

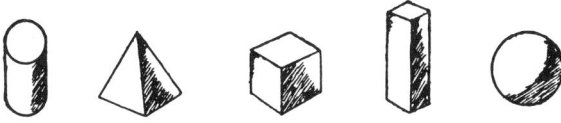

Le Corbusier's *Lessons of Rome* (half-page from *L' Esprit Nouveau,* later in *Vers une architecture,* 1923).

to these geometrical figures or abstract forms. Those produced by the architecture and arts of the twentieth century, though perpetuating the legacy of Plato, expressed the spirit of the century through mechanical imagery. Will it be possible to create new meaning by combining the abstraction of the twentieth century with the iconography of history and the cultural identity of *topos* in a "cosmology" of culture—a new symbolic abstraction, as a double code? This is the philosophical challenge of Abstract Symbolism.

The task confronted by contemporary architecture (architecture after modernism) is how to escape binomial oppositions and dualism and allow regional and international, past and present, the identity of *topos* and the universe to exist in symbiosis, in order to produce multivalent (or polyvalent) meaning. Abstract Symbolism may be able to provide the means to accomplish that task.

The meaning we can derive from such abstract forms is not a syntagmatic, linear process expressed as denotation but a paradigmatic, connotative potential. To put it simply, this is the difference between punning and original thought. For instance, the philosopher Adorno, known for his theory of discontinuity, in his *Logic of Beauty* refers to the nomadic relation attained through such correspondence with the universe: "mimesis," a harmonizing intelligence as opposed to the Platonic ruling intelligence. He cites the example of Joyce's *Ulysses*, which "by means of analogy that links the present and the past, gives meaning, form, and order to chaos."

In addition to the method of endowing abstraction and geometrical form with ambivalent and polyvalent meaning through a double code, it is also possible to do this by introducing distortions and discontinuities, say a twist that disrupts symmetry or interrupts rhythm. The curve of the wall in my Saitama Prefectural Museum of Modern Art (1982, see illustration p. 317) and the curved wall of the atrium of the Nagoya City Art Museum (1987)—indeed all the curving walls that figure prominently in my work—illustrate this attempt to interrupt rhythm.

I first employed a conical element when designing Melbourne Central in 1983. Since then, I have used the form frequently in my work, notably to mark an entrance, as in the Hiroshima City Museum of Contemporary Art (1986), the Aurora Hall of the Shirase Memorial Hall of the South Pole Expedition Party (1989), Lane Crawford Place in Singapore (1993), Ehime Prefectural Museum of General Science (1994), and Musée de Lōuvain-la-Neuve in Belgium (under construction). The cone is the shape of a compass, the nose of the supersonic jet, the tip of the rocket, the ziggurat, the tree. Asymmetry is created in the Hiroshima City Museum of Contemporary Art by cutting away one section of a circle, which otherwise would have suggested a Western rotunda. The circle and cone of the Shirase Memorial Hall of the South Pole Expedition Party are symbols of the movements of the stars as seen from the South Pole, and this circle, too, is cut away in front for the sake of asymmetry. The basic form of the Chinese-Japanese Youth Center in Beijing (1990), a combination of circles and rectangles, was determined by the ancient Chinese cosmological belief articulated in the *Huanianzi* that the Hheavens are round and the Earth is square.

The lattice, or modular grid, has a double image: the geometry of Plato or the plan of Miletus, as well as the latticework frequently encountered in Japanese architecture. My use of it extends from my 1960 "Agricultural City Plan," to the Japan Art Bank Plan (1981),

Kisho Kurokawa: Nagoya Municipal Museum of Modern Art (1987).

Kisho Kurokawa: Melbourne Central shopping plaza (Melbourne, Australia, completed 1991).

Kisho Kurokawa: Hiroshima City Museum of Contemporary Art (1988, above) and Memorial Hall for the Shirase South Pole Expedition Team, Yuri, Akita Prefecture (1990).

Kisho Kurokawa: Lane Crawford Place,
Singapore (1993, above left) and Ehime
Prefectural General Museum of Sci-
ence, Niihama (1994, right).

Kisho Kurokawa: Louvain-la-Neuve
Museum of Art, Belgium (architect's
model, under construction, above right).

and our entry for the Operation Sextus-Mirabeau International Nominated Competition, and the recent Osaka Prefectural Government Offices. The scale of my new Himeji City Shirotopia Park Senkantei (a rest area with public restrooms) is completely different from Pacific Tower at La Défense, but both are based on relational schemes. The Senkantei, in fact, uses a double code based on the curving walls of the northern part of the castle enclosure and the abstract geometry of the curve itself. Semicircles are set on two sides of a round pond. This unsettled, dynamic configuration exemplifies the contemporary holonic relationship—the independence of the part and the combinative order of the whole.

Part and Whole

The concept of order in the age of modernism is best represented by the Bourbakian model—an axiomatic order common to all modern systems. In his *Crisis of the European Sciences and Transcendental Phenomenology*, the philosopher Husserl stated that objective rationalism refers to a system in which an objective reality (order) is assumed to exist axiomatically. The thought of Euclid, Galileo, Descartes, Newton, and Darwin are all Bourbakian systems, emphasizing dualism and seeking established symmetry. In contrast to such systems, the new concept of order today challenging modernism may be called non-Bourbakian; it is a problematic system. Baroque natural science, which held that nature possessed within it the power to create itself, and the philosophies of, for example, Liebniz and Spinoza, must be reappraised in this light. The "implicated order" proposed by the "new science" of David Bohm, Koestler's Holon, the fractal geometry of Mandelbrot, Prigogine's Dissipative Structure, Haken's synergetics, Edgar Morin's theory of noise, and my philosophy of symbiosis are all *non*-Bourbakian.

What all these share is that disjunctive parts create a dynamic, floating, and ever-changing order, in which the part and the whole are in a mutually subsidiary relationship. For example, the word "Holon" contains the dual meaning of whole (*hol*) and part (*on*). Haken's synergetics refers to the principle that many partial systems generate, through their combined activity, an asymmetrical and symbiotic order.

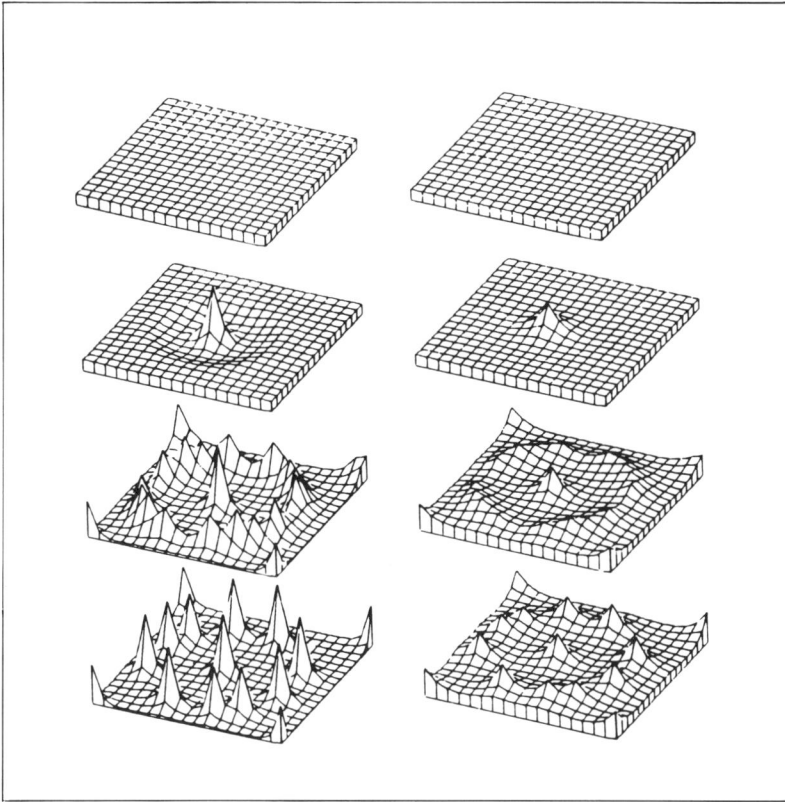

Illustration from *Synergetics: An Introduction* (third edition, Springer Verlag, Berlin, 1978) by Hermann Haken.

The segmental shape of Pacific Tower reflects the topography of the site, but was also based on the building's relationship to the rectangular Grande Arche. Pacific Tower perpetuates the geometry and abstraction of the rectangular Arche. It prolongs the concept of the gate, but by being set off axis from the Grande Arche, retains its independence. Meanwhile, it presents a flat façade to Jean Nouvel's four-hundred-meter-high cylindrical shaft, facing it across a cemetery. A similar generation of meaning through relationships can also be produced by deconstructing a single work of architecture—dividing it into its geometrical components and making these stand on their own before combining them in new relationships.

In the as yet unbuilt Louvain-la-Neuve Art Museum, the conical forum, rectangular exhibition wing, semicircular lecture hall, and semicircular amphitheater are quite independent of one another, but are placed just like the steppingstones in a Japanese garden, in random, free relationships. This asymmetry and displacement from a central axis creates a dynamic setting for each component. In all Japanese art, the greatest energy is poured into the invisible spaces between objects used to determine their position. In other words, it is not the objects but their relationships that provide the source of meaning. There are many examples of this: the stone garden at Ryoanji, the game of Go, calligraphy, and Zeami's *senuhima* (moment of stillness), the silent interval in Japanese music called *ma*. All are reflections of the Japanese aesthetic of asymmetry. We can call this an art of relationships.

Construction of our New Wing of the Van Gogh Museum has finally begun. The main building was the last work of Rietveld, and is a prime example of the abstractive geometry based on form and outline that is characteristic of modern architecture. The New Wing is completely separate from the old (though it is connected below grade). The New Wing employs ellipses and curving planes, in contrast to the straight lines of the main building. The wall facing the main building is subtly off axis, and the square exhibition hall on the mezzanine floor for Van Gogh's personal collection of Japanese woodblock prints is also slightly skewed. The façade facing the sunken water garden slopes at an angle, and the disjunctions among these parts of the building were designed to produce a work in tension—a Japanese-style, flowering, dynamic order of relationships.

In his book *Synchronicity: The Bridge Between Matter and Mind*, David Peat discusses how discoveries now explained by the Bernard instability—the collective unconscious morphogenesis—closely resemble the dreams of the Naskapi Indians and Chinese Taoism, in that both recognize the synchronicity and symbiosis of consciousness with the world of matter.

The world riven by Logocentrism is presently being reordered by Abstract Symbolism.

Kisho Kurokawa: new wing of the Van Gogh Museum of Art, Amsterdam (architect's model and site model).

Another Method

On the occasion of the completion of my Pacific Tower in Paris, I discussed the ideas upon which that project was based, suggesting that if I were to accept any part of the legacy of modern philosophy, art, or architecture, it would be abstraction; and I also pointed out, as in the preceding section, that the concept of abstract geometric forms already existed in Egypt, China, and other parts of the ancient world in the form of concepts of the universe. I proposed exploring the possibilities of combining modern abstraction and ancient views of the universe as a kind of double code to be embodied in architecture.

I have written many times of the need to overcome certain aspects of modernism and modern architecture: Eurocentrism, Logocentrism, and the universalism, authoritarianism, and homogenization that are their byproducts. The search for a postmodernism—not simply as new form but also a new philosophy, a new intellectual direction—has only just begun. If we are to accept abstraction as the best feature of modern architecture, how then are we to control the inherent tendency of abstraction toward universalization and homogenization, and redirect it creatively toward a new age?

The symbolism that manifests itself in *topos*, as well as regional cultures and traditions, will be a key concept in the new intercultural age of the twenty-first century. I have coined the phrase "abstract symbolism" precisely because I believe the symbiosis of these two ideas, abstraction and symbolism, marks the path for architecture in the twenty-first century.

Two major approaches in abstract symbolism can be distinguished. One is to use abstract geometric forms and manipulate, alter, and stagger their relationships to create completely novel meanings and narratives. For example, how is the axis of the building set? Is it symmetrical, does it establish the center, is it complete, has some other element or articulation (scenery, natural setting, an aperture, light, shadow, wind) been incorporated between it and an opposing element? We know that virtually an endless number of games, each unique, can be played by altering the placement of the black stones and white stones used in the game of *Go*. We also know great works of literature are composed of the ordinary, commonly understood words we find in the dictionary; again, it is the words' selection and arrangement that make for great literature. The equivalent in architecture is to employ geometrical abstractions, such as the helix, the cone, the cylinder, the four-sided and three-sided pyramid, the square, the triangle, the circle, the oval, and the grid to express *topos*, regional concerns, and even a view of the universe.

In the 1960s, my Helix City used the helix. I used the grid in the Agricultural City Plan, the ring in my Grand Spiral Project for Tokyo, and the cylinder in Cylinder City. In my work of the 1970s, I used tetrahedrons and helixes in the Toshiba IHI Pavilion for Expo '70 and a three-dimensional lattice for the Expo '70 Takara Beauty Pavilion. In the 1980s, I again used a three-dimensional lattice in the Saitama Prefectural Museum of Modern Art; the cone in the Mitsui Pavilion for the Universal Exposition of Science and Technology, held at Tsukuba; the rectangle, square-based pyramid, and sphere for the IBM Pavilion at the same exhibition; the cone, rectangle, and sphere for Melbourne Central; the cone for Fukuoka Seaside Momochi branch of the Fukuoka Bank; the cone, semicircle, and rectangle for the Louvain-la-Neuve Art Museum; the cone and circle for the Shirase Memorial Hall of the South Pole Expedition Party; the cone, circle, and triangle in the Hiroshima City Museum of Contemporary Art; the circle in the Honjin Memorial Museum of Art; the square and ellipse in the New Wing of the Van Gogh Museum; and the circle and rectangle in the Chinese-Japanese Youth Center in Beijing(1990). In the 1990s, I used the cone in Lane Crawford Place, Singapore; the cone, rectangle, semicircle, and sphere in the Ehime Prefectural Museum of General Science; the arc-and-chord in Pacific Tower; the helix in the Hachijoji Pagoda; and the semicircle and circle in the Shirotopia Memorial Park. All of these were attempts to create an architecture of abstract symbolism by the employment and manipulation of abstract geometrical forms.

The second method of achieving abstract symbolism is to abstract historical symbols, approaching the same goal from the opposite direction. Following this method, an architecture of abstract symbolism is arrived at through abstraction of symbolic forms, symbolic signs, and traditional symbols by way of intellectual manipulation.

Kisho Kurokawa: Helix City Plan for Tokyo (1961).

Expo '70, Osaka, Toshiba IHI Pavilion (1967–70, detail).

Kisho Kurokawa: Japan-China Youth Exchange Center, Beijing (1990).

In the following section, I mean to explore this second approach in greater detail.

Fragmentation of Historical Symbols

When we speak of historical symbols in the context of Japanese architecture, the first things that come to mind are temples such as Horyuji and Todaiji, shrines such as Ise and Izumo, a castle such as Himeji, the Katsura Detached Palace and other *sukiya*-style architecture. In all such buildings, the roof forms, post-and-beam structure and proportions, roof support systems, details of the entrance, and interplay of interior details afford extremely sophisticated "symbols," but, in addition, the ingenious relations inherent in the whole also create their own symbolism. Those relations, in the examples that we call masterpieces, have achieved an absolute perfection, making it impossible to modify any detail without spoiling the whole. Furthermore, each work as a whole is an expression of the spirit of its age, the social background, the technological expertise of the age, and the ideas and personality of its creator or creators. The preservation of historical architecture is important precisely because the

Kisho Kurokawa: Nara City Museum of Photography (1991, above) and plan for the K residence (architect's model, 1960).

buildings are witnesses to the spirit of the age in which they were built.

For us, who live in quite a different age, the challenge is whether we in turn can create architecture that will speak to future generations as our cultural legacy—an architecture that expresses the spirit of our age, its philosophy, level of technological achievement, and society. There is absolutely no creativity, then, in simply reproducing certain historical symbols, and it is equally meaningless to quote directly the system of relationships among such symbols. Like the Japanese, as part of the policy of the so-called Greater East Asia Prosperity Sphere[1] during World War II, certain developing nations are trying to employ an anachronistic method of combining past and present—for example, building a modern-style concrete box of a building and endowing it with a traditional-style roof and architectural details. This has never been a success. The "New Classicism" that has appeared in Western architecture of late is of the same type.

I experienced difficulty of this order in designing the Nara City Museum of Photography, which was to have a traditional roof. Though we did use a traditional Nara-style tile roof, by employing a newly developed type of roof tile we were able to achieve a clothoid closer to a straight line, and another clothoid with a much more arched line for the ceiling. This is an example of the method of deconstructing a historical symbol, in this case, a traditional roof form.

First the symbolic whole—made up of the roof tiles, their pitch, the eaves details, the roof, post-and-beam structures, and the distinctive façade—in all its relationships, was deconstructed. Then, the two clothoids, a tile roof, and an inner arc of curved metal sheeting were created. In addition, the beams and posts that would have supported the roof of the classical model were eliminated, their presence made undesirable by an exterior wall of transparent frameless glass. Thus the roof, which in the traditional building would have resisted the force of gravity on mighty pillars, seems to float from the heavens, as if held up by angels. In this manner classical Japanese architecture was simultaneously quoted and negated.

In 1960 my design for the K Residence had already attempted to abstract historical symbols following a method similar to that just described. The roof of the house was given a "traditional" up-curving

pitch based on a concrete shell, but instead of the pillars, beams, and other elements that would have supported such a roof in a traditional structure, it was hung from the central core. This project was never built, but I employed the same roof in my National Children's Land Central Lodge (1965), changing the construction from concrete to welded steel. In the Hans Christian Andersen Memorial Museum (1965) of National Children's Land, I tried another approach, making a straight roof out of four folded planes.

More recently, in the Hiroshima City Museum of Contemporary Art and Honjin Memorial Museum of Art, we used metal, such as titanium or aluminum, and concrete to construct the roofs, in a different attempt to abstract the historical symbolism of traditional roof forms. In the Museum of Modern Art, Wakayama / Wakayama Prefectural Museum, the historical symbol of the roof was further fragmented, the eaves being duly expressed. The use once more of a contemporary material, aluminum, contributed to an even more thorough abstraction.

The prominent "eaves" at the main entrance to the joint museum at Wakayama are made of three overlapping eave configurations, and they are an abstract expression of the overhangs that project far out from traditional Japanese structures, supported by rafter-and-beam elements. In fact, the rhythm of the repeating eaves echoes the roof line of Wakayama Castle, opposite the museum. The array of lighting towers between the main approach and the pond beside it also serve as vents for an underground parking area, and, at the same time, create a dramatic approach, suggesting traditional streetlighting. A device I often use, they are an abstraction of the stone lamps that line the pilgrimage pathway to a shrine or a temple. I have employed many other historical symbols, abstracting these and then placing them in as fragmentary a way as possible: a deep veranda on the second floor, snow-viewing sliding doors (*yukimi shoji*, a type of sliding door with a transparent lower panel and translucent or solid upper panels), a two-layer composition of tile at the wainscoting level that subtly alters surface texture, a Noh stage in the pond, and a stone stairway like that of Kumano Shrine.

◄ Eaves configuration of the Museum of Modern Art, Wakayama (1994) by Kisho Kurokawa; Wakayama Castle at right.

Familiar examples of "abstract symbolism": the Porsche crest (left); evolution of the Chinese character for "bird."

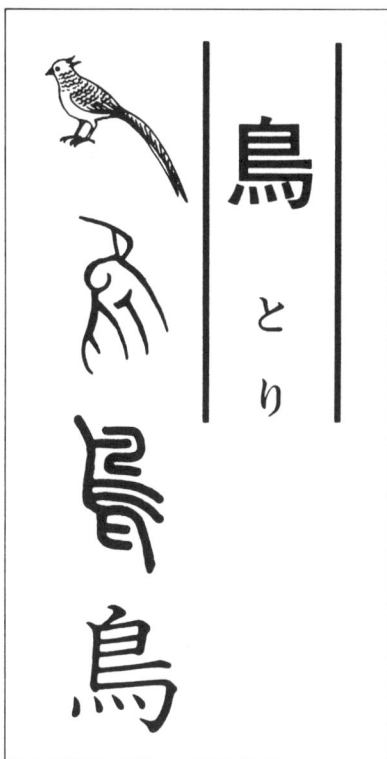

Pattern, Device, and Symbol

Other historical symbols include decor, decorative styles, or patterns such as family crests. At the time of their original use, specific rules governed where and how all these were applied, their measurements, and their placement—such as the location of designs and family crests on personal effects and kimono, the decorative detailing of buildings, door pulls and handles, and decorative windows. Each of these historical symbols has been endowed with a significance that contributes to a narrative quality.

It is also possible to incorporate the traditional feeling concentrated in such historical symbols into contemporary life. An easily grasped example is the heraldic symbol attached to the point of the hood of a Porsche automobile. This combination of a high-performance sports car, representative of our age, and an ancient heraldic symbol is a good example of abstract symbolism.

Chinese characters also provide a notable instance of abstract symbolism. Like letters of the Roman alphabet, the signs of the Japanese syllabary, have no independent meaning. They only produce meaning when combined according to certain preestablished rules. Chinese characters, on the other hand, were devised as ideographs. To take an example, the Chinese character for "bird" is a symbol in itself, an abstract representation of a bird (unlike the English B-I-R-D). Patterns, decorative motifs, and family crests are like Chinese characters in that many of them are abstract symbols derived from meaningful forms.

Just as we in Japan use a combination of Chinese ideographs and Japanese syllabary, each according to their own function, to create sentences and works of literature, it is possible to use historical symbols in contemporary architectural space to provide diachronicity, ambivalence, and multivalence.

Signs clearly express an established and shared meaning. A traffic indicator is a good example. A red light always means stop and needs no further interpretation. In many cases, signs such as letters of the alphabet and numbers have no independent meaning, only producing meaning in combination or relation with other signs. No one reads the statute books with the excitement that one might read a novel (with the possible exception of a legal expert or a criminal); that is only natural when we consider the care with which laws are recorded, so that all will read them with the same interpretation.

Literature, by contrast, is written in such a way that each reader can interpret and assign meaning to it in a unique fashion. The writer, of course, inscribes his own thoughts and feelings, but the meaning found in a work by its readers does not necessarily match these. Whether painting or music, whatever the art form, the greater the work of art, the greater multivalence and ambivalence it possesses. So, also, the greater its depth, which allows its reader, viewer, or listener maximum freedom of interpretation.

Abstraction by its very nature engenders a multivalence and ambivalence, allowing for a plurality of interpretations. When various methods are employed to further fragment such "symbolism," distribute it in novel arrangements, and create unexpected relationships, original meanings are transformed and new meaning is created.

For example, in my National Bunraku Theater (1983–94) in Osaka, multivalence and ambivalence are produced by intellectually manipulating decorative windows, lattice ceilings, a turret, and a bamboo fence that have been placed as fragments, their mutual relations severed. My intention was to evoke the feeling of the Edo period by a relationship of apparently random scattering. The silhouette of Hiunkaku may be quoted abstractly in the line of a building's roof. In both my Nagoya City Art Museum and the Wacoal Kojimachi Building in Tokyo, abstract fragments—the eighteenth-century Japanese philosopher Miura Baien's "Chart of Divisions and Opposites," the astronomical charts of Shunzo Yoshio, *torii*, lattices, geomancy charts, a façade à la Della Porta, UFOs, and primitive machines—are positioned to create humor, surprise, and *frisson*. I believe that through this trial-and-error process I have gradually established a method, or a code, for introducing symbols into contemporary architecture.

In the Museum of Modern Art, Wakayama/Wakayama Prefectural Museum, I restricted the number of symbols to a minimum and, at the same time, kept the layout of the buildings to the simplest geometrical figures—squares, rectangles, and semicircles. Through the repetition of a limited number of historical symbols, the abstract symbolism of the design came to be expressed more clearly. I purposely designed the elevator, the revolving door at the entrance, and the details of the reception counter to evoke an image of "gadgets or automata," reflecting a time in Japan when machines still had a human touch, thus injecting into the work a diachronicity reaching from the past up to the present.

Invisible Traditions, Invisible Technologies

There are visible traditions and invisible ones. Architecture, painting, craft, decoration, gardens, and such performing arts as Noh, Kabuki, and classical Japanese dance are all visible traditions. In the case of architecture and the decorative arts, the actual physical forms are their traditions; in performing arts such as Noh and Kabuki, the

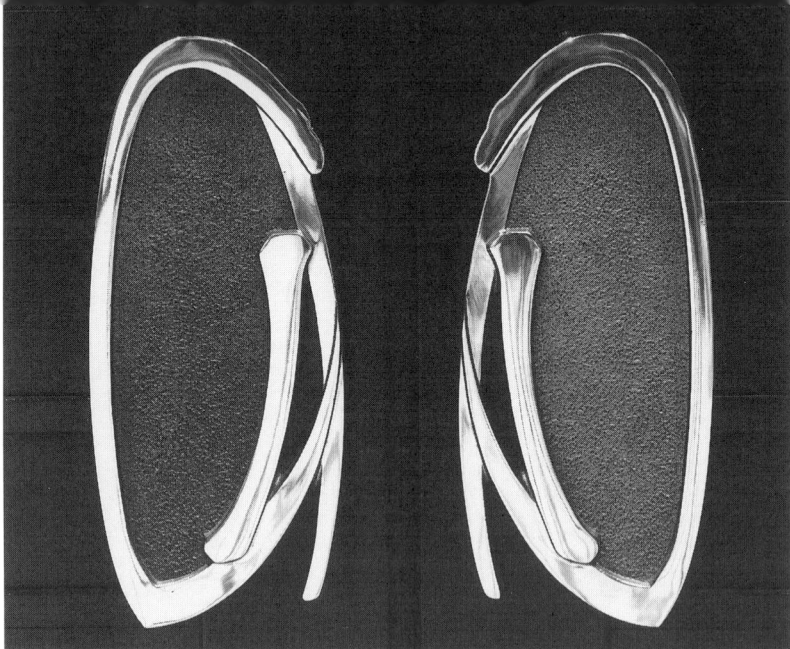

Door handles (above), decorative window (below), and turret (facing) of the National Bunraku Theater, Osaka (1983–94), by Kisho Kurokawa

INVISIBLE TRADITIONS, INVISIBLE TECHNOLOGIES | 373

tradition consists of the forms of expression and movement techniques transmitted from one generation of performer to the next. When we declare someone a "living national treasure," we are recognizing that in addition to the physical objects produced by that artist or craftsperson, the invisible techniques that he or she has mastered are also praiseworthy.

I have already discussed ways in which forms and symbols that are expressions of visible traditions can be abstracted. But ideas, philosophies, religions, aesthetic sensibilities, lifestyles, codes of etiquette, and skills are all invisible traditions. On a broader level, civilization as a whole is just such an invisible tradition. Indeed, the people of each nation and culture have over their long histories incorporated, so to speak, a distinct set of receptors in their communal DNA. In other words, each of us living today has been born with an invisibly coded tradition.

To characterize Western culture as materialist and Japanese, or Eastern, culture as spiritualist would be to fall victim to the evils of dualism. Yet compared to the cultural tradition of the West, that of Japan is unquestionably more spiritual. In pursuing this argument, I like to draw a contrast between Ise Shrine and the Parthenon.

Japanese regard Ise Shrine as a work of traditional architecture with a history of 1,300 years, and Todaiji as one of the world's oldest wooden buildings, dating from the Nara period. After saying that, they go on to admit that Ise Shrine has been rebuilt every twenty years from completely new materials and that Todaiji underwent major reconstruction in the Kamakura and Edo periods, so that its scale, proportions, and façade are quite different from the original. Non-Japanese are inevitably puzzled by such seeming contradiction.

For the West, a work must exist in its original form and materials to be considered authentic; if an exact model of the original is built using new materials, no matter how precise replication may be, it is regarded as a copy. Even if superior to the original, it will always remain a copy and, thus, a fake. If, for example, I were to build a new Parthenon next to the original, using precisely the same materials and replicating it in every detail, this would still be ridiculed as mere cleverness.

Such is the difference between the West and Japan with regard to cultural transmission. The West seeks to hand down the actual physical original, while Japan hands down the ideas, aesthetic sensibility, spirit, and technique behind the physical work, according superior importance to the invisible tradition and making every effort to keep it alive. This Japanese attitude helps explain why we have been so quick to destroy elements of our built heritage and replace them with new structures. Of course, we Japanese need to reconsider this tendency, but on the other hand, the importance our culture places on the invisible creates significant opportunities for the transmission of traditional culture to contemporary lifestyle and architecture.

Much of what is most distinctively Japanese belongs to the categories of thought, philosophy, religion, manners, and sensibility. This forms an invisible, spiritual tradition: the aesthetic of using materials in their natural state; minute attention to detail; the Buddhist idea that all living things possess the Buddha nature; the philosophy of Consciousness-Only, which resolves opposites in symbiotic relationships; a view of architecture and human beings as parts of the natural world; a curiosity that encourages the adoption of foreign cultures and new technologies; a concept of space as multivalent and ambivalent; a style of communication that values emotion, as well as reason; and a high regard for intermediary zones and ambiguity. Of course, visible and invisible traditions are both aspects of culture, but for architects and artists, whose role is to perpetuate cultural tradition, transmission of the invisible tradition is the central issue. Architecture, too, is an expression of thought and the spirit of the age.

We call the successive technologies, materials, and spirit of each age, "history" or "tradition." Only architecture expressing the spirit of the age in which it was created survives as a part of the greater cultural heritage. That being so, our creative role, even as we inherit and preserve tradition, is to employ the most advanced technologies and materials of our time, and, thus, to express symbolically the thought and spirit of our age. I have attempted to represent that invisible tradition in various ways, for instance, in the Museum of Modern Art, Wakayama/Wakayama Prefectural Museum.

The main approach, accessible by a flight of stairs leading up to the front of the building, derives from the traditional approach to a shrine or temple complex. A series of posts both divides and connects the approach and a pond set alongside it. This arrangement establishes an intermediary zone between architecture and nature. The pond border adjacent to the museum is straight, but the border on the garden side has a natural edge. The aim of each of these features is to make visitors feel the symbiosis with nature that is one of the bases of Japanese culture.

I personally designed the installation for the Philadelphia Museum of Art's recent exhibition on Japanese design. This is the first comprehensive Japanese design exhibition this century and included industrial, graphic, craft, and fashion design. Since industrial and product design is now by its very nature universal, we must ask the question whether there be any possibility of a distinctly Japanese identity in industrial products. The answer, surprisingly, is yes. By way of illustration, an American remarked to me once that just as Japanese love to take baths, Japanese cars seem to like being washed. He said that whenever he drove a Japanese car, he felt an inexplicable desire to wash it. Thus, Japanese aesthetic sensibilities and ideas are, ineffably yet without a doubt, expressed in Japanese-made products. Working within the time frame imposed on the Philadelphia exhibition by its sponsors, I used the central pillars of the exhibition hall to evoke by contrast the spiritual tradition and tentative quality of symbiosis, miniaturization, and multivalency that underlies Japanese culture—incorporating a linear display platform based on fractal geometry.

Resolving the issues contemporary architecture faces—symbiosis of tradition with the most advanced technology, of abstraction with symbolism, of local identity with international trends—while moving toward an architecture for the next era is by no means easy. Yet, as in the Philadelphia show, an additional path involving the most advanced technologies and materials to express an invisible or spiritual tradition is open to us.

Fractal Geometry

Fractal geometry was already employed in several instances in the Wakayama Museum of Modern Art. Through history, geometry evolved as the "reason of reason." It was the universal ideal that God had encoded in the natural world and humankind used its reasoning capacity to search for, test, and prove. From the time of Plato until quite recently, Euclidian geometry has signified a victory of reason over the many contradictions and the disorder prevailing in nature and human society.

Today, Mandelbrot's fractal geometry overcomes the dualism that the Bourbakian model had attempted to rescue from the irregularity and disorder within natural systems. Irregularity can at last be understood through a "geometry of irregularity." For example, the soliton wave, an irregular phenomenon of sudden change, has been explained by Prigogine's theory of sympathetic vibrations. The dualism that lies at the root of modernism is being dismantled on all fronts. In all fields of study—biology, physics, particle physics, mathematics, and philosophy—the theory of symbiosis is being confirmed. The dualistic notion that geometry presupposes abstraction but that symbolism cannot be expressed through geometry will be abandoned. Fractal geometry and non-Bourbakian models will make the symbiosis of abstraction and symbolism—in a word, abstract symbolism—possible.

In the Wakayama Museum of Modern Art, railings, reception counter, door handles, benches, and chairs (being manufactured in Germany under the name "Fractal Series") are all based on fractal geometry, suggesting a new age that is dawning.

Until quite recently, the concept of "organic architecture" was much discussed with reference to the work of architects who sought to liberate design from the constraints of geometry and make use of free, "natural" forms. Buildings by Frank Lloyd Wright, Alvar Aalto, Bruce Goff, Oscar Niemeyer, and Paolo Soleri were often linked with this concept of organic architecture. The leaders of the modern movement regarded these emotionally charged works as hyper-individualistic, symbolic, and pretentious. The modern age was predicated on an industrial society with its precision, homogenization, and universality.

Kisho Kurokawa: Museum of Modern Art, Wakayama (1994). Reception counter, railings, and doors.

That is why the modern movement rejected decorative craftsman-ship, personality, regional traits, and symbols based in a particular cul-ture. It labeled all such things "anti-modern" and regarded organic architecture as "impure."

But under "late modernism," all this began to change. Le Cor-busier built his pilgrimage church at Ronchamp, and Gropius began to make frequent use of the traditional arches of the Middle East. Industrial society had left the leaders of modern architecture behind and was rushing to place the highest value on homogenization and maximum profit. Yet the universality that was supposed to liberate people from feudalism met with resistance from the masses in search of an identity—those supposed to be its comrades and allies.

Art and culture themselves provide identity, having little affinity for the universal. The period of transformation and chaos in late modernism was also related to new invisible technologies. The age of the machine began with the visible technology of steam, moving on to automobiles, locomotives, aircraft, and giant bridges; every-where, the spirit of the modern age was expressed in these visible manifestations. Bridges, skyscrapers, and buildings with heroically

Le Corbusier's pilgrimage church at Ronchamp, France (1955).

exposed structures, like the Hong Kong and Shanghai Bank, Pompidou Center, and Lloyd's of London, as well as the older geodesic mode, were referred to as high-tech and regarded as heaven-sent by modern architecture. But do such buildings actually use the most advanced technology available? The answer is "no."

The main technologies responsible for the development of our present information society—biotechnology, computers, life science, satellite communications, and micro-engineering—have penetrated deeply into our daily lives, and these are all invisible technologies.

The leading technologies of each era have produced new architecture. Such works as the Crystal Palace, Eiffel Tower, Empire State Building, and Golden Gate Bridge, as well as Buckminster Fuller's domes, have at each stage expressed an advanced technology. High-tech architecture, however, no longer represents the technology and spirit of the present. With the inability of visible technologies to serve architectural expression, we have taken our first step into an age of a new philosophy, a new way of thinking.

Non-Bourbakian Systems

In the first section, I indicated means by which abstract geometrical forms might be used to express the identity of place (*topos*), regional context, and cultural traditions. The second has suggested how traditional forms and sensibilities could be abstracted or intellectually manipulated. In both, I have been concerned with the present challenge of accepting and working within modernism's greatest achievement, abstraction, while seeking ways to express such elements as *topos*, *genius loci*, context, individuality, and historical tradition that the modern spirit had lost or denied. I would now like to bring this discussion full circle by investigating the relationship between abstract symbolism and the philosophy of symbiosis.

The year 1993 was perhaps a milestone for the concept when the International Conference on the Environment was widely publicized as marking the first year of the age of symbiosis. The Treaty on the Diversity of Life that representatives of many nations signed at this environmental summit in Rio agrees to work to protect all species on the verge of extinction, such as the rhinoceros, buffalo, panda,

Japanese ibis, and Japanese river otter, and broadly to preserve as much of the diversity of the Earth's life forms as possible. On an intellectual level, this commitment represents a major revision of the Darwinian theory of evolution and survival of the fittest, so representative of the Bourbakian systems of the modern period. No one can deny that Darwin's theory of evolution—in particular the idea of the law of the survival of the fittest—served as an analogy that supported and justified the European dominance. That, in fact, is why the nations of the so-called Third World, which are seeking to promote and preserve cultural diversity, were the main forces behind the adoption of the Treaty on the Diversity of Life.

The philosophy of symbiosis seeks a symbiosis among all the different cultures on Earth and forces the reconsideration of Eurocentrism, Logocentrism, and rationalistic dualism. Logocentrism and rationalistic dualism have been the intellectual models of Western culture from the time of Aristotle, but only in the modern era have they become conjoined in a Bourbakian model, that embraces and defines all areas of learning. Both Logocentrism and Bourbakian-style thought posit an absolute truth, a single icon that is purportedly demonstrated by analysis, mathematical proof, and the scientific method. Euclid's geometry, Descartes's dualism, Newton's physics, Lavoisier's chemistry, and Darwin's theory of evolution are all representative of Bourbakian logic.

As opposed to the Bourbakian model of a rigid logical progression, a non-Bourbakian system employs the method of moving toward a whole by creating relationships among disjunctive parts.

Fractal geometry, the Holon, synchronicity, and the soliton wave are attracting attention as key concepts of the new age. The latest discoveries of this "new science" are all in accord with my concept of symbiosis. For example, the theory of serial symbiosis advanced by the American biologist Lynn Margulis as a major revision of Darwinism is attracting attention worldwide. Margulis hypothesizes that there were certain proto-nuclear organisms consisting of cells without nuclei—bacteria and algae are examples. These entities metabolized carbon and hydrogen compounds, as well as carbon dioxide in the atmosphere. When they had used up all the available carbon dioxide in the atmosphere and oxygen sulfide in the Earth, they turned to the primitive seas as a source of life. These chlorophyll-containing bacteria that had spread all over the Earth gave off oxygen as one of the waste products of their metabolism. Oxygen was a virulent poison to other organisms at this time, and the majority of life on Earth was exterminated. But some of the proto-nuclear organisms adapted to the presence of oxygen and survived, spreading over the Earth.

At the same time, there were organisms with nuclei. At that stage, 2.2 million years ago, when there was still only a small percentage of oxygen in the atmosphere, the oxygen-adapted proto-nuclear organisms entered the cells of the nuclear organisms and created the mitochondria, a part of the cell that can make use of oxygen in its metabolic processes. This compound organism in turn created the first stable, oxygen-consuming one-celled organisms. This is the serial symbiosis put forth by Margulis as an alternative to Darwin's theory of evolution based on genetic mutation and survival of the fittest.

William Donald Hamilton, who won the Kyoto Prize two years ago, has suggested that Darwin's theory of evolution based on survival of the fittest can be disproved. In his research on ants, he has discovered ant species that evolve not through competition, but through cooperation and symbiosis with other species. According to this theory, the life forms that have appeared on Earth since the most ancient times have overcome various difficulties by means of the symbiosis of different species.

Healthy Disorder

The word "fractal" derives from the Latin *fractus*, meaning irregular. The idea of a new fractal geometry was first proposed by the mathematician Mandelbrot in 1975. From the perspective of Cartesian reductionism, any complex, nonlinear realm is regarded as chaos or disorder and is excluded from consideration by science or reason. For example, ocean currents, shapes of clouds, forms of mountain ranges—or in the body, the structure of the brain or circulatory system—were all considered irregular or random features that

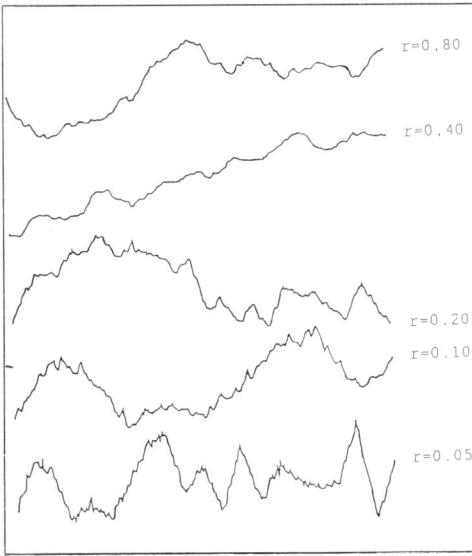
Fractal curves and their functional equations.

could not be recorded in any scientific or quantifiable manner. Mandelbrot's theory, which he discovered by examining the model of the stock market, states that not only is the whole composed of all its parts, but the structure of the whole is incorporated in each part as facsimile. Thus, complex natural forms never fully described by a Euclidian geometry were at last describable in terms of this new fractal geometry.

The fractal represents a symbiosis of order and disorder, yielding a dynamic equilibrium. The pulse of the human body, fractal variations, and "skips" of the pulse are the very proof of health. This idea is consistent with the concept of "noise" as put forth by Edgar Morin and Jean Piaget. Arthur Koestler's concept of the Holon (a portmanteau word that combines "whole" and "part") also describes a symbiosis, in which the whole is included inside each part. In his research on particle physics, the British physicist David Bohm calls the whole incorporated in the part "implicated order," another way of describing the symbiosis of part and whole. Symbiosis is the idea that all of these new philosophies and new sciences have in common.

The much discussed soliton wave was discovered in 1834, when

J. Scott Russell observed a single wave running down a narrow channel of water. The wave suddenly appeared on a still day, and it continued for two miles without diminishing in speed or changing in form. Only since 1980 has rigorous mathematical analysis been applied to this singular phenomenon. The soliton wave is a dramatic example of the part manifesting itself as a whole. Such nonlinear phenomena can be observed in air currents, tides, slime molds, heat transference within bodies, supercurrents, superconductors, and many other systems. What is common to them all is that, without losing sight of the context of the whole, the whole can be successfully analyzed or dissected into independent parts.

In his *Synchronicity: The Bridge between Matter and Mind* (1987), F. David Peat, particle physicist, as well as stage and radio dramatist, investigates the synchronicity between mind and matter, between points in different dimensions, and between system and chaos, from the perspective of quantum mechanics. Peat discusses the biologist Rupert Sheldrake's theory of morphic fields. According to this idea, all matter has an associated memory field, and the information in that shared memory governs all processes of formation. For example, when a new substance is first formed, the "crystallization" process takes time, but experiments have shown that when that substance is formed again, in another location, the process occurs more quickly. What is happening is that the second formation process, separated in time and place from the first, has acquired information from the first. There are innumerable examples of this synchronicity in the animal realm. For example, a certain animal faces danger, and, instantaneously, this information may be communicated to another animal separated by tens or even hundreds of kilometers, which then begins to take defensive measures. In other words, both matter and life are responding to an epigenetic background aimed at gradual formation. Growth and morphic formation do not respond, even in the case of living organisms, solely to the orders of DNA; formation takes place against an epigenetic background of an exchange of information which includes accident. That "morphic field" (field of information) is available to all matter and all life instantaneously throughout the universe, no matter how far separated the particular

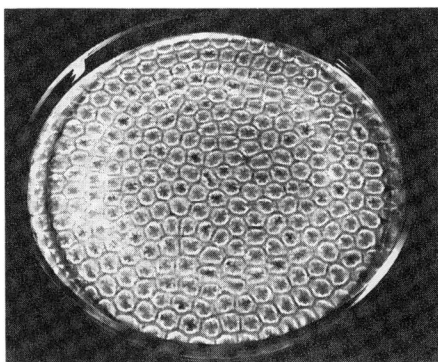

Bénard cell, example of heat exchange by convection first observed by Henri Bénard.

matter, or life, may be. It instructs matter in the process of formation in accordance with the principle of synchronicity. This dramatic concept of synchronicity that quantum mechanics has arrived at has been further extended to include a synchronicity of mind and matter and a synchronicity of mind and body.

Sympathetic phenomena such as the soliton, revealed by Haken's synergetics, and the Bénard instability discovered by Prigogine and the French physician Bénard, are clearly linked to synchronicity. The Bénard instability is a phenomenon that occurs when a liquid is heated. As it gradually begins to boil, a confused mix of whirlpools, eddies, and vortices of different sizes forms in a chaotic fashion, but at a certain point a barrier is passed and the randomness becomes a strong current, finally taking the form of a regular, ordered flow of hexagonal shapes. This phenomenon can be observed by watching a cup of coffee cool from the proper angle.

A corresponding phenomenon, by which the cells of mutant bacteria and the electrons in plasma suddenly shift from a random state to an all-embracing order, has also been discovered. These discoveries have all occurred in the last ten to fifteen years and are all distinguished by their evident contradiction of the Bourbakian model. The latter begins by establishing principles or hypotheses and then analyzing and proving these; it posits a single truth, and everything that does not fit within its symmetrical structure, or order, is labeled irrational and at once rejected; it is constructed clearly and rationally through binomial opposition and dualism. What all of the non-Bourbakian systems have in common is asymmetrical structure and order; orders that incorporate noise and randomness; orders that are interrupted and nonlinear; and symbiotic orders that reject binomial opposition and dualism.

Bourbaki was a name taken by a group of young mathematicians in the late 1930s. Their goal was to discover a unified wholeness in existence, a goal inherent in all modern science and philosophy. The Bourbakian model was an expression of the spirit of the modern age, its world view and world order; in contrast, non-Bourbakian systems express world views and world orders of the coming twenty-first century.

Architecture of the Age of Relations and the Age of Life Principle

In the modern age, people were interested in the visible and the substantial. Such symbols of material civilization as large houses, land, and luxury automobiles were valued for status. Monumental buildings, skyscrapers, and huge cities and factories characterized the era. The Bourbakian model of logic and learning that supported this age also placed the greatest importance on the visible and the substantial. Newton's Law of Universal Gravitation was concerned only with the mass of heavenly bodies and the distances separating them. The space between them was a void where nothing existed.

We now know that the void is full of a variety of substances, and that neutrons from the sun reach the Earth. On the other hand, things that were heretofore regarded as solid substances turn out to be surprisingly porous conglomerations of particles when viewed from the dimension of atomic structure; at the level of protons and neutrons, even surfaces and boundaries become difficult to define. Even the size and extent of planet Earth are now problematic. The spirit of rationalism based on dualism was established by oversimplifying the complexity of our world.

I have called the twentieth century the machine age, and the new age that follows modernism an age of the principle of life. All of the concepts and keywords that I have promoted over the past thirty-five years—Metabolism, then metamorphosis and symbiosis—express life principles. Today, life is regarded as a locus of ever-shifting relationships producing meaning. Even the link between one human cell and another is not merely physical or mechanical, but a flexible information link. I call the twenty-first century an age of relationships because the concept of relationship is fast becoming vital in explaining the principle of life.

The lifestyle of this age will not be one of large homes or fancy cars; an individual's relationships with other people and his freedom of movement will be of the highest value. For nomadic peoples always on the move, awareness of other groups with which they might come into contact, and whether those groups are friend or foe, is crucial. In addition, the survival of the tribe, or nation, may depend upon predicting weather by the direction or "feel" of the wind, or knowing where sufficient grass for grazing is located. In order to preserve the order of one's home, one's tribe, and one's nation, while constantly on the move, each individual must possess a sharp awareness of the environment and climate of human relationships. In the borderless twenty-first century, this sensitivity to relationships will be vital to us all.

If architecture is to express the spirit of the contemporary age, from now on our architecture, too, should be an architecture of relationship.

Though I said we are moving toward an age of the principle of life, this paradigm shift is occurring in tandem with a shift from industrial society to information society. While industrial society was directed toward the realization of a society of mass production and homogeneity, information society will be directed toward the production of unique differences and a pluralistic society. Recognition of this is equivalent to valuing relationships with others. As we make our way through the borderless world, the relationships we create— constantly reaffirming relations with our fellows and allies and keeping close watch on the distance we maintain from enemies—will always be fluid and infinitely complex. The new, non-Bourbakian systems based on the principle of life, that is, symbiosis, will naturally tend toward a science and culture of complex systems.

As I have frequently stated, symbiosis is distinct from mere coexistence, compromise, or harmony. Unlike these notions, symbiosis describes a situation in which two elements however opposing or even antagonistic, also need one another. A different way of describing symbiosis is to say that it only exists when an intermediary space, or relation, exists between two opposing elements, or when these two opposing elements recognize each other's sacred zones and observe certain mutually agreed upon rules of interaction. This explains my preoccupation with such ideas as street space, periphery, Rikyu grey, *ma* (or interval), ambiguity, ambivalence, and dual encoding, because all of those ideas are part of a theory of intermediary space. Creating relations is making an intermediary space between two opposing elements.

The problem that abstract symbolism seeks to resolve is how to bring several opposing elements into relations of symbiosis: the regularity of geometry and the irregularity of nature, the *genius loci* and a shared view of the universe, reason that analyzes and emotion that

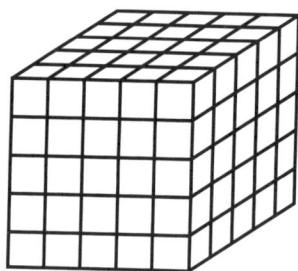

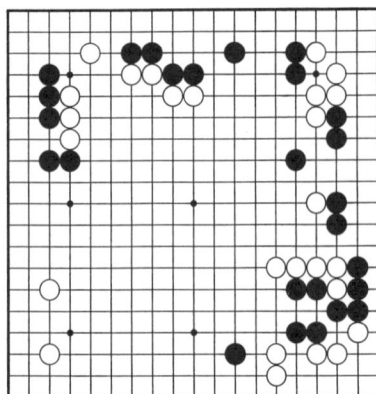

Diagram of lattice (left) and an arrangement of pieces ("stones") in the game of *Go*.

grasps things in their totality, historical tradition and international-ism, heterogeneous cultures, the part and the whole, and architec-ture and nature. In the beginning of this chapter I wrote that abstraction was a legacy we ought to accept from modern architec-ture. I also noted that it was possible to express traditional views of the universe through geometric forms.

Platonic geometry makes use of a hypothetical three-dimen-sional grid to demonstrate universal truths. In contrast, abstract sym-bolism would suggest that the world is built up of a variety of independent parts. A deconstructed architecture with a variety of abstract geometrical forms—cones, circles, rectangles, spheres, cylin-ders, semicircles, and triangles—expresses the rich variety of the world, as well as the variety and the pluralism of life itself. Abstract symbolism sets great store on the relations created by their place-

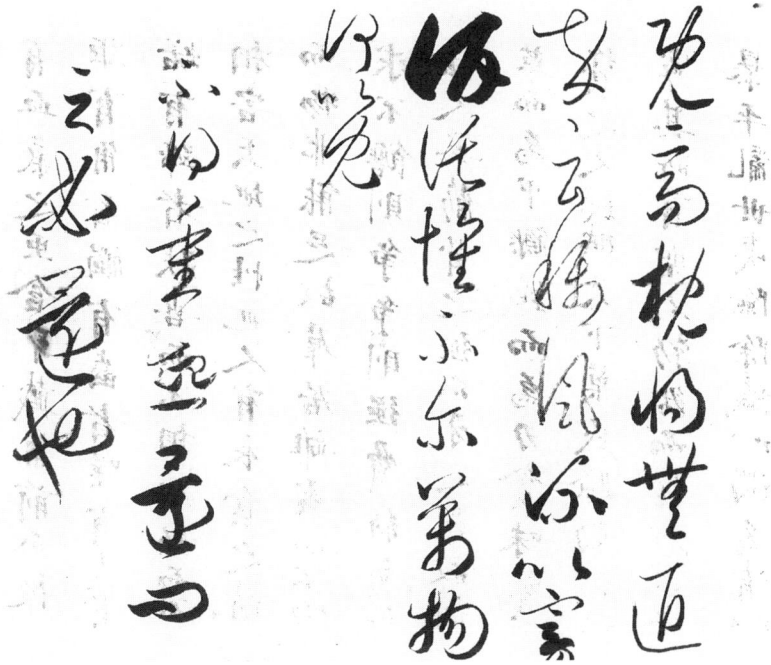

Akihagi-jo, extracts from poem anthologies and transcriptions of Wang Xi-zhi's letters, Heian period, eleventh century. Handscroll, ink on paper. National Treasure. Reverse side of scroll: Chinese classic *Huai-nan-zi* (eighth century, not shown).

The Japanese aesthetic of asymmetry and interval: sword guard with crab (above) and folding screen with trompe l'oeil kimono (both Edo period).

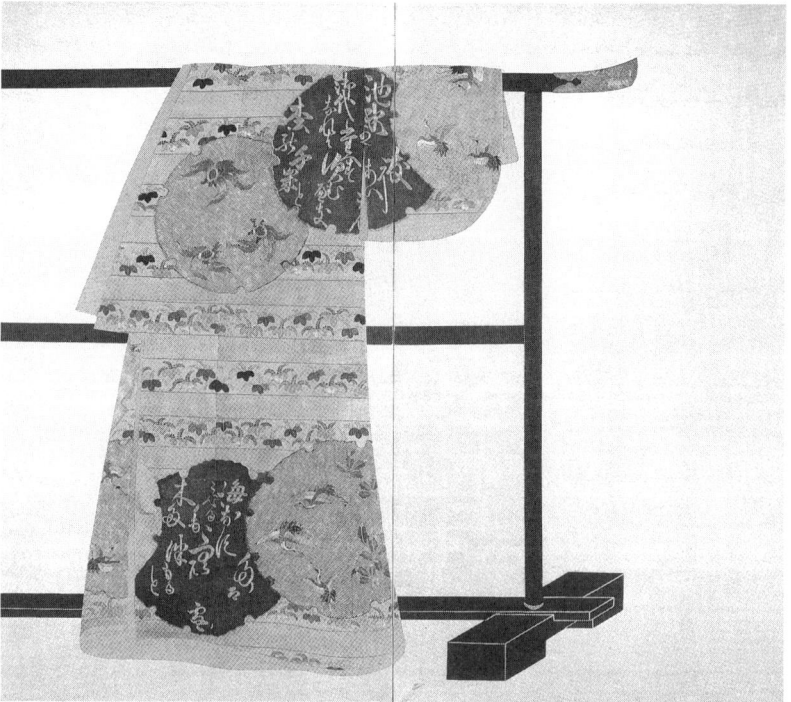

Arrangement of stepping stones at Katsura Detached Palace, Kyoto (Edo period).

ment between a variety of deconstructed elements and spaces. It values the mood, atmosphere, sense of space, and meaning created by the placement and relation of various elements, rather than simply trying to express meaning through the juxtaposition of independent spaces.

To symbolize the dynamic, floating field that is life, elements and their axes are twisted, bent, displaced, or tilted, and different materials and "noise" are introduced. The new order of this architecture arises just like the soliton wave and the Bernard instability, which crystallize out of chaos, and a fractal geometry may be employed in placing its elements. This asymmetry and nonlinear geometry can also be discovered pervading the depths of the traditional Japanese aesthetic of asymmetry and interval. As demonstrated earlier, these elements are deeply rooted in Japanese culture: from the logic of the game of Go to the significance of the empty spaces between strokes made by a calligraphy brush, the intermediary space between one object and another in the design of stone gardens and walkways, the aesthetic of relationships, a strategically dense society, and the sociological nuances of consideration for others observable during the Edo period. Thus, abstract symbolism bids fair as a Japanese contribution to the methodology of a twenty-first century architecture.

15

TWO EXPERIMENTAL COMMUNITIES

Why Bedouin Can't Live in California-style Housing

A project I was involved with some twenty years ago for the design of a desert city in Libya provides an interesting instance of putting the philosophy of symbiosis into practice. The town, in the Sarir region of southwest Libya, offered a blueprint for the symbiosis of Arab and Japanese culture, tradition and the latest technology. During the 1970s I had been asked to design an international conference center in Abu Dhabi. Although the project never materialized owing to local political problems, my planning work in Abu Dhabi helped prepare me for further work in the Middle East. One day the leader of one of the emirates invited me to look at some recently built housing. He explained that to encourage the establishment of towns in the desert an American architect had been engaged, but the scheme wasn't working out very well.

The population of the United Arab Emirates at the time was still only about 1.3 million, and per capita income was the highest in the world. The nation was trying to encourage its Bedouin population to settle in towns and villages by providing housing without cost. The Bedouin are a migratory people who live by hunting and pasturing livestock. Though they sometimes build shelters of sun-dried brick, they frequently move from place to place and usually live in tents. This large migrant population had made it difficult for the UAE to achieve the modernization its leaders desired–providing a basic education for Bedouin children, for example, was clearly a problem and the government wished to encourage the Bedouin to settle permanently.

When we arrived at the new American-built homes, a strange scene greeted my eyes. I found two-story, concrete American-style units of the kind one might encounter in California. Each was completely air-conditioned, with an attached garage. And they stood there in a row, in the middle of the Arabian desert.

As we approached, however, I saw Bedouin tents set up *next* to the houses; there were sheep, together with a supply of livestock feed, inside the units. I proceeded to investigate the reasons for this. The first problem, as it turned out, was with the air conditioning. In the desert, the temperature rises as high as forty degrees centigrade. Air conditioning works at low efficiency in such temperatures, and of course it breaks down; but you can't call a repairman to come out and fix it the same day—repairs take at least a month. Meanwhile, the concrete boxes turn into ovens. Not only that, but the heat that builds up through the day is released by the walls at night. Though it is already cool outside, the concrete is a powerful heat retainer, roasting anyone inside the walls. Of course no human being could live in this environment, so the owners had set up their tents outside and given the California-style housing over to their animals.

When I looked at the Bedouin tents, however, I was struck by how very well suited they were for life in the desert. While the surface temperature in the desert rises and falls dramatically, there is almost no temperature variance below ground level. When the air temperature rises to forty degrees centigrade during the day, it is only twenty degrees at three meters underground; and when the air grows cold at night, say, to five degrees, it is still twenty degrees three meters below ground. During the day, when the Bedouin sit in the shade of their tents, a cool breeze rises from the ground. At night, they sleep on skins and rugs spread on the ground and the relative warmth from underground protects them from the cold night air. The Bedouin exploit their centuries of experience in the desert to achieve the most pleasant and comfortable life they can manage in their habitat. To these masters of desert ecology, the American architect had brought California-style suburban housing.

Value of Regional Culture

When I met the American architect, I asked him why he had designed buildings no one could live in. He replied that he didn't expect the Bedouin to be able to live in the houses at once, but that eventually peoples of the developing nations, like these nomads, would need to exchange their camels for cars and their tents for modern homes. This being inevitable, it was important to instruct them as quickly as possible, and these houses were one step toward that goal.

Here we see an extreme application of the dogma of modernism, based on Western values. According to this way of thinking, the application of technology produced by industrial society has raised the quality of human life and is bound, sooner or later, to spread throughout the world. But such ideas were repudiated early on by anthropologists who rejected the idea of stages in cultural evolution and insisted that each culture possesses an autonomous value—their research culminating in the theory of Lévi-Strauss that all cultures share a common structure. His study of myths and family structures in cultural anthropology set Western culture alongside others in a larger context as part of a spectrum.

Of course, at certain times in history, one culture may be especially strong and may influence other cultures. At one time Egypt possessed such power; later, China had an equal importance. Yet in no case should one culture dominate the planet. We must recognize that human life is the richer when each region maintains a cultural identity suited to its people, climate, geography, and history.

Symbiosis of New Technology and Desert Culture

From the time of this experience, I continued to ponder how I might meet the challenge of building a community in the desert. Several years later, by chance, the opportunity came to put those ideas into practice. The Sarir region is several hundred kilometers to the south of Libya's third-largest city, Benghazi. Great quantities of

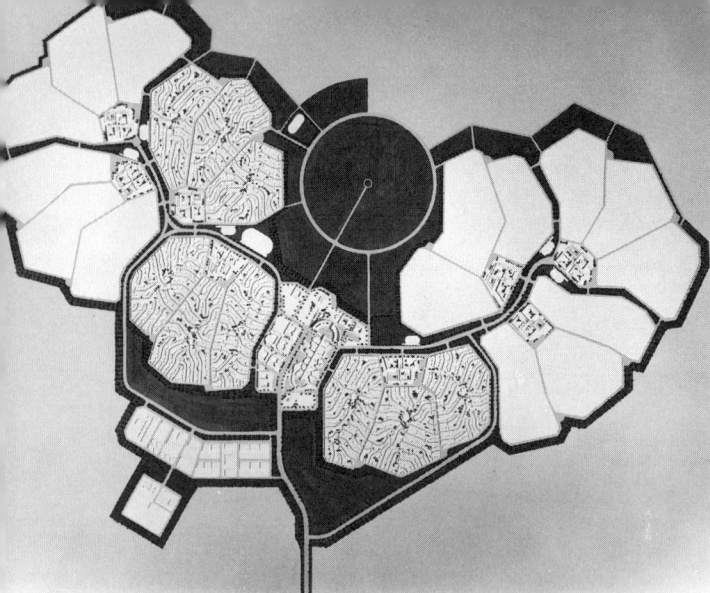

As–Sarir New Town, Libya, planned by Kisho Kurokawa (architect's model, below, and proposed layout).

As–Sarir New Town, Libya: experimental prototype unit with wind tower (below), exploded axonometric (right), and worker with prefabricated elements.

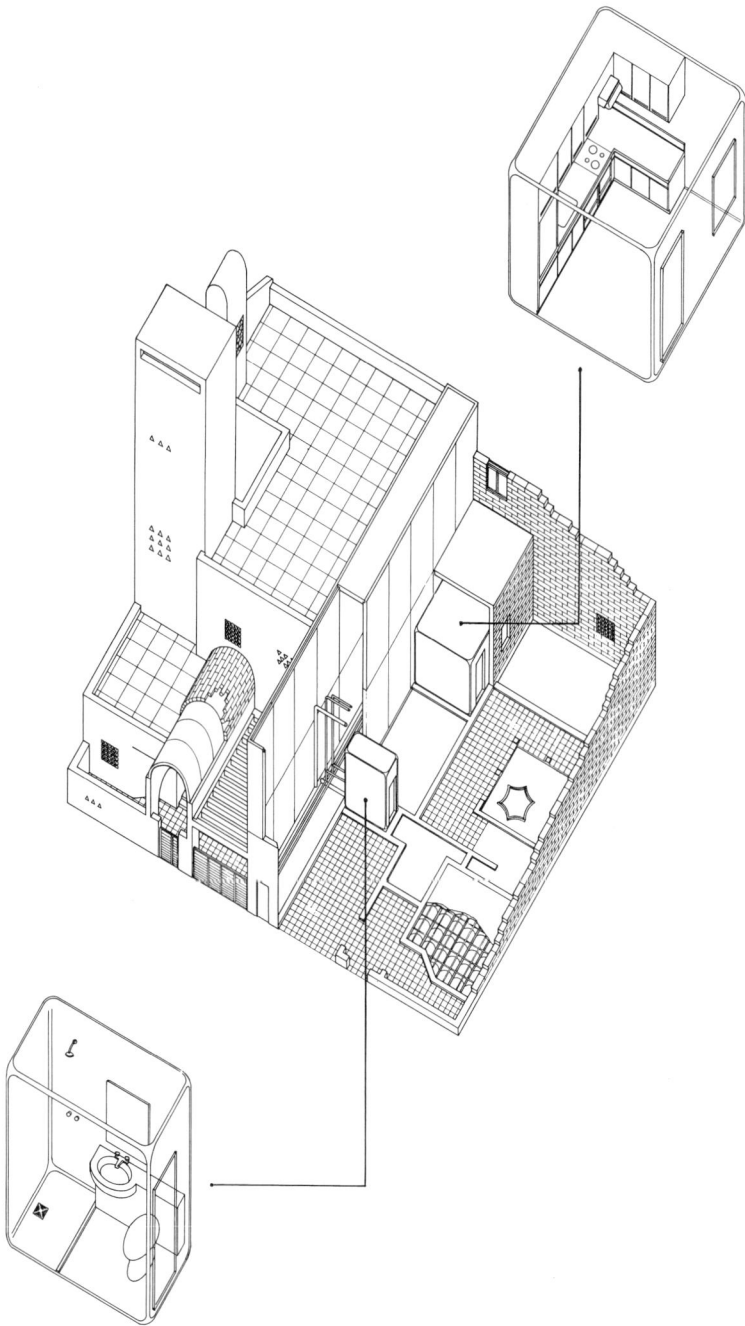

As–Sarir New Town, Libya: researcher with brick mold (left) and sun-dried bricks (above, facing), wall construction (facing below), and prefabricated roof vaulting and beams (this page).

underground water were discovered there in channels that moved as much water as a river, and a plan was devised to use it to farm the desert. There were also oil fields near Sarir, which employed large numbers of workers. The government of Libya therefore decided on an ambitious plan for a city in the desert, to house workers, engineers, farmers, and the Bedouin of the region.

I was asked to design and oversee the project. My first thought was to develop a brick from sand—an infinite resource in the desert—as a building material. The Bedouin had been making sun-dried mud bricks from antiquity, but these were perishable and hardly suited for housing of any permanency. After three years of cooperative work with a British research center, we perfected a process for casting sand bricks able to last several decades. Our idea was that the houses we planned would be built on a "do-it-yourself" basis by the owners, using these sand bricks.

The most difficult items for amateurs would be the roof, electrical wiring, and plumbing. In particular, an arched roof of brick would be very hard to erect. So we decided on a thin, prefabricated roofing that could simply be set and anchored on top of the house. We developed a comparatively simple method: a hollow dug in the sand served to mold a mixture of concrete and fiberglass reinforcement.

As far as plumbing and electricity were concerned, we decided on a single wall of service ducts—all plumbing and wiring were placed inside this sandwich-walled unit, to minimize costs and maintenance. The builders had only to situate kitchen and bathroom adjacent to this wall; otherwise, they were free to build whatever sort of house they liked. Unlike typical public housing, each home in this community might assume the design and layout its owners wanted— each different from its neighbors.

To find out if amateur builders could actually put together our design, we conducted an experiment. Some members of my staff who had never done anything but desk work lived at the site for three weeks, and with the help of an English assistant, attempted to assemble a house. The experiment was a success. Three weeks was insufficient for construction, but aside from final finishing, the houses were entirely buildable by unskilled labor.

The houses I designed had one remarkable feature, a wind tower. This was a chimney-like tower, some fifteen meters in height with open slots at the top. When the wind blew through the top of the tower, warm air inside the house was sucked out and more temperate air from the floor was drawn upward to cool the interior. This design exploited the natural temperature patterns of the desert, which the Bedouins put to such excellent use in their tents. Thus, our community in Sarir marked the encounter between the latest industrial technology from the West and the age-old desert culture of the Arabs.

New Community Development

When I drew up the master plan for the Sarir settlement, I gave greater importance to streets—though not necessarily straight—than to open squares. For I believe strongly in the superiority of streets to squares as public urban space. In the Japanese tradition, the street is the "front," and streets, gently unfolding from one house to another, are the source of the city's enjoyment. I wanted that Japanese-style "street as façade" to exist in symbiosis with local features of the community in Sarir. After all, the concept of the street, intersection, or market (in Japanese, *tsuji*) as a public space was firmly established in Islamic cultures as the *souk*, or bazaar—the shopping district in Islamic cities. In old French films you often see a criminal dashing into the streets of the bazaar and disappearing in the crowd. That crowded, seemingly confused maze of streets and shops is what I am talking about—a conception of public space identical to Japan's meeting space, or *tsuji*. A maze of streets in a town set in the midst of the desert has the advantage of blocking sandstorms and winds, and its also creates much-needed shade. At the peak of summer's heat, you can walk comfortably through such well-ventilated, shaded streets.

In Sarir, my philosophy of symbiosis was realized at a wide range of levels, from conceptual to practical. The scale of the project was large: we were building an entire city from scratch in the middle of the desert. It is still not finished. But this, so to speak, was no castle built on sand. And, gradually, the sand-colored city will rise from the desert; and then, just as inevitably, it will one day return to the sands whence it came.

Symbiosis of Past and Future

Shonan Life Town in the northern part of the city of Fujisawa in Kanagawa Prefecture, near Yokohama, is another of the town projects our firm designed some twenty years ago. It was then planned for a population of 45,000. Some 35,000 are already living there, and over time the place is acquiring the lived in aspect of a real town. Before construction began, about five hundred farming families lived in the district, mostly cultivating rice. Their farmhouses have been preserved, together with 50 percent of the area of each paddy. One of the aims of the project was to permit the symbiosis of urban and farming districts, the present and the past. This meant developing parcels of land that became available at widely separated locations according to area, and often swapping farm plots for housing lots throughout the site.

In every Japanese farming community there is a wooded area or sacred mountain. To preserve the natural environment along with this traditional topography, we decided against leveling all the ground and building a grid of straight roads, which would have destroyed the history and environment of the area. Carefully selecting our rights of way at a uniform grade, we built meandering roads, leaving as much greenery as possible and preserving the historical appearance of the agricultural village. As a result, Shonan Life Town has proved a successful symbiosis of farm and town, with roads as irregularly winding as you could find anywhere. At one stage, the Ministry of Construction, which was overseeing the project, objected to the twisting roads, and—because it was to supply the funds for site preparation—issued an order to revise our plan. But we stubbornly held to the original scheme and were at last able to carry it out. Now twenty years later, Shonan Life Town is recognized as a model of new community development.

Publicly we stressed that the preservation of the local farming economy was essential in the design of Shonan Life Town, but in fact this presupposed the preservation of the historical community—the human ecology—of the area.

Today, Brasilia and Canberra are both regarded as inadequate; in Japan, Tsukuba Academic New Town is another unfortunate case.

What is wrong with these new cities? Many complaints are voiced that they are one-dimensional, dominated by the automobile, isolated from other cities. They lack human warmth, their populations are too uniform, there is no community. In sum, these cities are all without symbiosis or, put another way, they have no history. In fifty or hundred years, they will accumulate their own histories. But is that any reason why they need be unpleasant to live in for a century? Is there no way to allow these new towns a symbiosis with history from the start?

There is, indeed. For, as in Shonan Life Town, new communities must be built as much as possible in symbiosis with the existing historical context, so the entire city ought *not* to be planned in advance. At least one district must be set aside and allowed to develop in a natural way. Such growth inevitably results in a mazelike pattern. New communities that possess such mazes—that live in symbiosis with history—will be attractive and enjoyable to live in.

16

SYMBIOSIS OF LAND-USE PLANNING AND REDEVELOPMENT

"Livability Factors" in Regional Planning

The ancient and beautiful towns of Vasto and San Salvo on the Adriatic coast of southern Italy still look as they did in Roman times. Agriculture is their mainstay, but since they have not succeeded in introducing any secondary industries, per capita income is low compared to industrialized centers in the north. At a public meeting on regional planning in the provincial assembly, people declared that high per capita income was not their aim. They didn't want to bring all sorts of factories into the area and make it like the north, but wanted instead to preserve their splendid coastline, lovely towns, and delicious seafood—in short, their lifestyle. They sought, accordingly, a plan for the region grounded in a full understanding of these aims.

I was deeply impressed by this declaration of the people of Vasto and San Salvo. When we hear the same sentiments expressed by the people of various regions in Japan, we too will be able to have regional plans that respect the unique character of each area. As long as every city aims to match and mimic Tokyo, we are bound to see thousands of mini-Tokyos sprout across Japan; but how much more attractive is the image of regional communities, each distinct and rich in local character. If increase in per capita income is the guiding principle of most regional development, preservation of local character and lifestyle, in contrast, are decidedly noneconomic notions.

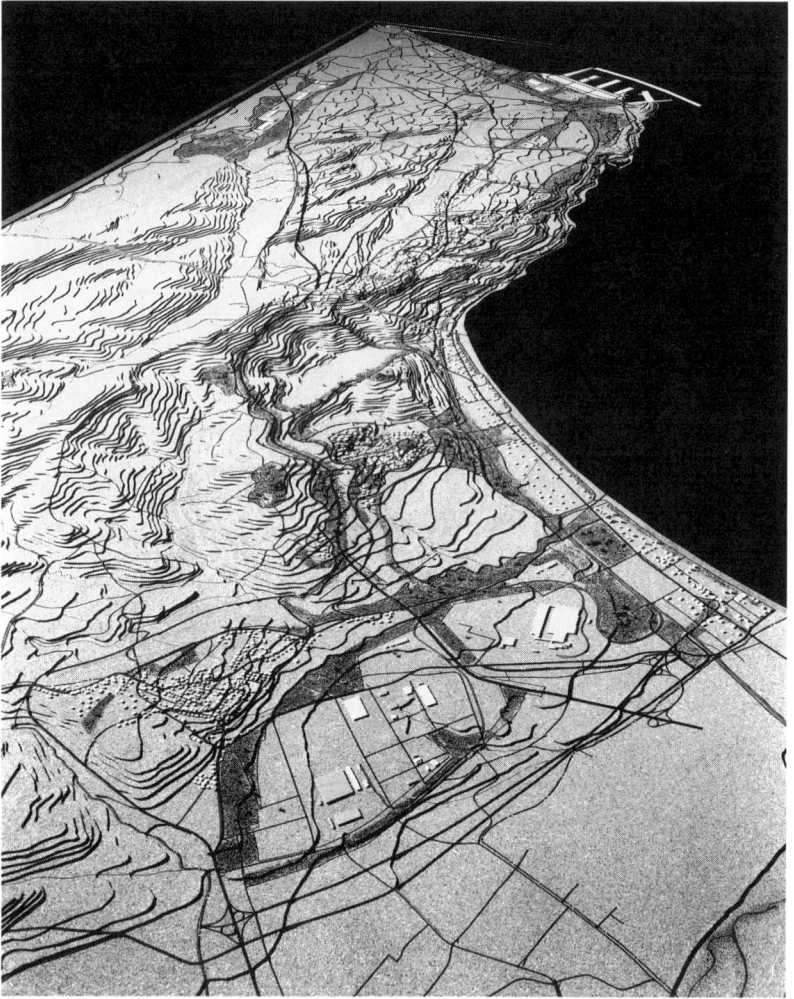

Kisho Kurokawa: regional plan for Vasto–San Salvo, Italy (model, 1975).

"Character" and "lifestyle" are instead livability factors which reflect the local residents' pride in their history and surroundings. We cannot afford to ignore such goals: indeed, we need plans for regional development that balance economic with noneconomic factors.

From the 1960s, Japan's national planning has consistently been linked to a policy of achieving more or less standard per capita income throughout the country. The Ikeda cabinet (1960–64)[1] was the first to make this a national goal. Its "Plan for Doubling Per Capita Income" (1961–70) spurred the Japanese on toward ever greater productivity, a policy clearly graspable by anyone. That government instituted what is now known as "the Pacific coast industrial belt." The region was chosen for development because of its excellent harbors, ready supply of labor, and large market catchment. It was eminently well suited for the secondary processing of raw materials, which made up Japan's leading industrial growth sector at the time. The intensive development of a region so rich in potential led, in the end, to an overconcentration of Japan's capital, industrial power, and workforce. In response, there arose a cry from other regions of the country, particularly those along the Japan Sea coast, for a fairer share of the national productivity and a rectification of the gap between per capita income on the Pacific coast and elsewhere in Japan.

The slogan of the succeeding Sato cabinet (1964–72) became "Social Development." The new government sought to decentralize industry, planning and building new industrial centers throughout Japan—intended to stop the flow of labor, especially younger workers, from local areas to Tokyo and the Pacific belt. If that exodus could be stemmed, local economies would revive and tax revenues increase, public works projects would be generated and local environments improved. Indeed, the gap between earnings in Tokyo and other regions shrank.

But any real decentralization of Japan had certain major disadvantages for local areas, too. First, it was extremely wasteful in terms of the investment required in public works and facilities. The ideal at that time of a regional city was a self-sufficient unit that could meet all the needs of its residents, from cradle to grave. People were born, educated, and married, raised families, and died in such towns, where a strong community spirit, almost a family feeling, used to be promoted. However, communities of this sort need all the goods and services of modern life brought in, despite limited available markets. In its most extreme form, this implies amenities, from cinemas and department stores to universities and research centers. Even Kabuki theaters and opera houses would have to be constructed and supported in each region, for a limited local population. It had to be concluded that entirely self-supporting small, or even medium-sized, regional cities were economically unfeasible.

Network Cities for the Age of *Homo Movens*

The second disadvantage of complete decentralization is that it makes it unnecessary for people to move between regions. The title of my book *Homo Movens* (1969; meaning of course, "man on the move," after the models *Homo sapiens*, man as thinker, and *Homo faber*, man as maker) expresses the importance of mobility as the special characteristic of contemporary humankind. Just as the concept of *Homo faber* is linked to those principles on which industrial society was based, *Homo movens* is linked to the principle of a post-industrial society.

The mobility that characterizes present-day society cannot be explained simply in terms of transport development. The fact is that in our information society, mobility has begun to possess considerable value of its own. It is choice that makes movement possible. According to individual inclinations and values, you can now choose things not found in your hometown. People today look on the availability of choice as one of the riches of life—"a wealth of choices." The city of the future, as we continue to evolve toward an information society, should be the sort of place that guarantees freedom of choice and makes positive provisions for movement.

A third disadvantage of decentralization is that, economically speaking, a small city simply cannot compete with a big one. There is no way a small city can match a larger one in capital flow, population, or consumer activity; decentralization only encourages smaller cities to strive for what they can never achieve.

All in all, a policy of total decentralization has many disadvantages and is no better than the competing policy of total concentration. A truly ideal scheme can never be achieved by *either* total decentralization *or* centralization. Japan has been grappling with this problem, and has at last produced a New National General Development Plan. A completely new policy for all regions—neither centralization nor decentralization, but a network city—is finally taking shape. The concept of the urban locality as an independent and self-sufficient unit will need to be abandoned and we shall create a web of linked cities, in symbiosis.

The network theory of cities is based on two major assumptions. One is that an information society will supersede our outmoded industrial society. The second is that each city in the network will establish its own cultural identity and pursue its own culturally based development. If the kind of network we are proposing is formed in an industrial society, there is danger of a "siphon phenomenon" occurring between large and small cities: the economies of the smaller cities, which have less accumulated capital and labor, may be siphoned off by the larger cities with their concentrated resources. This has actually happened along the high-speed bullet-train trunk lines. The leading sector of industrial society today, finished manufacturing, depends to a great extent on concentrated capital, productivity, and consumption.

By contrast, in an information society, the leading sector comprises such tertiary industries as broadcasting, publishing, education, and services. These depend mostly on cultural acumen, and so the economies of small cities are less likely to fall victim to the "siphon phenomenon"; they may even take a substantial lead over large cities. Kyoto, for example, cannot be compared economically with Tokyo or Osaka, but its accumulated cultural wealth is celebrated worldwide. In the twenty-first century, the information value of cultural properties, skills, and scholarship will grow apace. As a "data base," Kyoto offers a vast repository of information, and this will be a powerful weapon for Kyoto, and cities like it, in the coming age.

An "Event Economy" for the Regions

In the information age, the local character of each regional city, no matter what its size, will be a source of economic strength. Moreover, the evolution from an industrial to an information society represents a move from economic priority to the priority of knowledge and expertise. Already it is becoming possible to enlarge regional economies, which have been strictly limited up to now, through the power of such knowledge.

The "event economy" that I propose is an example. A calendar of local events can generate enormous income by attracting visitors from outside the region. The economic scope of tourism and resort industries is virtually unrelated to the size of the local population. An intriguing example of this is the sweet-potato liquor "Downtown Napoleon," which expanded its market nationally. Similarly, the governor of Oita Prefecture, Morihiko Hiramatsu, led a successful "village product" campaign, structured on events. When local groups hold exhibitions and fairs, promote international conferences and film festivals, and encourage local civic and religious festivals, they are often able to sell their agricultural and other products on a nationwide scale. Regional efforts to expand local markets now frequently achieve success with these kinds of events.

Local tax revenues were, until recently, determined by certain fixed and inflexible items: forestry, farming, and local population figures. In the future, however, local governments might start offering their financial support for ideas. The conduct of regional govern-

A naming event made "Downtown Napoleon" sweet-potato liquor instantly famous nationwide in Japan.

ment itself will be modified as it turns to supporting ideas and events that will get the region's economy moving. In an age of information—and ideas—networks between big and small cities will avoid a one-way siphon phenomenon, promoting symbiosis. As this continues, small cities will increase their own information-generating capacity and exploit the markets of larger areas. This is but a single reason why regional planning should adopt the network concept.

Cities with High Informational Capacity

The Fourth National Japan Development Plan (1983–2000) focuses mainly on the Tokyo metropolitan area, and many have criticized the plan as an attempt to recentralize Japan around the capital. Let us look at a portion of the plan's intermediate report, under the heading "Tokyo as an International Center," that has stirred considerable controversy:

> Tokyo is not only the nation's capital but also, in such matters as international finance, for example, an international center. It provides information of international import to other cities of Japan, contributing to the development of the economies of Japan and the world. To ensure that greater Tokyo is able to function as an international center, we recommend the general development of Tokyo Bay, for which high-use demand continues to increase, and the adjacent coastal areas. We encourage at the same time the selective decentralization of various functions and the reform of regional structures. We also recommend the development of more sophisticated access by regional cities to Tokyo, so that Tokyo's developed skills and technologies may eventually reach out across the nation. We especially recommend that a base of high-priority government and business data be concentrated in Tokyo, with a lowering of access costs, for the benefit of other regions.

This section of the report caused noisy dissatisfaction among regional governments, and we cannot fail to recognize various difficulties for implementation. My own suggestion is that, since this plan has spotlighted Tokyo as an international center, it must at the same time offer the other regions methods for resisting Tokyo's dominance. Concretely speaking, there is a need to rethink the traditional allocation of public works projects uniformly across the country. By way of remedy, the national government ought to invest more regional cities that have already achieved a certain concentration of population and resources: namely, Osaka, Nagoya, and Kyoto, as well as Sapporo, Sendai, Kanazawa, Hiroshima, Takamatsu, Oita, and Kumamoto. These cities must be enabled to develop the same appeal as living and working environments as Tokyo.

An attractive city, in other words a city with a strong information-generating capacity, contributes enormously to establishing regional identity and is linked as well to the economic development of its own region. One reason regional cities lack Tokyo's attraction is their relative poverty of choice: they offer citizens far too little. People are drawn to a city that has more than one department store, or more than a single university. My second suggestion regarding the Fourth National Plan follows from the first. This is to look for specific large-scale projects to initiate in regions other than the capital.

Symbiosis of Three Networks

Following the deregulation of finance, Japan's short-term money market continues to grow at a rapid pace. With the total from trade in foreign currencies and interbank transactions, excluding reciprocal trading, added to that of the open market, Japan's short-term money market surpassed that of West Germany and Great Britain, becoming second only to the United States.

Another reason that Tokyo has found itself in the center of the international financial network is geographical. In the age of twenty-four-hour dealing, trading activity moves on to Tokyo after New York closes, and then to London after Tokyo. Lights may remain on all night in the offices of major trading companies and banks. The international money market needed an opening in time somewhere between New York and London—somewhere in Asia. Hong Kong and Singapore were both regarded as promising, but Tokyo, with its superior investment capability, has taken the lead. Tokyo now exists in symbiosis with three networks—a federation of Japanese regional cities; the three major urban centres: Nagoya, Osaka, and Tokyo; and an international money market network of entirely new dimensions.

This stratified network has resulted in the following predictions. According to the estimates of the Fourth National Plan, by 2025 the number of non-Japanese residing in Japan will have reached 2.3 million. This is a conservative estimate, and I believe that 2.5 million is closer to the mark—equivalent to a city the size of Osaka. The "internationalization" that had been little more than a vague slogan will take literal form before our eyes. The majority of overseas residents will be living in the international financial capital, Tokyo. Just as today New York has become a thoroughly international, global city, Tokyo will support its end of the network. As a city, it will no longer belong completely to Japan.

While some insist that other regions of Japan must also internationalize to counterbalance the concentration of human and economic resources, Tokyo's development is itself inextricably linked with that of the regions. In France, for example, there has been no resistance from other parts of the country to the further concentration of cultural facilities in Paris, already so richly blessed with them. Thus, a new Bastille Opera House was completed; the largest museum of science in the world and a unique music center have been constructed in the new Parc de La Villette; the Musée d'Orsay has opened in the restored Orsay station; the Institute of the Arab World has been built on the Seine; an international competition (of which I was one of the judges) was held for the design of an international communications center (La Tête Défense). Major additions were made to the Louvre, after the move of the Ministry of the Treasury, which had long occupied part of the Louvre's space. These new cultural facilities commemorated the second centennial of the French Revolution, just as the Eiffel Tower had commemorated the first anniversary in 1889. At all events, as long as Paris continues as one of the leaders in the international network of global cities, the rest of France will have access to the same level of information through domestic networks. Other regions of France are confident that they will prosper—their

Redevelopment at La Défense, Paris. The Grande Arche, foreground, with Arc de Triomphe toward the horizon.

unique local cultures intact—by remaining linked to Paris.

As regards Berlin, after the wall, consensus has been less readily attained—though in 1987 the 750th anniversary of the founding of the city was marked by an international architectural exhibition, the IBA. Some fifty architects from around the world were invited to participate in this ambitious project, including myself representing Japan. Each was given a site and asked to design a plan for its redevelopment, which should be left as architectural exhibits for the twenty-first century. More recently, the entire city has been transformed into a vast building site in anticipation of the transfer of the capital.

In any case, Tokyo *must* continue to develop; through its participation in an international network of cities, all of Japan will in consequence be linked to the rest of the world.

Tokyo Plan 2025: Man-made Island in Tokyo Bay

A major redevelopment is required to enable Tokyo to interface with the international network of cities, thus helping promote a new

Redevelopment in Berlin: IBA (International Building Exhibition, 1987), with Kisho Kurokawa representing Japan.

age in every region of Japan. Millions of overseas residents will pour into the city, yet even now Tokyo has insufficient housing. The bayshore areas are being recommended for new schemes, but it is not ecologically sound to increase landfill along the shore—a method which also drives up land prices in adjacent areas and makes public works more expensive.

I believe it is much wiser to preserve the shoreline and raise a man-made island off Tokyo, similar to Portopia at Kobe. Let us assume an island of 30,000 hectares in Tokyo Bay. At its deepest, the bay is twenty meters, and it is estimated that the sludge on the bay floor extends another seven meters, so for an island five meters above sea level, landfill would be needed to a depth of thirty-two meters. The amount of landfill to create an island of 30,000 hectares—approximately two-thirds the size of the present twenty-three wards of Tokyo—would be nine billion cubic yards. This is equivalent to two-thirds of Mount Fuji. Where could this amount of landfill be obtained?

First, from the dredging of Tokyo Bay itself: that alone would

"Tokyo Plan 2025" (1988), including Boso Canal (right) and 30,000-hectare New Tokyo Island (center). Two concentric canals would encircle "old Tokyo" (upper left), inside Intercity Ring Road. See also page 267.

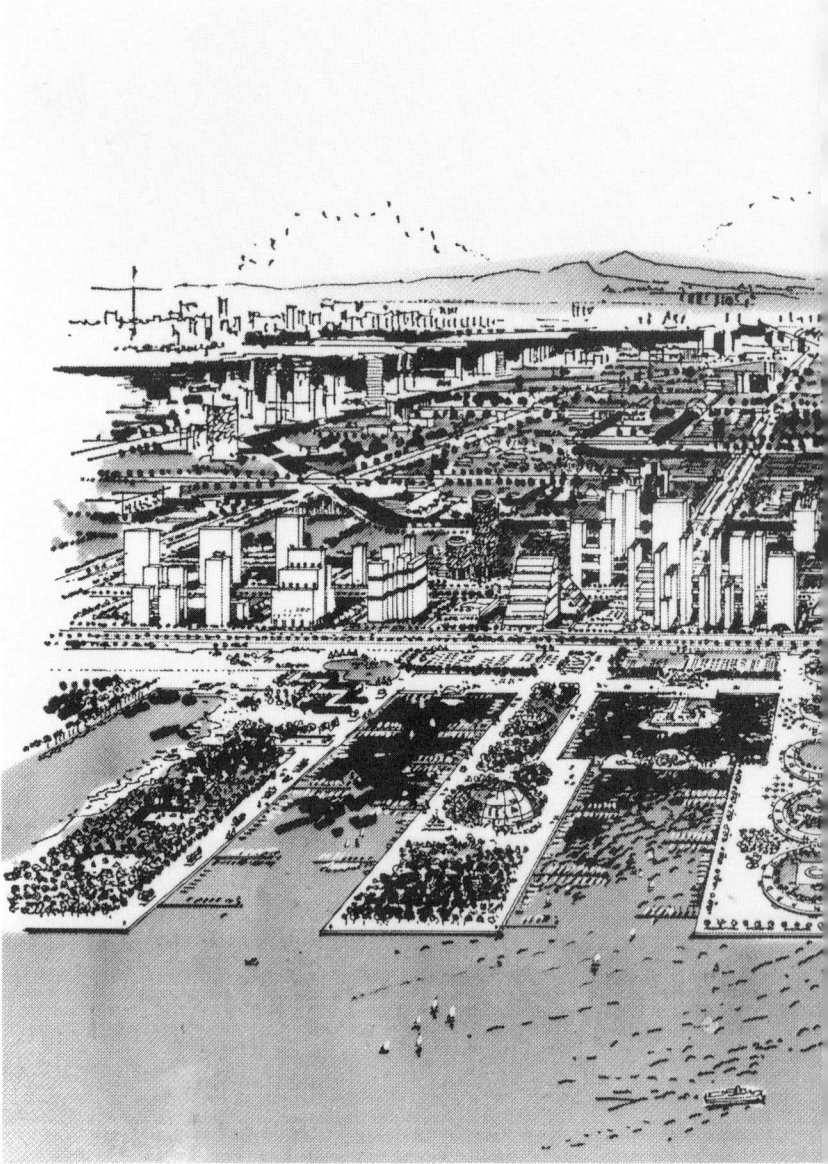

"Tokyo Plan 2025": New Tokyo Island (artist's rendering)
intended to rehouse five million persons.

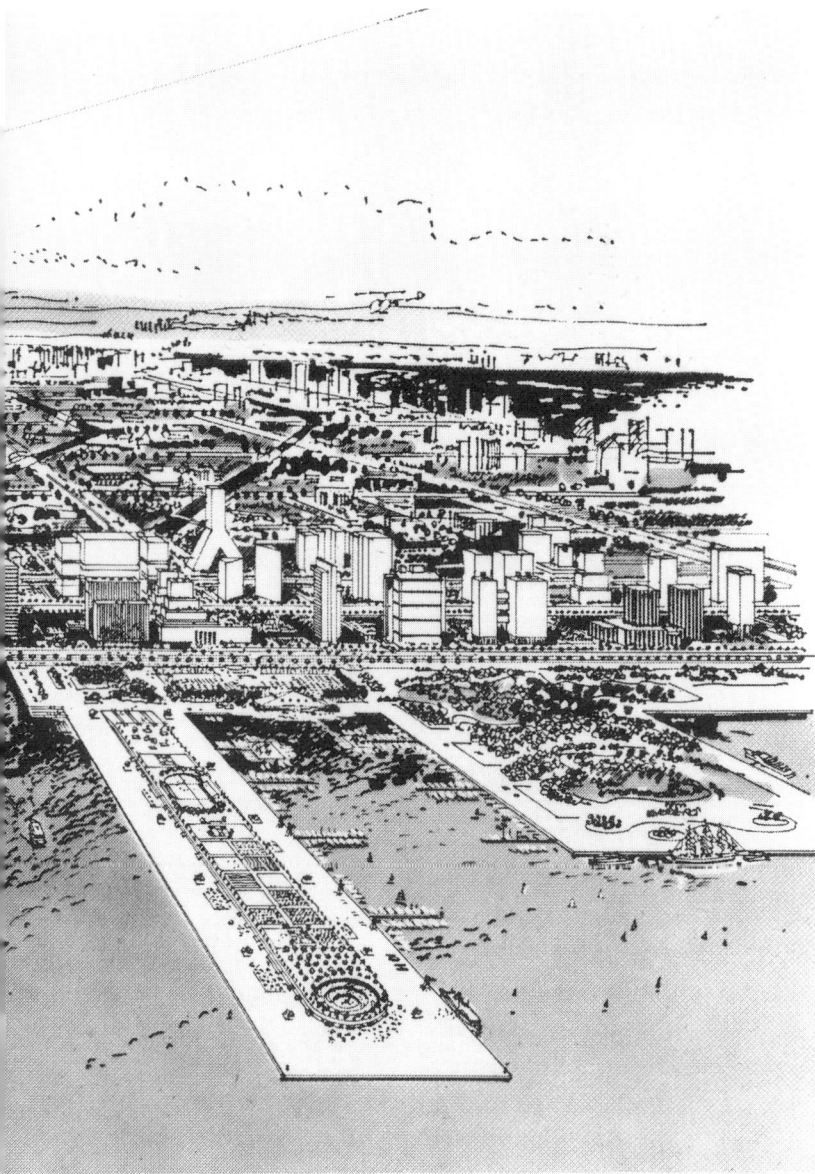

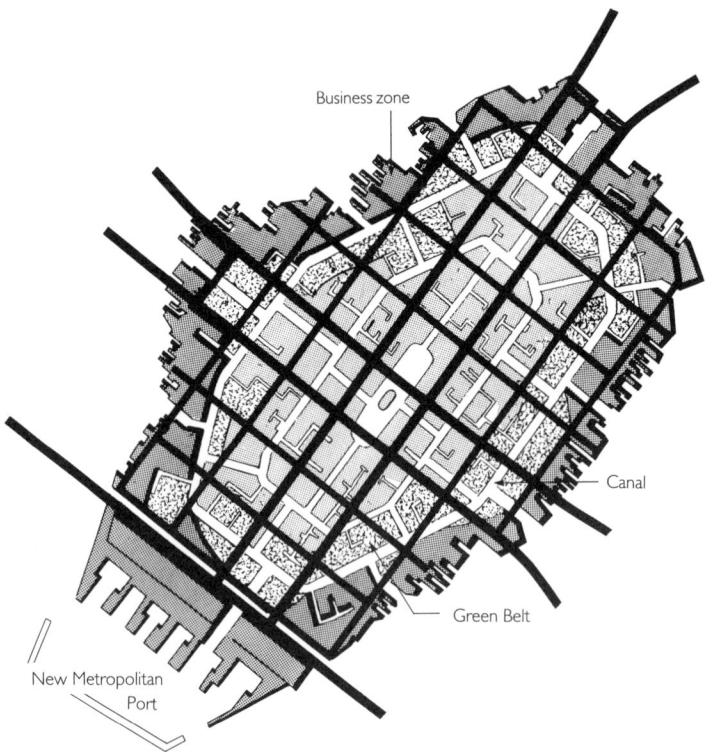

Business zone

Canal

Green Belt

New Metropolitan
Port

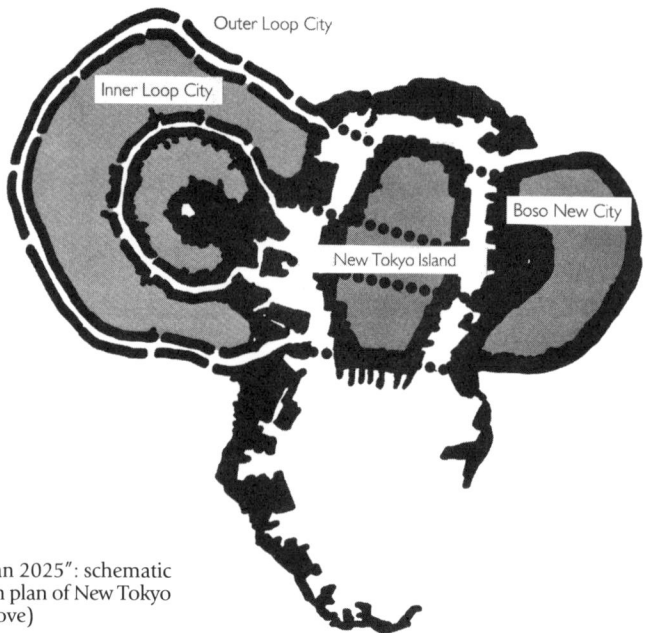

Outer Loop City

Inner Loop City

Boso New City

New Tokyo Island

"Tokyo Plan 2025": schematic
layout, with plan of New Tokyo
Island (above)

produce 4.5 billion cubic meters of soil. The other half of the needed total could be had by excavating a Boso Canal—a canal five hundred meters across, connecting Tokyo Bay with the Pacific Ocean through the Boso Peninsula. If the Boso Canal were to be built, the resulting difference in tides would assure that three or four meters of water would come rushing in and out of Tokyo Bay daily. This would cleanse the bay and increase its marine life, in a symbiosis with development.

At present, several hundreds of thousands of boats ply the waters of Tokyo Bay annually. The creation of a man-made island would disrupt their traffic, so the port of Tokyo would have to be moved to the tip of the island. At the same time, an outer port facility would be constructed at the Pacific mouth of the Boso Canal. Products that do not have to be unloaded in Tokyo Bay could be sent by pipeline.

The cost of putting this 30,000-hectare man-made island in place would be about ¥80 trillion. Computing the net land cost based on that figure, 3.3 square meters would cost about ¥2 million. If we suppose a land-use ratio of 400 percent, that is reduced to ¥500,000, a cost that would permit the average white-collar worker to buy a condominium. In that projected cost of ¥2 million per 3.3 square meters, all construction and support facility costs are included: light rail, bridges, roads, parks, water, and energy plants. A pleasant, liveable apartment from which one could commute by underground, car, or even boat need not be an impossible dream.

Nor does the intent of this project go against the comprehensive policy of decentralizing population and technological capacity across the archipelago. It is merely a plan to improve the appalling living circumstances of Tokyo's workforce, meet the needs of a growing influx of overseas employees, and improve the efficiency of Tokyo as an international business and financial center.

The projected population for our man-made island is five million. Of that total, 1.5 million will be non-Japanese. The projected population increase for the *native* Tokyo population by 2025 is another 1.5 million. The remaining two million will be accounted for by previous residents of "mainland" Tokyo, actually reducing its population density. As far as the ¥8 trillion construction cost is concerned, we can see that, given the enormous quantity of Japanese capital invested overseas, this is a far from impossible figure. Furthermore, there is a clear and definite demand for this new island. Land sells for about ¥12.7 million per 3.3 square meters today, so the profit to be had from this project is approximately ¥200 trillion at current rates. If the project were carried out by private enterprise, capital now floating in domestic stocks and foreign bonds could be attracted. The tax revenues from this ¥200 trillion could be used for further redevelopment of Tokyo and the major regional cities. In other parts of Japan, the same pattern could be followed: encouraging projects based on private enterprise, and reinvesting the profits in still other projects—as has been handled so successfully in Kobe for a number of years. This would be a way to channel funds that today float like disembodied spirits through the stock market and other foreign investment centers down to earth, within Japan.

For the Japanese government, facing the challenges of institutional reform and replenishment of the tax base, large-scale regional projects and the redevelopment of Tokyo are burdens too heavy to bear. It is in the best national interests to push surplus funds from profitable enterprises into increased circulation and pursue regional development through private means. In future, this new strategy will attract considerable support.

Preserving the Jumble of Tokyo's Rhizome

The new island in Tokyo Bay will provide the elbow room necessary for redevelopment and resuscitation of the city. The aims of Tokyo's redevelopment must be: to make the city safer in the case of a natural disaster on the scale of the Great Kanto earthquake; to increase housing space per person, currently far below the national average; and to add to the city's green spaces. If two or three million people are eventually drawn away from Tokyo to the new island, a pair of loop-shaped canals can be excavated from the land they vacate. A belt of high-rise buildings can even be constructed along both sides of these canals to form effective firebreaks in case of a new earthquake disaster.

Aside from the canals and their high-rise loop developments, Tokyo can be left as it is. The mazelike chaos of Tokyo is a natural rhizome with the potential to evolve as a genuinely postmodern city of symbiosis. Tokyo today seems chaotic, without order. If order means the Champs-Elysées in Paris, where the buildings on both sides of the avenue are more or less standard in height and reasonably consistent in design, then indeed Tokyo is chaotic. While nothing is wrong with broad boulevards and high-rise buildings, we also want cluttered, mazelike districts to explore. Tokyo's attraction is in its complexity, its variety, and its wide range of choices. Its constant transformation is also enjoyable. It is a city that doesn't distinguish between the wealthy, the middle class, or indigent students; a city that is fun and interesting to walk through (unlike Los Angeles, for example); it also has buses, a vast underground railway, and myriad taxis, and this wide range of choice is what makes Tokyo human.

Modern Tokyo is a city where old things and places are occasionally preserved, even if lacking historical value—but at the same time a city being rebuilt with the most advanced technology, to weird and sometimes pioneering designs. We must not sacrifice this source of Tokyo's attraction to redevelopment. If we supplement its lacks and proceed pragmatically with required changes, Tokyo may well become the most attractive and interesting of world capitals by the twenty-first century. Aside from doubling the amount of parkland and greenery and increasing the average standard living space, the city should be left alone. In so doing, we can proceed slowly, taking our time with Tokyo's revitalization.

Our loop developments along the new canals and the preservation of the present city represent a single package. We might call this symbiosis of development and preservation. There is also a need to invest in the suburban areas outside the present Number Eight Beltway and foster a more urban network there. In addition, as I have proposed, we should restore the Musashino Forest, creating a ten-thousand-hectare deciduous reserve that is a combination of royal park and sacred forest in its design.

The contemporary city of Tokyo has three important overlapping meanings for the Japanese: it is their greatest metropolis, the political capital, and home of the emperor, who is the nation's figurehead. This degree of concentration is unnatural. The nation's capital will be transferred in large part to the new island in the bay, which would be classified a special administrative district. Kyoto celebrated its twelfth centennial in 1994—why not commemorate that occasion by building a new imperial palace in Kyoto? It could become the first imperial residence, and the present palace in Tokyo could be a secondary palace. Could we not well afford to have the emperor spending half the year in Kyoto?

A direct track connecting Tokyo with Osaka by "linear motor car" in only an hour should be built, and the functions of the nation's capital split among Tokyo, Osaka, and Nagoya. Even now several government entities—the Imperial Household Agency, the Ministries of Education, Science, Sport, and Culture, the Agency for Cultural Affairs, and the Science and Technology Agency—have relocated one or another of their divisions. In this sense, the belt from Tokyo to Osaka can already be regarded as a "capital corridor." One way of invigorating Hokkaido and the Tohoku region would be, in addition, to extend the bullet train through the Seikan tunnel, build a "super port" in Hakodate, and relocate the Supreme Court to Sapporo.

It is widely held that the Japanese balance-of-trade surplus cannot last indefinitely; now is our chance to engage in building for future generations. In any event, Japan should not end its age in the sun as a mere economic giant. In the age of symbiosis dawning today across the world, Japan will for the first time make an assured contribution to present-day thought and culture.

CHAPTER

17

SYMBIOSIS IN ASIA: Promising Future for an Asian Renaissance

Roles of Structuralism and Post-Structuralism

Asia has been receiving a great deal of attention recently. Much of what is newsworthy relates to the philosophy of symbiosis, which in turn is closely linked to Buddhism. In addition, symbiosis seeks to revise several important tenets that have upheld the world order in the past, one being the notion of Eurocentrism. Such philosophers as Jacques Derrida, Gilles Deleuze, and Felix Guattari—following Claude Lévi-Strauss and Michel Foucault—have focused a lively debate on this subject. This generation, wishing to bring about a new era and overcome the modernism that the West itself had created, has now practically resolved these issues.

Lévi-Strauss first formulated a positive notion of "primitive thought" in the context of structuralism, because cultural anthropology had—almost up to that time—regarded other lesser cultures as "primitive" in comparison with the culture of Europe, and France in particular. These other cultures were classified according to an ethnographical scale indicating their proximity to the French standard. Clearly, this viewpoint mirrored that of the Chinese, who had from ancient times considered their civilization to be the center of the world. With the thought of Derrida, Guattari, and Deleuze, as well as Foucault, Barthes, and Lacan—who might all be classed as post-structuralists—the death of Eurocentrism seems certain.

Symbiosis at the Leading Edge of Physics and Biology

Since the Meiji Restoration, Japan has strived to model itself on Europe by imitating things European—from our school system to the Constitution. Likeness to Europe was the equivalent of modernization and progress. The same has applied in China, the countries of Southeast Asia, the Islamic countries of the Middle East, and throughout Africa since the mid-nineteenth century. Had this continued into the twenty-first century, the world would have become quite homogeneous, abnormally so. Extreme Eurocentrism would have ended in the global adoption of European norms everywhere, with only minor differences among the races. Since the mid-1950s, I have repeatedly voiced objections to this trend and have continuously emphasized rehabilitation of traditional cultures as the alternative. The world contains countless distinct cultures of varying degrees of influence and age. My thesis of symbiosis among different cultures maintains that the world would be far richer were these cultures helped to survive, resisting the drift toward homogeneity.

This philosophy of symbiosis has become a key concept, even if on occasion only lip service was paid to it. Earnest research and dialogue are now pursued, notably in the *Kyosei Jiyu Togi*[1] (Free Roundtable Discussion of Symbiosis) founded in the autumn of 1993. This is a gathering of Japanese university professors from various academic disciplines; it hosts symposia on the concept of symbiosis as this relates to Buddhism, economics, Taoism, Consciousness-Only, and other topics. A further example is the forum the architectural critic Charles Jencks and I initiated in London for elementary particle physicists, economists, philosophers, and other Nobel Prize–caliber scholars based on a scenario called "New World View," with symbiosis as its key concept. Television programs about this forum will eventually appear in Japan, Europe, and the U.S.

Research on symbiosis is now well underway, exerting an influence in the fields of medicine, biology, and quantum physics. Many leading academics have advocated the concept of symbiosis. In the field of elementary particle physics, such theories include F. David Peat's concept of synchronicity and David Bohm's "implicate order." In biology, there is the theory of symbiotic evolution put forth by

Lynn Margulis in the U.S. Others are the Holon theory, which Arthur Koestler proposed in his *Ghost in the Machine*, Hermann Haken's theory of synergetics, Ilya Prigogine's concept of dissipative structure, and Mandelbrot's fractal geometry. Such a Copernican shift in scientific views of the world, and the universe, has occurred only upon rare occasions since classical times. Evidently, the next paradigm shift is virtually complete and in place.

After Logocentrism: Environment and Multimedia

Computers epitomize dualistic technology, as they use 0's and 1's exclusively. In 1960, however, I predicted that the next generation of computers would take a giant leap and adopt a system that uses neither 0's nor 1's, or one that includes both 0's and 1's among others. Such a prediction is only natural according to the philosophy of symbiosis, and the appearance of "fuzzy-logic" computing has gone a long way to validate my prediction. Using fuzzy logic, computers can process imprecise concepts not easily dealt with otherwise. In fuzzy programming, the machine itself—through trial and error—accumulates experience and loosely formulates conclusions, only gradually working its way toward precision. In the process, it can obtain a marvelous grasp of something as fluid and indefinite as a marshmallow or a raw egg.

The conventional computer excels at grasping hard-edge concepts. However, since intermediary regions are not within the scope of such programming, anything like an egg is crushed in its grasp. That imprecise or "soft" entities are crushed by this dualistic rationalism of 0's and 1's—"yes" or "no"— is in fact an attribute of reason. In the age of symbiosis, an eventual correction will be accomplished through a symbiosis between reason and sensibility. By mobilizing the powers of sensibility, ambiguous areas hitherto overlooked by reason will be regained.

The essence of an industrialized consumer society is to manufacture large quantities of identical items by applying universal principles. Reason, science, and technology are therefore of the essence. The birth of information society, however, is shifting the emphasis to creative ability, design, and other areas of sensibility. The focus is shifting from mere production to added value, indicating an age of symbiosis between sensibility and reason. As the twenty-first century approaches, then, two new industrial domains will acquire importance: environmental industries and multimedia industries.

The Japanese government has forecast that, by the year 2010, environmental industries—including genetic engineering, biotechnology, pharmacology, bioelectronics, and biomechatronics—will obtain at least a ¥120 trillion market, while the multimedia sector will have gained a market of about ¥123 trillion. To compare: the television and radio industries combined now register sales of ¥2.9 trillion; newspaper, publishing, and video software industries, ¥6.3 trillion; and telephone and cellular industries, ¥6.2 trillion. Clearly, the potential field and scope are enormous. In an era in which such industries take center stage, sensibility will be considered determinant. Moreover, the birth of fuzzy-logic computing ushered in an era of symbiosis between digital and analogue approaches, leading to revolutionary changes. The age has arrived in which virtually any image can be exchanged. The ability to read and process holography and virtual reality is a sensitive skill, and the workers most needed in the age of multimedia will be those rich in sensibility.

In addition, environmental industries are rapidly multiplying—addressing resources such as forests, oceans, soil, animals, and microorganisms. Western society in the past has considered nature opposed to humanity. Humans have constructed buildings and cities, while nature has remained outside and in opposition. However, in Asia, including Japan, people have long considered themselves part of nature. This has given rise to a strong sense of gratitude for the benefits of nature and recognition of nature as a precious gift. Moreover, Asians have traditionally protected such resources. For example, in the West, people do not ordinarily eat bamboo shoots in season or freshly picked cucumbers in fermented soybean paste. However, such seasonal foods are still very popular in Japan—albeit at high prices. Although cucumbers abound in Bulgaria, it is difficult to explain to Bulgarians the custom of purchasing cucumbers the size of one's little finger at $20 apiece, simply because they are the first of the season.

The many ethnic groups of Asia have continued to live in ways that value human sensibilities in the abstract, while actively cultivating a sensibility toward nature. This is expressed in divers cultures, which adapt without too much effort to an age of symbiosis with nature. For such reasons, Asians are well suited to working in environmental and multimedia industries.

Close of the U.S.-Soviet Era: End of the Age of Dinosaurs

Aircraft, vehicles, and ships are industrial products built with the power of reason and with a universal capacity for science and technology. Thus it is only natural that these flourished in Europe, and that the industrial revolution occurred there. In the twenty-first century, when the sun will again shine on nature and sensibility, environmental industries and multimedia industries will bloom in Asia—new industries of sensibility likely to develop in close relation to Asian cultures and lifestyles. An age of symbiosis among nature, culture, and economics is about to begin in Asia. This is happening for the first time, since in modern Western-oriented society, no such phenomenon occurred. Capitalism and socialism (ultimately, Stalinism) are philosophies that grew out of the modern age. These pursued opposing viewpoints and vied to conquer the world. One side aimed at creating a socialist world community, while the other sought civilization through freedom and capitalism, giving rise to the Cold War.

In the struggle between the U.S. and the Soviet Union—two dinosaurs—one superpower has emerged victorious. However, this is not inevitable. The age of dinosaurs has ended, including both victor and vanquished. The U.S. and its capitalist ideology have not triumphed over the Soviet Union and its socialist ideology; rather, an age has ended for the U.S., as the leader of the West who sought to impose the American way of life, a single universal rule of freedom and democracy.

The U.S. has vigorously pushed for free competition—a type of competition that is, in fact, Darwinistic. The American ideal is as if all Sumo wrestlers were to compete in the same ring, from grand champions to second-class wrestlers, and that even a second-class wrestler could become a champion if he won all his matches—an extremely unlikely scenario. In the kind of free competition intended by the U.S., the U.S. with its enormous economic and military power is sure to win. Countries such as Croatia, Serbia, and the newly industrialized economies of Asia cannot succeed so easily in this game of survival of the fittest.

In Asia, the situation has led to a major problem in the relationship between APEC (Asia Pacific Economic Co-operation Conference) and EAEC (East Asia Economic Caucus). EAEC was conceived by Prime Minister Mahathir of Malaysia in opposition to U.S. dominance of the APEC member nations.

Concerning the overlap of APEC, directed by the U.S., and EAEC, led by its own member countries, he affirmed that "Each region has a different identity, and each region should be able to determine its own speed of development and its own culture." In addition, he stated, "The relationship between APEC and EAEC is neither hostile nor competitive. EACE should be able to exist within APEC as a subgroup of nations sharing common cultural ground."

I agree thoroughly with Prime Minister Mahathir of Malaysia's concept of the East Asia Economic Caucus (EAEC), since it accords well with my philosophy of symbiosis. Together with Prime Minister Mahathir and Vice-Premier Anwar, I am now promoting several concepts centered around Malaysia, including Eco-Media City 2020, and an Asian Internet. The objective is to align the scope of the Asian satellite and Asian Internet concepts with that of EAEC, so that the latter is not simply an economic consortium but also furthers communication and cultural exchange via multimedia channels.

Eco-Media City 2020

Eco-Media City 2020 is to be the base of these various activities. I have designed for it an international hub airport that is among the world's largest—currently under construction fifty kilometers south of Kuala Lumpur. A number of small villages that exist on the outskirts of the airport will be left as they are, and an enormous man-made tropical rain forest will be created. Trees grow three times faster in Malaysia than in Japan, so the forest will grow to a height of

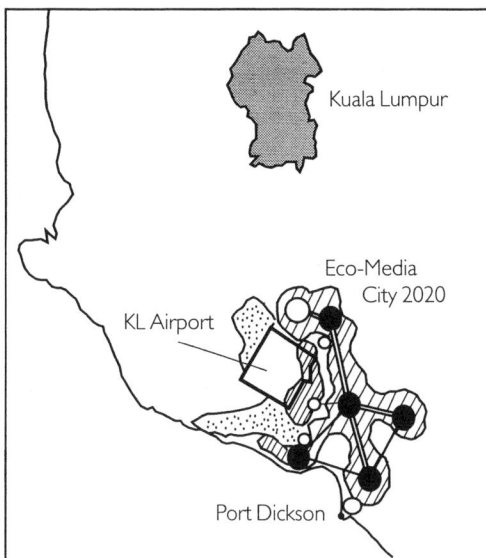

Linear Capital Corridor for Malaysia: sketch map by Kisho Kurokawa (1995, below) and locator key (at left).

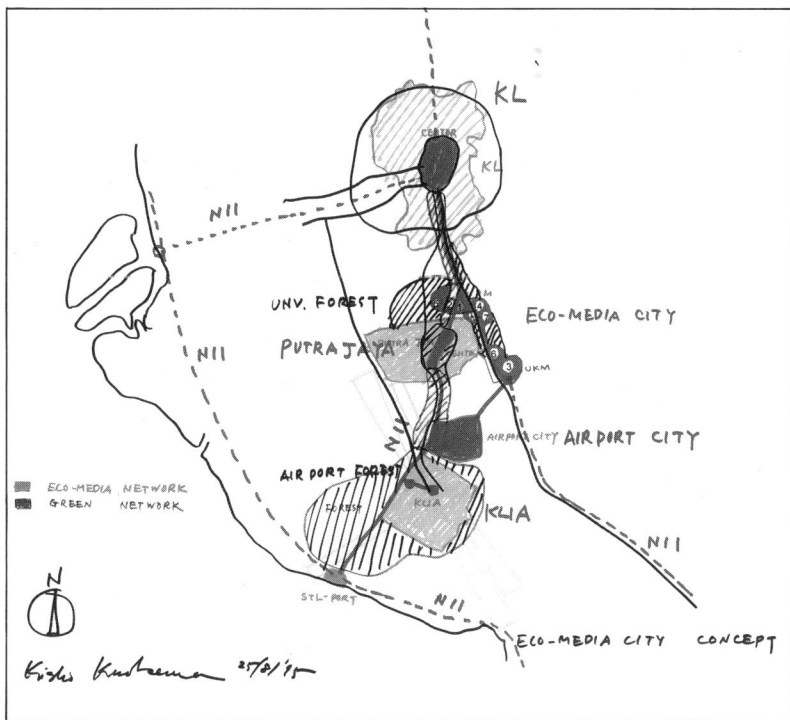

thirty meters within just twenty years. Small-scale, highly advanced cities will be built within that forest, connected by silent monorail as well as by the information highway. Leading-edge multimedia research institutes and universities are to be established. As the name Eco-Media City 2020 suggests, the city is scheduled for completion by 2020 and will make full use of ecotechnologies and multimedia technologies.

The Culture Shock of "Wawasan 2020"

When one walks along a street in Malaysia these days, one can see the number 2020 everywhere. It refers to "Wawasan 2020," a development target that Malaysia has set for itself, Wawasan being Malay for "vision." The aim of the nation as a whole is to become fully developed by 2020, and all efforts are being focused on that goal. When a ministerial-level APEC meeting was held in nextdoor Indonesia, the declaration adopted was: "We aim to achieve complete liberalization of trade by the year 2020." Here again, the year 2020 was selected as a milestone. Even more important, when Prime Minister Mahathir announced the decision to become a "developed nation" by 2020, thorough consideration was given to what this means. That, in turn, led to the setting of the Wawasan 2020 target. The Malaysia of Prime Minister Mahathir does not equate "rich" with "advanced," as Malaysia believes that wealth and technology alone cannot make a spiritually, or morally, backward nation "advanced." Accordingly, Europe and the U.S. must be weighed in the balance, since their societies currently demonstrate such unconcern over moral degeneration—a policy that does not augur well for continuing development.

APEC, NAFTA, and the EU were equally based on the viewpoint that the world order of the latter half of the twentieth century and beyond should be built using economic yardsticks. Therefore, the goals of these major consortia are merely economic. The intention of the U.S., as the leading force behind APEC, seems to be to gain a foothold for itself in Asia—which is demonstrating such remarkable economic growth—by forming an economic body encompassing Asia, the Americas, and Oceania. President Clinton continues assiduously to promote APEC for this reason. However, Prime Minister Mahathir of Malaysia has set before Asia as a whole the fundamental question of whether Asia ought silently to accede to this U.S. economic-centered strategy. Such bodes a particula, warning to Japan.

Consultation with Prime Minister Mahathir and Vice-Premier Anwar

Construction of the gigantic airport I have mentioned is one of Malaysia's projects targeted for completion by 2020. An enormous tract of land measuring ten kilometers square has been acquired near the coast about forty kilometers south of the capital, Kuala Lumpur, large enough for this huge hub airport with four 4,000-meter runways.

In addition, to decentralize functions from the nation's capital, plans are underway to move a portion of these to a location about twenty kilometers distant from Kuala Lumpur to a new Government City. In conjunction with the move, a new City Center Plan calls for redevelopment of downtown Kuala Lumpur. This will be built on the former site of the racing club. Some ten new super high-rise buildings, two hotels, and a new municipal office building are initially to be constructed.

The city terminal for the airport, which I am currently designing, is planned as a redevelopment of Brook Field Station; functionally it will resemble Tokyo City Air Terminal at Hakozaki. Travelers will be able to check-in with luggage, and then proceed by ERL (Express Rail Link) directly to the new airport. A densely populated district will be constructed around and above the ERL tracks. Eventual plans call for integrated development of a financial center here—more than fifteen office buildings as well as hotels, department stores, and residences.

In 1998, the Commonwealth Games will be held in Malaysia, so the first terminal building and two runways of the new airport must be complete, along with one satellite and the transport link to the airport by ERL and highway. This is envisioned as one part of Eco-Media City 2020, a symbol for the whole Malaysian nation which I myself have proposed after beginning the City Center Plan for redevelopment of downtown Kuala Lumpur. At that time, in 1989, Prime Minister Mahathir contacted me to request advice. The original commission was for the new airport and we began work on the design in 1992.

Meanwhile, Vice-Premier Anwar, also Minister of Finance, has become party to the debate concerning a new world order. He happened to have read the first English edition of *The Philosophy of Symbiosis*, and explained how my book had made a deep impression on him, even going so far as to declare, "The philosophy of symbiosis can become the future political slogan for Malaysia. Our target in the twenty-first century is symbiosis." From that moment, the distance between us seemed to diminish. Indeed, I now have the privilege of advising him not only on architecture and urban planning, but also on overall national policy, such as an ecomedia-oriented society.

Eco-Media City 2020: "Incubator" for Eco-Industry and Multimedia Industry

In October 1995, the government of Malaysia held an international symposium entitled "Intercultural Conference for Eco-Media City." Following the conference, leading specialists in multimedia and environmental technology from Japan, Malaysia, and the U.S. began their research. Eco-Media City 2020 will be the world's first "network agglomeration" with a twenty-first century airport as its core. It will include an industrialized airport city, a government city, and a university and research city, and will have the capacity to house between 250,000 and 500,000 persons. An information highway using communications satellites and optical-fiber cable, a high-speed wireless digital network, and other informational infrastructure components will be variously combined. The objective is to draw up and confirm optimal future directions for this resulting hybrid system of communication-linked satellites. We intend to study the arrangement on a practical level while proceeding with detailed design, in order to arrive at a twenty-first century lifestyle prototype. In other words, this city itself will serve as an "incubator" for the future eco-industry and multimedia industry. The project may incorporate tax advantages to draw business ventures from around the world and will provide a favorable research environment to attract leading research scholars from other countries.

Clearly, the success of this experiment will be felt throughout the Malaysian system of private and government enterprise. Additionally, it will provide feedback for Japan as well as for the Information Superhighway advocated by U.S. Vice President Albert Gore.

Symbiosis between Forests and Cities

Another notable feature of Eco-Media City 2020 is its inclusion of a massive experiment in environmental and multimedia technology. Environmental research will generate new industries by harnessing the power of nature. Eco-Media City 2020 will make use of this cutting-edge environmental resource capacity to recycle items that are currently being discarded as waste and carry out experiments toward a new fishery industry that takes into account forest and ocean cycles.

The most crucial element in such an experiment is abundance of natural resources. In the case of Japan, unfortunately even such cities as Tama New Town, Senri New Town, and Tsukuba Academic New Town are not situated in areas richly blessed by nature. However, these conditions are present in Malaysia, and can be exploited almost at once. Malaysia's environment is particularly well suited to forestry. Its long hours of sunlight, optimal humidity, and ample rain are responsible for some of the world's outstanding tracts of rain forest, with trees growing far faster than in Japan. The land to be made into forest in Eco-Media City 2020 is presently used to grow rubber trees and coconut palms cultivated for their oil. If this parkland is reforested now, a magnificent new cover will develop by the year 2020.

In many modern cities, especially in Asia, there are few trees and shade is scarce. This lowers the efficiency of air conditioning equipment, which gives off further heat and raises the local ambient temperature. Such cities should seek the shelter provided by forests. Though success in this area, as easy as it could be to achieve, would result in immediate energy savings, little or no thought has been given to the combination of cities and afforestation in modern urban planning. A metropolis such as Tokyo is therefore unable to function without air conditioning in summer. Heat released by air conditioners combines with heat radiated from concrete, automobile exhaust, and other sources to further increase temperatures. Thus, it has been estimated that temperatures in Tokyo today are about five degrees higher than during the Edo period.

The forest projected for Eco-Media City 2020 will enhance the city's functioning as a modern metropolis. Residents will be able to live and work without air conditioning in summer. Although housing complexes have been built in the midst of forested areas in Northern Europe, there are as yet no modern cities based on a conscious environmental strategy of incorporating forests or animal life. Our experiment is therefore expected to achieve a first by realizing such symbiosis between the city and nature and high tech and nature, such as bioelectronics, biosensors, bioreactors, and biomass.

In all modern cities, there are major problems associated with waste water and runoff control. As is clear enough in Tokyo, most modern roads are of concrete or asphalt. Rainwater flows from such roads along gutters, is collected in drains, and from there flows into Tokyo Bay. Practically none is returned to the soil. Meanwhile, processing of wastewater, including liquid industrial wastes, has already reached saturation. At present, wastewater sludge is transported in its raw state to processing sites, where chemicals are added. This wastewater is aerated and sludge removed by sedimentation, all at great cost. In the past, rain soaked into the soil and was purified, then rose to the surface at various sites. Well water was potable, and indeed clean, naturally pure water was available almost anywhere; there was no need for massive reservoirs or runoff systems. If rainwater purification through soil filtration can be revived and a supply system developed to use and recirculate well water, it will become possible at great ecological savings once more to plan for a more localized water distribution.

All in creating a sense of the preciousness of nature, environmental technology helps people enjoy the fruits of high technology by relying on nature's strengths. Such are the demands and privileges of a sustainable city.

Twenty-First Century Ship of Dreams—the Techno-Superliner

In Malaysia, the area of Port Dickson and Kulang, at the southern edge of Kuala Lumpur, is being considered as the site of a new world-class harbor of fifteen meter in debth. Meanwhile, in Japan, research is proceeding apace on next-generation ships and ports. One such ship is the superconductor electromagnetic thrust vessel propelled by a superconductive electromagnet affixed to the ship's hull. The *Yamato*—the world's first such experimental ship—was completed in July 1990. Measuring thirty meters in length with a 2.5-meter hull and projected full load draught of 1.5 meters, the *Yamato* underwent successful water trials in Kobe Port in June 1992. Since this type of vessel has no screws, it can be designed with a shallow draught. The successful commercial launch of such a large, high-speed freighter would be a revolutionary accomplishment, especially considering the numerous shallow ports of Southeast Asia.

The second possibility is a high-performance freighter dubbed the Techno-Superliner, which surpasses the capabilities of all existing vessels. It boasts a top speed of fifty kilometers per hour—about five times that of conventional freighters—and would be capable of carrying 1000 tons of freight over distances exceeding 500 nautical miles (about 930 kilometers). One difficulty is its fifteen-meter draught, deeper than that of existing ships. However, since the Techno-Superliner would navigate with its hull raised through a combination of buoyancy, lift, and pneumatic force, it would be the equivalent of an ocean-going truck. This would be ideal for freight transport in Asia, with its many islands. Since the majority of Malaysian ports are shoalbound, it would be necessary to deepen these. However, if harbors were built for the Techno-Superliner and shipping lines established throughout Asia, the benefits of a new age of ocean freight transport would surely justify this cost. The demand for freight transportation to and from Southeast Asia in the twenty-first century will become the fastest-growing anywhere in the world; futhermore, there is a strong tendency toward gigantic container ships reaching one million tons in freight. Therefore, combining harbors for the Techno-Superliner with the opening of the world's most advanced airport would be highly appropriate.

Techno-Superliner prototype, the *Hisho*.

Artist's rendering of Techno-Superliner in port.

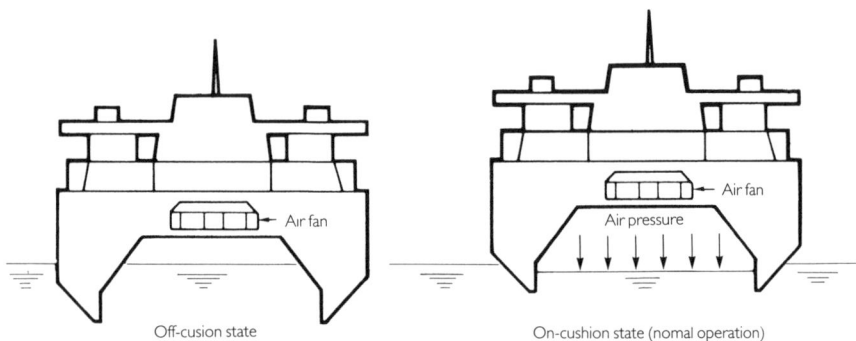

Off-cusion state

On-cushion state (nomal operation)

Air fan

Air fan

Air pressure

Cross section of hull.

Wake Up, Japan!

As I warned in late 1994 in *Jiyu Shinpo*, an organ of the Liberal Democratic Party, Japan lacks the clear goals and strategies that encourage Malaysia's citizens to dream!

In Malaysia, Prime Minister Mahathir has established exceptionally clear national goals for the year 2020. He has originated the EAEC concept, placing limits on APEC participation, in pursuit of Malaysia's vision for the future of Asia, as well as recent aggressive policies for multimedia supercorridors between Kuala Lumpur and the Kuala Lumpur international airport. The same is true of Vice-Premier and Finance Minister Anwar,[2] who, during a previous visit to Japan, stressed the notion of an Asian Renaissance. He is clearly predicting that the world order of the twenty-first century will be different from that of the twentieth century.

Japan, however, has as yet proposed nothing like this; we shall hardly be able to lead Asia under these circumstances. Not only Dr. Mahathir, but the whole of Asia finds this unfortunate. Today, we urgently need politicians and leaders with an original Japanese philosophy and world strategy. During the twentieth century, we have been able to solve most problems through the joint application of economics and technology. In the areas of overseas development aid and creation of domestic policy, the only question heretofore was how best to manage the economy. Consequently, the nation entered a decline following the burst of the economic bubble in 1991, largely because it had no extra-economic goals.

In China, where economic growth has been extremely robust, annual income per capita remains at about $360, or some 1 percent of Japan's. Still, China is self-assured and takes a truly assertive attitude when negotiating with the U.S., Russia, and South Korea. Why is China so confident? Surely because the Chinese nation has a clear outlook and goals for the future based on traditional ideals, not on external influences. When Prime Minister Li Peng of China met with Prime Minister Mahathir, he stated his wholehearted support for Dr. Mahathir's EAEC proposal. When I contrast this with the vague attitude of Japanese politicians who simply parrot the U.S. stance, I am envious. To be sure, China is aware that, although no one has openly criticized the twentieth-century world order with its economic priorities, the coming century will focus jointly on economy *and* culture.

Throughout the world, governing by economic or military might alone has become nearly impossible. Such might has now to be combined with the authority that stems from culture and tradition. Moreover, the world is entering an age of symbiosis among different cultures, and economic development will stagnate unless the identities of individual cultures are respected. The bilateral understanding between Malaysia and China has two significant aspects that almost no one has pointed to. First, since the EAEC concept rests on the twin pillars of economics and culture, any notion of a bloc based on economics alone is excluded. In other words, APEC will be unable to compete effectively with EAEC. Second, although Japan possesses economic and technological strength far exceeding the rest of Asia, we will be unable to exert leadership—unless we develop a philosophy and strategies rooted in Japanese culture and, indeed, in the cultures of the Asian region for helping to create a new world order.

An "Asian Renaissance" Rooted in Economics and Culture

Throughout the twentieth century, European culture was viewed as the most advanced, and overseas development aid has focused on transferring developed technology to developing countries. The aim was to foster a Western lifestyle—and, thereby, develop markets for the products of Western nations. As we approach the end of the twentieth century, however, the scenario of an entire world moving toward European culture is beginning to lose its luster. In its place, the new light of the age of symbiosis is beginning to shine from Asia itself.

All the world's diverse cultures must shun homogeneity to remain viable for future generations, including, for example, the cultures of Bosnia, Herzegovina, Serbia, Iran, China, and Malaysia. Many have begun to realize that the preservation of different cultures—like the genes of more than a single species—serves to enrich the world. Since this change is well underway, the goal of overseas development aid must change in the direction of respecting the culture of each country and allowing it scope. Rather than mere technological transfer, a kind of technological transformation is needed to rearrange means and goals to suit the culture of each country. For some years now I have advocated such an approach as a symbiosis between technology and culture.

In the area of electrical power, for example, the development efforts of Japan and the U.S. have focused on nuclear power generation. Japan's nuclear power plants are considered quite safe, and Japan is viewed as a developed country in this regard. Japan's nuclear power generation technology was expected to be transferred to Asia with increasing speed, as it was believed that developing countries would follow the paths of developed countries. In line with my philosophy of symbiosis, however, this has not proved the case. India, for example, has nuclear, thermal, and hydroelectric power plants. Nevertheless, cow dung still provides more than 70 percent of the fuel for household use in rural areas. Cow dung is collected, dried, baked until it resembles charcoal, and used as a household fuel for cooking and the like. This could scarcely be imitated in other countries, where cows do not freely walk about the streets. In India, cows are considered sacred, and if a cow blocks the middle of the road, vehicles must yield right of way. Consequently, cow dung is widely and freely available. From this I conclude that the most viable solution for India would be a hybrid energy supply system that includes cow-dung fuel as well as hydroelectric, thermal, and nuclear power generation. Conversely, if India were to construct a comprehensive nuclear power system capable of meeting the country's entire demand for electricity, the need for cow dung would disappear, while both funds and energy would be wasted in disposing of enormous amounts of this fuel.

Moreover, the use of cow dung as a cooking fuel has long been part of Indian lifestyle and is a practice well suited to the land's climate and ecology. If all cooking were done by electricity supplied from nuclear power sources, India's traditional lifestyle would suddenly be modified and the destruction of Indian culture accelerated.

The twentieth century has seen the destruction of certain cultures owing to economic factors and the increasing influence of the cultures of developed nations. This is no longer acceptable. Japan, which has been providing support for economic development, must initiate a form of assistance that ensures continued cultural diversity and development. This will favor an "Asian Renaissance" founded on both economic and cultural factors. If the twenty-first century is to flourish as an age of symbiosis, we must preserve cultural differences while building a new world order.

Formation of Three Asian Blocs: Japan Plus China and Malaysia Plus Indonesia as Nodes

The term "Asia" has long been used primarily in reference to the South or Southeast. However, Asia should logically be seen as comprising at least three blocs: Southeast Asia, Northeast Asia, and Southern Asia.

Southeast Asia currently refers to Vietnam, Thailand, Myanmar, Cambodia, the Philippines, Brunei, Singapore, Malaysia, and Indonesia. However, China, Japan, Taiwan, and India all need to be included

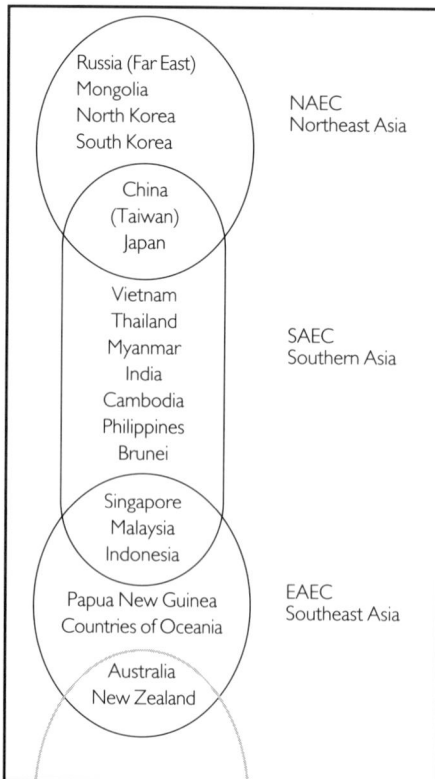

Proposed organization of new Asian economic spheres.

here. This is often pointed out with regard to China, but India's market liberalization has led to rapid modernization and the forging of closer ties with those nations conventionally considered part of the Southeast. India, a former British colony, possesses an unmistakable pool of scientific and technical talent; nor is this surprising when one remembers India as the country that invented the concept of zero. Not coincidentally, a media park modeled on California's Silicon Valley is being built on the Deccan Plateau, which enjoys clean air. In the near future India is expected to post the highest growth in Southeast Asia.

A second new group of countries should be referred to as Northeast Asia, in contrast to the Southeast. One development in support of this is the increasing economic activity of the sphere bordering the Sea of Japan since the mid-1980s. It comprises seven regions in six countries arranged around the Sea of Japan: the Far Eastern region of the Russian Federation; China's Shandong Province; China's northeastern provinces of Liaoning, Jilin, and Heilongjiang; North Korea; South Korea; Japan; and Mongolia. The economic strength of all these regions is substantial, and international joint development projects are in place both at the mouth of the Douman River and in the Far Eastern region of the Russian Federation. The latter, formerly known as the Soviet Far East, must be reckoned as a powerful new factor in the Asian sphere.

I suggest that the term Northeast Asian bloc include Taiwan's cooperation with this economic sphere bordering the Sea of Japan. Prime Minister Mahathir of Malaysia has proposed and implemented an East Asia Economic Caucus, centered around ASEAN countries; a parallel to this EAEC formation could be termed North Asia Economic Caucus (NAEC).

The key to the classification of Southeast and Northeast Asian blocs I have described is that China, Japan, and Taiwan would belong to both groups. China and Japan would thus serve as the principal link between the two regions of Asia, assuming the roles of political buffer and hub in the flow of people and goods. They also form a direct political link to the developed nations of the West. In fact, the U.S. already consistently treats China and Japan as the twin foci of its Asia policy.

More thought is needed to create scenarios in which Japan, along with China, might coordinate the economic, cultural, environmental, and military order of the Northeast and Southeast Asian blocs. Japan's leaders, from politicians to financial magnates, have a tendency to concentrate on economics, forever thinking of nothing but financial matters—while China at present is regarded primarily as a developing country or as potential military threat. I believe this to be a critical mistake.

China is a country with a preponderant political strategy. When Prime Minister Mahathir first proposed the EAEC concept, Prime Minister Li Peng immediately spoke with him in Myanmar, specifying that the countries of Southeast Asia might indeed hold views on development, as well as human rights, differing from those of the West. In modernization and economic policy then, China clearly believes that Asia has its own unique culture, which should be nurtured toward development. Instead of following the path set by Western nations, China has long supported "Chinese-style" modernization. Nor has it escaped notice that the country's leadership feel unable to accept some aspects of the human rights policy championed by the West.

The third Asian bloc is Southern Asia. Although it has not yet clearly emerged, Papua New Guinea, other nations of Oceania, Australia, and New Zealand may well link up with Singapore, Malaysia, Indonesia, and others to form a future South Asia Economic Caucus (SAEC). Many countries of Oceania have only just achieved independence yet are certain to mature economically, politically, and culturally as the twenty-first century begins.

Singapore, Malaysia, and Indonesia all belong to *both* Southeast and Southern Asia. These three countries could serve as a node connecting the two blocs. The relationship is evident at a geographical level, while at present almost as many students from the three countries now study in Australia as in Britain. Furthermore, Singapore, Malaysia, and Indonesia are easily accessible to developed nations further west, including the U.S.—an additional reason for their potential as buffer between the South and Southeast.

In Southern Asia, treatment of Australia and New Zealand is currently vague and undefined. Though members of APEC, Australia and New Zealand are not part of EAEC. Indeed, this is one reason the U.S., Australia, and New Zealand have voiced opposition to the EAEC concept. Although EAEC encompasses divers religions, races, and cultures, broadly speaking it is non-European. Australia and New Zealand are the opposite and presently favor APEC. For the time being, any form of membership in EAEC on their part is highly problematic.

I indicated that China and Japan might serve as a hub between Southeast and Northeast Asia. The U.S. is soon to use Singapore as Asian hub for the Global Information Infrastructure (GII), since it is a former British colony and has many Chinese inhabitants, is politically stable, and is generally rich in human resources. In this sense, India also has the potential to become an Asian information hub easily accessible to the West. Meanwhile, Singapore has made satellite and cable television programming available to foreign companies and introduced tax incentives for overseas firms. Moreover, Singapore's harbor already handles the largest volume of container traffic in Asia—not to mention the efficiency of its financial markets.

Security within Asia and the World

In considering Asia in the next century, we cannot afford to ignore the security issue, traditionally viewed only from a military perspective; my own view, however, differs. I first became interested in problems of security while the late Masayoshi Ohira was prime minister of Japan. The policy study group advising him included subcommittees on cultural policy, security, urban policy, family issues, and so on. I was invited to join those on city policy, cultural policy, and security, and I proposed that we regard the concept of security in the broadest possible sense. Later on, I also submitted reports to the Hosokawa and Murayama cabinets. As I see it, security encompasses economic, environmental, and cultural issues in addition to basic military considerations. Without such a comprehensive perspective, it is virtually impossible to ensure a realistic approach.

While the "two dragons"—the then Soviet Union and the U.S. with their nuclear arsenals—carried on a tacit war of ideological opposition backed by an overwhelming array of force, security discussions would inevitably open with debate about which "nuclear umbrella" one was under. Such debates were realistic enough at the time, but more recently I have advocated the importance of economic security. As I am not an economist, my position was never readily accepted—understandably so. Nowadays, however, economic crises rather than military ones are producing refugees, leading to deaths from starvation, and causing debilitating political instability. The recent Mexican peso crisis illustrated how frequently the world is liable to encounter such crises, and if the U.S. itself were to suffer a serious economic panic, global confusion far greater than that engendered by the Gulf War could occur. Clearly, the paucity of economic security measures in place outside the G-7 conference membership area is a grave mistake.

Moreover, in the area of environmental security, global problems severe enough to threaten human existence are surfacing. For example, as China rapidly industrializes, factories, motor vehicles, and coal-fired power plants are dramatically increasing nitrogen oxide and carbon dioxide emissions in the atmosphere. In addition, the world's forest areas continue to recede. China is hardly alone in feeling the repercussions of this situation, especially as the effects of environmental destruction are wafted over Japan by westerly winds. Correcting the situation on the Chinese mainland is a security issue of regional and global import. All this fails even to mention the problem of the ozone hole that continues to expand owing to our use of chlorofluorocarbons.

It has gradually been determined that nuclear power plants built by developed countries are not as safe as had once been believed. Soviet-constructed nuclear plants as well as the more general issue of nuclear waste processing, require particular attention. The former Soviet Union, however, is not the only site of unsafe nuclear generators; India and Eastern Europe also possess Soviet-style nuclear power installations. Compounding this problem are the many difficulties with storage and disposal systems for the old Soviet-produced nuclear weapons.

Risks associated with potential environmental destruction are at a peak, and the global environment's warning lights are flashing furiously. With regard to culture, there is an increasing possibility that religious and cultural disputes could upset the balance of world security at a point in the near future. An especially unsettling aspect of this is the explosive growth of militant Islam. One tends to think of the Middle East in this connection, but in fact Asia is home to the world's largest Muslim population. Many Muslims are citizens of Indonesia, Malaysia, China, and the countries of the former Soviet Union. Their political importance is increasing due to the loosened bonds of socialism.

It thus becomes clear that policies integrating military, economic, environmental, and cultural issues are vital to world security. However, because most security studies were carried out during the Cold War, they tend to emphasize military considerations. In my opinion, security policies taking into account economic and cultural factors are now urgently needed to prevent the deterioration of world order.

Need for Aid to Developed Nations

Japan assigns large sums of economic aid to many countries every year, but almost exclusively to developing nations. Not long ago, I wrote in a leader for the popular magazine *Koron* that, in an emergency, aid may also need to be directed to other developed nations, since, despite the current lull, economic risk has greatly increased during the past five years or so. Since the bursting of Japan's economic bubble in 1991, both the local economy and Japanese overseas investment have weakened. Adverse effects, however, have not been limited to Japan. Until our economy recovers and Japan begins once more to channel funds to the world as it did before the bubble ended, the world economy will probably continue to stagnate.

What is to be done? First, Japan must regain strength by commitment to substantial domestic investment. However, as with investment in the U.S., this carries the risk of temporarily diminishing assets, and cannot always be easily accomplished. In the public sector, vast funds have been budgeted many times over in an attempt to spark economic growth, which has not been forthcoming. In the recent past, one unit of public spending could be depended upon to produce a tenfold ripple effect, but this no longer works.

Clearly, conventional economic recovery measures have lost much of their effectiveness, and some more revolutionary strategy is in order. For such reasons, I believe that "aid to developed nations" is an idea whose time has come. The aim of such aid is global stability and mutual security, no longer merely to draw developing societies into the orbit of developed nations. Aid in the coming century must preserve and nurture existing lifestyles and cultures instead of pressuring developing countries to adopt a Western lifestyle, thus turning them into markets for developed nations. Symbiosis, mutual cooperation, and cultural exchange among diverse, heterogeneous cultures must become the basis for aid.

Specifically, to bring a quick end to current global economic stagnation, we must revive the three engines that in the past have driven the world's economy: the U.S., Japan, and Germany. When the economies of these three nations recover, the global economy will at last be revitalized. The U.S. economy is experiencing a lull, and Japan is still in the depths of a recession. However, the Japanese recession is not of a kind that can be improved with financial aid. A fundamental change is needed in the old-fashioned societal, political, and industrial structures we Japanese have inherited from the age of industrialization. Germany and the U.S., however, might realize great short-term benefits from financial aid. If Japan could invest ¥2 trillion in German real estate and ¥1 trillion in the U.S. automobile and entertainment industries, their economies would quickly rebound. Japan's export-based economy would also inevitably be pulled along by this joint recovery.

To accomplish this, it would seem practical during two or three years to halt aid to developing nations, which amounts to ¥1 trillion annually. Since aid to developing nations must in the long run be resumed, it could be halted temporarily as an emergency measure; when the economies of the U.S., Japan, and Germany had recovered, former overseas development aid would be restored and increased. Admittedly, the concept of aid to developed nations seems somehow preposterous. However, there is a recent example. During the Gulf

War, Japan donated substantial funds to the allied effort, and these went into the U.S. treasury. This was done for the excellent reason that the U.S. was using military means to secure imported petroleum for Japan. And, briefly, that "aid" exceeded Japan's own annual overseas development aid expenditure.

Large Corporations Retreat to the Sidelines

Although the countries of Southeast Asia are grouped in a single region, they are truly diverse in terms of religion, ethnicity, climate, and language. Still, they share certain qualities and a measure of common identity, which I shall refer to overall as a "culture of density."

European culture is psychologically opposed to this Asian culture of density, for Europe maintains the thinning out of density to be consistent with rational development. For example, when cities such as Manchester became too densely populated during the Industrial Revolution, the concept emerged of garden cities, such as theorized by Ebenezard Howard, where people could live in pastoral, low-density suburbs. Moreover, postwar redevelopment tended, in theory, to set aside vast areas of greenery for recreation. Thus, the Radiant City concept originated by Le Corbusier, arguably the most important architect-planner of the twentieth century, features super high-rise buildings scattered over wide expanses of parkland.

This concept has been visited upon Japan as well, and now the most densely populated areas are the older downtown areas, while tall buildings surrounded by vacant land are found in modern towns. Viewed from this perspective, Asia's major cities still consist of dense concentrations of low-rise buildings. Some believe that such arrangements can never adapt to the twenty-first century or to economic development.

Nevertheless, Asia remains today the world's major growth center—despite the conventional view that modern economic conditions emerge only from a context of rational functionalism. The fallacy of twentieth-century modernism in architecture and city-planning is that humanity will develop only through a precise logic of zoning. Since the early 1960s, however, I have repeatedly stated that density must triumph as a theme of twenty-first century physical planning. Crowded downtown districts, for instance, should be retained and street stalls allowed to flourish. Gradually, my prediction is now beginning to be verified.

The most important factor in Asia's development has been its high-density societies. In the twenty-first century—an age led by Asia—large corporations, giant financial and scientific organizations, and the large-scale computers that support those activities will retreat to the sidelines. Within Asia, only Japan has produced a developed Western-style nation instead of pursuing an "Asian" style of development. Therefore, just as Western industrialized societies with their rationalistic systems are discovering limits, Japan likewise is beginning to reach an impasse.

The Twenty-first Century as an Age of Smaller Firms

When I was researching Baigan Ishida (1685–1744), the originator of what can be termed *chomin* (townsfolk) ethical philosophy during the Edo period, I came to understand how in China and Japan, making money was not thought to be a bad thing, while in the West, being a merchant may be considered somewhat vulgar. In Western society, a person who has profited from commerce is expected to return some of this gain in the spirit of public service as philanthropy. People who only make money are despised, and prejudice and contempt have long been focused on merchants and moneylenders.

In Asia, however, making money is not necessarily felt to be vulgar, as reason and sensibility have intertwined in a complex way to produce a unique ethical stance in the matter. For, however good someone may be at business, the reality is that customers will only respond if sensitivity to duty and a feeling for others is demonstrated, and the person is considered approachable. In contrast, the U.S. is a bleakly rational, contract-based society, where even a cold-hearted individual can do business if the product or service alone is outstanding. In Japan, if someone is perceived as not caring enough to make a point of exchanging pleasantries, it may be hard to attract and hold customers.

In the modern age, this Asian emphasis on human relationships has been considered a weak, or negative, factor. In an information society, however, that is not necessarily the case. The most valuable element in the exchange of information is communication, and Asia is more highly developed than the West in terms of relationships and a subtle sensitivity to human nature.

In his *Third Wave*, the futurologist Alvin Toffler[2] described a vision of the computer age as one that would allow people to accomplish their work easily, even if living in some isolated spot, as long as they possessed a computer terminal. Life would be comfortable, and people would work in "electronic cottages." However, this trend has not yet materialized. When the telephone was invented, some predicted that the new device would make it unnecessary for people to be in contact directly, and that cities would implode as a result. In the event, telephones provided an increased stimulus for people to meet, so that contrary to expectations more opportunities were created for person-to-person encounters.

The information society is certain to launch a new age of cities because the highest-quality, raw information—born of contact among human beings—accumulates in the metropolis. The important issue is how to build comfortable, high-density societies and still remain in symbiosis with nature.

Pacific Axis and Sea of Japan Axis

I have long held that Japan needs a second national axis of prioritized development linking major cities, in addition to the Sanyodo and Tokaido industrial axes. After pursuing this issue for nearly ten years, I am pleased to note that new axes, such as the so-called Pacific prioritized development axis, are to be incorporated as major items in the next national plan. Research funds have already been appropriated for this project, expected to be Japan's largest of the twenty-first century.

This Pacific axis will also link Japan directly with Southeast Asia. Specifically, a tunnel joining the islands of Kyushu and Shikoku will be dug from Oita under the Bungo Channel, one of the world's most hazardous straits. The axis will eventually run from Ehime to

Prioritized development axes for Japan in the twenty-first century.

Tokushima, span Osaka Bay by bridge, extend from the new Kansai Airport to the Kii Peninsula, cross another bridge from Ise over the Ise Gulf, and continue to Toyohashi. It is estimated that the entire project will require a budget of ¥17 trillion.

In addition, a new Japan Sea prioritized development axis with infrastructural extensions in the Tohoku region is being studied. It will pass through Shimane, Tottori, Niigata, and Akita along the coast of the Japan Sea, and ultimately reach as far north as Sapporo. During the 1960s and into the 1970s, the original Tokaido/Sanyodo axis provided the framework for Japan's newly industrialized society. However, in the recent major earthquake in southern Hyogo Prefecture, this infrastructure became completely impassable, pointing to the need for a more complex network of infrastructural axes criss-crossing the entire country.

Japanese Industry in the Twenty-First Century: Agriculture, Fishery, and Forestry

Taking the human body as an analogy, the first prioritized development axis running from Sanyodo along the Tokaido, nearly to the Tohoku region, may be thought of as the backbone, while future axes will play the role of nerves or skin, linking islands and the tips of promontories throughout the archipelago. Along this skinlike band, we must work to revitalize our agricultural, fishery, and forestry industries at the same as the information industry is served.

Potentially, agriculture, fishery, and forestry can be updated as important economic activities in the twenty-first century by calling on advances in biotechnology, genetic engineering, and environmental technology. Mountains cover 80 percent of the surface area of Japan and their afforestation is already underway. Although some persons claim that Japan has too few resources, forests are indeed valuable—it is only that modern Japan has failed to realize this.

Japan's agriculture, fishery, and forestry are in a sorry state. The case of forestry is particularly tragic, as it has ceased to be economically viable, and the environmental damage this causes is a further concern. Since the Meiji era, Japan has consistently replanted mountain forests of deciduous and broadleaf trees with Japanese cedar and cypress for harvest as timber for construction. These species both have shallow, fragile root systems, and in torrential rains, they become uprooted and quickly topple. In Nagasaki Prefecture and elsewhere throughout Japan, repeated flood damage can be traced to this problem. Meanwhile, the soil of deciduous forests is needed to provide nutrients for the plankton fed on by fish in our rivers and seas. The replacement of Japan's deciduous forests has suppressed the growth of plankton, robbing fish of their food and forcing Japan's fishing industry to resort to deep-sea trawling as a livelihood.

I tour forests all around Japan each year with branch forestry officials, but there is nothing enjoyable about visiting plantations of

Japanese cedar and cypress. They are dark, and damp year-round. One cannot walk without pushing low undergrowth aside and trying to avoid snakes, mosquitoes, and centipedes. As a result, few enter these forests of Japanese cedar or cypress to hike or picnic.

Eco-Media City Project at Amagasaki

With all this in mind, I undertook to design and build an "Eco-Media City" at the request of Hyogo Prefecture and the municipality of Amagasaki, agreeing to chair a group of national experts and local professionals.

A twenty-first century city will be constructed on about 800 hectares of oceanfront land in Amagasaki—to be encircled eventually by three airports. Osaka and Kansai International Airports are now both in operation, and funds have already been appropriated for a new Kobe Airport for domestic routes. Chubu International Airport will also be tied to this project. A monorail will assure transport from Shin Kobe Station to Kobe Airport, extending through the Amagasaki oceanfront district and on to Osaka Airport. Kansai International, Kobe, and Osaka Airports will be further linked by a loop road encircling Osaka Bay to form a segment of the new Pacific infrastructural axis.

Kansai International Airport will serve as an approach to the bridge carrying the axis over Osaka Bay. The axis will then cut across the Kii Peninsula and the New Chubu Airport will be located across projected Ise Bay bridge. A high-speed train will also travel between the two airports in just twenty minutes.

Kansai International Airport is to have three runways, and two are planned for the New Chubu Airport. Eventually, three domestic airports, including Nagoya's Komaki Airport, would become part of the Pacific axis. These will form Asia's largest international air hub, unsurpassed by any in South Korea, Hong Kong, China, Singapore, or Malaysia. At present this remains my own personal proposal, yet the decision on whether to proceed may well influence Japan's position in the world in the coming century.

Malaysia has neither earthquakes nor typhoons, while Japan is hit by numerous typhoons every year. If a typhoon struck Kansai International Airport, Japan's sole twenty-four-hour facility, it would have to close, but if two international airports were linked via the scheme I am proposing, one of these might still continue to function. The combination I have in mind would serve not only the Kansai and Chubu regions locally, but also function as an international hub airport for all of western Japan.

Making Amagasaki into a Living Industrial Museum

A number of the previous generation of factories, active until the 1960s, remain in Amagasaki. Since all operations are to be withdrawn, or terminated, an Amagasaki Oceanfront Redevelopment Grand Plan has already been prepared. This comprises several proposals, the first of which entails symbiosis. As Amagasaki is a coastal city, symbiosis with the ocean is desirable—one could access one's apartment from one's private yacht by elevator. Symbiosis between the old industrial town and new information city is also conceivable.

Another proposal is to link Amagasaki directly to Southeast Asia. Recent popular opinion has concentrated entirely on information industries or conversion of cities into centers of tourism, based on the view that the older industry has no future. However, this approach makes it difficult to preserve and improve older features while also attracting advanced industries in order to create cities of symbiosis.

In the future, regions with existing industries may be preserved, with a spectrum of emphasis on small, medium sized, and large businesses. Joint undertakings with Southeast Asia would be stressed in order to increase production efficiency. Production will thrive if new types of industry are networked with Southeast Asia. For instance, parts could be made in Southeast Asia for assembly in Amagasaki, or products could be manufactured that would combine advanced technologies with the sort of craft-intensive traditional industries found only in Japan.

Such a connection with Southeast Asia could reduce the costs of conventional production while encouraging new environmental and multimedia industries. This would make Amagasaki a "living industrial museum" that encompasses all stages of industrial development from the 1950s well into the future. If such a city is actually built,

Southeast Asian investors are likely to vie for the chance to invest. I would like to fashion it into an "incubator city" for new industries in Asia, where unique policies for other countries might be modeled on those of Amagasaki.

European culture came early to Japan through Kobe and other locations in Hyogo Prefecture. I would like to see a European village constructed in Kobe and international schools relocated here, thus further stressing Kobe's role as a city of international exchange.

Future of Asia / Future of Japan

Amagasaki's canals, once used for moving goods to and from factories, remain a rare feature making for an attractive residential and commercial environment. While preserving these, I would like to see roads built alongside in order to foster shopping streets like those of Amsterdam, where visitors to Amagasaki would be able to stroll beside the canals as they shop. Behind these shopping areas, the older factories would perhaps continue to function alongside leading information and service industries. Recreational areas and parks should include as many deciduous trees as possible, with the goal of achieving symbiosis between nature and the city in a European mode.

A crisis mentality has arisen recently regarding the "hollowing-out" of Japanese industry. We should recognize, however, that this can be either desirable or undesirable. This recent trend represents the globalization of Japanese industry, and certainly should not be reason for alarm. As Japan's population ages and decreases in the future, labor supply will decline and industry's drift overseas will be a good thing. We must remember that, even if located abroad, a Japanese industry remains just that. Although goods produced within Malaysia are "made in Malaysia," they are still the products of Japanese firms. Since Japan will form increasingly close relationships in the near future with other countries, particularly in Southeast Asia, I believe that a research center should be constructed in Amagasaki—open to all of Asia as well as to the West. One theme could be the expansion of small and medium-sized companies toward the world market via the Internet.

I would also like to build a superblock as educational center. Schools would be able to rent floors of this building at low cost. Small private schools, including Japanese language schools, could be concentrated there, as well as research institutes and specialized schools for interior decorating, design, cooking, motorboat and aircraft pilot's licenses, and so on. Sports facilities, gymnasiums, social facilities, and cafeterias would be installed for shared use. This would result in an incubation center for multimedia industries, while simultaneously benefiting other small and medium-sized private companies. As we expect an increase of these in the twenty-first century, a city that neglects them is sure to become deserted.

Close contact with nature is essential to *any* eco-media city experiment. In Malaysia, climatic advantages—including ocean and tropical rain forests—will actually be utilized to recreate nature. Amagasaki is on the seacoast, possesses canals, is near several larger cities, has rapid access to the nearby Osaka and Kansai International Airports, and will be close to the future Kobe and Chubu International Airports. A location so well suited to this kind of future experiment is indeed rare. If the Eco-Media City in Amagasaki is successful, it will serve as a test case and concrete example for the rest of Asia, and the expertise thus acquired could be disseminated. The Asian twenty-first century is bright. If Japan joins hands with Asia in a set of constructive moves forward, we will be guaranteed a role in this future.

18

CHALLENGE OF ASIA, CHALLENGE OF ECO-MEDIA CITY

Fruit of the "Eco-Media Tree"

Taking into consideration the future of multimedia technology and industry, there will be no gap between Asia and the West. Moreover, in the combination of natural resources, ecotechnology, and ecoindustry with multimedia, micromachines, and electronics, such countries as Japan and Malaysia—rich in water resources, forests, and the sea—possess an overwhelming advantage. The twenty-first century will be an age of symbiosis between nature, or life, and electronics: biochips, biomechatronics, bioelectronics, biosensors, genetic engineering, and biotechnology will replace today's integrated circuits. My Eco-Media City aims to foster these industries of the new century, and promote network cities to create a revolutionary mode of life for the information age.

We shall have to construct both a Global Information Infrastructure (GII), and a National Information Infrastructure (NII) to connect with it, in order to establish and exploit the communications potential of the age of information. To function fully, these information infrastructures must be interconnected with transportation and logistics infrastructures for the use of *people*. All three infrastructures are required to maintain and foster life, industry, and culture, as well as to allot natural resources. In short, infrastructures are the foundation for establishing network cities and maintaining them. The Eco-Media City concept has double significance—first, for the symbiosis between development and the preservation of nature, and second, for the symbiosis between ecotechnology and multimedia technology. In addition, Eco-Media City itself requires natural forests to protect its resources and ecology. Eco-Media City is a new urban paradigm: a grouping, or association, that serves as a network between individual, small- and medium-sized cities, and cities of different functions. Based on the idea of symbiosis, Eco-Media City seeks to integrate the following features into a new twenty-first century metropolis: preservation of nature, global environmental issues, biotechnology, genetic engineering, and information and multimedia industry policies—all of which have evolved at different rates.

The initial conditions to achieve this integration will be found in a region with an abundance of unspoiled nature, that is actively searching to create a multimedia industry. In such a situation, observers believe that nature and ecotechnology will develop a symbiotic relationship and, finally, merge with multimedia technology in an "age of bioelectronics and *biomechatronics.*" It will be necessary to set up coordinated standards based on an understanding of this merger. For example, research and incubation facilities will be required enabling joint research into biotechnology and multimedia technology. Eco-Media City will be a twenty-first century metropolis that provides an industrial base, living space, and a research environment for the new age; it will be just one of the fruits of the "Eco-Media tree." Conventional cities developed into metropolises by layering these functions. The Eco-Media City concept, however, is of small- to medium-sized cities that form networks specializing in one, or more, such functions. Existing natural spaces, man-made forests, and farmland will lie between these urban units. Network cities will coexist with nature and constitute a symbiotic cluster of cities each complementing the other.

Malaysia/Japan

The trunk and branches of each Eco-Media city will comprise an optical fiber information infrastructure, a transportation infrastructure, and a logistical infrastructure. Meanwhile, the information age will be a borderless era linking the world through GII. Therefore, Eco-Media cities cannot be realized if the construction of these infrastructures are limited to a single prefecture, state, or country. There must be a direct global interlinkage through hub airports, hub ports, and information trunk lines (at the terabit class, or above).

An extremely limited number of areas meet these various initial specifications, whether overseas or in Japan. Singapore is one of the most advanced countries in Asia in terms of information infrastructure, but has no natural resources. The country in Asia with the most potential is Malaysia, where a Multimedia Super Corridor project is being advanced under the leadership of its prime minister. Malaysia also has an abundance of natural terrain, including tropical rain forest, as well as the world's largest international hub airport and ocean port.

Major projects will be underway for the next ten years in the Chubu region of Japan. This region meets all the conditions for Eco-Media city implantation. The first phase of a new airport will be completed here by 2005. There also will be the Aichi Expo in 2005, the new Pacific prioritized development axis, the Maglev (i. e., superconductor) Shinkansen, renovation of the Nagoya and Yokkaichi harbors for the TSL (Techno-Superliner one-thousand-ton container ship) era, and the Tokai Loop Highway.

A Multilevel Network

In the information age, the flow of three different resources—information, people, and goods—will be intertwined, It will be an age of high-speed, superior quality, interactive, integrated networks. These may be termed multilevel networks.

More schematically, the first infrastructural level is a transportation network for people. Specifically, this will comprise new high-speed railways and highways linking core cities with international hub airports and local airports. The second level of the infrastructure is a goods-distribution network. This will include an air-cargo containerization module, or system for matching air cargo with container sizes, that will guarantee access to the transportation infrastructure linking ports and airports. It also will include a logistics system (freight-shipment net-

• Eco-Media City for Malaysia designed by Kisho Kurokawa, extending from the capital, Kuala Lumpur, to Port Dickson on the Straits of Malacca. The scheme shows existing city areas, development areas, educational facilities, nature and forest reserves, and new and existing transport infrastructures—all in the context of the Multimedia Super Corridor (see also sketch map, p. 433) for the capital.

• Eco-Media City projected by Kisho Kurokawa for the Chubu region of Japan showing the Bay of Ise, Nagoya and Yokkaichi harbors, and Tokai Loop Highway system (pp. 466–67). ▶

Eco-Media City
A UPM University
   (Universiti Pertanian Malaysia)
B UKM
   (Universiti Kebangsaan Malaysia)
C UTM
   (Universiti Tenaga National Malaysia)
   University Forest
   Express Way
   Express Way
   (Future Development)
   ERL
   (Express Rail line)
   LRT
   (Light Railway Transit)
   MARDI
   (Malaysia Agricultural Research Development Institute)
   MINT
   (Malaysia Institute of Nuclear Technology)
   PORIM
   (Palm Oil Research Institute Malaysia)
   Airport
   Existing City Area
   Development Area
   Nature Reserve
   Forest Reserve

N

0 1 2   4   6   8

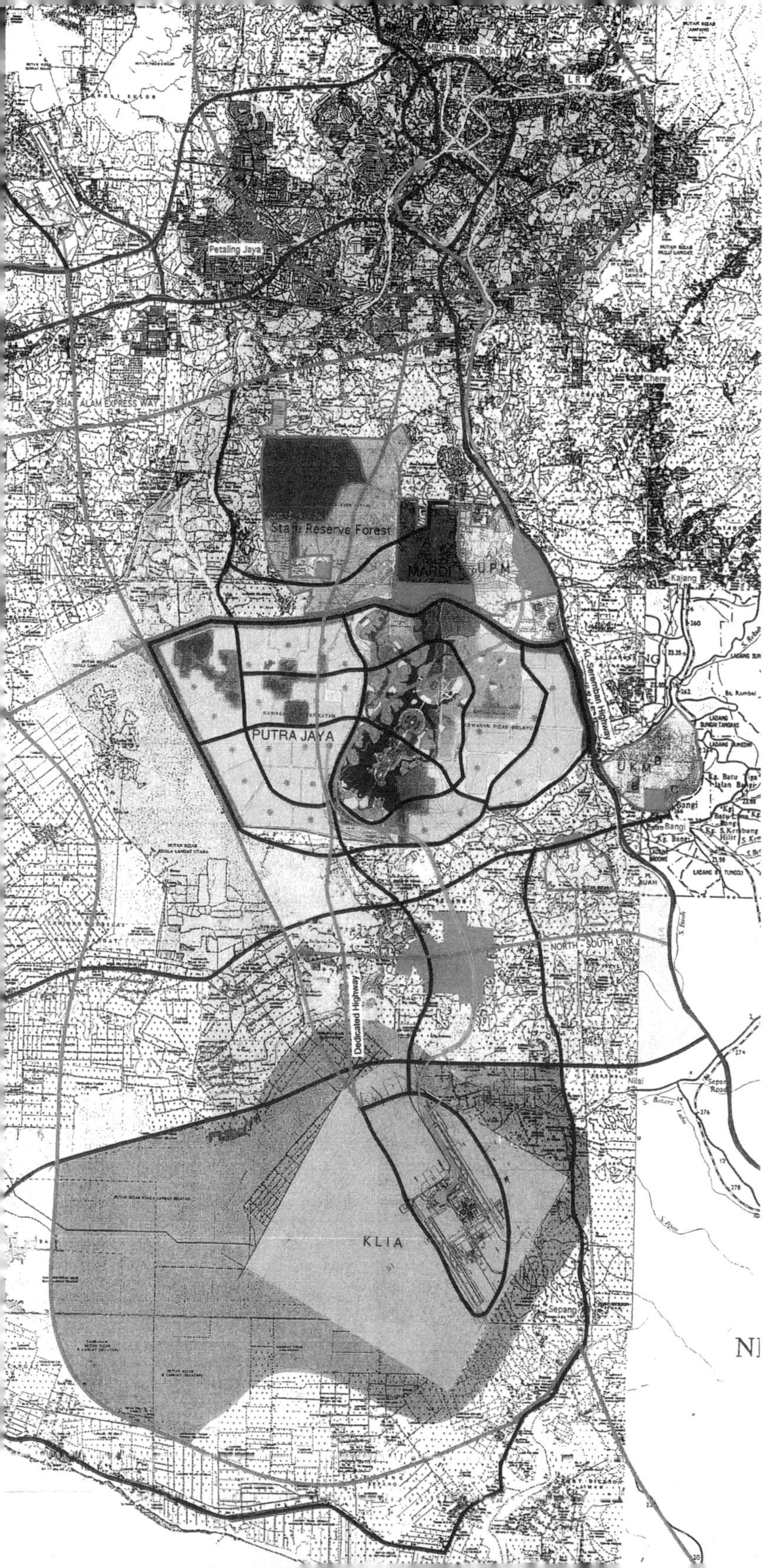
MIDDLE RING ROAD
LRT
Petaling Jaya
SHAH ALAM EXPRESS WAY
Cheras
State Reserve Forest
MARDI
UPM
Kajang
KL-Seremban Highway
PUTRA JAYA
UKM
Bangi
NORTH - SOUTH LINK
Dedicated Highway
Nilai
KLIA
Sepang

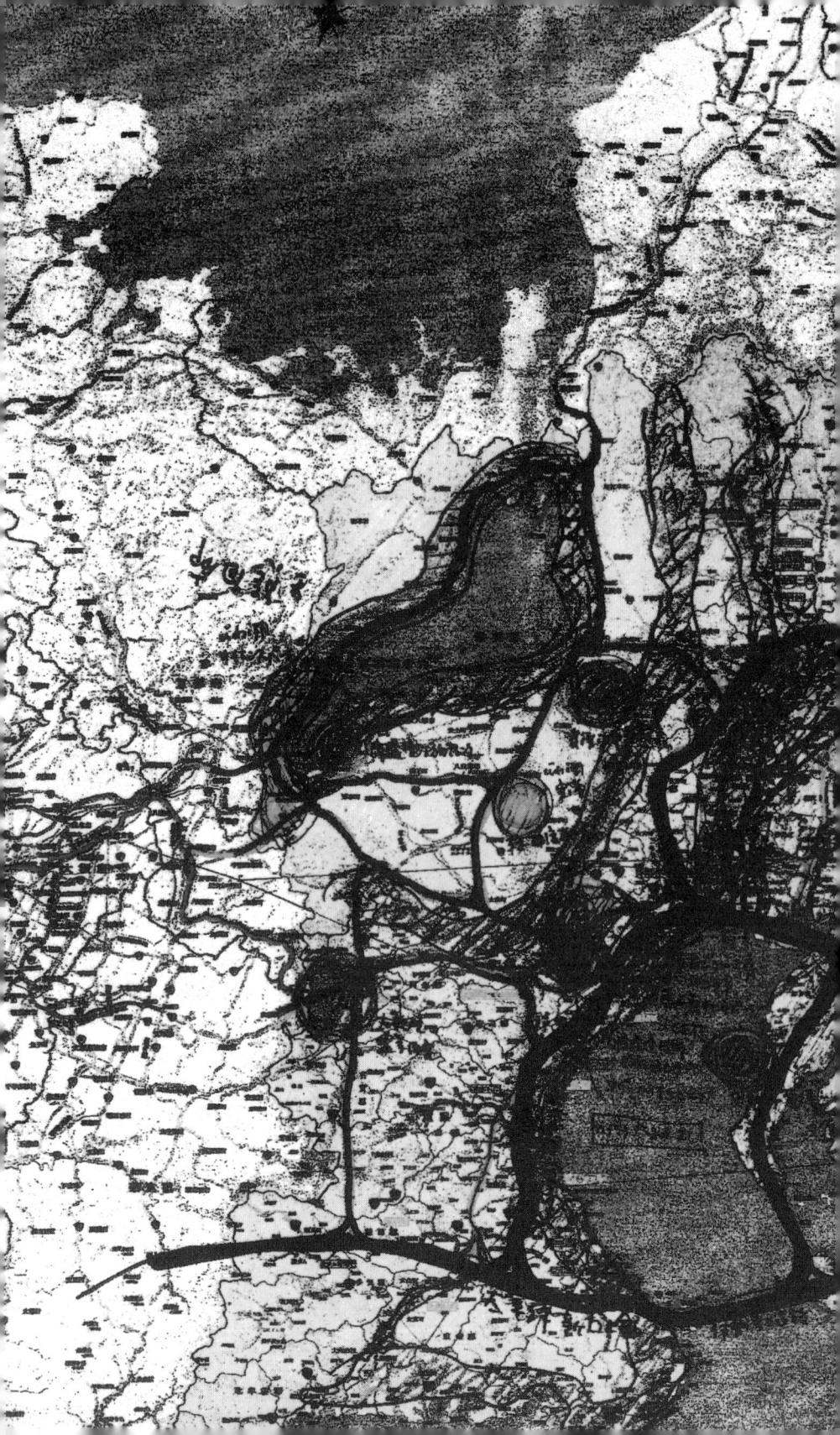

work), maintaining a network between, say, Kuala Lumpur, and truck terminals and distribution centers of every other city. Another requirement will be a computer control system to channel cargoes by the best and shortest possible route to factories using the "just-in-time" system pioneered in Japan. The third infrastructural level is the information network. This will require a high-speed, large-volume digital information infrastructure of optical fiber. The Multilevel Network will combine these three types of traffic and communication services.

To take an example, by combining the beltway spur linking the new Chubu Airport and Nagoya Harbor, with an information superhighway of the future and a superexpressway, an Eco-Media Ring Corridor will result namely, here, the Tokai Loop Highway. The Eco-Media City served by this loop network will be a prime candidate for the transfer of capital functions from Tokyo.

Such a multilevel network can be described using the analogy of a tree. The information network is best termed a multimedia network, or "multimedia computer communication network" based on the worldwide interconnection of computers. One such network already exists in the Internet, but the appearance of other satellite and wireless networks is virtually certain. The conditions required for a multimedia network of this type are that the network must be digital, it must have a large capacity (gigabits/terabits per second), it must be interactive, and it must be capable of handling all other types of media content. The latter include television and radio broadcasts, data telecommunications, telephone, and electronic mail, as well as visual images, videos, CDs, DVDs, and CD-ROMs. Domestically, this multimedia network must be accessible by every household and corporate consumer. Internationally, it must be connected to the GII through a linkage capable of high speeds and large capacity (gigabits/terabits per second). Internet connections through modems on telephone lines take time, and are only useful for e-mail or a home page. High-speed, large-volume, digital optical fiber lines or wireless networks will be indispensable for transmitting and receiving superior quality still images, video, and audio.

The information superhighway is like a utilities pipe, or cable, through which information passes. The significance of building such a network derives from the fact that there are now facilities, structures, and even cities for consuming information, to the same extent as water, gas, or electricity. If a multilevel network, or particularly a multimedia network, is compared to the trunk of a tree, the forest and natural areas surrounding a city would be its leaves. The city is, then, the fruit that a tree produces at the tips of its branches, or an incubator for the production of information.

Sophisticated and Self-Sustainable

Each of the cities of the Eco-Media City cluster will have a specialized function. These will include a Research and Development City, Expo City, Auto City, Sports City, Port City, High-tech City, Multimedia City, Aerospacial City, Agribusiness City, and Art City. The metropolis must be linked internally by its own multilevel network; that is, high-speed railways, expressways, a logistics network, and an information highway. This will facilitate the integration of people, goods, and information. Their interaction will ensure a multimedia industry and an ecomedia industry utilizing natural resources, human resources (intellectual and creative), processed goods and raw materials, and data content. A further condition for such a metropolis will be comfortable and sophisticated urban amenities encouraging a globally sophisticated populace to gather, visit, and live there. As has been said, forests and plentiful natural spaces will permit a symbiosis between nature and the most modern technology. These natural areas and forests will also be a condition for the food processing and pharmaceutical industries that make use of such ecotechnologies as biotechnology and genetic engineering. Information bases and incubation structures for each industrial sector will be needed to attract specific multinational firms to the city. This will require a type of urban planning different from what we know today. The cities of the information age will, therefore, be made possible through combined superior multilevel networks and superior urban planning.

The Eco-Media Cities will promote a symbiosis of biotechnology, genetic engineering, and biosensors with multimedia and ecotechnology. They will be completely new, experimental cities open to the world, attracting new cutting-edge industries from inside and outside the country, as well as vast R&D facilities. Eco-Media Cities will preserve the natural environment. Their objective will be symbiosis of nature with the city, preservation with development, and nature with advanced technology through the dynamic creation of more forests and the effective use of natural resources. They will aim to become self-sustainable cities.

Great Expectations

In terms of multimedia industry and information infrastructure alone, the Western countries and Japan have an overwhelming lead in basic technology-related industries, and such human resources as researchers. It will be extremely difficult for the developing countries to catch up. This is, above all, because educated and trained company personnel, specialists, and a public capable of utilizing multimedia in their daily lives are needed to establish a market for the multimedia industry. Yet, ecotechnology requires abundant natural resources, favorable climatic conditions, and water resources, such as forested mountains, rivers, seas, and lakes. Thus, Malaysia, Japan, and other Asian nations have a major headstart in the conditions for creating an ecomedia industry and Eco-Media Cities able to assure symbiosis between nature and advanced technology.

Great expectations are focused on Malaysia, and a few other countries, for preserving the tropical rain forest and creating new forests to resolve global environmental problems. Even Japan, which has less favorable topographical, climatic, and land conditions than the ASEAN countries, is forecast to have an annual market of 20 trillion yen in 2010 for industries using ecotechnology.

Though smaller than the annual multimedia market of 123 trillion yen forecast for 2010 in Japan, it will still be an extremely large market.

Included in ecotechnology are the following:

- Rain-water recycling systems
- Waste-disposal recycling systems
- Air-purification systems using soil

- Soil-purification system using bacteria
- Use of solar heat
- Energy-saving systems using sensors
- Energy-saving systems using cogeneration and area climate control

More agressive ecotechnology includes:

- Agriculture and forestry cross-breeding, and production improvements using biotechnology
- Promotion of forest development using biotechnology
- Food-product improvement, and a food-product processing industry, using biotechnology
- Genetic preservation of plant and animal varieties in the rain forest
- Application of biosensors in the multimedia industry
- Biochips, predicted to be one of the most important technologies of the twenty-first century (integrated circuits using living tissue) and *biomechatronics* (micromachines based on the principles of living tissue)
- Gene pools and a global gene registration center

Asian Identity and Asian Wisdom

The combination of multimedia and ecotechnology technology in the twenty-first century is expected to establish an entirely new ecomedia industry.

Sophisticated *multi*media cities will almost certainly be built in the U.S. and Japan. The conditions for building Eco-Media Cities, however, are limited to Asia, especially Malaysia and Japan, with its abundance of sea, forested mountains, level forests, rivers, lakes, and water resources. It is possible now to begin the Eco-Media City experiment in Japan in Gifu, Hyogo, Mie, Aichi, and Shiga Prefectures, notably in the city of Seto in Aichi Prefecture, site of the forthcoming "2005 Expo."

A fierce competition is currently underway among the worlds universities and private laboratories for preserving and registering genes and species. The global passion for this genetic analysis and registration has profound academic value in providing clues for understanding the history of the development of humankind and biological life in general. The analysis, registration, and pooling (preservation) of genes will certainly enable researchers to shed new light on pathogens, develop new pharmaceuticals, cross-breed and develop new varieties of agricultural products, and generate a decisive transformation of the food-processing industry. Put bluntly, ability to control the world's genes would permit the domination of global agriculture. Of all the world's continents, Asia has a natural environment capable of providing sustenance to a variety of species with its lush tropical rain forest. We believe it is the optimum location for a global gene and species preservation-and-registration center.

Today, the foodstuffs required by the human race each year include 90 million tons of grain for human diet, 90 million tons of grain for livestock feed, and 100 million tons of fish. Grain demand is skyrocketing in Asia, and shortages are forecast to become a grave problem in countries with high rates of economic growth, including China. That country became a net importer of grains two years ago; the U.S. is the only net grain exporter in the world today. While rice consumption in Japan is 10 million tons annually, the country imports 25 million tons of grain every year for feed. Thus, humankind is in the extremely precarious position of relying wholly on American weather conditions in this matter.

In addition to expansion of population, the dramatic increase in grain demand in Asia is due to the recent economic growth in Asian countries and resultant changes in dietary habits. Meat consumption inevitably climbs when standards of living rise and more grain is used as livestock feed. The global foodstuffs problem, particularly in Asia, cannot be resolved with conventional agriculture based on the use of inexpensive manpower and land. A new type of agriculture is required that combines ecotechnology, including biotechnology and sensor technology, with computer communications networks, such as the Internet, and multimedia marketing. This can no longer be termed agriculture; it is more appropriately referred to as "agri-industry."

Agriculture, that is "agri-industry," in the twenty-first century could rank with the multimedia industry as one of the world's leading economic activities. In addition, many people throughout the world are looking to biochips as a symbiosis of ecotechnology and multimedia technology. The production volume of integrated circuit chips based on actual semiconductor use will reach a limit in the future. The new age—the age of the high-performance biochip—will feature integrated circuits combined with living tissue (artificial protein). Research has already begun in both Japan and the U.S.

Asia is blessed with natural resources, and is aggressively developing information technology and a Multimedia Super Corridor. Eco-Media City is an entirely new concept for combining multimedia and ecotechnology, promoting the symbiosis of conservation with development, and promising an active role in the contemporary global environment. It is the ultimate project for demonstrating Asian identity and traditional Asian wisdom to the world, through a symbiosis between high-technology and nature.

E P I L O G U E

LIBERATION FROM CRAVING
AND IGNORANCE

From Coexistence to the Philosophy of Symbiosis
I began systematizing the philosophy of symbiosis around 1958, and it was in the 1960s that I began to discuss the "concept of coexistence." In *Toshi Dezain* (Urban Design), a book I published in the early sixties, the section entitled "Philosophy of Coexistence" includes the following:

> Isn't dualism a sickness that has taken root in all areas of modern thought and methodology? Broadly speaking, we cannot conceive of European civilization without Christianity. European civilization is, in other words, Christian civilization. Christianity presupposes dualism—a good and an evil deity, the god of goodness and light versus the evil material world, or the Creator and his imperfect creation. This is true of all Western philosophy as well. The philosophical dualism of which the fundamental principle is the separation of existence into mind and matter was already established in ancient Greece. In modern times, Descartes refined this dualism between mind as a separate faculty depending on God for its essence, on the one hand, and matter, on the other. Kant—who divided existence into the thing in itself and phenomena, freedom, and necessity—was also a characteristically dualist thinker.

European rationalism provided the spiritual backbone that has supported the industrialization and modernization of society. This rationalism has been articulated from head to tail in dualistic forms: spirit and body, art and science, man and machine, sensitivity and logic. Humanity has relentlessly pursued these extremes, terrified of the deep chasm it has discovered between them. Without a doubt, the world's impressive modern civilization born of European rationalism is the product of the recognition of this deep abyss—and the will, somehow or other, to bridge it.

Advances in contemporary design, too, are based on dualism, giving us such pairs of contrasting terms as beauty and utility, form and function, and architecture (human scale) and the city (urban, or "superhuman" scale). All debates about design up to now have been pendulumlike, swinging back and forth between these notions. Yet the upshot of the matter is that beauty may be found only in what is "functional." Narrow as that view may seem, the contrary notion that humanity, sensitivity, and beauty are independent entities *opposed* to function represents the net defeat of humanity. From all this the debate is then reduced to a simple head count, from which no creative thinking is likely to result.

When we try to resolve problems through dualism, the concept of harmony comes into play. Here is an example from urban planning: there are two scales, one human and the other "superhuman," regarded as antithetical. To bridge the gap between them, a hierarchy of several graded scales leading from the human to the superhuman is posited, and that is how the extremes are harmonized.

If these two scales are really antithetical, there will always remain an unbridgeable gap between them, no matter how many intermediary steps are constructed. Conversely, if the gap can be bridged, that means that the two scales were never truly opposed in the first place. As long as dualism is exploited as creative logic, one will always arrive at either compromise or escape.

Our task is to move from dualism to pluralism, and from there to advance to a new philosophy.

My advocacy of coexistence began here; its roots are in the Indian philosophy of absolute non-dualism that can be traced to the Vedanta philosopher Nagarjuna and to the Mahayana Buddhist concept of emptiness. These are the sources of my current concept of symbiosis, which first began to take shape as early as 1959 and has been growing and developing ever since.

I began sytematizing the philosophy of symbiosis around 1958. I wrote the books *Homo Movens, Michi no Kenchiku—Chukan Ryoiki e* (Architecture of the Street: Towards Intermediate Space), *Guree no Bunka* (A Culture of Greys), *Nomado no Jidai* (The Nomad Era), *Kenchikuron I—Nihonteki Kukan e* (Thesis on Architecture I: Toward Japanese Space), *Kenchikuron—Imi no Seisei e* (Thesis on Architecture: The Evocation of Meaning), and *Hanasuki* (Hanasuki: Reflections on Traditional Architecture).

I edited the book *Kyosei no Jidai* (Toward an Age of Symbiosis), published by Kodansha Ltd. in 1981, as a record of the Inter-Design Conference, Yokohama, in 1980, at which I served as chairperson. I have also written many articles, including *Ryogisei no Geijutsu* (The Art of Ambiguity) in a special edition of *Geijutsu Shincho*; and *Rikyu Nezumi Ko* (Rikyu Grey), *Kyosei no Shiso* (The Philosophy of Symbiosis), *Kikai no Jidai kara Seimei no Jidai e* (From the Machine Age to the Age of Life), and *Abstract Symbolism* in *Shin Kenchiku*. I intended all these as chapters that would eventually be included in my book *Kyosei no Shiso* (The Philosophy of Symbiosis). Published by Tokuma Shoten Publishing Co., Ltd., this book went through many editions, was revised, and has finally reached some degree of systematization in *Shin Kyosei no Shiso* (The New Philosophy of Symbiosis), upon which *Each One a Hero: The Philosophy of Symbiosis* is based.

City of Symbiosis: A Way to Liberation

In the early 1960s, together with Noboru Kawazoe,[1] Masato Otaka,[2] Fumihiko Maki,[3] Kiyonori Kikutake,[4] Kiyoshi Awazu,[5] Kenji Ekuan,[6] Shomei Tomatsu,[7] and others, I laid the foundations of the Metabolist movement. We borrowed the term metabolism from biology in the belief that cities and architecture—like living organisms—grew and metabolized. The Metabolist movement touched many different fronts and although it is impossible to summarize it in a word, it is fair to say that the issue of the symbiosis of past, present, and future, of human beings and technology—in other words, the issues of diachronicity and synchronicity—were central to it.

As I stated in this edition, since the latter half of the 1950s I have predicted that the "age of machine" principle would evolve into the "age of life" principle.

The principles of life are metabolism, metamorphosis, and symbiosis. During my forty years as an architect, I have delved deeply into the philosophy of life principles, and the cities and architecture of life principles. The principle of symbiosis can be said to be the most important of the life principles.

Benkyo Shiio, who introduced me to the philosophy of co-living when I was a middle school student, formed Zaidan Hojin Tomoiki Kai, or the Foundation for Co-living. This foundation published *Tomoiki Hoku-Shu* (Collection of Verses on Co-Living) and *Tomoiki Kyohon* (Text of Co-Living), the theme of which is as follows:

> We take the truth of coexistence as our guide and concentrate on the realization of the Co-living Pure Land—both for the sharp and the dull, for the strong and the weak, hand in hand. No one exists divorced from the thoughts of those around him. All comes into existence through an assembly of causes. All things are interrelated. In accordance with this principle, it is our aim to build an ideal world, step by step.

This is the true teaching of co-living. In Shiio's Buddhism of co-living, he reads the Chinese characters *kyosei* as *tomoiki* (living together). At the base of his philosophy is the conviction that all living things not only exist but are given sustenance by the rest of existence. Even inorganic substances such as minerals are essential to human life; if just one vital mineral is lacking, we cannot survive. Human beings live and are kept alive through their coexistence with animals, plants, and minerals. Shiio calls this essentially Buddhist vision of life "true life."

In Buddhism, human suffering is said to be caused by two things: craving and ignorance. Craving is attachment to things and the delusions that arise from that attachment. Ignorance means not to know what our universe *is*, what our self *is*. When you believe you are living entirely on your own, you cling to life and fear death—in other words, craving arises. The arrogant attitude that one knows everything there is to know is based on ignorance. The escape from those two kinds of suffering is called liberation, and that escape is based on first grasping and, then, living out the concept of symbiosis.

Buddhist circles cannot be said to have emphasized the existence of Co-living Buddhism. However, my philosophy of co-living has led to a re-evaluation of Benkyo Shiio's concept of *tomoiki* at my alma mater, Tokai Gakuen. I have also been given the opportunity to discuss and teach the philosophy of symbiosis at Buddhist and related schools such as Chionin.

My aim is for the philosophy of symbiosis to be a philosophy of the world, beyond Buddhism. However, I believe the time has come for a recognition of the philosophical contributions and services that Buddhist circles have provided to society.

* * *

It was through the kind help of Hiroshi Moriya of the editorial department of Tokuma Shoten that I was able to complete the first edition of *Kyosei no Shiso* (The Philosophy of Symbiosis). In preparing the revised edition of that book, Takayoshi Hasegawa of Tokuma Shoten provided invaluable support. And I could not have realized *Shin Kyosei no Shiso* (The New Philosophy of Symbiosis) without the help of Naohiko Akashi, also of Tokuma Shoten. Last, for his consistent support in the publishing of these works, which are so thick and difficult to sell, I would like to express my heartfelt thanks to my friend Yasuyoshi Tokuma. I would also like to thank Professor David

B. Stewart of Tokyo Institute of Technology and Shigeyoshi Suzuki and Michael Brase of Kodansha International for their efforts on behalf of *Each One a Hero*.

NOTES TO THE TEXT

INTRODUCTION

1. The term "paradigm shift" was coined by the American historian of science Thomas Kuhn in *The Structure of Scientific Revolutions* (1962, rev. 1970). Today, it is also used to refer to changes that mark the social framework by overturning conventional views. Or, it may signal transformations in modern art and philosophy—yet, sometimes, without sufficient regard for the evolution of past artistic expression or thought.

2. Paolo Soleri (b. 1919) is an American architect born in Turin, Italy. He has been involved in many self-build "arcology" schemes constructed on the theme of energy conservation, especially the ongoing Arcosanti project in the Arizona desert.

3. Andrzej Wajda (b. 1926) is a Polish film producer and director. Major works include the early *Canal* (1957) and *Ashes and Diamonds* (1958). He became a member of the Polish senate in 1989.

4. Renzo Piano (b. 1937) is an Italian architect. Major works include the Centre Pompidou in Paris (co-designed with Richard Rogers) and the Kansai International Airport Passenger Terminal Building.

CHAPTER 1

Toward an Age of Symbiosis

1. NIES were initially termed NICS (Newly Industrializing Countries); however, the name was changed in 1988 in consideration of China's relationship with Taiwan and Hong Kong. These economies rose from the ranks of the "backward," or developing, countries through rapid industri-

alization during the 1970s. Industry came to account for 25 to 40 percent of GNP, a proportion nearly as high as in the developed nations.

2. The Baht Economic bloc is that regional economic sphere based on the *baht*, the Thai unit of currency. It is currently spreading in Indonesia. This is one manifestation of the regionalism existing alongside globalization, characteristic of the world economy in the 1990s. Similarly, a Hwang Ho (Yellow River) economic sphere is emerging among China, Korea, and Japan, and a Southern China economic sphere is developing among Hong Kong, Taiwan, and the Chinese provinces of Guangdong and Hainan. The regional economic sphere comprising Singapore, Indonesia, and Malaysia is a remarkable growth triangle. The region is referred to as the "golden triangle of Southern Asia," while the Southern China region is called simply the "northern triangle."

3. The G7 is a conference of the finance ministers of seven countries: those five nations having the largest allotments in the IMF (International Monetary Fund)—the U.S., Japan, Germany, France, and the U.K.—as well as Canada and Italy. The term "G7" is also used in other contexts to refer to these participants in the economic summit.

4. In particular, I have in mind the following figures in the history of Western ideas:

Euclides (or Euclid, fl. 300 B.C.) who was, of course, "father of geometry." His *Elements*, in 13 books, contributed a deductive system of proof; this work would have been lost but for its preservation in Arabic and subsequent retranslation into the world's major languages. His five postulates remained the basis of geometry until in the last century the fifth postulate was replaced, radically affecting propositions regarding parallel lines, thus introducing a "non-Euclidean" geometry.

Sir Issac Newton (1642–1727), the English mathematician, physicist, and astronomer, who completed the study of dynamics, established mathematical physics, and contributed to the study of fluid mechanics, light, and tides. He was president of the Royal Society from 1703 until his death.

Immanuel Kant (1724–1804), pioneer of modern philosophy and one of the greatest figures in the history of metaphysics. He taught at the University of Königsberg. Kant maintained objective awareness to be possible in the experiential, phenomenal world, whereas things lying beyond experience, *noumena*, were unknowable and could not be scientifically demonstrated.

Antoine Laurent Lavoisier (1743–94), French chemist and physicist, today called "father of modern chemistry." He established the theory of combustion and systematized methods of organic analysis. In addition to devising the principle of the constancy of mass, he was responsible for the nomenclature used in chemistry today.

Charles Robert Darwin (1809–82), English naturalist who established the theory of evolution on the principle of natural selection.

5. *Gemeinschaft* can be translated as "shared society." The German sociologist Ferdinand Tönnies used the term to express a type of society in which divers members share an emotional bond. It may refer to families, based on blood ties, and villages, based on community ties. Its opposite is the word *Gesellschaft*, which describes a society comprising groups and individuals who pursue only their own interests. This refers to the present organization of large cities, nations, and, indeed, the world.

6. The EAEC (East Asia Economic Caucus), proposed by Malaysia in December 1990, is based on the concept of an East Asia economic sphere. It is composed of the members of APEC (the Asia-Pacific Economic Cooperation group, founded in 1989, with 14 countries and regions)—with the exception of the U.S., Canada, Australia, and New Zealand. Misgivings and restrictions on the part of the U.S. within APEC gave rise to EAEC in its present form. Finally, in 1994 preparations began toward a departure from the internal structure and aims of APEC.

7. NAFTA, the North American Free Trade Agreement, came into effect on January 1, 1994, with the inclusion of Mexico in the U.S.-Canada Free Trade Agreement. A manifestation of regional economics, it allows duty-free marketing of products throughout North America.

8. CIAM (Congrès Internationaux d'Architecture Moderne, pronounced "*SEE-am*") was formed in 1928 under the leadership of Siegfried Giedion (1888–1968), a Swiss architect, and the Swiss-born Le Corbusier. It advocated a radically anti-traditional approach in architecture and planning, pursuing the goals of "social architecture" and "functional" cities.

C H A P T E R   2

From the Machine Age to an Age of Life

1. Le Corbusier (1887–1965), born in Switzerland, was active as an architect in France. He is also famous as a painter and publicist. In architecture, his work spanned many areas, from housing design to city planning. He was likewise a major theorist of modern architecture, setting forth its five principles: *pilotis*, independent modular structures, unobstructed interior space, free façades, and rooftop gardens.

2. Sergei Mikhailovich Eisenstein (1898–1948) was a Russian film director born in Riga (son of the city architect). His 1925 film *The Battleship Potemkin* was a story of revolutionary sailors on a ship in the Black Sea in 1905. A silent movie, it shocked the world with its theme and montage methods.

3. Filippo Tommaso Marinetti, (1876–1944) was an Italian poet born in Egypt and the founder of Futurism, a movement that profoundly influenced the Russian formalists and other European writers, as well as modern art and even architecture. His major ideological work was *Mafarka the Futurist* (1910) and a series of manifestoes. He later became an active Fascist and backer of Mussolini.

4. Togo Murano (1891–1984) was a well-known Japanese architect whose major works include the World Peace Memorial Cathedral and the Nippon Life Insurance Hibiya Building, Tokyo. He was awarded the Order of Cultural Merit, Japan, and the Art Academy Award Blue Ribbon Medal.

5. Seiichi Shirai (1905–83) was a hermetic Japanese architect whose Head Office of Shinwa Bank and Shoto Museum are major works. His work has been recognized by the Kotaro Takamura Award and the Japan Architecture Academy Award.

6. Kunio Maekawa (1905–86) was a disciple of Le Corbusier. Major works are Nippon Sogo Bank and the Tokyo Metropolitan Museum. Awards include the Japan Art Academy Award, Mainichi Art Prize, and Japan Architecture Academy Award.

7. Kenzo Tange (b. 1913) established his reputation with the Olympic Yoyogi Gymnasiums, Tokyo, and Tokyo Metropolitan Government Offices. He has been awarded the Japan Architecture Academy Award, the Order of Cultural Merit, Japan, and the Royal Gold Medal for Architecture of the RIBA.

8. The most important works of the Japanese architect Arata Isozaki (b. 1931) are the Saint Jordí Sports Palace, Barcelona, and Art Tower Mito, Mito. His work has been recognized by the Architectural Institute of Japan, who awarded him its prize for design. He has also been awarded the Royal Gold Medal for Architecture of the RIBA.

9. The Austrian architect Hans Hollein (b. 1934) is well known for his Jewellers Shop Schullin I & II and the Austrian Travel Agency headquarters, Vienna. Awards include the Reynolds Memorial Award and the German Architecture Award.

10. American linguist and political critic, Auram Noam Chomsky (b. 1928) has had a profound impact on the field of linguistics with his theory of transformational generative grammar. Writings include *Aspects of the Theory of Syntax* (Cambridge, Massachusetts, 1965) and *Language and Mind* (New York, 1968).

11. Written by Liu An, who, vested with the title Huai-nan, was the grandson of the founder of the Han dynasty (ca. 200 B.C.–200 A.D.). The origi-

nal work was entitled *Hong Lie*, but the title *Huai-nan-zi* refers to the surviving 21 chapters. It now indicates both the person and his book.

12. Isoya Yoshida (1894–1974) was a noted Tokyo architect. Major works include the Nihon Geijutsuin Kaikan, Goto Museum of Art, Yamato Bunkakan, and the residence of the painter Ryuzaburo Umehara.

13. Robert Venturi (b. 1925) is a leading American postmodernist practitioner, along with his wife, Denise Scott Brown. His book *Complexity and Contradiction in Architecture* (New York, 1966) placed him at the theoretical forefront of the anti-modernist architectural movement.

14. Michael Graves (b. 1934) is a noted American postmodern architect and professor at Princeton University. Because he designs stagelike versions of classical European architecture, he became controversial as a historicist. Major works include the Fargo Moorhead Culture Centre, the Portland Building, and hotels at Disneyworld.

C H A P T E R   3

Symbiosis in the Economy

1. Sakyo Komatsu (b. 1931), pen name of Minoru Komatsu, who writes primarily science fiction novels. His *Nihon Chinbotsu* (Eng. tran., *Japan Sinks*, Kodansha International, Tokyo, 1995) was a record-setting bestseller in the original Japanese version.

2. Heisuke Hironaka (b. 1931), a mathematician, won the Fields Medal in 1970, an award in the field of mathematics comparable to the Nobel Prize. He is a professor at Kyoto University.

3. Issei Miyake (b. 1938) is a world renowned fashion designer (see also note 2, ch. 12).

4. Toru Haga (b. 1931), professor at Tokyo University, is a scholar of comparative literature. He is the author of *Taikun no Shisetsu*.

5. Nagisa Oshima (b. 1932) is a film director, whose major works include *Cruel Story of Youth* (1960) and *Merry Christmas, Mr. Lawrence* (1983).

6. Masuo Ikeda (1934–97) was a printmaker, author, film director, and ceramic artist. He won the coveted Akutagawa Award in 1977 for his novel *Egekai ni Sasagu*.

7. Toshi Ichiyanagi (b. 1933) is a composer who introduced Japan to music with an element of randomness. His work covers a broad range, from avant-garde music to "acoustic design" and environmental music.

8. Tadanori Yokoo (b. 1936) is a world famous graphic designer, illustrator, and painter. He has achieved a unique mode of expression within the pop art genre.

9. Yotaro Kobayashi (b. 1933) is a businessman and CEO of Fuji Xerox Corporation.

10. Alias Adonis (b. 1930), born in Syria, is a Lebanese poet and author of *Miyahar Song of Damascus*.

11. Takeshi Umehara (b. 1925) has developed a unique doctrine known as "Umehara Japanology." His collected works (20 volumes) of philosophy cover a wide range of fields, including literature, art, Buddhism, and antiquity.

12. Daizo Kusayanagi (b. 1924) is a critic and essayist. Major works include *Yamakawa ni Geijutsu Arite*.

13. Shuji Takashina (b. 1932) is an art historian and critic, whose unique comparative study of Japanese and Western art is highly regarded. A major work is *Runessansu no Hikari to Yami*.

14. Ichiro Hariu (b. 1925) is a critic of art, literature, and society as well as professor at Wako University. His oeuvre includes the six-volume *Ichiro Shinsho Hyoronshu*.

15. Shichihei Yamamoto (1921–95) was a publisher and critic. He developed a unique theory about the Japanese, expounded in the two-volume *Watashi no Naka no Nihongun* and other works.

16. Hideo Kanze (b. 1927) is a Noh performer of the Kanze school. He also performs and acts in *Shingeki* ("new" theater) and opera.

17. Taichi Sakaiya (b. 1935) is an author and economics critic. Born Kotaro Ikeguchi, he pioneered the field of futurological economic novels. His main works include *Yudan* and *Chika Kakumei* (Eng. trans., *The Knowledge-Value Revolution*, Kodansha International, Tokyo, 1991).

18. Hisashi Inoue (b. 1934) is a popular author and self-styled revivalist of *gesaku* (popular fiction as written from mid eighteenth to early nineteenth centuries). He is also well regarded as a playwright. Major works include *Dogen no Boken* and *Tegusari Shinju*.

19. Yasushi Akutagawa (1925–89) was a composer. Among his works *Triptych for Strings* is particularly well known.

20. Masahiro Shinoda (b. 1931) is a film director. Major works include *Love Suicide at Amijima* (1969) and *MacArthur's Children* (1984). His interpretations of traditional plays have also been well received.

21. Yusuke Fukada (b. 1931) is a writer popular for his sympathetic portrayals of the tragicomedy arising from differences between Japanese and Western culture and customs. A well-known work is *Ennetsu Shonin*.

22. Tadao Ando (b. 1941), an architect based in Osaka, focuses on the beauty of exposed concrete. Major works include Sumiyoshi Rowhouse and Suntory Museum of Art, both in Osaka.

23. The Bauhaus was a comprehensive art school in Dessau led by Walter Gropius, the German architect (see note 22, ch. 7). It became a stronghold of the International Style of modern architecture, emphasizing functionalism—having been founded originally in 1919 as an art-and-craft school in Weimar.

C H A P T E R   4

Transcending Modernism

1. Ludwik L. Zamenhof (1859–1919), a Polish Jew, invented this international language in 1887. The word "Esperanto" signified "one who hopes." Esperanto is the most popular of the international languages devised so far, though its use is increasingly rare in politically and culturally developed countries.

2. Gilles Deleuze (b. 1925) is professor of philosophy at the University of Paris. His philosophical method is characterized by a rejection of the consciousness theories of traditional metaphysics and a focus on will and desire, from which he proceeds to analyze modern society. In *Anti-Oedipus*, coauthored with Felix Guattari (see below), he postulates the two principles of schizophrenia and paraphrenia in contemporary society. According to Deleuze, the "modern intellect" seeks to know all, ignoring the fact that life itself is inherently anti-hierarchical. In modern capitalist society, the desire to view all existence as orderly has become a self-sustaining quest affecting interpersonal relations and expressed as a feeling of pressure and anxiety.

3. Felix Guattari (1930–92) was a French psychoanalyst at the La Borde Clinic in Cour-Cheverny since 1953. He was in the forefront of the development of a new, revolutionary psychoanalysis based on the notion of a sociopolitical content of the unconscious, in the face of the perceived reactionary tendencies of Anglo-saxon psychiatry. His major works are co-authored with Gilles Deleuze (see above): *Anti-Oedipe* (1972), *Kafka* (1975), and *Rhizome* (1976), and *Mille-plateaux* (1980).

4. René Girard (b. 1923) set the image of the scapegoat at the core of human culture and also developed a theory of culture as the "imitation of

desire." According to Girard, desire cannot exit at the level of the individual. He offers the love triangle as an example. In a love triangle, the desire of B for C is linked to B's awareness that A desires C. In this triangle of desire, a reciprocal imitation of desire is manifested, and this paradigmatic relationship extends universally until it produces violent confusion, exposing all human groups to danger.

In reaction, the natural defence mechanisms of groups are activated, and reciprocal imitations among groups are transferred to a relation between the group and a single individual. This person, Christlike, becomes a scapegoat and the symbol of the evil which has wrought chaos. At the same time, paradoxically, he may be emblematic of the group's salvation.

5. Claude Lévi-Strauss (b. 1908) held that we must look at cultural phenomena not from the viewpoint of an established theory but from the perspective of their own structure. The system of distinctions among phenomena reflects the structure of relationships among different things. Lévi-Strauss applied these ideas broadly to the study of anthropology, especially kinship relationships and mythology. He is sharply critical of the modern notion of the self as a discrete entity, and refuses to accord a higher value to civilization than to the quality he refers to as "the unknown." He discovered so called "savage thought," that is, *non-rational* logic, and stressed that the equation of thinking with rationality only applies to the European cultural context. He went on to criticize all notions of substance and existence based on rationality, as an oppressive ideology.

6. Jan Mukarovsky was a Czech dialectical thinker of the 1930s. Mukarovsky held that while any structure possesses a tendency towards integrity it also possesses factors that seek to destroy continuity and regularity. A structure is forever repeating a cycle of stasis, upset, and restoration. Its integrity is preserved by the opposition of the forces of harmony (affirmation) and conflict (negation), but Mukarovsky places the stronger emphasis on negation. In other words, dominant structural elements are renewed via the introduction of negation of tension into the system, and the subsequent upset of the system's balance. In this model, structure is self-rehabilitating.

7. William Morris (1834–96), the English poet, painter, craftsman, and social reformer established the household and ecclesiastical decorating firm of Morris, Marshall, Faulkner & Company in 1861. This enterprise embarked on the production of celebrated room interiors, stained glass, metalwork, textiles, and wallpaper. Morris was opposed, in theory, to industrialization and sought to bring beauty to daily life through the influence of handicrafts. As a poet and artist, he promoted medievalism and believed that its revival was possible in the context of socialism.

8. Arthur Koestler (1905–83) was imprisoned as a spy in 1937 during the Spanish Civil War. He claimed to have experienced "the third reality" in prison. Koestler writes in *The Holon Revolution*:

> The third reality cannot be explained on either the perceptual or conceptual levels. It is like a magical meteorite perceived by primitive man streaking across the round dome of the heavens, and it is when we have occasion to gain access to that level that we encounter occult phenomena.... Just as we cannot feel the pull of a magnet with our skin, we cannot hope to understand this ultimate level of reality through language. It is a text written with invisible ink.

Koestler's essay "The Tree and the Candle," to which I shall have occasion to refer, was published in *Unity Through Diversity*—a collection of papers published to commemorate the seventieth anniversary of the birth of the Austrian-Canadian biologist Ludwig von Bertalanffy, the originator of general systems theory.

9. Carl Gustaf Jung (1875–1961) posited the so-called collective unconscious as a generalized source of consciousness comprising all memories of human history and linked in synchronicity to the mind of each individual. According to Jung, if one perceives by intuition that a close friend has died, this is the action of synchronicity joining the subconscious of both persons. He also held that the sensation of déjà vu could be the synchronous consciousness of past experience transcending time.

10. Wolfgang Pauli (1900–1958), an Austrian physicist, made many contributions to the theory of relativity and molecular theory, including the discovery of the Pauli exclusion principle.

11. David Bohm (b. 1917) is an American physicist who has suggested that both mind and matter have an "implicated order," which links the two. Bohm uses the image of a drop of ink in a glass of water. If we stir slowly, the ink will spread out until part and whole are completely inseparable. This is the world of implicated order. If we could gently stir the water backwards, the ink would slowly separate from the water and return to its form as a single drop, becoming a mere part again. According to Bohm, this is the process through which atomic particles are constituted, as well as mental process and nerve impulses.

12. Daisetz Suzuki (1870–1966) was perhaps the best-known popularizer of Zen in the West. According to Suzuki, the total self-identity of "I am I" is the state of non-time, equivalent to the emptiness of Buddhist philosophy. In this state, the mountain is the mountain, so to speak: I see it as it is; it sees me as I am. In other words, my experience of seeing the

mountain is identical to the mountain seeing me. From this, Suzuki moves to the conclusion that absolute subjectivity and objectivity are identical. That which is inside me is at the same time that which stands opposed to, and outside of, me. Human beings and nature, God and nature, are one; and the many and the one are also one. In this way, Suzuki arrives at an absolute monism.

13. Miura Baien (1723–89) was a physician by profession, but studied a wide range of subjects, from Confucianism to traditional astronomy to mathematics. The originality and profundity of Baien's philosophical trilogy (see chapter 9) marks him as a universal philosopher who transcends all genres and his age.

14. Georg Wilhelm Friedrich Hegel (1770–1831) considered human history to be the process of realizing ideas and systemized the movement of concepts within human history as a dialectical process of development. No thing, or phenomenon, can subsist in an original form, since it always harbors within itself an element opposed to it. This opposing element will sublate it and change it into an opposing phenomenon, thus tracing a dialectical movement. According to Hegel, consciousness placed *outside* the self is able to develop on its own even to the point of becoming a "national" idea.

CHAPTER 5

The Philosophy of Consciousness-Only and Symbiosis

1. The Upanishads are a group of sacred texts appended to the Vedas, the ancient texts of the Brahman religion in India. One of its most striking teachings is that each human being possesses an absolute self (*atman*) identical to the great universal self (*Brahma*), and that the two can be unified through religious practice. The Upanishads are also the first Indian texts to offer a theory of *karma*, that is, deeds and their ethical consequences.

In the Rig Veda, the earliest Hindu scripture, the word *atman* is used in the sense of the soul, center of respiration or one's inner self. Later, it was thought to be a soul that transcends the self. Eventually it was considered to be identical to *Brahma*, the centre of the universe.

2. The *alaya* was conceived of as a stream of discontinuous instants, but in orthodox Buddhist philosophy it is said to be "empty"—that is, to have no substantial existence. The concept of the *alaya* is, in any case, a recognition of process apart from substance.

3. Nagarjuna lived in the second century in southern India. Of Brahman birth, he converted to Mahayana Buddhism. The central concepts of Nagarjuna's writings are the "mean" and emptiness. Emptiness implies

that no phenomenon has substantial existence; and the mean refers to the esoteric Buddhist Middle Way between all dualistic extremes, such as illusion and enlightenment, or non-existence and existence.

4. Maitreya (not to be confused with the Boddhisattva of that name) was a Buddhist scholar of fourth-century India. Asanga, his pupil, a scholar of northwestern India (Gandhara), also lived in the fourth century, and taught that the stream of the *alaya* consciousness could be purified, transforming our consciousness into enlightenment itself. Asanga's brother Vasubhandhu was the most prolific writer of the three and with him the philosophy of Consciousness-Only reached completion. His doctrinal innovations included distinguishing the sense of self from the *alaya* consciousness and his encyclopaedic listing of the afflictions that pollute the human mind.

5. Susumu Hani (b. 1928) stresses freedom, naturalness, and the realities of everyday life in his films, which include *Bad Boys* (1961), *Bwana Toshi* (1965), and *Bride of the Andes* (1966).

C H A P T E R   6

Edo: Pre-text for an Age of Symbiosis

1. The Edo period, or Tokugawa period, is usually dated from 1603, when Tokugawa Ieyasu assumed the title of shogun and established the Tokugawa shogunate in Edo (now Tokyo), to 1867, when the last Tokugawa shogun resigned. It is also sometimes dated from 1600 to 1868, the year of the Meiji Restoration.

Japanese designate the Edo period as "early modern," to distinguish it from the "medieval age" from the twelfth to the sixteenth centuries, and from "modern," which commences with the Meiji Restoration. Following more than a century of civil strife, the Edo period was called in its own time the era of Great Peace.

The Edo period saw the development of a literate, hereditary ruling elite of *samurai*, a complex bureaucratic government, a network of major cities (Edo, Osaka, and Kyoto), a thriving urban merchant class with its own characteristic culture, and a national monetary economy that linked the 85 percent of the population who were peasants to the 15 percent in cities and towns. It was also an age of flourishing cultural activity in letters and the arts.

2. Shitamachi, the "low city" or "downtown," is now east central and northeast Tokyo. It was traditionally where townsmen and craftsmen lived, as opposed to the feudal lords and their entourages, who lived "in the hills," the Yamanote area. The Shitamachi district preserves more of the old character of Tokyo-Edo than other parts of the city.

3. The Royal Academy of Arts was founded in 1768 to teach painting, sculpture, and architecture, and promote progress in these arts. Its initial patron was George III (r. 1760–1820) and its model was the French institution of the same name. The content of lectures at the academy under its first director, Sir Joshua Reynolds, amounted to an eighteenth-century theory of art. In addition to providing education, the academy supported impoverished artists and their families.

4. Yamagata Banto (1748–1821) was a scholar of the merchant class. He was adopted at thirteen by his uncle and moved to Osaka, where he became the manager of a rice business. While carrying on this trade he also studied Confucianism, astronomy and Western science, or *rangaku*, and wrote *Instead of Dreams*. This work is divided into twelve sections, devoted to astronomy, geography, mythology, history, government policies, economics and other subjects. The section on astronomy is especially well-known. Banto's achievements as an economist and a thinker rank him with his contemporaries in Europe, America, and Asia.

5. Shizuki Tadao (1760–1808) was a scholar of Western science, or *rangaku*, who translated many Dutch works in addition to his own writings. His main work is *Rekisho Shinsho*, a translation from Dutch of Keill's English commentary on Newton's *Principia*. Tadao's own appended theory of nebula rivals the Kant-Laplace hypothesis.

6. Ino Tadataka (1745–1818) is famous as a cartographer, although until he was fifty he was manager of a brewery. It was only after retirement that he began to study astronomy, geography, and mathematics and also to draw maps. In sixteen years starting from 1800, he spent 3,736 days traveling around Japan and charted 43,708 miles, taking hundreds of thousands of readings. His maps are accurate to about a thousandth of a degree. Ino's maps became the standard maps of the country during the Meiji era.

7. Joruri is Japanese puppet theater, also called Bunraku. In the Joruri theaters, serious dramas were enacted for an audience of adults. The large puppets were eventually operated by three puppeteers dressed in black and visible from the waist up. The drama was accompanied by a balled narrative called Joruri, which gave its name to the theatrical genre.

8. The dates of the artist Toshusai Sharaku's birth and death are unknown, but he was active in the late Edo period. His output of more than 140 prints is concentrated between May 1794 and January 1795; after that we know little more of him. Various theories about his true identity have been suggested, but there is not enough evidence to confirm any of these.

9. Rinpa is a school of painting founded by Sotatsu about 1600 and revived in the early eighteenth century by Korin. Works characteristically incorporate precious materials, notably gold or silver ground, and are highly decorative; yet they retain a keen sense of the visible world of nature. Korin, from whose name the style's name derives, first trained as a textile designer.

10. *Kumadori* makeup, in contrast to the makeup of Peking Opera, for example, is based on the muscles of the face, abstracted in stylization. It is said to have been influenced by the iconography of Buddhist images, especially those of fierce guardian deities such as Fudo Myoo.

11. Suzuki Harunobu (d. 1770) was the originator of the multicolored woodblock print, or *nishiki-e*. In addition to his prints of beautiful women (*bijinga*), he devised scenes of amorous couples and sights of daily life about town. He is regarded as having introduced the sophistication of aristocratic art into the woodblock print, but his role in commercializing the genre is probably even more important.

12. Rekisai Kobayashi (1884–1959) was a maker of miniatures, including tiny, perfectly crafted ink boxes, incense stands, dressers, samisens, and other furniture and accessories.

13. The architecture of Shinto religious structures (shrines) changed substantially with the introduction of Buddhism during the Nara and Heian periods, from the eighth century onward. In the Heian period the *ishinoma* style (later called the *gongen* style, or *gongen-zukuri*) separated the main shrine building from a worship hall by an intervening space paved in stone and covered by a transversal gabled roof joining the two structures. The ultimate exemplar of *gongen-zukuri* is the seventeenth-century Toshogu mausoleum at Nikko, consisting of an elaborate and ornate series of buildings forming courtyards staggered up the mountainside.

14. Yukichi Fukuzawa (1835–1901) was a scholar of Western enlightenment, leader of the Meiji era, and founder of Keio University. Although he lacked the political power of Shigenobu Okuma, founder of Waseda University, nor was he as devoted to education as Jo Niijima, founder of Doshisha University, it may be a reflection of Fukuzawa's individuality that Keio today produces graduates active in economic circles, even though he himself was a leader in the field of journalism, publishing the journal *Meiroku Zasshi*.

CHAPTER 7

Hanasuki: Aesthetic of Symbiosis

1. A tea room in Japan is a unique architectural entity where the tea ceremony and related arts, such as flower arrangement, are practiced. However, it is also a place for quiet contemplation and the appreciation of works of calligraphy, painting, and ceramics. *An* means "hut" and is often used to describe a tea room or tea house.

2. These key terms in Japanese aesthetics are notoriously difficult to define in English. *Wabi* suggests a highly austere, severe aesthetic—a sort of sacred poverty. *Sabi* carries additional connotations of sadness and loneliness, reflection and isolation. These highly emotional sensibilities— for they are not rigorously defined concepts in any sense—are more often associated than accurately distinguished. They are applied to a wide range of visual and literary art.

3. Shokado Shojo (1584–1639) took up residence in Takimotobo when he was seventeen. Later he became head monk of Takimotobo, but he is better known for his tea room and collection of tea utensils, paintings, and works of calligraphy, now preserved at Iwashimizu Hachimangu shrine. Shokado is also credited as the inventor of the traditional Japanese lunch box, the *bento*. This is a rectangular lacquer box divided into four compartments for rice and various delicacies. Shokado was a noted connoisseur and man of taste of his age.

4. Kan'unken was built in the style favored by Kobori Enshu. Though destroyed in 1773, it was reconstructed in almost identical fashion in 1922, in the form of the present tea room in Takimotobo. It is often confused with another tea house designed by Shojo (see above), which stands on the property of the Atsuda family in Kyoto and is called the Shokado. The latter tea house was built by Shojo in his last years, after retiring from Takimotobo to take up residence in Izumibo.

5. Kobori Enshu (1579–1647), though a member of the samurai class, was best known as a master of tea and founder of one of the established schools. He was also commissioned by the Tokugawa shogunate and the imperial house to design major buildings, such as the dungeons of Edo Castle and Nagoya Castle, the central compound of Fushimi Castle, and the Sento Gosho palace in Kyoto, as well as numerous gardens and tea rooms. He introduced his personal taste, which he called *kirei sabi*, or gorgeous *sabi*, into the tea ceremony.

The private library of Sutemi Horiguchi, editor of the encyclopaedic *Chashitsu Okoshiezu Shu* (Fold-out Plans of Tea Rooms), contained a work called *Sukiya Mansions*, that includes a floor plan with the annotation "the

Takimotobo in Hachimangu shrine is built from the same plan as Enshu's Fushimi tea room." *Sukiya* is a style of architecture characterized by a sophisticated taste that blends formal and informal, the ponderously ornate and the light. It was strongly influenced by the evolving aesthetic of the tea ceremony and is the prevailing style of non-official architecture in the Edo period. *Suki* connotes "taste" or "style" and is used in compounds such as *wabisuki* and my coinage *hanasuki*.

6. A *daime*-sized mat is slightly smaller than an ordinary tatami mat, roughly three-quarters. It was an approximation of the distance from the host's mat to the *daisu* tea-utensil stand.

7. A *kaiki* is a detailed record (*ki*) of a tea gathering (*kai*). The *Matsuya Kaiki* is one of the most valuable of these records, a rich historical source for the development of the aesthetic of the tea ceremony.

8. The tea room Jo'an, a National Treasure, is located in Yurakuen in the castle town of Inuyama, Aichi Prefecture. This is said to be the *sukiya* portion of the hermitage that Oda Uraku built in the Shoden'in of Kennin-ji Temple, Kyoto. The name derives from Uraku's Christian baptismal name, Joao. After being taken over by the Mitsui household in 1908, it was moved to its present location in 1971.

9. Oda Uraku (1547–1621) was the eleventh son of the warlord Oda Nobuhide and the younger brother of Oda Nobunaga, who ruled Japan in the mid-sixteenth century. He survived the reigns of his brother and the two rulers who came after him in succession, Toyotomi Hideyoshi and Tokugawa Ieyasu, and was made a feudal lord of a moderate-sized domain. Born Oda Nagamasu, he adopted the name Uraku, by which he is usually known, after joining the Buddhist order late in life. His line continued to the Meiji period. The names of the present central Tokyo districts, Yurakucho and Sukiyabashi, derive from his mansion, which was located in the heart of the city. He is also founder of the Uraku school of the tea ceremony.

10. Nanbo Sokei (dates unknown), a master of the tea ceremony from the port of Sakai (near modern Osaka), was active during the rules of Oda Nobunaga and Toyotomi Hideyoshi. He describes himself as a Zen monk, the second-generation head priest of the Shuun'an at Nanshuji. He was the foremost disciple of Sen no Rikyu and regarded as his successor, but disappeared after the third annual memorial observance of Rikyu's death. He was devoted to an aesthetic expression, through the art of tea, of his Zen ethic of "pure poverty."

The *Nanpo Roku* is a secretly transmitted manual of Sen no Rikyu's school of tea, regarded as having been composed by Nanbo Sokei. The earliest copy we possess is in the hand of Tachibana Jitsuzan, a senior minister of the Kuroda clan in Fukuoka fief. Because of the strange "coincidence" that the work was discovered on the first centenary of Rikyu's death its authenticity is suspect. Nevertheless, it offers an accurate record of the world of tea, and based on this work, Jitsuzan inaugurated the Nanbo school of tea. Though the Tachibana family line terminated eight generations later, the school has continued in Kyoto and other areas as the Nanboryu Meikyoan school.

11. Takeno Joo (1502–55) was a wealthy merchant of the port city of Sakai who made a name for himself as a leader and patron of the art of tea. He taught the great tea masters of the age, including Imai Sokyu, Tsuda Sogyu, and Sen no Rikyu. With the wealth to support his innovations, he promoted the aesthetic of linked-poetry (*renga*) gatherings, which had been popular for many years in the form of contests. Significantly, he also brought Zen to the tea ceremony. Joo is the leading figure in the period of the evolution of the so-called *wabi*-style tea ceremony (*wabi cha*). His three disciples mentioned above were also all from merchant families, and they eventually became tea masters to the samurai class, thus spreading the art far and wide.

12. Murata Juko (1422–1502) is traditionally regarded as founder of the tea ceremony. After becoming a monk at Shomyoji in Nara, he returned to lay status and began to practice the art of tea. He cannot be directly associated with Sen no Rikyu or his followers and descendants, but he is indisputably linked to the *wabi* style of tea. Juko was instructed in Zen by the famous monk Ikkyu Sojun, and he was also a curator of Chinese art and tea master to the shogun Ashikaga Yoshimasa. He succeeded in creating a tea for the common people based on his deep knowledge of the tea ceremony as practiced among the elite.

13. Yamanoue Soji (1544–1590) was a tea practitioner during the reigns of Nobunaga Oda and Hideyoshi Toyotomi. He was Sen no Rikyu's earliest pupil, and Hideyoshi's guide to the tea ceremony. However, being both unsightly and sharp of tongue, he was banished. He became the guest of Hojo, feudal lord at Odawara, where he continued to promote and influence the tea ceremony. When Hideyoshi attacked Hojo, Soji's ears and nose were cut off in the Odawara camp and he met his end. His famous chronicle, *Yamanoue Soji Ki*, is a record of important tea appurtenances and a commentary on the philosophy of Murata Juko, Takeno Joo, and Sen no Rikyu.

14. *In'ei Kaisan* dates from 1933–34 and was translated by Thomas J. Harper and Edward G. Seidensticker.

15. Matsuo Basho (1644–94) is the most famous of all haiku poets. He traveled throughout Japan composing haiku and poetical prose called *hai-*

bun, and he also contributed significantly to the aesthetic of these genres.

16. Mukai Kyorai (1651–1704) was Basho's disciple. Basho placed great faith in him, and he edited the schools' collection of haiku called *Sarumino* (Monkey's Raincoat). Kyorai's greatest achievements, however, were in the criticism and theory of haiku. He was born to the samurai class, but gave up his status to become a geomancer, which remained his profession for the rest of his life. *Kyorai Sho* is Kyorai's masterwork, in which he identifies and discusses many of the distinctive properties of the haiku and *haibun* genre, including "unchanging flux."

17. Zeami (1363–1443) was a Noh actor, theorist, director, and composer. Together with his father Kan'ami, he created the theatrical genre of Noh. Zeami made his first real debut as a performer at the age of twelve, when he and his father performed for the shogun Ashikaga Yoshimasa, who was much taken with Zeami. In fact, Yoshimasa showed such affection for and protection of Zeami that it was widely thought they were lovers.

Zeami based his Noh on that of his father, which had a broad popular appeal, but placed strong emphasis on beauty, raising the art to great heights. After suffering persecution from Yoshimasa's successor, Zeami increased the intellectual content of Noh, formulating the art as we have it today. *Fushi Kaden* is a systemization of the theories of Noh that Zeami inherited from his father. It is a practical work, dividing the life of an actor into seven periods and prescribing the appropriate practice for each. Zeami wrote *Kakyo* when persecution by the new shogun threatened to destroy his theatrical troupe; it contains the marrow of Zeami's thoughts. The "flower" (*ka*) in the titles of both works refers to the performer's continued ability to be attractive on the Noh stage, and it is related to Zeami's key conceptual ideal of beauty—*yugen*, or mysterious beauty.

18. Sen no Rikyu (1522–91) was born into a merchant family in Sakai, the port city near Osaka. He studied tea under Takeno Joo. When Oda Nobunaga demanded payment of a huge indemnity from Sakai, Rikyu and Imai Sogyu were sent as members of a party to negotiate a settlement. After Nobunaga's death, Rikyu became tea master to Toyotomi Hideyoshi.

Rikyu is known as the prime formulator of the art of tea; we owe the transmission of this art not only to his aesthetic vision but also to his success in promoting tea among ranking samurai. Thus, Rikyu's seven disciples, called the Seven Sages of Rikyu, were mainly of samurai origin, and he also taught tea to such well-known feudal lords as Date Masamune. It is believed that this increasing political influence may have played a part in Hideyoshi's decision to sentence Rikyu to death by *seppuku*, or self-disembowelment.

19. Genealogy of the Tea Ceremony (*Sadō ryakukei zu*)

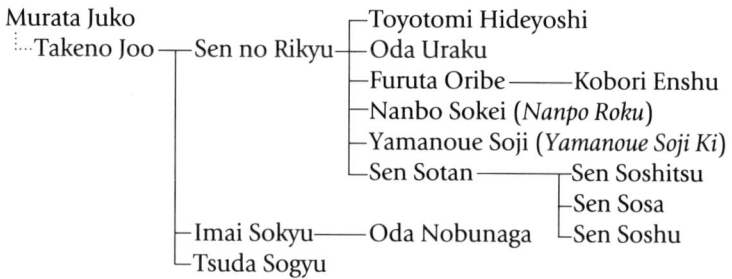

```
Murata Juko                      ┌─Toyotomi Hideyoshi
 ┊··Takeno Joo ──┬─Sen no Rikyu──┼─Oda Uraku
                 │               ├─Furuta Oribe────────Kobori Enshu
                 │               ├─Nanbo Sokei (Nanpo Roku)
                 │               ├─Yamanoue Soji (Yamanoue Soji Ki)
                 │               └─Sen Sotan────────┬─Sen Soshitsu
                 │                                  ├─Sen Sosa
                 ├─Imai Sokyu────Oda Nobunaga       └─Sen Soshu
                 └─Tsuda Sogyu
```

The *major masters* and schools of tea are as follows: Murata Juko (1422–1502), Takeno Joo (1502–55), Sen no Rikyu (1522–91), Oda Uraku (1547–1621), Furuta Oribe (1544–1615), Hosokawa Tadaoki (1563–1646), and Kobori Enshu (1579–1647).

20. Furuta Oribe (1544–1615) was of samurai birth, and he served under both Oda Nobunaga and Toyotomi Hideyoshi, rising well up into the feudal hierarchy. Oribe studied under Rikyu, but he transformed Rikyu's essentially quietist style of tea, which found beauty in stillness, into a more dynamic style that would please members of his own class. He is said even to have purposely broken tea utensils and had them repaired with gold. His disciples included Kobori Enshu and Hon'ami Koetsu, and a type of pottery has been named after him. He was tea master to the second Tokugawa shogun, Hidetada, but when, at the age of seventy-two, his involvement in plans for a *coup d'état* in Osaka was discovered, he was forced to commit suicide.

21. This structure (today an Important Cultural Property) was offered, without a name, by Furuta Oribe to Kenchu, founder of the Yabunouchi school of tea. Later on, a panel inscribed with the words "Swallow Hut" (Ennan) was erected by Murata Juko, and this eventually came into general use as both a proper name and a style name—the Ennan style being one of those preferred by Oribe.

22. Bruno Taut (1880–1938), the German expressionist architect, came to Japan from working in Russia in 1933. He extolled what he called "emperor art," by which he meant Katsura Detached Palace and Ise Shrine, as opposed to "shogun art," referring to the Toshogu shrine at Nikko. His writings include the book *Nippon* with his own illustrations. Taut left Japan in 1936 to teach in Istanbul, where he died.

The German architect Walter Gropius (1883–1969) started out with an architecture based on the techniques of modern industry, and while advocating progressive and rational methods of building, he sought a unification of handcraft and the industrial arts. While director of the celebrated Bauhaus school, he assembled a number of highly creative personalities, such as Wassily Kandinsky, Oskar Schlemmer, Paul Klee, and Laszlo Moholy-Nagy, and sought to create a unified contemporary design. Gropius's buildings and his writings, notably the book *International Architecture* (1925), constitute one of the bases of the modern movement.

The Katsura Detached Palace was originally a country villa of the Hachijo no Miya family. As remodeled and extended in the seventeenth century, the main house has four sections, as well as four pavilions, several belvederes, and a Buddhist chapel arranged about the gardens. A combination of the *shoin* (palatial) and *sukiya* styles, Katsura is regarded by many as the supreme example of residential architecture in Japan.

23. The Grand Ise Shrine is located at Ise in Mie Prefecture and is one of the two or three most important Shinto foundations in Japan. It is associated with the imperial deity, the Sun Goddess Amaterasu. Made of unpainted Japanese cypress wood, it has a bold, simple design vaguely suggestive of South Pacific origins. Ise Shrine is carefully dismantled and rebuilt every twenty-one years, always following the same specifications, though some changes have crept in over the centuries.

24. The Toshogu shrine at Nikko serves as the mausoleum of Tokugawa Ieyasu, the founder of the Tokugawa shogunate, which ruled Japan from 1600 to 1868. It was completed in 1636, and the shrine building and gateways are highly ornate.

25. Taro Okamoto (1911–96) was a painter and sculptor. Born into an artistic family, he spent his youth in Paris, studying at the Sorbonne. After his return to Japan he fought in the Second World War in China, and when the war was over became active not only in the art world but in politics, and as a writer and critic. His sculptures include the *Tower of the Sun* at Expo '70 (Osaka) and the sculptures decorating the Children's Castle in Aoyama, Tokyo.

26. The Jomon period, from about 10,000 B.C. to 300 B.C. (Japan's Neolithic period), is characterized by the dynamic and dramatic clay figurines and pottery that have been discovered dating from that time. "Jomon" means rope patterns, which are one of the commonly found decorative techniques on pottery of the period. The following Yayoi period, from about 300 B.C. to 300 A.D., was when rice production was first introduced to Japan. Its pottery is simpler, more austere and delicate.

27. Todaiji was erected by the emperor Shomu (r. 724–29) at Nara to serve as the directing Buddhist institution within the hierarchical network of provincial monasteries and convents throughout Japan. By its immense scale, the temple demonstrated its position at the acme of imperial sponsorship; although rebuilt, it still houses the colossal bronze statue known as the Great Buddha of Nara, dating to 752. This image compared so

favorably in size and magnificence with contemporary Buddhist statues produced in Tang China that it came to be regarded as the symbol of Japan's rise from a backward country to a highly developed one.

28. Toshodaiji was funded in 759 in the western sector of Nara by the Chinese monk Jianzhen, and Todaiji was built between 710 and 784 in the eastern sector of the same city, largely by Emperor Shomu.

CHAPTER 8

Rikyu Grey: Art of Ambiguity

1. Hishikawa Moronobu (ca. 1618–94) was an ukiyoe artist of the early to mid Edo period. He entered his family's textile painting business and became popular for his portrayals of scenes of the thriving capital, including courtesans in the Yoshiwara district as well as the world of Kabuki. In depicting the social conditions and customs of Edo, he was supported by the rising fortunes of the townspeople. Consequently, Moronobu specialized in paintings for printmaking and virtually created the style and market of Edo ukiyoe.

2. Fujiwara no Teika (also Sadaie, 1162–1241) was a distinguished poet and compiler of the *Shin Kokin Shu*, also renowned for his critical writings. The full title of his anthology is the *Shin Kokin Waka Shu* (New Anthology of Ancient and Modern Poetry). Compiled by Teika in or around 1205, it is one of the greatest of the twenty-one imperial poetry anthologies.

3. Giacomo della Porta (1540–1604) was an Italian architect and sculptor who studied with Michelangelo and Vignola; he became the official "Architect to the Roman People." As a builder he is considered to have spanned the late Renaissance and baroque periods. As Vignola's successor, he became architect in charge of St. Peter's in 1573 and completed the dome along with Fontana. His best-known works include the façade of Santa Maria dei Monti and the interior of the Farnese palace in Rome, both of which are strongly baroque in character.

4. Baldassare Peruzzi (1481–1536) was a Sienese architect and painter. He became a disciple of Bramante in 1503 and later, after the death of Raphael in 1520, his coworker in the construction of St. Peter's in Rome. He was appointed architect in charge in 1536. Peruzzi attempted the use of false perspective (illusionist architectural painting, *quadratura*) for the first time in Rome. As a painter, he created both frescoes and easel works, just as Pinturicchio and Raphael had done. His first work of architecture was the Villa Farnesina (1509–21) in Rome, where he also participated in the cycle of fresco decoration. He is believed as well to be the architect of the Palazzo Massimo alle Colonne (ca. 1535) in Rome.

5. Nicolas Poussin (1594–1665), the most significant painter of seventeenth-century France, was devoted to study of the Italian Renaissance masters Raphael and Titian, and spent most of his life in Rome. His well-polished and architecturally balanced compositions had a great influence on later generations and became a model for nineteenth-century classicists. Among his best-known works are *Parnassus* and *Arcadian Shepherds*.

6. Herbert Read (1893–1966) was an English poet and critic active in the 1930s. In addition to poetry, he wrote extensively on the fine arts and produced literary criticism. His most influential works of art criticism include *The Philosophy of Modern Art* and *Art and Society*. His writings reflect his belief that works of art are the highest expression of inherent meaning. After World War II, he also wrote political works that are strongly anarchist in character.

7. William Empson (1906–1984) was an English poet and critic, whose poems were modernized versions of the John Donne school of seventeenth-century metaphysical poetry; his work pursues the unification of sensibility and reason. As a critic, he exerted a great influence on the methodology of the New Criticism. His *Seven Kinds of Diversity of Meaning* (1930) is a classic of modern literary criticism, whose fame has passed to general domain. Empson lived in Japan from 1931 to 1934, lecturing on English literature at Tokyo Bunri University and Tokyo Imperial University.

8. Masao Yamaguchi (b. 1931) has, since the 1970s, investigated new ways of perceiving issues in linguistics and cultural anthropology. Among his concepts is that of "core and periphery." Yamaguchi claims that a culture develops from peripheral strength rather than from a concentration of power at its core. In fact, the core tries to reject the periphery, while the periphery continues to stimulate and enliven the core. This ambivalence characterizes all binomial relations: sacred and profane, heaven and earth, order and chaos, man and woman, regulation and freedom.

9. Kunio Yanagida (1875–1962) recognized a continuous, folk-transmitted history behind all documentation. He surveyed and studied the customs, beliefs, lifestyles, and ceremonies of villages in mountainous, coastal, and plains regions all over Japan—founding so-called Yanagida ethnology. Folk customs do not merely evolve in successive stages; instead, they are layered and persist even in modern times.

10. Aldo van Eyck (b. 1918) is a well-known Dutch architect, a driving force behind the Team 10 organization that during the 1950s evolved from CIAM. He was active in the architectural scene of the 1960s. Major works include the former Amsterdam Orphanage and the campus of Arbino Bon University.

11. Louis I. Kahn (1901–1974), born in Estonia, was an American architect of great international fame, who taught for many years at the University of Pennsylvania. Major works include Yale University Art Gallery, Richards Medical Research Laboratories of the University of Pennsylvania, Salk Institute, Indian Institute of Management, Kimbell Art Museum, and Yale Center for British Art.

12. James Stirling (1926–1992) was a British architect, principal of the London firm of Stirling and Gowan, and for many years adjunct professor at Yale University. Major works include the Leicester University College of Engineering, the Faculty of History Building at Cambridge University, the Stuttgart Museum of Modern Art, and the Arthur M. Sackler Museum of Art at Harvard University.

13. Charles Jencks (b. 1939) is an American architectural critic, who lectures at the London Architectural Association School of Architecture and at UCLA. His major works include *The Meaning of Architecture, Le Corbusier and the Tragic View of Architecture*, and *The Language of Post-Modern Architecture*.

14. C. R. Mackintosh (1868–1928) was a Scottish architect who, together with the MacDonald sisters and Andrew MacNair, pioneered a new style of proto-Art Noveau in the 1890s in Glasgow. Its newness, recognized on the Continent before Britain, played a leading role in the emergence of modern architecture. Mackintosh's best-known work is the Glasgow School of Art, in addition to several residences in Scotland. His work is noted for a decorativeness not bound by past styles and comprehensively applied to furniture and objects of all sorts.

15. Otto Wagner (1841–1918) was an Austrian architect, who played a guiding role in theory and design as professor, from 1894, at the Vienna School of Art. He advocated a "practical style," the point of departure for which is to be found in modern life, and emphasized the social function of architecture. Major works include Vienna's Karlsplatz Station and the Vienna Post Office Savings Bank.

16. Caravaggio (Michelangelo Mersi, 1573–1610) was a unique representative of Italian Baroque painting. The Caravaggio style is based on starkly contrastive compositions of light and dark, resembling works in relief, and sculpturelike depictions of people. This manner had an important influence not only in Italy, but also on the baroque art of Spain, Flanders, and Holland. Major works include *Bacchus, Fortune-teller, Calling of St. Matthew, Martyrdom of St. Matthew*, and *Madonna of the Serpent*.

C H A P T E R   9

Intermediary Spaces

1. Commercial or artisanal cooperatives of persons in the same occupation, dating from medieval times, the *za* were a Japanese form of guild. *Za* were under the protection of a noble family, temple, or shrine (for example, the *za* of oil-sellers were under the Oyamazaki Shrine) and had exclusive rights to manufacture or sell certain products or commodities. The system survived into the age of civil war, but since it posed an obstacle to distribution, during the process of unification under Nobunaga Oda *za* fell into decline and were forced into liberalization as *rakuza*. The free markets formed in this way were called *rakuichi*, the spread of which was promoted throughout Japan by Hideyoshi Toyotomi.

2. The German mathematician G. F. B. Riemann (1826–66) created a new world of mathematics, the primary components of which are Riemannian geometry and the Riemann integral. The former transcended Euclidean geometry, while the latter superseded the classical mathematics of Leibniz and Newton. This prepared the way for a paradigm shift in science, as Riemannian geometry provided the earliest definitions of manifold and curvature.

3. These terms from German philosophy mean, respectively, "having many values" and "having dual values." When used as modifiers, *multivalent* indicates that divers emotions and attitudes are present simultaneously, while *ambivalent* points to two emotions or attitudes.

4. Japan's population numbered approximately 12 million at the beginning of the Edo shogunate. It had grown to more than 30 million by the early eighteenth century, and reached 35 million by the latter half of the nineteenth century toward the end of the shogunate. Japan by that time was more populous than any European nation except Russia.
   Edo's population growth was particularly rapid, eventually reaching the one million mark. That number included about 580,000 *chonin*, or tradesmen. As these people lived on 20.9 percent of the land in Edo, they were subjected to severe overcrowding.
   The Edo period saw a great focus on travel and information about travel, a trend cultivated mainly by *ko*, or religious organizations. Many types of *ko* existed, and those of famous temples and major shrines, such as the Ise *ko*, attracted a particularly large following. For example, records state that as many as 3.62 million people, or about 20 percent of the population in 1705, participated in the Hoei pilgrimage of that year to the Ise Shrine. Even more remarkably, by 1756 4.39 million households reportedly participated in *ko*, including *ko* pilgrimages by proxy. In such pilgrimages, a representative was selected from the members of the *ko*, by lot or in

turn, to visit the temple or shrine that was the object of faith. This representative would use the accumulated funds of the *ko* for travel expenses and to provide shrine or temple contributions, and would bring back *ofuda*, or Shinto talismans, for the other members.

Incidentally, there existed a great variety of *ko* corresponding to various aims and occupations. Some took on a financial nature, such as the Tanomoshi *ko*. There were also the Koyasu *ko*, for women who wanted to have children; the Tenjin *ko*, run by children; and the Ebisu *ko*, run by a group of merchants. Some also had the character of a salon gathering, such as the *cha ko* (tea *ko*).

5. The SII (Structural Impediments Initiative) was a series of bilateral conferences, begun in 1989, to probe the structural reasons for the gross trade imbalance between Japan and the U.S.

C H A P T E R 1 0

Man and Nature

1. Yoshida Kenko (fl. first half of the fourteenth century) was first employed as a poet by the emperor Go-Nijo (r. 1301–08), but about age 30 he chose to become a hermit monk. *Tsurezuregusa*, written in his late forties, has come to be a model of the Japanese aesthetic consciousness. Translated as *Essays in Idleness*, the work reflects Kenko's wide range of friendships, which extended from clergy and laity, nobility and commoners, to military commanders in the eastern hinterlands. The essays, celebrating enlightenment and solitude, cherish the memory of the royal court but also indicate an awareness of the beginnings of a new era. The 243 brief entries recall both the quiet beauty of the royal court found in the earlier *Pillow Book of Sei Shonagon* and the philosophy of mutability explored in *A Tale of a Ten-Foot Square Hut*. In this way, Yoshida's work formulated an aesthetic consciousness for the new Muromachi era.

2. Seiji Tsutsumi (b. 1927), chairman of the large Seison Corporation of merchandisers, is also a poet. Under the pen name Hashi Tsujii, he has authored *Ihojin* (Stranger) and other works.

3. Under the Building Standards Act, before one can build housing in an area designated an "urban replanning zone," application must be made for approval in regard, particularly, to structural codes and means of disaster prevention. In addition, approval must be obtained for height, road frontage, building-to-land ratio, occupancy ratio, and direct and indirect sunlight obstruction.

C H A P T E R   1 1

Philosophy of *Karakuri*

1. The great French philosopher Jean Jacques Rousseau (1712–78), in works such as *Social Contract* and *Origins of Human Inequality*, became a leading influence for democracy and helped inspire the French Revolution. His philosophy, which maintains that human unhappiness begins when people deviate from nature, has had a major influence on contemporary philosophers, notably Lévi-Strauss.

C H A P T E R   1 2

From Postmodernism to Symbiosis

1. Jean-François Lyotard (b. 1924) is one of the French so-called new philosophers, professor at Paris University, and Director of the International Institute of Philosophy.

2. Issei Miyake (b. 1938) is a fashion designer. After his graduation from Tama Arts University, he worked in Paris and then New York. In 1971 he established the acclaimed Issey Miyake label, and by 1975 he had opened his first boutique in Paris. His fashions are marked by an elegant simplicity combining Japanese and Western notions of style.

3. Rei Kawakubo (b. 1942) is a fashion designer, who graduated from Keio University and then worked for the Asahi Kasei Corporation. His fashions were first shown in Paris (1981) and then New York (1983). They have a beauty that disregards the rest of the fashion world, at one time featuring a vagrantlike appearance and sweaters with holes.

4. Michel Foucault (1926–64) was a celebrated French philosopher, author of *The Order of Things* and *The Archaeology of Knowledge*. He was influenced by Nietzsche and preoccupied with identifying the forces that shape human institutions, carrying out studies on early forms of treatment of the insane and criminals and writing a history of human sexuality. In *The Archaeology of Knowledge* this disciple of Jean Hippolyte showed how different ages are characterized by different styles of knowledge.

5. Giambattista Piranesi (1720–78), an Italian architect and engraver, was active mostly in Rome and produced many views of that city, but he is also well known for his series of *Imaginary Prisons*, containing fantastic and macabre variations on Roman architecture.

6. Antonio Sant'Elia (1888–1916) argued for a new architecture free from all past conventions, and exhibited his ideas as sketches in the 1914 Nuove Tendenze group exhibition under the title *New City*. His concepts

were visionary, and although his work had few links to contemporary building practice many of his ideas uncannily have been realized decades later. He was killed in the First World War at the age of twenty-eight.

7. Roger Caillois (1913–1978) was a French critic, thinker, author, sociologist, and anthropologist. He used his wide-ranging knowledge to blaze a trail in the study of the human sciences, cofounded the Collège de Sociologie, and directed the social sciences review *Diogène*. Major works include *Sociology of the Sacred* and *People and Play*.

8. The German philosopher Martin Heidegger (1889–1976) considered the everyday existence of *das Mann* (the ordinary individual) to be intertwined with a variety of social problems. He used the word *Sorge* to describe man's basic state. Humans do not confront a pre-existing world order; instead, human experience (*Sorge*) gives form to the world and verifies it. This is what it means for humans to inhabit the world, a view known in Heidegger's terminology as "existence in the world."

9. François Marie Charles Fourier (1772–1837), a French Utopian socialist, influenced anarchists such as Proudhon and Kropotkin. The ideal society described by Fourier was known as a *phalanx*, or cooperative society, in which the central authorities were managers. Cooperative living units were based on agricultural production, each having at its center a Phalanstère with residential quarters for members, a large hothouse with indoor gardens, a theater, classrooms, a school, a library, and a hospital.

10. Edward Robert de Zurko was an American architect active in the 1950s and professor of architecture at Rice Institute of Technology.

11. Leon Battista Alberti (1404–72) was a humanist, poet, painter, and architect of the early Renaissance in Italy. He became well known for his principles of architectural theory, which he first applied to the remodeling of the Church of San Francesco at Rimini.

12. Andrea Palladio (1508–80), an Italian architect, became a leading figure in classical studies and Roman archaeology. His style of building, which rehabilitated the antique orders, was termed Palladian. His works include the Church of Saint Giorgio Maggiore in Venice and numerous villas on the mainland.

13. Claude-Nicolas Ledoux (1736–1806) was the court architect to Louis XVI of France. He produced many works characterized by the clarity of their geometrical forms, as well as a posthumous treatise celebrated today for its illustrations.

14. Gotthold Ephraim Lessing (1729–81) was a German playwright, art critic, and philosopher of the Enlightenment. His *Hamburg Dramaturgy*, a

treatise on dramatic theory, is pervaded by the critical insight that, instead of worshiping the cultures of other countries, a nation should create its own.

15. Karl Friedrich Schinkel (1781–1841) was the German architect who recreated classical Greek architecture in Berlin, as well as elsewhere in Prussia and parts of today's Poland. His works include the Berlin Royal Theatre and the Museum of Ancient History. He was also a stage designer and neo-Gothic church architect; he is celebrated for the engraved version of his drawings and projects.

16. Horatio Greenough (1805–52) was an American sculptor and architectural theorist. He is known as a functionalist thinker.

17. Louis Sullivan (1856–1924) was the leading architect of the Chicago school and famous for the slogan "form follows function." His works include the Guaranty Building in St. Louis and the Carson, Pirrie, Scott department store in Chicago. He was especially talented as a designer of architectural ornament.

18. Jean Baudrillard (b. 1929) wrote *The Consumer Society* in 1970, which announced that modern capitalist society is entering a completely new era, that of the exchange of symbols. His later works propose that any direct equivalence between symbols and actual content is nearing an end; ours is an "age of simulation," in which symbols are exchanged without any real meaning. This is seen to indicate a collapse of the economic and social doctrine that priority be given to productive labor. Instead, consumption becomes the pre-eminent fact of economic life.

19. Ferdinand de Saussure (1857–1913) was a Swiss linguist who in this century has exerted a fundamental influence on modern thinking via the dimension of semiology, or the study of signs. He was also involved in the study of anagrams in his later years. Through this study, Saussure was moving purportedly from the attention to *langue* (language as rules and a common code) to the study of *parole* (language as an act manifest in speech and writing), but this work remained unfinished.

20. Shuhei Aida (b. 1932) has written extensively on cybernetics and ecotechnology.

21. Gaston Bachelard (1884–1962) was an eminent French philosopher and historian of science who exerted a wide-ranging influence in areas extending from literature to philosophy. Bachelard held that no limits can be placed on the imagination, owing to human ability to twist and bend the images offered by perception. Taking the concept of "fire," for example, he traced its images back to ancient mythology in an attempt to discover "archetypes," or original elements of human consciousness. His

work had a decisive influence on twentieth-century cultural anthropology and literary criticism.

22. The concept of the *fractal* was originated by Mandelbrot in 1977. Fractal geometry serves to express shapes difficult, or impossible, to measure; not mere parallelograms or spheres but instead clouds, shorelines, and the meandering of rivers. The word means "broken." According to Mandelbrot, the broken that protrudes from the integral realm is called the fractal dimension. The fractal dimension "D" expresses the index of complexity of a drawing produced by the combination of complex elements having the dimension "d."

23. Jiddu Krishnamurti (1895–1985) was born in India. At the age of fourteen, he was put forward by Annie Besant, second leader of the Theosophical Society founded by Mme. Blavatsky. Krishnamurti's teachings, which state that one should conquer the self and walk the path of absolute freedom, contain elements similar to the theory of Zen. He speaks from deep meditative experience, and his thought has created a lasting impression on those involved in the New Science and New Age movements.

24. Advocates of the New Science favor a holistic approach to health, linked to the study of organic systems in light of the "bootstrap theory" and other views relating the new physics and the world. Its origins lie in the holonic philosophy of Kestra and his colleagues, according to whom modern medicine sees the body only as a collection of organs and other parts. By contrast, they value the Oriental view that conceives of body and mind as a "whole," as well as traditional folk healing methods.

C H A P T E R   1 3

Toward the Evocation of Meaning through Symbiosis

1. Thomas Aquinas (1225–74) was an Italian scholasticist and theologian. He devised the harmonization of faith with reason, based on Aristotelian doctrines developed in accordance with the principles of the Christian religion.

2. Roger Bacon (fl. thirteenth century) was a medieval English philosopher whose thought and achievements forged a path for the natural science of the Middle Ages.

3. Meister Eckhart (ca.1260–1327), a German theologian, was a mysticist who belonged to the Dominican Order.

4. Sir Arthur Conan Doyle (1859–1930), the English detective novelist, is renowned for his series of books about Sherlock Holmes.

5. Julia Kristeva (b. 1941) was born into a Jewish family in Bulgaria. She traveled to Paris in 1966, where she studied semiology and psychoanalysis. Active in semiotic criticism and a practicing psychoanalyst, her beauty and talent were admired by Roland Barthes. She is married to Philippe Sollers, and much of the success of the magazine *Tel Quel* is due to the efforts of this couple.

6. Henry Moore (1899–1986), the greatest English sculptor of the twentieth century, was famed for large, semiabstract sculptures that convey an impression of the organic force of life.

CHAPTER 14

Abstraction Rendered Symbolic

1. The "Greater East Asia Co-Prosperity Sphere" sprang from the idea of liberating China and Southeast Asia from the dominance of Western imperialist nations and building a vast economic sphere of influence and "co-prosperity," led by Japan. This was nothing more than a slogan advocated by Japan toward the end of the Pacific War to rationalize its aggressive tactics toward Asia. An echo of this movement resounded in architectural circles, and an architectural style in keeping with the slogan was born. This was the Greater East Asia Co-Prosperity Sphere "style," an offshoot of the Imperial Crown Style of prewar institutional building—both aesthetically meaningless, these styles produced pastiches of various traditional motifs grafted onto modern techniques of construction.

CHAPTER 16

Symbiosis of Land-Use Planning and Redevelopment

1. The Ikeda cabinet was formed in 1960 and took over the reins of government from the Nobusuke Kishi cabinet when Prime Minister Kishi resigned following conclusion of the new Japan-U.S. security treaty. Its members served three terms until the resignation of Hayato Ikeda due to illness in 1964, having concentrated mainly on economic policy. During its first term, the cabinet promoted an income-doubling plan. During its second term, foreign economic policy was central, including visits to the U.S. and France. It was then that President de Gaulle of France commented, "I was visited by a salesman of transistor radios, not by the leader of a country," thus stirring up public censure. The Tokyo Olympics of 1964 were held during the final year of the cabinet's third term of office.

C H A P T E R   1 7

Symbiosis in Asia

1. The first meeting of *Kyosei Jiyu Kaigi* (Open Symposium on Symbiosis) was held on September 7, 1993, in Room 1105 on the eleventh floor of Keidanren Kaikan in Tokyo. Lectures were presented by Koshiro Tamaki, professor emeritus of Tokyo University, on "The Prototype of Omens"; by Shigeru Okamura, professor* at Kurume University, on "The *I-Ching*: The Book of Changes and the Concept of Symbiosis"; and by Kisho Kurokawa on "The Philosophy of Symbiosis." Discussion followed. Thereafter, meetings were held at several leading universities. Members included Koshiro Tamaki; Shigeru Okamura; Hiromichi Serikawa, professor at Shukutoku Junior College; Hidefumi Imura, professor at Kyushu University; Shunji Yokota, professor at Chikushi Jogakuen; Masaru Akimoto, assistant professor at Chikushi Jogakuen; Masayuki Okubo, assistant professor at Kurume University; Akio Mineshima, professor at Waseda University; Noboru Kajimura, professor at Asia University; Sho Kawanami, professor at Toyo University; Noriteru Tanaka, professor at Musashino Women's University; Yuichi Ukita, assistant professor at Bunkyo Women's Junior College; Ikko Fukui, assistant professor at Tamagawa University; Tsunehisa Kumehara, lecturer at Shukutoku Junior College; Shunji Hosaka, lecturer at Reitaku University; Katsuhito Okamoto, director of the Planning Department, Head Office Business Bureau; Shiro Hattori, vice-director of the Nuclear Power Safety System Research Institute; Jifuji Misumi, director of the Social System Research Institute; Akira Yamada, vice-director of the Social System Research Institute; Yasuhiro Haruna, director of research at the Social System Research Institute; Eiko Hanabusa, vice-director of research at the Social System Research Institute; and Kisho Kurokawa.

*Titles are as of September 1993.

2. Ibrahim Anwar, born in Penang in 1947, is Vice-Premier and Finance Minister of Malaysia. He is also president of the International Islamic University, Malaysia, and has served as president of the General Assembly of UNESCO.

In 1996 Anwar published his *Asian Renaissance* (Times Books International, Singapore and Kuala Lumpur), in which he goes beyond the simple concept of an East Asian Economic Miracle to subject the recent, vast social and cultural transformation of the region to close scrutiny.

3. Alvin Toffler (b. 1928) is an American futurologist and sociologist. His book *The Third Wave* (1984) became an international best-seller.

EPILOGUE

1. Noboru Kawazoe (b. 1926) is an architectural critic and the director of the Kawazoe Research Institute. His main writings include *Tami to Kami no Sumai* (The Dwellings of the People and the Gods), *Kenchiku to Dento* (Architecture and Tradition), *Seikatsugaku no Teisho* (A Proposal for a Science of Lifestyle), and *Toshi Kukan no Bunka* (The Culture of City Space).

2. Masato Otaka (b. 1923) is an independent architect. Major works include redevelopment of Sakaide (Kagawa Prefecture), Bunka Kaikan (Chiba Prefecture), Tochigi Prefectural Government Building, Gumma Prefectural Museum of History, Fukushima Prefectural Museum of Art, and redevelopment of the Motomachi district in Hiroshima.

3. Fumihiko Maki (b. 1929) is an architect, director of the firm of Maki and Associates. A graduate of Tokyo University, his main works are Toyota Memorial Lecture Hall at Nagoya University, Kumagaya campus of Rissho University, Daikanyama Terrace housing complex in Tokyo, the libraries of the Hiyoshi and Mita campuses of Keio University, the Spiral Building in Tokyo, Kyoto National Museum of Modern Art, Fujisawa Gymnasium, Tokyo Gymnasium, Nihon Convention Center at Makuhari, and Shonan Fujisawa campus of Keio University.

4. Kiyonori Kikutake (b. 1928) is an independent architect. His main works include the Izumo Taisha visitor's reception hall, Kyoto Community Bank, Aquapolis, Tanabe Art Museum, Karuizawa Takanawa Art Museum, and Edo Historical Museum in Tokyo.

5. Kiyoshi Awazu (b. 1929) is a graphic designer, director of Awazu Design Institute. He is professor at Musashino College of Art and a member of the steering committee for the National Ethnological Museum in Osaka. His writings include: *Dezain ni Nani ga Dekiru ka?* (What Can Design Do?), *Gaudi Sanka* (A Tribute to Gaudí), and an illustrated collection of his own works.

6. Kenji Ekuan (b. 1929) is an industrial designer, president of GK Industrial Design Institute and head of Kuwasawa Research Institute. He was special consultant for exhibit design at the Tsukuba International Science Fair and producer for the Japan IBM exhibit. His major writings include *Dogu Ko* (On Tools), *Indasutoriaru Dezain* (Industrial Design), *Makunouchi Bento no Bigaku* (The Aesthetics of the Box Lunch), and *Dogu no Shiso* (The Philosophy of Tools).

7. Shomei Tomatsu (b. 1930) is a photographer. In the 1960s his work focused on Tokyo street scenes and he is regarded as the founder of that genre in Japan. He received the Ministry of Education Special Prize for his work, among which are the famous *Taiyo no Empitsu* (The Sun's Pencil) and *11:02 Nagasaki*.

ACKNOWLEDGMENTS

The publisher wishes to express its gratitude to all of the following people and institutions for graciously granting permission to use the photographic images and illustrations in the present volume: In some instances, the publisher was unsuccessful in locating copyright holders or in receiving responses to queries. Any information on material not credited would be welcome.

Bokusuishobo: page 164 (both)

Cordon Art B.V., Holland: page 319 (above)

Ford Moter Company: page 46

Fondation du Corbusier: pages 91, 163 (below), 294, 351

Garland Publishing, Inc.: page 52

Idemitsu Museum of Arts, Tokyo: page 350

Imperial Household Agency: pages 152, 153 (both), 238 (below), 391

Ise Shrine: page 154 (above)

Ishikawa Pension Hall: page 166

Itsukushimajinja: page 324

Itsuo Art Museum, Osaka: page 148 (below)

Kairyuoji: page 313 (above)

Kanda Myojin: page 130

Kinokuniya shoten: page 193

MOA Museum of Art, Shizuoka Prefecture: page 121

Murata Isamu: page 123

Nagoya Railroad Co., Ltd.: pages 150, 151, 314 (above)

National Museum of Japanese History, Chiba Prefecture: page 390 (below)

Nezu Gongen: page 131 (below)

Nishihonganji: page 176

Paul Theobald & Co.: page 194 (center)

Saioin: pages 175, 328

Seibundo shinkosha: page 388 (below)

Springer–Verlag Borlin Heidelberg: page 357

Sumiya hozonkai: page 334 (above)

Takahashi Masayasu: page 221

Tatsukawa Shoji: page 275 (both)

Thames & Hudson Ltd., London: pages 97, 98, 292 (below)

Todaiji: page 157

Tokugawa Art Museum, Nagoya: pages 134–5, 230 (above)

Tokyo National Museum: pages 120 (above), 122 (right), 126, 127, 145, 155, 156, 230 (below), 316, 389, 390 (above)

Tokyo Sogensha: page 308

Toshogu Shrine: page 154 (below)

Urasenke Foundation: page 148 (above)

Yabuuchisoke: page 149

Yushima Tenmangu: page 131 (above)

PHOTO CREDITS

© ADAGP Paris & SPDA Tokyo, 1997: pages 91, 163 (below), 351, 347

Camera Tokyo Service: page 227 (below)

© Cordon Art-Baarn-Holland: page 319 (above)

© Ford Moter Company: page 46
© Futagawa Yukio: page 180 (below)
© Hibi Sadao: page 328 (above)
© Hunting Aerofilms Limited, London: page 292 (above)
© Inouye Koichi: page 369 (left)
Kanda Myojin: page 130
© Kyodo Photo: page 49
© Matsuoka Mitsuo: page 136
© Misawa Nobuhiko: page 385
© Murai Osamu: page 200
© Ohashi Tomio: pages 124–5, 138, 166, 167 (both), 186, 201, 202, 217 (both) 312 (below), 313 (below), 314 (below), 317, 318, 319 (below), 322–3, 325, 328 (below), 330, 332, 333 (below), 334 (below), 335 (below), 338–9, 340, 341, 353 (both), 354 (both), 355 (above right and below), 359 (both), 362 (both), 364 (above), 366–7, 372 (both), 373, 378 (all), 396–7, 412, 417

© Ota Seiroku: page 349
SCALA Instituto Fotogarafico Dditoriale S. P. A.: page 172
Shibundo: pages 149, 150, 151, 154, 175, 238, 313, 324, 391
Shogakukan Inc.: page 157
Shokokusha Publishing Co., Inc.: page 209 (above)
© Sautter, Hans: page 197
© Takase Yoshio (GA Photographers): page 276
The Japan Architect Shinkenchiku-sha Co., Ltd.: pages 131 (both), 180 (above), 181 (both), 209 (below), 355 (above left) 379
The Mainichi Papers: pages 68, 251, 252, 260, 263 (both)
The Metropolitan Museum of Art: page 347
© Takahashi Toshitake: page 396
© Torihata Eitaro: page 364 (below)

Back flap of jacket: © *Shintoshi Journal*; photographer, Kaoru Namekawa

AUTHOR'S PROFILE

Kisho Kurokawa
Architect, City Planner, and Critic

Born in Nagoya, 1934.
Graduated Kyoto University, Department of Architecture, and Tokyo
University, Graduate School of Architecture

President CEO, Kisho Kurokawa Architect and Associates
Chairman CEO, Urban Design Consultant
Principal, Institute for Social Engineering, Inc.

Architect and City Planner
At the age of 26 Kisho Kurokawa made an astonishing debut as one of the
founders of the Metabolism Movement in 1960. Since then, he has
earnestly solicited recognition of the paradigm shift from the Machine Age
to an Age of Life Principle.

Kurokawa's own works are highly distinguished, and he has received
the Gold Medal (1986) from the Academy of Architecture in France. He
was also given the Richard Neutra Award (1988) by California State Poly-
technic University in Pomona. He has been the recipient of numerous
awards in Japan, such as the Prize of the Architectural Institute of Japan,
Mainichi Art Prize, Takamura Kotaro Design Award, and the Building
Contractors Society Award, among others. Most recently, he earned the
highest prize from the Japan Art Academy for his Nara City Museum of
Photography (1992).

Kurokawa is an Honorary Fellow of the American Institute of Architects
(AIA) and the Royal Institute of British Architects (RIBA), the first Japan-
ese architect to be thus honored by the RIBA. He is also an Honorary
Member of the Union of Architects of Bulgaria.

He has become the first nonresident member of the Ordre des Archi-
tectes in France and was awarded the "Chevalier de L'Ordre des Arts et des
Lettres" (1989) by the French Ministry of Culture, "Commandeur de l'Ordre du Lion de Finlande" (1988), and "Mandara First Order" (1979) in
Bulgaria.

Kisho Kurokawa is chair of the Board of Trustees of the Advanced
Research Center for Japanese Architectural Studies of Columbia University
in the City of New York campaign, Board Member of the Architectural
Association School of Architecture, London, Visiting Professor at Tsinghua

University in Beijing, Honorary Professor of Tongji University in Shanghai, Honorary Professor of the University of Buenos Aires, Honorary Professor of the Georgian Technical University, Republic of Georgia, and Visiting Professor at Musashi Institute of Technology in Tokyo.

Major works are the National Ethnological Museum, National Bunraku Theater, Nagoya City Art Museum, Hiroshima City Museum of Contemporary Art, and Museum of Modern Art, Wakayama. Works realized abroad include the Japanese-German Center, Berlin, the Chinese-Japanese Youth Center, Beijing, Melbourne Central in Australia, and Pacific Tower, Paris.

At the moment, Kisho Kurokawa is chief design-architect for Kuala Lumpur International Airport, Kuala Lumpur Central and Central Station, Republic Plaza in Singapore, the new wing of the Vincent Van Gogh Museum in the Netherlands, the Musée de Louvain-la-Neuve in Belgium, and Le Colisée, in Nimes, France.

Critic

Kurokawa's publications include *Urban Design, The Archipelago of Information: The Future of Japan, Homo Movens, The Culture of Greys, Thesis on Architecture I and II, The New Nomad Era, Toward an Era of Symbiosis, Philosophy of Symbiosis, Hanasuki, Poems of Architecture,* and *Kisho Kurokawa Note.* His *Philosophy of Symbiosis,* which was awarded the Japan Grand Prix of Literature, was first published in 1987 and revised in 1991.

An English version of *Philosophy of Symbiosis* was cited for "Excellence" by the AIA, and selected as one of the ten best architectural publications by the RIBA in 1992.

Exhibitions and Media

The works of Kisho Kurokawa have been published by Moniteur in France, Academy Editions in the U.K., Rizzoli International in the U.S., Electa and L'Arcaedizioni in Italy, and Tongji University in China.

In 1993, an American firm, Michael Blackwood Productions, produced the documentary film *Kisho Kurokawa,* telecast in several countries.

In 1994, the Art Institute of Chicago dedicated a new architecture gallery as the Kisho Kurokawa Gallery of Architecture.

A Kisho Kurokawa Retrospective Exhibition will be opened in 1998 at Maison de la Culture du Japon in Paris, traveling to the Royal Institute of British Architects and other venues in Europe, then to the Art Institute of Chicago.

Activities

Kisho Kurokawa's activities as a public figure include the following:
He has acted as advisor to Japan Air Lines (1970–74) and Japan National Railways (1970–81), Councilor to the Science and Technology Agency

(1971–73), Commentator for Japan Broadcasting Corporation (NHK, 1974–91), and member of the Advisory Committee to the Prime Minister (1971 to the present).

He is also a member of the Advisory Committees for the Ministry of Education, Ministry of Construction, Ministry of International Trade and Industry, Ministry of Health and Welfare, and Agency for Cultural Affairs, while he acts as advisor and councilor for Hyogo Prefecture, Gifu Prefecture, Nagoya City, and Inuyama City, among others.

Through these activities, Kurokawa has influenced not only the architectural field but also the financial world, the business world, and the press. His Philosophy of Symbiosis, in particular, has become the key concept of this age in politics, finance, culture, and the arts.

BOOKS, MEDIA PUBLICATIONS, AND LECTURES

Reference list of Kisho Kurokawa's major books, articles, lectures, television programs, films, and so on concerning the philosophy of symbiosis.

BOOKS

YEAR	TITLE ETC.	PUBLISHING COMPANY ETC.
1965	*Toshi Dezain* (Urban Design)	Kinokuniya Shoten
1969	*Homo Movens*	Chuo Koron Sha
1972	*Metaborizumu no Hasso* (Conception of Metabolism)	Hakuba Publishing Co.
1977	*Toshi no Shiso* (Concept of Cities)	Hakuba Publishing Co.
1981	*Kyosei no Jidai* (Toward the Age of Symbiosis) (Report of the Nihon Bunka Dezain Kaigi, Japan Culture and Design Conference)	Kodansha Publishing Co. (co-author)
1982	*Kenchikuron I—Nihon-teki Kukan e* (Thesis on Architecture I: Towards Japanese Space)	Kajima Publishing Co.
1983	*Michi no Kenchiku—Chukan Ryoiki e* (Architecture of the Street: Towards Intermediate Space)	Maruzen
	Jihyo: Nihon no Danmen (Social Commentaries: A Cross Section of Japan)	Kajima Publishing Co.
1985	*Do Suru 21 Seiki 1, 2* (Prospective Dialogues for the 21st Century, Volumes 1 and 2)	Efuei Publishing Co.
1987	*Kyosei no Shiso* (The Philosophy of Symbiosis)	Tokuma Publishing Co.
	Kisho Kurokawa: Architecture de la Symbiose	Moniteur, France
	Kisho Kurokawa: Architecture of Symbiosis	Rizzoli International Publication, U.S.
1988	*Tokyo Dai Kaizo* (Tokyo Large Reformation)	Tokuma Publishing Co.
1989	*Nomado no Jidai* (The Era of Nomad)	Tokuma Publishing Co.
	Rediscovering Japanese Space	John Weatherhill, U.S. and Japan

YEAR	TITLE ETC.	PUBLISHING COMPANY ETC.
1990	*Kenchikuron II—Imi no Seisei e* (Thesis on Architecture II: Towards the Evocation of Meaning)	Kajima Publishing Co.
	Kisho Kurokawa 1978–1989, Gendai no Kenchikuka: Kurokawa Kisho (A Contemporary Japanese Architect: Kisho Kurokawa) (2)	Kajima Publishing Co.
1991	*Hanasuki*	Shokoku Sha
	Intercultural Architecture: The Philosophy of Symbiosis	Academy Editions, England and A.I.A. Press, U.S.
1992	*Kurokawa Kisho Sakuhin Shu—Taisha kara Kyosei e* (Kisho Kurokawa Monograph: From Metabolism to Symbiosis)	Bijutsu Shuppan Sha
	Kisho Kurokawa: From Metabolism to Symbiosis	Academy Editions, England
1993	*Kenchiku no Shi* (Poem of Architecture)	Mainichi Shimbun Sha
	New Wave Japanese Architecture	Academy Editions, England
1994	*The Philosophy of Symbiosis*	Academy Editions, England

ARTICLES AND ESSAYS

YEAR	NAME OF PUBLICATION ETC.	SUBJECT, TITLE, ETC.
1967	*Geijutsu Seikatsu, 6/67*	*Kyoson no Bigaku* (Aesthetics of Symbiosis)
1970	*Industrial Japan, 1/70*	*Concord of Man and Technology*
1976	*Kenchiku Zasshi, 5/76*	*Kyozon no Shiso to Giho* (Concept and Techniques of Symbiosis)
1977	*Kumamoto Nichinichi Shimbun, 5/9/77*	*Ketsuraku Shita Kyoyu no Shiso* (Disappearance of the Concept of Common Ownership)
	Shin Kenchiku, 7/77	*Kyozon no Giho* (Techniques of Coexistence)
	Nikkei Architecture, 7/25/77	*Rekishiteki Fudo to no Kyoson* (Coexistence with Historic Natural Features)
	The Japan Architect, 10/11/77	*The Philosophy of Coexistence*

YEAR	NAME OF PUBLICATION ETC.	SUBJECT, TITLE, ETC.
1980	*Nikkan Fukui*, 4/14/80	*Seigen, Kyosei no Jidai e* (Toward the Age of Symbiosis)
	Zaikai Koron, 6/80	*Kenchiku Tokushu* (Special Edition on Architecture) (1), review: *Kaiteki Kankyo Mezasu Toshi Kossogaku—Kyosei no Jidai e Minkan Shudo no Daisan Sekuta o* (Urban Physiognomy Toward a Comfortable Environment: Third Sector Led by Private Enterprise Toward the Age of Symbiosis)
	Sankei Shimbun, 7/14/80	*Kyosei no Jidai e—Daiikkai Nihon Bunka Dezain Kaigi Yokohama Kaigi Kara* (Toward the Age of Symbiosis: From the First Yokohama Meeting of the Japan Culture and Design Conference)
1981	*Sanyo Shimbun*, 3/31/81 and other local newspapers	*Tairitsu kara Kyosei e* (From Opposition to Symbiosis)
	Winds, 8/81	*Special edition, Toshi no Shiso—Ningensei Kaifuku o Motomeru Kyosei Toshi* (Urban Philosophy: Cities of Symbiosis Seeking Restoration of Humanity)
	Symposium Ehime 1981 Report	*21 Seiki wa Kyosei no Jidai* (The 21st Century As an Age of Symbiosis)
1982	*Sekai Nippo*, 1/1/82	*Kyosei no Jidai ga Torai Shita* (The Age of Symbiosis Has Arrived)
	Kyosei no Kenchiku, 5/82	*Kyosei no Kenchiku* (Architecture of Symbiosis)
1983	*Montana State Architectural Review, Spring '83 Kyosei Kenchiku Ron*	*Architecture of Symbiosis*
		Kyosei no Kenchiku (Architecture of Symbiosis)
1984	*Nihon Keizai Shimbun* (evening), Osaka edition, 1/31/84	*Bunraku Gekijo, Dento to Gendai ga Kyosei* (Tradition and Modernity Coexist in a Bunraku Puppet Theater)
	Tokyo University, Kyoyo Gakubu Ho, 4/16/84	*Dai-11 Kai Kyoyo Gakubu Kokai Koza, Kyosei no Shiso* (11th Liberal Arts Department Open Lecture: The Philosophy of Symbiosis)

YEAR	NAME OF PUBLICATION ETC.	SUBJECT, TITLE, ETC.
	Shin Kenchiku, 5/84	*Rekishi to Gendai no Kyosei—Kokuritsu Bunraku Gekijo no Sekkei Ito* (Symbiosis of History and Modernity: Intentions in Designing the National Bunraku Theater)
1985	*Kenchiku Bunka*, 1/85	*Kyosei no Shiso—Kokusai Yoshiki kara Kyosei Yoshiki e* (The Philosophy of Symbiosis: From International Style to the Style of Symbiosis)
	The Japan Architect, 2/85	*The Philosophy of Symbiosis: From Internationalism to Interculturalism*
	Chunichi Shimbun, 3/29/85	*Kurashi no Naka no Enerugi—21 Seiki wa Kyosei no Jidai ni* (Energy within Life: The 21st Century as the Age of Symbiosis)
	Yokohama Shoko Geppo, 7/85	Keynote address, *Kyosei no Jidai no Toshi* (Cities of the Age of Symbiosis) at the symposium *Renkei suru Toshi—Sono Mirai* (The Future of Collaborating Cities)
	Arquitetura Urbanismo, 11/85	*Integrar a Parte eo Tado*
1986	*Shin Kenchiku*, 7/86	*Kyosei no Kenchiku—Nimenshin Yanusu* (Architecture of Symbiosis: Janus, God with Two Faces)
	Universidad de Belgrano, Ideas en Arte y Tecnologia, No. 4, 1986	*La arquitectura de la simbiosis*
	Shin Kenchiku, extra number, No. 10, 1986, *Gendai Kenchikuka Shirizu* (Modern Architect Series)	*Kyosei no Shiso* (The Philosophy of Symbiosis)
1987	*Soka Kenko to Jinsei*, Vol. 7, 1987	*Bunkasai—Atarashii Bunka to Kachi no Kyosei no Sekai* (Cultural Festival: World of Symbiosis Between New Cultures and Values)
	Odra, 7/8/87	*Architektura Symbizy*
	Sumitomo Kensetsu Geppo, 11/20/87	Lecture: *Kyosei no Shiso* (The Philosophy of Symbiosis)
1988	*Shin Kenchiku*, 1/88	*Kyosei no Kenchiku e* (Towards an Architecture of Symbiosis)

YEAR	NAME OF PUBLICATION ETC.	SUBJECT, TITLE, ETC.
	Yukan Yomiuri Shimbun, 1/14/88	*Rekishi to Gendai no Kyosei* (Symbiosis of History and Modernity), The German-Japanese Center in Berlin
	FESAE Journal, 5/88	*The Architecture of Symbiosis*
	Shin Kenchiku, 7/88	*Rekishi to Gendai no Kyosei* (Symbiosis of History and Modernity)
	Nikkei Architecture, 7/11/88	*Ishitsu Bunka no Kyosei* (Symbiosis of Different Cultures)
	Weekly Report, Rotary Club of Nagoya, No. 276, 1988	*Kyosei no Shiso* (The Philosophy of Symbiosis)
1989	*Kari,* 3/89	*Kyosei no Shiso* (The Philosophy of Symbiosis)
	Kyoto Shimbun, 3/15/89	*Kyoto Saiko Sono 3, Dento to Mirai no Kyosei o* (Kyoto Reconsiderations No. 3, Symbiosis of Tradition and the Future)
	Shin Kenchiku, 6/89	*Shizen, Rekishi to no Kyosei* (Symbiosis with Nature and History)
	Rekishi Kaido, 9/89	*Kinosei to Soshokusei no Kyosei* (Symbiosis of Functionality and Decorativeness)
	Mitsui Symposia, Tomorrow, No. 10, 1989	Theme essay of 25 instructors in Mitsui symposia, *Kyosei no Shiso* (The Philosophy of Symbiosis)
1990	*Shin Kenchiku,* 1/90	*Kenchiku Rondan* (Architectural Criticism), *Kyosei no Jidai no Kaika* (Enlightenment of the Age of Symbiosis)
	50 Oku, 2/90	*Chiiki no Jiritsu ga Nihon o Kaeru—Ishitsu Bunka o Kyosei Saseru Machizukuri* (Regional Independence to Change Japan: City Building that Promotes Symbiosis among Different Cultures)
	A&I Report, 24, 1990	*Tairitsu suru Hikari no Kyosei* (Symbiosis of Opposing Lights)
	Mitsui Symposia Tomorrow, No. 11, 1990	*Kyosei no Shiso* (The Philosophy of Symbiosis)
	Kyosei no Toshizukuri, published by Palais Blanc Koshi Kaikan	*Palais Blanc Symposium: Kyosei no Toshizukuri* (City Building of Symbiosis)
	Shin Kenchiku, 9/90	*Chiikisei to Sekaisei no Kyosei* (Symbiosis of Regionalism and Globalism)

YEAR	NAME OF PUBLICATION ETC.	SUBJECT, TITLE, ETC.
	Shin Kenchiku, 9/90	Rekishi to Gendai no Kyosei (Symbiosis of History and Modernity)
	VIA 11	Shadows, Symbiosis, and a Culture of Wood
	Jidai no Kenchikuka II (book), published by Aika Kogyo	Aika Gendai Kenchiku Seminar—Kokusai Yoshiki kara Kyosei Yoshiki e (Aika Modern Architecture Seminar: From International Style to the Style of Symbiosis)
1991	Mainichi Shimbun, 1/1/91	Raito Kaiko Ten—Shizen to Gijutsu no Kyosei Mezashita Raito (Retrospective Wright Exhibition: Wright's Symbiosis of Nature and Technology)
	Shin Kenchiku, 3/91	Kyosei no Shiso (The Philosophy of Symbiosis)
	Gendai Kenchiku no Choryu ni Tsuite (On Trends in Modern Architecture), published by Property Custodianship Department II, Kanto Local Finance Bureau, Ministry of Finance	Komuin Shukusha Kenkyukai, Dainikai Koen Yoshi, Gendai Kenchiku no Choryu ni Tsuite—Kyosei no Shiso (Study Group on Lodging for Public Officials, Second Lecture Abstract, On Trends in Modern Architecture: The Philosophy of Symbiosis)
	Kyosei no Shiso, booklet, published by Sohonzan Chionin	Otetsugi Koen Hyo 1, Kyosei no Shiso (Otetsugi Lecture Table 1, The Philosophy of Symbiosis)
	Approach, Winter 1991	Metabolism 1960–1990 special edition, Kyosei no Shiso—Metaborizumu kara Shinbioshisu e (The Philosophy of Symbiosis: From Metabolism to Symbiosis)
	L'immaginario tecnologico metropolitano (book), published by Fronco Angel	La Filosofia Della Simbiosi
1992	The Japan Architect, 3/92, No. 7	Kikai no Jidai kara Seimei no Jidai e—Kyosei no Shiso (From the Age of Machine to the Age of Life: The Philosophy of Symbiosis)
	Mainichi Shimbun, 4/6/92	Shiken Chokugen (Speaking Out on Personal Views), 21 Seiki e no Kakehashi, Kyosei no Shiso (The Philosophy of Symbiosis, Bridge to the 21st Century)

YEAR	NAME OF PUBLICATION ETC.	SUBJECT, TITLE, ETC.
	Light Up, 4/92	*21 Seiki e no Teigen—Tokyo to Chiho no Kyosei* (Proposal for the 21st Century: Symbiosis of Tokyo and Hinterlands)
	Hirakawa Forum, 9/92	*62nd Hirakawa Forum, Sekai ga Chumoku Shihajimeta Watashi no Kyosei no Shiso* (My Philosophy of Symbiosis, Beginning to Draw Worldwide Attention)
	Gekkan Keidanren, 10/92	*Kyosei no Shiso* (The Philosophy of Symbiosis)
	Bungei Shunju, 10/92	*Gokai Sareru Kyosei Rongi* (Misunderstood Symbiosis Discussion)
1993	*Kenchikushi*, 1/93	*Kenchikuteki Kyosei Kan* (Constructive Views of Symbiosis)
	Sansara, 3/93	*Kome wa Nihon no Seiiki ka—Kome no Goji Koso Kyosei e no Michi da* (Is Rice a Japanese Sacred Zone? Defense of Rice is the Path to Symbiosis)
	Chugai Nippo, 3/23–3/31, 1993	*Kyosei no Shiso to Gendai Bunmei 1–5* (The Philosophy of Symbiosis and Modern Civilization 1–5)
	Naniwa, 6/93	*Kyosei no Shiso* (The Philosophy of Symbiosis)
	Gifu-ken Shokuin Kenchiku Kankei Gijutsu Kyogi Kai 10 Shunen Kinen Koenkai Kirokushu (Gifu Prefecture Employee Discussion Group on Construction Related Technology, Record of Tenth Anniversary Memorial Lectures)	*Kyosei no Shiso* (The Philosophy of Symbiosis)
	Hoseki, 10/93	*Nihon no Seiji Dokan-to 55-nin no Dai Ronso* (Major Debate by 55 Persons on Japanese Politics): *Hosokawa-san Kyosei no Shiso de Ashita no Nihon o* (Mr. Hosokawa, Build Japan's Future on the Philosophy of Symbiosis)
	Keidanren Club Kai, 10/93, No. 276	*Kyosei no Jidai* (The Age of Symbiosis)

YEAR	NAME OF PUBLICATION ETC.	SUBJECT, TITLE, ETC.
	Riburu, 11/93	*Essay: Nara-shi Shashin Bijutsukan—Rekishi no Machi ni Mirai to no Kyosei o Hakaru* (Nara Photography Museum: Toward Symbiosis of a Historical City with the Future)
	Gekkan Keidanren, 11/93	*Keizaikai ni Motomerareru Tetsugaku to Kodo—Kyosei no Tetsugaku no Zehi* (The Philosophy and Conduct Demanded of the Economic Sphere: Merits of the Philosophy of Symbiosis)
	Shidai Jianzhu, 4/93 (Shanghai, China)	*Chouxiang de Xianghu Meixi* (Abstract Mutual Aesthetics)
	Musashi Kodai Tayori, 12/93, No. 110	*1993 Nendo Daisan-kai Bunka Koenkai—Kyosei no Jidai* (Third 1993 Cultural Lecture: The Philosophy of Symbiosis)
1994	*Powaru,* No. 8, 1994, New Year	*Kokoro no Rashinban 8* (Compass of the Heart 8), *Watakushi ga Inoru Toki—Kyosei e no Imeji* (When I Pray: An Image of Symbiosis)
	Shin Kenchiku, 1/94	*Abusutorakuto Shinborizumu* (Abstract Symbolism)
	Tenkanki o Ikiru—7-nin ga Kataru Gendai (Living in a Time of Transition: Seven Persons Discuss the Modern Age)	*21 Seiki wa Kyosei no Jidai da* (The 21st Century as an Age of Symbiosis)
	Kojun Zasshi, 4/94, No. 362	*Kyosei no Shiso* (The Philosophy of Symbiosis)
	Wakayama Shinpo, 5/19/94	*Rekishi, Shizen to Kenchiku no Kyosei I* (Symbiosis of History, Nature and Architecture I)
	Wakayama Shinpo, 5/20/94	*Rekishi, Shizen to Kenchiku no Kyosei II* (Symbiosis of History, Nature and Architecture II)
	Furusato Sosei Bunka Koenkai, Kyosei no Jidai, 1994 Lecture Series I	*Kyosei no Shiso* (The Philosophy of Symbiosis)
	Shin Toshi Journal, 6/15/94, No. 24	*Kyosei Shiso o Kataru* (On the Philosophy of Symbiosis)

YEAR	NAME OF PUBLICATION ETC.	SUBJECT, TITLE, ETC.
	Togokai Kaiho, 9/94	*Warera Kanreki no Kotobuki—Kyosei no Shiso* (Our Sixtieth Birthday Congratulations: The Philosophy of Symbiosis)
	Shin Kenchiku, 10/94	*Absutorakuto Shinborizumu II* (Abstract Symbolism II)
	Nihon no Ronten '94 (book) *Bungei Shunju Sha*	*Seio Gorishugi no Genkai o Koeru no wa Nihon Kara Hasshin Suru Kyosei no Shiso da* (Philosophy of Symbiosis from Japan Will Overcome the Limitations of Western Rationalism)
	Mainichi Shimbun, 12/18/94	*Ima Nani ga Towarete Iru no ka—Seimei no Jidai no Kenchiku* (What is Now in Question: Architecture of the Age of Life)
1995	*Sansara,* 1/95	*Ajia Runessansu to Kyosei no Shiso I* (The Asian Renaissance and the Philosophy of Symbiosis I)
	Shin Kenchiku, 1/95	*Absutorakuto Shinborizumu III* (Abstract Symbolism III)
	JIA News, 1/95	*Kenchiku Sekkei Ron—Kyosei no Shiso* (Views on Architectural Design: The Philosophy of Symbiosis)
	Sansara, 2/95	*Ajia Runessansu to Kyosei no Shiso II* (The Asian Renaissance and the Philosophy of Symbiosis II)
	NTT Plaza, 2/95	*Eco-Media City*
	Sansara, 3/95	*Ajia Runessansu to Kyosei no Shiso III* (The Asian Renaissance and the Philosophy of Symbiosis III)
	Japan Forum, No. 24, 1995 (Korea)	*Translation of The Philosophy of Symbiosis* (*Sansara* 1/3/95) into Korean
	Louvre Auditorium Musée-Musée	*Art Museum of Nagoya, Aichi: The Philosophy of Symbiosis and Museums of Art*
	Kyoto Shimbun, 4/15/95	*Bunka no Fudo 245, Kyosei no Jidai e 13* (Cultural Features 245, Toward the Age of Symbiosis 13)
	Cahiers du Japon, No. 64, 1995	*Le concept de symbiose et l'architecture des musées*
	The Japan Architect, Vol. 18, 1995	*The Architecture of the Age of Life Principle*

YEAR	NAME OF PUBLICATION ETC.	SUBJECT, TITLE, ETC.
	Fourth Toyoda Inter-City Forum 1995	Keynote address, *Kokochi Toshi—Kyosei no Jidai no Toshi Zo* (Feeling Cities: Image of Cities in the Age of Symbiosis)
	Furusato Sosei Bunka Koenkai, Collection of 1994 Lectures	*Kyosei no Jidai* (The Age of Symbiosis)
	Osaka-fu Shokuin Kenshujo 30-nen no Ayumi '95 (30-year history of the Osaka Prefectural Employee Training Institute, 1995)	Lecture commemmorating the opening of the new Training institute: *Kyosei no Jidai ni Okeru Toshi Keikaku* (City Planning in the Age of Symbiosis)
	L&G Ladies and Gentlemen, 12/95	*Otoko no Dokei—Kyosei no Biishiki* (Male Aspirations: Aesthetic Consciousness of Symbiosis)
	Chunichi Shimbun, 12/17/95	Forum commemorating the opening of Tokai Gakuen University: *21 Seiki no Chikyu Shakai—Kyosei to Kyoso o Megutte* (Global Society in the 21st Century: On Symbiosis and Competition)

SYMPOSIA AND DIALOGUES

YEAR	NAME OF PUBLICATION ETC.	SUBJECT, TITLE, ETC.	PERSONS IN ATTENDANCE, ETC.
1978	*Komei Sekai,* 7/78	*Kyoson to Chowa no Sekai* (A World of Coexistence and Harmony)	Kancho Goto
1979	*Zaikai Koron,* 6/79	Special edition on housing, *Toshi to Noson Kyoson no Denen Toshi Koso— Taira ni Sumu ka Rittaiteki ni Sumu ka* (Concept of a Pastoral City with Symbiosis between the City and Farming Villages: Single-level or Multistory Living)	Genzaburo Tokai

YEAR	NAME OF PUBLICATION ETC.	SUBJECT, TITLE, ETC.	PERSONS IN ATTENDANCE, ETC.
1984	*Nikkan Kensetsu Tsushin,* 9/21/84	*Kyosei no Jidai e* (Toward the Age of Symbiosis)	Teijiro Muramatsu
1987	*Sumai Omoshiro Hakken,* book by Takeo Morimoto, published by Maruzen	*Kyosei no Shiso* (The Philosophy of Symbiosis)	Takeo Morimoto
1988	*Rinsho no Ayumi,* 3/88	*Shiten, Tairitsu o Koete Kyosei no Jidai e* (Viewpoint: Past Opposition Toward the Age of Symbiosis)	Kazuhiko Atsumi
	Let's Love Oita, Vol. 33, 1988	*L.L.O. Talk, Kyosei no Jidai* (The Age of Symbiosis)	Morihiko Hiramatsu
1989	*Abashiri Shisei Yoran*	*Big Taidan, Abashiri 21 Seiki, Kyosei suru Ningen Toshizukuri* (Dialogue, Abashiri City in the 21st Century: Building a Human City of Symbiosis)	Tetsuro Ando
1990	*DHL World '90,* Vol. 18	*Toppu Interijento to Kataru 8* (Speaking with Top Intellectuals 8): *Kyosei no Shiso o Minna no Mono ni* (Making the Philosophy of Symbiosis Accessible to Everyone)	Shinichi Momose
1991	*Kokusai Kyoryoku,* 1/91	*Henka suru Kokusai Shakai to Nippon, Kyosei no Jidai ni Mukete* (Japan and Changing International Society: Toward an Age of Symbiosis)	Kensuke Yanagiya
	Nihon Bunka Dezain Kaigi, 1991 Shimane	*Bunka Konwakai, Rekishi to Senshinsei no Kyosei* (Culture Discussion: Symbiosis of History and Progress)	Nobuyoshi Sumida, Keiko Aoyama

YEAR	NAME OF PUBLICATION ETC.	SUBJECT, TITLE, ETC.	PERSONS IN ATTENDANCE, ETC.
1992	*Shimane ni Tsudou Bunka to Dezain* *Jinsei o Kataru* (Speaking About Life), book by Shiro Yoshizaki, published by Raicho kai	*Atarashii Shimane Bunka no Sozo e* (Toward the Creation of New Shimane Culture) *Kyosei no Toshizukuri* (City Building of Symbiosis)	Tomoko Kaneoka, Shiro Yoshizaki
1993	*Toshi Mirai, Summer 1992*, Vol. 14 *Nihon no Sentaku '93*, Vol. 17, No. 39	*Ima, Naze Kyosei na no Ka* (Why Symbiosis Now?) *Kyosei no Jidai to Nihon no Yakuwari* (The Age of Symbiosis and Japan's Role)	Riyako Godai Masaya Miyoshi, Toshio Shishido, Kazuo Aichi, Hisayoshi Higuchi (moderator)
1994	*Dandan Bunko 1, Kakucho Suru Dezain* (Expanding Design), book, Eiko Education and Culture Research Institute	*Dezain suru Kyosei no Shiso* (The Philosophy of Symbiosis in Design)	Katsumi Asaba, Katsuhiko Hibino, Marie Christine
1995	*Kokoro no Chikyu Gi* (book), *Simul Publishing Co.* *Kobe Shimbun*, 1/1/95 *Sankei Shimbun*, 2/3/95	*Kyosei no Jidai ni Mukete* (Toward the Age of Symbiosis) *Shin Jidai no Seishin o Kataru, Tomo ni Ikiru Shiso o Sekai ni* (On the Spirit of the New Era: Bringing the Philosophy of Living Together to the World) *Kyoiku Runessansu, Hirakareta Gakko o Mezashite* (Educational Renaissance: Toward Open Schools)	Kensuke Yanagiya Toshitami Kaibara, Itsuko Yamamoto Junji Ito

YEAR	NAME OF PUBLICATION ETC.	SUBJECT, TITLE, ETC.	PERSONS IN ATTENDANCE, ETC.
	Dandan Bunko 9, Chitsujo no Dainamizumu (Dynamism of Order), book, Eiko Education and Culture Research Institute	*Kyosei suru Sekai* (World of Symbiosis)	Sumet Jumsai, Ken Young

INTERVIEWS

YEAR	NAME OF PUBLICATION ETC.	SUBJECT, TITLE, ETC.
1981	*Kobe Shimbun* (evening), 3/31/81	*80 Nendai wa Kyosei no Jidai* (The 80s as an Age of Symbiosis)
1990	*Sankei Shimbun*, 5/28/90	*Hiroshima-shi Gendai Bijutsukan no Kyosei no Shiso ni Tsuite* (On the Philosophy of Symbiosis of the Hiroshima Museum of Modern Art)
	Home Living, 6/30/90	Special interview: *Dezain no Kaku wa Kyosei no Shiso* (The Philosophy of Symbiosis Is the Core of Design)
	Toyo Keizai Nippo, 7/6/90	*Annyon, The Philosophy of Symbiosis in Korea Also*
1992	*Nikkei Executive Life*, Spring 1992, Vol. 3	Hiroshima Museum of Modern Art: *Seimei no Kyosei* (Symbiosis of Life)
	Nihon Nogyo Shimbun, 11/6/92	*21 Seiki e no Torendo, Kyosei no Jidai I* (The Age of Symbiosis, a Trend toward the 21st Century I)
	Nihon Nogyo Shimbun, 11/13/92	*21 Seiki e no Torendo, Kyosei no Jidai II* (The Age of Symbiosis, a Trend toward the 21st Century II)
1993	*Mahoroba*, 10/93, No. 33	*Kyosei no Kokoro* (Heart of Symbiosis)
	Arakitoryo, 10/93, No. 173	*Kansei to Kyosei no Jidai—Nihon Saikochiku no Kozu* (The Age of Sensibility and Symbiosis: Conception for the Reconstruction of Japan)
1994	*Tri-View*, 7/94	*Seijuku Shakai ni Okeru Kyosei to wa* (What is Symbiosis in a Mature Society?)

YEAR	NAME OF PUBLICATION ETC.	SUBJECT, TITLE, ETC.
1995	*Big Smile*, 4/95	*Kosei to Kyosei 8, Jidai no Shiso o Hyo-gen Shitsuzukeru Kenchikuka* (Individuality and Symbiosis 8: An Architect Continues to Express the Philosophy of the Era)
	Kensetsu Tsushin Shimbun, 5/19/95	*Sekaikan no Kochiku e* (Toward Construction of World Views)
	Nihon Keizai Shimbun, 6/19/95	*Toshi 33, Dai 6-wa, Sekai to no Kyosei—Ajia Sumiyasusa Kisou* (Cities 33, No. 6, Symbiosis with the World: Asia Competes on Ease of Living)
	Intelligence, 9/95	Front Interview, Kisho Kurokawa
	Famusu Tsushin, No. 2 1995	Interview with Kisho Kurokawa
	Nikkan Kensetsu Kogyo Shimbun, 9/6/95	Interview: *21 Seiki no Kokudo Keikaku o Sasaeru Kyosei no Shiso* (The Philosophy of Symbiosis Supports National Land Planning of the 21st Century)

LECTURES AND SYMPOSIA

YEAR	NAME OF LECTURE OR SYMPOSIUM	PLACE OF LECTURE OR SYMPOSIUM, ETC.
1976	*Rekishiteki Kenchiku, Kankyo Hozen no Rinen to Giho—Kyoson no Shiso to Giho* (Concepts and Methods of Historical Building/Environmental Conservation: The Philosophy and Methods of Coexistence)	General Research Conference Commemorating the 90th Anniversary of the Establishment of Japanese Architecture
1980	*Kyosei no Jidai e* (Toward the Age of Symbiosis)	Nihon Bunka Dezain Kaigi, Yokohama Kaigi (Japan Culture and Design Conference, Yokohama Conference)
	Kyosei no Jidai (The Age of Symbiosis)	Nagoya Rotary Club
	Kyosei no Jidai (The Age of Symbiosis)	Sumitomo Kensetsu

YEAR	NAME OF LECTURE OR SYMPOSIUM	PLACE OF LECTURE OR SYMPOSIUM, ETC.
1981	*Kyosei no Jidai e* (Toward the Age of Symbiosis)	Japan-Libya Friendship Association
	Symposium Ehime '81—21 Seiki wa Kyosei no Jidai (The 21st Century as an Age of Symbiosis)	*Ehime Shimbun*
1982	*Kyosei no Jidai* (The Age of Symbiosis)	Kashiwa City, Chiba Prefecture
	Kyosei no Toshi (Cities of Symbiosis)	Nihon Kokokugyo Kyokai (Japan Advertising Industry Association)
	Kyosei no Shiso (The Philosophy of Symbiosis)	Wakayama Prefecture Architectural Design Direction Association
	Kyosei no Shiso—21 Seiki no Toshizukuri (The Philosophy of Symbiosis: City Building of the 21st Century)	Osaka Gas
	Kyosei no Jidai (The Age of Symbiosis)	International Commercial University
	Kyosei no Shiso (The Philosophy of Symbiosis)	Ube City Education Committee
	Kyosei no Jidai (The Age of Symbiosis)	Hagi City Chamber of Youth
	Kyosei no Jidai (The Age of Symbiosis)	Yokohama Education Committee
	Kyosei no Jidai (The Age of Symbiosis)	Ehime Prefecture Education Service Center
	Kyosei no Jidai (The Age of Symbiosis)	Hyogo-ken Shogakko Kokugo Renmei (Hyogo Prefecture elementary school Japanese language federation)
	Kyosei no Shiso (The Philosophy of Symbiosis)	Otake City Education Committee, Hiroshima Prefecture
	Kyosei no Toshi (Cities of Symbiosis)	Industrial Technology Institute, Tsukuba Management Office, Yomiuri Shimbun Sha
	Kyosei no Jidai (The Age of Symbiosis)	Ogaki Commercial Senior High School
	Kyosei no Toshi (Cities of Symbiosis)	NHK Television
	Kyosei no Kenchiku (The Architecture of Symbiosis)	National Development Research Institute, Korea

YEAR	NAME OF LECTURE OR SYMPOSIUM	PLACE OF LECTURE OR SYMPOSIUM, ETC.
	Kyosei no Kenchiku (The Architecture of Symbiosis)	L'Academie d'Architecture (Paris)
	Kyosei no Kenchiku (The Architecture of Symbiosis)	Royal Australian Institute of Architects (Singapore Convention)
1983	*Kyosei no Jidai* (The Age of Symbiosis)	Hokkaido High School Education Study Group
	Kyosei no Shiso (The Philosophy of Symbiosis)	JMA Salon
	Kyosei no Toshi (Cities of Symbiosis)	Japan YPO
	Kyosei no Shiso (The Philosophy of Symbiosis)	Ad Hoc Conference Group, National City Inspection Committee
	Kyosei no Kenchiku (The Architecture of Symbiosis)	Shin Kenchiku Yoshioka Bunko (Yoshioka New Architecture Library)
	Kyosei no Jidai (The Age of Symbiosis)	Hogyo General Research Institute
	Kyosei no Kenchiku (The Architecture of Symbiosis)	Keisho Nando, Korea
	Kyosei no Kenchiku (The Architecture of Symbiosis)	Union of Architects Bulgaria (Sofia)
	Kyosei no Kenchiku (The Architecture of Symbiosis)	Bulgarian Chamber of Commerce and Industry (Sofia)
	Kyosei no Kenchiku (The Architecture of Symbiosis)	Istituto Nazionale di Architecttura (Rome)
	Kyosei no Kenchiku (The Architecture of Symbiosis)	Comune de Pistoia / Assessorato agli Istituti (Rome)
1984	*Kyosei no Shiso* (The Philosophy of Symbiosis)	Saiko Sai Shiho Kenshujo (Supreme Court Judicature Study Center)
	Dai-11 Kai Kyoyo Gakubu Kokai Koza, Kyosei no Shiso (11th Liberal Arts Department Open Lecture: The Philosophy of Symbiosis)	Liberal Arts Department, Tokyo University

YEAR	NAME OF LECTURE OR SYMPOSIUM	PLACE OF LECTURE OR SYMPOSIUM, ETC.
	Kyosei no Jidai (The Age of Symbiosis)	Chunichi Shinkin Bank
	Kyosei no Shiso (The Philosophy of Symbiosis)	Tokyo University May Festival
	Kyosei no Giho (The Methods of Symbiosis)	Misawa Home General Reasearch Institute
	Kyosei no Shiso (The Philosophy of Symbiosis)	Fujitsu Fakomu Family Kai
	Kyosei no Shiso (The Philosophy of Symbiosis)	Bunka Women's University
	Kyosei no Kenchiku (The Architecture of Symbiosis)	Kajima Corporation
	Kyosei no Shiso (The Philosophy of Symbiosis)	Anjo City
	Kyosei no Kenchiku (The Architecture of Symbiosis)	Fratelli Fiorentino (Naples, Italy)
1985	*Kyosei no Jidai no Toshi* (Cities in the Age of Symbiosis)	Yokohama Chamber of Commerce and Industry
	Kurashi no Naka no Enerugi: 21 Seiki wa Kyosei no Jidai ni (Energy within Life: The 21st Century as the Age of Symbiosis)	Chunichi Shimbun
	Kyosei no Shiso (The Philosophy of Symbiosis)	Okinawa Union of Architects
	Kyosei no Kenchiku (The Architecture of Symbiosis)	Romanian Union of Architects (Bucharest)
	Kyosei no Kenchiku (The Architecture of Symbiosis)	Finland National Museum of Architecture (Helsinki)
1986	*Kyosei no Shiso* (The Philosophy of Symbiosis)	Tokyo Rotary Club
	Kyosei no Shiso (The Philosophy of Symbiosis)	Bunkyojin Kondankai

YEAR	NAME OF LECTURE OR SYMPOSIUM	PLACE OF LECTURE OR SYMPOSIUM, ETC.
	Aika Gendai Kenchiku Seminar—Kokusai Yoshiki kara Kyosei Yoshiki e (Aika Modern Architecture Seminar: From International Style to the Style of Symbiosis)	Aika Gendai Kenchiku Seminar Executive Committee
	Kyosei no Kenchiku (The Architecture of Symbiosis)	Yugoslavian Association of Architects (Sarajevo)
	Kyosei no Kenchiku (The Architecture of Symbiosis)	Museum of Architecture (Wroclaw, Poland)
	Kyosei no Kenchiku (The Architecture of Symbiosis)	Hong Kong Union of Architects (Hong Kong)
1987	*Kyosei no Shiso* (The Philosophy of Symbiosis)	Shizuoka Copy Center
	Kyosei no Shiso (The Philosophy of Symbiosis)	Sumitomo Kensetsu
	Kyosei no Kenchiku (The Architecture of Symbiosis)	University of California (Los Angeles)
	Kyosei no Kenchiku (The Architecture of Symbiosis)	Executive Committee, Los Angeles Japan Week (Los Angeles)
	Kyosei no Kenchiku (The Architecture of Symbiosis)	Union of Architects Bulgaria (Sofia)
	Mirai no Toshi—Kyosei no Shiso (Cities of the Future: The Philosophy of Symbiosis)	Group Panorama (Buenos Aires)
	Kyosei no Kenchiku (The Architecture of Symbiosis)	Center of Art and Communication (CAYC)
1988	*Kyosei no Jidai no Toshi* (Cities in the Age of Symbiosis)	Nara Nichinichi Shimbun
	Kyosei no Shiso (The Philosophy of Symbiosis)	Kari

YEAR	NAME OF LECTURE OR SYMPOSIUM	PLACE OF LECTURE OR SYMPOSIUM, ETC.
	Kyosei no Shiso (The Philosophy of Symbiosis)	Nagoya Rotary Club
	Kyosei no Shiso (The Philosophy of Symbiosis)	California State Polytechnic University
	Kyosei no Kenchiku (The Architecture of Symbiosis)	Domar Laminated Products Co., Ltd. (Vancouver)
	Kyosei no Shiso (The Philosophy of Symbiosis)	Japan Society (New York)
	Kyosei no Shiso—Intakarucharizumu ni Tsuite (The Philosophy of Symbiosis: On Interculturalism)	Sophia University
1989	*Mitsui Symposia: Kyosei no Shiso* (The Philosophy of Symbiosis)	Mitsui Symposia
	Kyosei no Toshi (Cities of Symbiosis)	Palais Blanc Koshi Kaikan
	Kyosei no Bi (The Beauty of Symbiosis)	Nihon Kangyo Kakumaru Shoken
1990	*Kyosei no Shiso* (The Philosophy of Symbiosis)	Kinki University
	Kyosei no Shiso (The Philosophy of Symbiosis)	Musashi Intelligent Building
	Kyosei no Toshi (Cities of Symbiosis)	Fukui City, Fukui Prefecture
	Kyosei no Jidai (The Age of Symbiosis)	Mitsubishi Motors Corp.
	Kyosei no Shiso to Keikan Sekkei (The Philosophy of Symbiosis and Landscape Architecture)	21 Seiki Chiiki Koso Kenkyukai (21st Century Regional Concept Study Group)
	Kyosei no Shiso to Hakubamura no Keikan (The Philosophy of Symbiosis and the Scenery of Hakuba Village)	Hakuba Village, Nagano Prefecture
	Kyosei no Shiso (The Philosophy of Symbiosis)	Kinki Post Office

YEAR	NAME OF LECTURE OR SYMPOSIUM	PLACE OF LECTURE OR SYMPOSIUM, ETC.
1991	*21 Seiki ni Okeru Nihon—Kyosei no Toshi* (Japan in the 21st Century: Cities of Symbiosis)	Hiroshima Shoko Rengokai (Hiroshima Commercial and Industrial Union)
	Kyosei no Jidai (The Age of Symbiosis)	IBM Japan
	Kyosei no Shiso (The Philosophy of Symbiosis)	Japan Industrial Designers Association, Asahi Shimbun Sha
	Kyosei no Shiso (The Philosophy of Symbiosis)	Sohonzan Chion-in, Otetsugi Undo Honbu
	Rekishi to Mirai no Kyosei—Sekai Kenchikuhaku 1998 Nara e Mukete (Symbiosis of History and the Future: Toward the World Architecture Exposition, Nara 1998)	*Nara Shimbun*, Seikei Konwakai (Discussion group on politics and economics)
	Kyosei no Jidai (The Age of Symbiosis)	Fuji Sash
	Kyosei no Machizukuri (City Building of Symbiosis)	Nagasaki Prefecture Union of Architects
	Kyosei no Shiso to Kenchiku (The Philosophy of Symbiosis and Architecture)	Tomei Lease Kensetsu
	Kyosei no Jidai (The Age of Symbiosis)	Kaneura-machi
	Kyosei no Jidai (The Age of Symbiosis)	Aichi Prefecture, Chita-gun, Akuhi-machi
	Kyosei no Jidai—Nihon o Do Suru, Todai o Do Suru (The Age of Symbiosis: What Should be Done in Japan and at Tokyo University)	Study Group on Government Structure, Tokyo University

YEAR	NAME OF LECTURE OR SYMPOSIUM	PLACE OF LECTURE OR SYMPOSIUM, ETC.
	Komuin Shukusha Kenkyukai, Dainikai Koen—Gendai Kenchiku no Choryu ni Tsuite, Kyosei no Shiso—Taisha kara Kyosei e (Study Group on Lodging for Public Officials, Second Lecture: On Trends in Modern Architecture, The Philosophy of Symbiosis)	Property Custodianship Department II, Kanto Local Finance Bureau, Ministry of Finance
	From Metabolism to Symbiosis	Royal Institute of British Architects (London)
1992	*Kyosei no Shiso* (The Philosophy of Symbiosis)	Grail Academy
	Kyosei no Shiso (The Philosophy of Symbiosis)	NTT Toshi Kaihatsu (NTT Urban Development)
	Kyosei no Shiso (The Philosophy of Symbiosis)	Kisho Kai
	62nd Hirakawa Forum, Sekai ga Chumoku Shihajimeta Watakushi no Kyosei no Shiso (My Philosophy of Symbiosis, Beginning to Draw Worldwide Attention)	Hirakawa Forum
	Kyosei no Shiso (The Philosophy of Symbiosis)	Nishi Nihon Shimbun Sha
	Kyosei no Shiso (The Philosophy of Symbiosis)	Gifu-ken Shokuin Kenchiku Kankei Gijutsu Kyogi Kai (Gifu Prefecture Employee Discussion Group on Construction Related Technology)
	Kyosei no Shiso (The Philosophy of Symbiosis)	Keidanren Shohisha Seikatsusha Iinkai (Keidanren consumer committee)
	Kyosei no Shiso (The Philosophy of Symbiosis)	Yotsuya Rotary Club
	Kyosei no Shiso (The Philosophy of Symbiosis)	Kochi Prefecture

YEAR	NAME OF LECTURE OR SYMPOSIUM	PLACE OF LECTURE OR SYMPOSIUM, ETC.
1993	*Shukutoku Kokai Koza— Kyosei no Shiso to Gendai Bunmei* (Shukutoku Open Lecture: The Philosophy of Symbiosis and Modern Civilization)	Daijo Shukutoku Gakuen
	Kyosei no Shiso (The Philosophy of Symbiosis)	Police Headquarters, Osaka Prefecture
	Taisha kara Kyosei e (From Metabolism to Symbiosis)	Columbia University (New York)
	Kyosei no Kenchiku (The Architecture of Symbiosis)	Chinese Culture University, Taipei, Taiwan R.O.C.
	Taisha kara Kyosei e (From Metabolism to Symbiosis)	Delft University of Technology (Delft, Netherlands)
	Kyosei no Shiso to Hanasuki (The Philosophy of Symbiosis and Hanasuki)	Shiho Kenshujo (Judicature Study Center)
	Kyosei no Shiso to Hanasuki (The Philosophy of Symbiosis and Hanasuki)	Asahi Culture Center
	Kyosei no Shiso (The Philosophy of Symbiosis)	Token Corporation
	Kyosei no Shiso (The Philosophy of Symbiosis)	Minsei Shogai Gakushu Kareji (Public continuing education college), Toyama Prefecture
	Kyosei no Kenchiku, Toshi (The Architecture and Cities of Symbiosis)	Palais Blanc Koshi Kaikan
	Kyosei no Jidai (The Age of Symbiosis)	Keidanren Club
	Kyosei no Shiso—Hanasuki (The Philosophy of Symbiosis: Hanasuki)	Ken'o Chiiki Chijo Sangyo Shinko Senta (Mid-Prefecture local industry promotion center), Niigata Prefecture
	Kyosei no Jidai (The Age of Symbiosis)	Musashi Institute of Technology

YEAR	NAME OF LECTURE OR SYMPOSIUM	PLACE OF LECTURE OR SYMPOSIUM, ETC.
	Kyosei no Shiso (The Philosophy of Symbiosis)	Maebashi City Education Committee
	Kyosei no Shiso (The Philosophy of Symbiosis) *Kyosei no Jidai no Kenchiku* (Architecture in the Age of Symbiosis)	Architecture Festival Executive Committee, Tokai University, Hokkaido Public Building Association
	Kyosei no Shiso (The Philosophy of Symbiosis)	Supreme Court Secretariat Training Institute
	Kyosei no Shiso—Kikai no Jidai kara Seimei no Jidai e (The Philosophy of Symbiosis: From the Age of Machine to the Age of Life)	Tongji University (Shanghai, China)
	Kyosei no Shiso—Kikai no Jidai kara Seimei no Jidai e (The Philosophy of Symbiosis: From the Age of Machine to the Age of Life)	Royal Academy of Arts (London)
	Kyosei no Shiso—Kikai no Jidai kara Seimei no Jidai e (The Philosophy of Symbiosis: From the Age of Machine to the Age of Life)	AA School (London)
	Kyosei no Shiso—Kikai no Jidai kara Seimei no Jidai e (The Philosophy of Symbiosis: From the Age of Machine to the Age of Life)	Stuttgart University (Stuttgart, Germany)
1994	*Kyosei no Shiso* (The Philosophy of Symbiosis)	Kojun Sha luncheon
	Dai 74-kai Toshi Keiei Foramu—Kyosei no Shiso (74th City Management Forum: The Philosophy of Symbiosis)	Nikken Sekkei Keikaku Jimusho

YEAR	NAME OF LECTURE OR SYMPOSIUM	PLACE OF LECTURE OR SYMPOSIUM, ETC.
	Rekishi, Shizen to no Kyo-sei—Wakayama to Toshizukuri (Symbiosis with History and Nature: Wakayama and City Building)	Wakayama Chamber of Youth
	Kyosei no Jidai (The Age of Symbiosis)	Musashi Institute of Technology
	Kyosei no Jidai (The Age of Symbiosis)	Furusato Challenge Jigyo Suishin Kyogikai (Furusato Challenge Project Promotion Conference Group), Beppu City
	Kyosei no Machizukuri (City Building of Symbiosis)	Wakayama Prefecture
	Kyosei no Jidai no Chiiki Keikaku (The Age of Symbiosis and Community Planning)	New national land axis formation study group, Ibaraki Prefecture
	Kyosei no Jidai (The Age of Symbiosis)	Jutoku Senior High School
	Kyosei no Jidai e (Toward the Age of Symbiosis)	Shukutoku Yono Senior High School
	Kyosei no Jidai no Toshi Zo (City Image of the Age of Symbiosis)	Toyoda Inter-City Forum
	Kyosei no Shiso (The Philosophy of Symbiosis)	Setagaya Rotary Club
	Kyosei no Shiso—Kikai no Jidai kara Seimei no Jidai e (The Philosophy of Symbiosis: From the Age of Machine to the Age of Life)	Architectural Institute of Malaysia (Kuala Lumpur, Malaysia)
	Kenchiku to Dezain ni Okeru Kyosei no Shiso (The Philosophy of Symbiosis in Architecture and Design)	Philadelphia Museum of Art (Philadelphia, U.S.)

YEAR	NAME OF LECTURE OR SYMPOSIUM	PLACE OF LECTURE OR SYMPOSIUM, ETC.
	Kyosei no Shiso—Kikai no Jidai kara Seimei no Jidai e (The Philosophy of Symbiosis: From the Age of Machine to the Age of Life)	Chicago Museum of Art (Chicago, U.S.)
	Kyosei no Shiso—Kikai no Jidai kara Seimei no Jidai e (The Philosophy of Symbiosis: From the Age of Machine to the Age of Life)	Lincoln University (Nebraska, U.S.)
	Kyosei no Shiso—Kikai no Jidai kara Seimei no Jidai e (The Philosophy of Symbiosis: From the Age of Machine to the Age of Life)	Tongji University (Shanghai, China)
1995	*Kyosei no Shiso—Osaka no Machizukuri* (The Philosophy of Symbiosis: City Building in Osaka)	Osaka Chamber of Youth
	Kyosei no Shiso to Toshi (The Philosophy of Symbiosis and Cities)	Kansai Electric Power Co. Inc.
	Kyosei no Shiso to Toshi—Maebashi no Miryoku o Motto Suteki ni (The Philosophy of Symbiosis and Cities: Enhancing the Charm of Maebashi)	Maebashi City
	Kyosei no Jidai (The Age of Symbiosis)	Interior Center School
	Kyosei no Shiso to Kenchiku (The Philosophy of Symbiosis and Architecture)	Tokyo Gas
	Sumai to Shizen to Jinsei to no Kyosei (Symbiosis of Housing, Nature, and Human Life)	Japan Housing Information Exchange Center
	Kyosei no Shiso (The Philosophy of Symbiosis)	Fukui City

YEAR	NAME OF LECTURE OR SYMPOSIUM	PLACE OF LECTURE OR SYMPOSIUM, ETC.
	Kyosei no Jidai ni Okeru Toshi Keikaku (City Planning in the Age of Symbiosis)	Osaka Prefecture Employees Training Center
	Ajia to no Kyosei (Symbiosis with Asia)	Ajia Minzoku Zokei Bunka Kenkyujo (Asia Ethnic Group Formation and Culture Research Institute)
	Kyosei no Jidai e (Toward the Age of Symbiosis)	Nagoya Institute of Technology
	Kyosei no Jidai (The Age of Symbiosis)	Inuyama Chamber of Commerce and Industry
	Gendai Kenchiku wa Doko e Iku ka (Where is Modern Architecture Headed?)	Komani
	Keizai no Kyoso to Ningen no Kyosei (Economic Competition and Human Symbiosis)	Tokai Gakuen University and Chunichi Shimbun
	Kyosei no Shiso to Toshi Keikaku no Atarashii Rinen (The Philosophy of Symbiosis and a New Conception of Urban Planning)	Kuala Lumpur City Planning Bureau (Kuala Lumpur, Malaysia)
	Kyosei no Shiso to Bijutsukan (The Philosophy of Symbiosis and Museums of Art)	Louvre Museum of Art, Nagoya, Aichi Council (Paris, France)
	Kyosei no Shiso (The Philosophy of Symbiosis)	Princeton University (Princeton, U.S.)
	Nihon Bunka to Gendai Kenchiku (Japanese Culture and Modern Architecture)	Institut de France (Paris, France)
	Kyosei no Shiso to Eco-Media City (The Philosophy of Symbiosis and Eco-Media City)	Infotech, Malaysia '95 (Kuala Lumpur, Malaysia)
	Nihon Bunka to Gendai Kenchiku (Japanese Culture and Modern Architecture)	Tongji University (Shanghai, China)

TELEVISION, RADIO, AND FILM

YEAR	NAME OF PROGRAM, ETC.	NAME OF BROADCASTING NETWORK, ETC.
1979	*Toki no Wadai–Kyoson no Jidai e* (Topic of the Times: Toward the Age of Coexistence)	NHK Radio
1980	*Toki no Wadai–Kyosei no Jidai e* (Topic of the Times: Toward the Age of Symbiosis)	NHK Radio
1985	*Kyosei no Shiso* (The Philosophy of Symbiosis)	Bulgaria Broadcasting (Bulgaria, film)
1988	*Torendi Naito–21 Seiki wa Kyosei no Jidai* (Trendy Night: The 21st Century as an Age of Symbiosis)	Aichi Television (with Mamoru Horiuchi)
1991	Television column: *Kyosei no Seiiki* (Sacred Zones of Symbiosis)	NHK Educational Television
1993	*Taisha kara Kyosei e* (From Metabolism to Symbiosis)	Blackwood Pro (U.S., film)
1994	Interview: *Kyosei no Kenchiku* (The Architecture of Symbiosis)	Vitosha Radio (Bulgaria)